Learning Science in the Schools:
Research Reforming Practice

Learning Science in the Schools:
Research Reforming Practice

Edited by

Shawn M. Glynn
University of Georgia

Reinders Duit
IPN, University of Kiel, Germany

LEA
1995
Lawrence Erlbaum Associates, Publishers
Mahwah, New Jersey

Lawrence Erlbaum Associates, Inc., Publishers
10 Industrial Avenue
Mahwah, New Jersey 07430

Library of Congress Cataloging-in-Publication Data

Learning science in the schools : research reforming practice / edited
by Shawn M. Glynn, Reinders Duit.
    p. cm.
  Includes bibliographical references and indexes.
  ISBN 0-8058-1807-3. — ISBN 0-8058-1808-1 (pbk.)
  1. Science—Study and teaching (Elementary) 2. Science—Study and
teaching (Secondary) 3. Learning, Psychology of. I. Glynn, Shawn
M. II. Duit, Reinders.
LB1585.L36 1995
372.3—dc20
                                        94-44784
                                          CIP

Printed in the United States of America
10 9 8 7 6 5 4 3 2 1

Contents

List of Contributors

JOHN BAXTER • Science Department, St. Lukes College, South Cloisters 13, Exeter University, Devon, England

BEVERLEY BELL • Centre for Science and Mathematics Education Research, Private Bag 3105, University of Waikato, Hamilton, Aotearoa New Zealand

REINDERS DUIT • Physics Education, IPN—Institute for Science Education at the University of Kiel, Olshausenstrasse 62, 24098 Kiel, Germany

RICHARD A. DUSCHL • Department of Instruction and Learning and Center for Philosophy of Science, University of Pittsburgh, Pittsburgh, PA 15260

DREW H. GITOMER • Educational Testing Service 18-R, Princeton, NJ 08541

SHAWN M. GLYNN • Departments of Educational Psychology and Science Education, 325 Aderhold Hall, University of Georgia, Athens, GA 30602

KARL S. HOOK • Department of Science, Florida State University, Tallahassee, FL 32306-3025

SOFIA KESIDOU • Project 2061, American Association for the Advancement of Science, 1333 H St. NW, Washington, DC 20005

THOMAS R. KOBALLA, JR. • Department of Science Education, University of Georgia, Athens, GA 30602

JOSEPH D. NOVAK • Science Education and Biological Sciences, Department of Education — Kennedy Hall, Cornell University, Ithaca, NY 14853-4203

RODNEY B. THIELE • Science and Mathematics Education Centre, GPO Box U 1987, Curtin University of Technology, Perth 6001, Western Australia, Australia

DEBORAH J. TIPPINS • Department of Science Education, 212 Aderhold Hall, University of Georgia, Athens, GA 30602

KENNETH TOBIN • Science Education Program, Department of Curriculum and Instruction, 203 Milton Carothers Hall, Florida State University, Tallahassee, FL 32306-3032

DAVID F. TREAGUST • Science and Mathematics Education Center, GPO Box U 1987, Curtin University of Technology, Perth 6001, Western Australia, Australia

RUTH STAVY • School of Education, Tel Aviv University, P.O.B. 39040, Ramat-Aviv, Tel Aviv 69978, Israel

ARTHUR STINNER • Faculty of Education, Curriculum: Mathematics and Natural Sciences, University of Manitoba, Winnipeg, Manitoba R3T 2N2, Canada

BARBARA Y. WHITE • Education and Computer Science, Tolman Hall, EMST, School of Education, University of California at Berkeley, Berkeley, CA 94720

COLIN WOOD-ROBINSON • Centre for Studies in Science and Mathematics Education, School of Education, University of Leeds, Leeds, LS2 9JT, England

ROBERT E. YAGER • Science Education Center, 769 Van Allen Hall, University of Iowa, Iowa City, IA 52242-1478

Preface

Innovative research is reforming how science is learned in schools. This book is about that research. The researchers who have contributed chapters are leading authorities in science education. In their chapters, they have drawn clear connections among research, theory, and classroom practice. They have provided excellent examples from science classes in which their research has reformed practice.

This book is intended for science teachers, teacher educators, researchers, and administrators. It is ideal for use in pre-service and in-service courses for science teachers. This book bridges the gap between cutting-edge research and classroom practice to provide teachers with the knowledge they need to foster students' scientific literacy.

The book is organized in four parts: Part I, *Learning Science Meaningfully*; Part II, *Conceptual Development in Science Domains*; Part III, *Conceptual Tools for Learning Science*, and Part IV, *Assessing Learners' Science Knowledge*. In each part, the chapters provide overviews of current research and illustrate how the findings of this research are being applied in schools. This research is helping to bring about powerful changes in science instruction.

This book will be particularly useful to educators concerned about the scientific literacy of students. Science — and the technology derived from it — is having a dramatic impact on the quality of our personal lives and on the environment around us. Science will have an even greater impact on the lives of our students. To prosper in the near future, all of our students must become scientifically literate and embrace the notion of life-long learning in science.

What does it mean to be scientifically literate? Scientifically literate students understand the basic concepts and principles of science. They realize that science makes technology possible and that technology can be a double-edged sword. The lives of scientifically literate students are enriched by their understanding, appreciation, and enjoyment of the natural world. Scientifically literate students care for and protect the natural environment.

Unfortunately, many of our students, perhaps most of them, are not scientifically literate. Without scientific literacy, it will be impossible for our students to make informed decisions about the interrelated educational, scientific, and social issues that will confront them in the future. An example of one of these issues is population growth. Before the year 1800 the world population was less than 1 billion. By 1900, the population had grown to 1.7 billion; by 1970 to 3.7 billion; and by 1994 to 5.7 billion. By 2050, if left unchecked, the population will grow to 12.5 billion. Not only is our population increasing, but our natural resources are decreasing due to land deforestation, overgrazing, and pollution. In order to solve the problems associated with decreasing resources and increasing population, our students—all of them—must become scientifically literate.

The cutting-edge research discussed in this book is based on the view that students must actively construct their knowledge for it to be meaningful. In this view, the goal of the teacher is to facilitate learning, not dispense knowledge. When planning lessons in the various science domains, the teacher takes into account the conceptual development of the students. The teacher strategically creates a rich, authentic environment in which students interact and build their knowledge in a meaningful way. This environment is both "hands on" and "minds on"—in other words, it is an environment that stresses both knowing how and knowing why. Assessment is an integral part of this environment. Assessment provides challenging opportunities for students to learn and it guides students towards the attainment of their instructional goals in science. These goals include an understanding, appreciation, and enjoyment of the natural world. To prosper in the 21st century, our students—all of them—must achieve these goals.

The content of all the chapters—including student quotes—was edited for instructional purposes and consistency of style. We very much appreciate the understanding and flexibility of our international authors because our editing included the use of American spelling and terminology throughout the book.

ACKNOWLEDGMENTS

We wish to thank Hollis Heimbouch, Amy Olener, and Debra Ruel of Lawrence Erlbaum Associates for their expertise and support. We also wish to thank the following exemplary science teachers who read chapter drafts and provided advice: Dava Coleman, Nicole Gibson, and Kim Nichols.

Shawn M. Glynn
Reinders Duit

I Learning Science Meaningfully

The view that students must actively construct their science knowledge for it to be meaningful is being widely advocated by science education researchers. According to this view, students should play an active role in building knowledge and making sense of the natural world. This view has roots in philosophy and psychology, but it is taking a powerful new form in the field of science education, where researchers are examining students' mental models of concepts, constructive processes, attitudes toward science, and beliefs about the nature of learning. The chapters in Part I highlight this research and its implications for instruction.

1 Learning Science Meaningfully: Constructing Conceptual Models

Shawn M. Glynn
University of Georgia

Reinders Duit
IPN, University of Kiel, Germany

> The greatest value of models is their contribution to the process of originating new ideas — developing the imagination. (Pauling, 1983)

One of the questions most often asked by both new and seasoned science teachers is: How can I help my students learn science meaningfully? The answer is to ensure that learning is constructive, rather than rote. We define the *constructive learning of science* as a dynamic process of building, organizing, and elaborating knowledge of the natural world. The cornerstones of this knowledge are conceptual models.

A conceptual model is a cognitive representation of a real-world process (e.g., photosynthesis) or thing (e.g., a cell). A conceptual model can be actualized in a variety of forms, such as a diagram, a flow chart, a computer program, a physical replica, or a mathematical equation.

Teachers introduce students to conceptual models in order to simplify natural phenomena, making the phenomena more understandable to students. Generally speaking, conceptual models are scientifically valid; they are consistent with scientists' understanding of the phenomena.

When students learn science meaningfully in schools, they construct conceptual models consisting of related concepts, not lists of unrelated facts (Glynn, Yeany, & Britton, 1991). Science teachers often realize this, but are not sure how to facilitate constructive learning in their students, particularly when the number of students in a class is large, lesson plans are rigid, time is short, and concepts are complex. Complexity is the rule rather than the exception in biology (e.g., respiration), chemistry (e.g., elements), physics (e.g., energy), earth science (e.g., weather), and astronomy (e.g., the sun). Complex science concepts are introduced to elementary school students, who are expected to understand these concepts by the time they are in high school. Teachers at all levels play a critical role in ensuring that students develop valid conceptual models and an awareness of the purpose of science:

> Science is the attempt to make the chaotic diversity of our sense-experience correspond to a logically uniform system of thought. In this system single experiences must be correlated with the theoretic structure in such a way that the resulting coordination is unique and convincing.
>
> The sense-experiences are the given subject-matter. But the theory that shall interpret them is man-made. It is the result of an extremely laborious process of adaptation: hypothetical, never completely final, always subject to question and doubt. (Einstein, 1940, p. 487)

In the first part of this chapter, we introduce what we call a *constructive view of learning science.* Then we review briefly some relevant background information on constructivist philosophy and the psychology of learning. Next, we explain how students construct and use conceptual models in learning science. Finally, we apply our constructive view and propose a model of science instruction that can serve as a guide in planning successful science lessons.

A CONSTRUCTIVE VIEW OF LEARNING SCIENCE IN SCHOOLS

We believe the learning of science facts and procedures is important; however, the construction of valid conceptual models is the hallmark of students' science achievement. When students construct conceptual models they are making sense of their experiences — they are constructing meaning. Scientifically literate students are those who can construct and apply valid conceptual models of the world around them.

Our view of learning science is based on recent findings in cognitive science concerning students' cognitive architecture (e.g., Anderson, 1989, 1990, 1993; Newell, 1990), development of expertise (e.g., Ericsson & Charness, 1994; Schmidt & Boshuizen, 1993), scientific reasoning (e.g., Carey & Smith, 1993; Gigerenzer, 1991; Kaplan & Simon, 1990), conceptual models (e.g., Anderson, Boyle, Corbett, & Lewis, 1990; Grosslight, Unger, Jay, & Smith, 1991; White, 1993), constructive processes (e.g., Kintsch, 1988, 1992), and persistent misconceptions (e.g., Duit, 1991a; Griffiths & Preston, 1992). In our view, students learn science meaningfully when they activate their existing knowledge, relate it to educational experiences, and construct new knowledge in the form of conceptual models. The process of relating existing knowledge to new experiences should be intrinsically motivating and students should continually apply, evaluate, and revise the conceptual models they have constructed. In sum, we believe that five conditions are present when students learn science meaningfully. These conditions are outlined in Table 1.1.

Conceptual models are cognitive systems of related concepts and features that are scientifically valid, but simpler than the natural phenomena they represent. In science instruction, several conceptual models of the same phenomenon can be valid, particularly when the developmental level of the students requires simple representations. Thus, students learn a progression of conceptual models:

> A further characteristic of models is that in any one clearly-defined instance, a number of them can be useful as aids in clarifying the concept. For example, in the specific instance of atomic structure, the Rutherford, Bohr and Schrödinger model can all be useful. The Schrödinger model is considered to be the most accurate, because it generates conclusions that match observation most closely. . . . Each newly understood observation dealing with atomic structure requires a more sophisticated model. An understanding of atomic spectra requires a model which includes energy levels. An understanding of Heisenberg's Uncertainty Principle requires a model for the atom in which electrons occupy orbitals and not orbits. This ordered set of models leads ultimately to the model of the atom as the purely mathematical treatment of atomic structure in terms of the Schrödinger wave equation. (Levine, 1974, p. 84)

Students vary in the nature and extent of their experiences and therefore come to science class with personal mental models that vary in the degree to which they correspond to the scientifically valid conceptual models being introduced by teachers and textbook authors (see Fig. 1.1). For this reason, we distinguish between *conceptual models* and *mental models*, as did Norman (1983):

> Conceptual models are devised as tools for the understanding or teaching of physical systems. Mental models are what people really have in their heads

TABLE 1.1
Conditions for Learning Science Meaningfully

1. Existing knowledge is activated.
2. Existing knowledge is related to educational experiences.
3. Intrinsic motivation is developed.
4. New knowledge is constructed.
5. New knowledge is applied, evaluated, and revised.

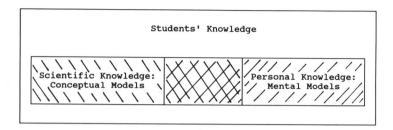

FIG. 1.1   Students' personal mental models vary in the degree to which they correspond to the scientifically valid conceptual models learned in school.

and what guides their use of things. Ideally, there ought to be a direct and simple relationship between the conceptual and the mental model. All too often, however, this is not the case. (p. 12)

As Fig. 1.1 implies, the conceptual models that are taught in science class can be either identical to, similar to, or quite different from the students' mental models. For science instruction to be effective, it is important for teachers and textbook authors to be aware that significant differences often exist between their conceptual models and students' mental models.

In order to illustrate the difference between a conceptual model and a mental model, we asked an eighth-grade science teacher to draw the conceptual model she uses when teaching a lesson on animal cells (see Fig. 1.2). We also asked her three classes of students ($N = 53$) to draw their mental models of animal cells (see Figs.1.3–1.6) and explain what animal cells are (see Table 1.2). We asked the students to do this at the very

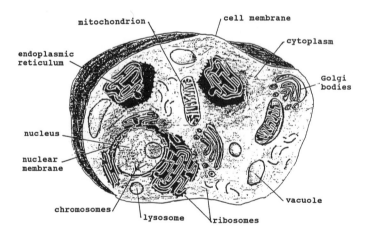

FIG. 1.2   An eighth-grade science teacher has drawn a conceptual model of an animal cell.

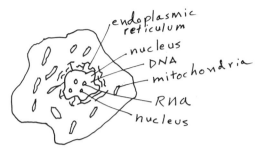

FIG. 1.3 Mike, an eighth grader, drew his mental model of an animal cell and explained, "Animal cells make up the tissues of the animal."

beginning of the school year, 2 weeks after returning from their 3-month summer vacation. They had not yet been taught a lesson on animal cells that year, but they had been taught lessons on animal cells in previous years. The instructions given to the students were:

On one side of a paper, draw a typical cell from an animal (e.g., a bear or fox) and all the things inside the cell. Write the names of those things, using arrows to point to the things. It's ok to guess. On the other side of the paper, explain what an animal cell is.

The "things inside an animal cell" identified by students and the percentage of students identifying those things were as follows: nucleus (94%), cell

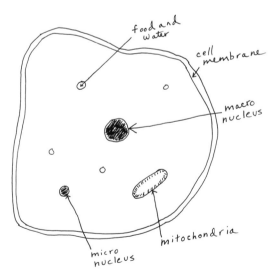

FIG. 1.4 Ginna, an eighth grader, drew her mental model of an animal cell and explained, "An animal cell is the building block of the animal."

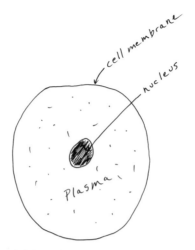

FIG. 1.5 Shannon, an eighth grader, drew his mental model of an animal cell and explained, "Animal cells make up the animal."

membrane (57%), mitochondria (47%), nucleus membrane (26%), plasma (21%), cell wall (11%), DNA (11%), chromosomes (8%), protoplasm (8%), cytoplasm (6%), food (6%), macronucleus (6%), micronucleus (6%), RNA (6%), cilia (4%), ectoplasm (4%), electrons (4%), endoplasmic reticulum (4%), neutrons (4%), protons (4%), ribosome (4%), vacuole (4%), air bubble (2%), chloroplasts (2%), cytoplast (2%), endoplasm (2%), Golgi body (2%), nuclear envelope (2%), nucleoid (2%), nucleolus (2%), paramecia (2%), and water (2%). A nucleus and cell membrane were present in most students' drawings, but otherwise the cells drawn by students varied a great deal from each other. The students' drawings and explanations revealed a variety of misconceptions. For example, one student thought that animal cells contain chloroplasts, and another thought that animal cells exist only in the blood. Two students' mental models of animal cells even included components of an atom (neutrons, protons, and electrons); the students mixed components of a cell with those of an atom

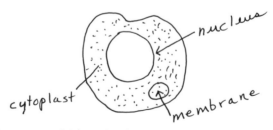

FIG. 1.6 Courtney, an eighth grader, drew her mental model of an animal cell and explained, "Animal cells are parts of an animal which keep it functioning."

TABLE 1.2
Sample Sentences from 15 Students' (Ss) Essays Explaining Animal Cells

---

S1: An animal cell is what the whole animal is made of. Every single part of an animal is made of cells. The cells contain and store energy and contain DNA.

S2: An animal cell is a living organism which makes up the body of the animal. They come in different shapes and sizes and do different things.

S3: [An animal cell is] the basic unit of life. The building block of tissues like an atom in science. It carries out jobs like respiration, carrying messages, getting food, making the body go.

S4: An animal cell is the organism that keeps the animal alive. It conducts the functions of the animal and sends signals to the brain.

S5: An animal cell is part of an animal that makes new cells. It helps an animal grow.

S6: It is a part of the animal that keeps it alive. An animal cell flows through the animal's body through the blood vessels.

S7: An animal cell is the start of life. It can be a bone cell, a muscle cell, a brain cell, etc. They all have different functions.

S8: An animal cell is a thing in the blood. It keeps the animal alive somehow.

S9: An animal cell makes up the inside of an animal's body to make energy.

S10: It is the smallest part of an animal's body. It has different parts which do certain things.

S11: An animal cell is something in an animal that helps the animal fight off sickness and death and it is one of the many cells which make or help the animal live and be healthy.

S12: The smallest particle in an animal that can complete all the functions of an animal.

S13: An animal cell is a part of an animal that reproduces itself to help the animal grow.

S14: It makes animals live. An animal cell fights off bacteria.

S15: An animal cell makes up different parts of an animal such as tissues, skin, blood, etc. It helps wounds and the animal to grow.

---

because both have nuclei, are circular (Bohr's model), and are often connected in textbooks:

> Tiny particles make up all matter. . . . The cells of your body are living matter, so your body cells, too, are made up of tiny particles. The tiny particles making up all matter are called atoms. (Jantzen & Michel, 1989, p. 31)

In sum, the preceding findings illustrate how students' mental models of a science concept can vary considerably and contain a variety of misconceptions, even when the concept has been the focus of lessons in previous school years. When teachers introduce a concept, they should help students to activate their existing mental models and reflect on them. Strategies for doing this are described later in this chapter.

NEW WINE IN OLD BOTTLES

Philosophy, the study of ultimate reality, shapes both psychology, the science of mind and behavior, and education, the study of teaching and learning pedagogy. Our view of learning science is consistent in many ways with earlier philosophical, psychological, and educational views of learning in general. Our thinking has been influenced by the constructivism of Kant and later epistemologists who posit that mental processes and experience interact to produce knowledge (Kant, 1781/1964; Knorr-Cetina, 1981; Piaget, 1954; von Glasersfeld, 1992; Vygotsky, 1962). We call our view of learning *constructive* rather than *constructivist* because it is a psychological rather than philosophical view of learning science; it is empirically based and focuses on the behavior of students. Our view is practical, not radical. We believe that students of science should work toward an adaptive understanding of natural phenomena:

> Reality is subject to many alternative constructions, some of which may prove to be more fruitful than others. The discovery of an ultimate correspondence between the constructions we are able to devise and the flow of actual events is an infinitely long way off. In the meantime, we shall have to be content to make a little progress at a time, to invent new alternative constructions—even before we have become dissatisfied with the old ones, and hope that, in general, we are moving in the right direction. (Kelly, 1961/1969, p. 96)

We also believe that students of science should develop an appreciation of constructivist epistemology. It is not yet clear, however, at what stage of cognitive development students can understand constructivist epistemology, much less appreciate it. It may be that students go through stages in developing their views of learning. Students may begin school with a common-sense epistemology in which they view knowledge as coming simply and directly from sensory experiences and, ultimately, forming a collection of true beliefs (Chandler, 1987; Kitchener & King, 1981; Kuhn, Amsel, & O'Loughlin, 1988). Later, students may come to understand the role that interpretative frameworks play in knowledge acquisition and the justification of beliefs (Kitchener & King, 1981). Until students understand interpretative frameworks, they cannot begin to understand constructivist epistemology and its implications for science. Carey and Smith (1993) reviewed the literature in this area and concluded it is questionable if even junior high school students could grasp the following constructivist epistemology:

> Knowledge consists of theories about the world that are useful in providing a sense of understanding and/or predicting or explaining events. Individuals actively develop their theories through a process of critical inquiry. Conjectures derived from interpretative frameworks merit testing; the results constitute evidence for or against the interpretative framework and associated specific beliefs. Different people may draw different conclusions from the same perceptual experiences because they hold different theories that affect

their interpretation of evidence. Reality exists, but our knowledge of it is elusive and uncertain. Theories are judged to be more or less useful, not strictly right or wrong. Canons of justification are framework relative. (p. 249)

Another reason why we call our view of learning science constructive rather than constructivist is to avoid the recent confusion caused by myriad characterizations of constructivist epistemology in science instruction (Good, Wandersee, & St. Julien, 1993; Lawson, 1993; von Glasersfeld, 1992). These characterizations include a "constructivism theory" (e.g., Ledbetter, 1993, p. 612) and a "constructivist learning theory" (Prawat & Floden, 1994, p. 37). But it is doubtful if constructivism qualifies as a theory, much less a learning theory:

Constructivism has become one of the main philosophies of mathematics education research, as well as in science education and cognitive psychology. I use the term "philosophy" deliberately, for I do not believe that constructivism is well enough defined to be termed a theory. (Ernest, 1993, p. 87)

There is yet another reason why we call our view constructive rather than constructivist. We are not calling for radical revisions of the way research in science instruction is conducted, but some advocates of constructivism are (Duschl, 1990). For example, consider Roth's (1993) criticisms of an empirical research study conducted by Lawson et al. (1991):

The use of the word *subject* to describe the participants in the research project is further evidence for the nonconstructivist position of the researchers. It hints at the distinction between the objective researcher and the observed reality. Such a position is incompatible with constructivism. (p. 799)

Even more importantly, constructivists do not use the inferential statistics employed by Lawson et al., "since causal linkages implied by such statistics are contrary to the position on causality that phenomenologically oriented and constructivist inquiry takes" (Guba & Lincoln, 1989, p. 259). Interestingly enough, Lawson et al. supplemented their quantitative work with a qualitative analysis of a few interview transcripts. However, a constructivist would have started by analyzing these transcripts without bringing to the analysis a theoretical framework, here hypothetico-deductive reasoning. (p. 800)

Lawson (1993) responded to Roth's criticisms in the following way:

The crux of the issue seems to me to be that students should be given several opportunities to raise *causal* (yes, I said causal) questions, *construct* a variety of alternative answers (hypotheses), and attempt to put these to the test. And by test I do not mean that the students should merely sit around and discuss which idea they like the best (like a band of Roth's extreme constructivists would). Scientific research is not some sort of armchair democratic process. Thus, contrary to Roth's belief that discourse is the most important mechanism for testing knowledge claims, knowledge claims are tested through the deduction of their implied consequences and through a comparison of the consequences with data gathered from experiments conducted in the "world out there" in as controlled a fashion as possible. Of course, this is not to say that thought experiments and theoretical discussions may not be productive; however, they are far from being the most important element in testing the alternatives. (p. 806)

I understand that the constructivist movement is strong in science education. Indeed it may turn out to be more than just another "ism" in a long line of rejected "isms" and become something of lasting value. To do so, however, extreme views, such as that advocated by Roth, cannot be taken seriously. (p. 807)

As Lawson's comments suggest, extreme characterizations of constructivism in science instruction appear to be leading to a renewed interest in an *unguided discovery* method where students attempt to construct conceptual models more or less on their own. Our constructive view of learning does not support unguided discovery. This method had been found to be ineffective because students get sidetracked and become frustrated (Anastasiow, Bibley, Leonhardt, & Borish, 1970; Gagne & Brown, 1961). Unguided discovery might benefit preschool children, but *guided discovery* is preferable for students learning science:

A distinction is usually made between discovery learning, in which the students work on their own to a very great extent, and *guided discovery*, in which the teacher provides some direction. Unguided discovery is appropriate for preschool children, but in a typical elementary or secondary classroom, unguided activities usually prove unmanageable and unproductive, so for these situations, guided discovery is preferable. Students are presented with intriguing questions, baffling situations, or interesting problems: Why does the flame go out when we cover it with a jar? Instead of explaining how to solve the problem, the teacher provides the appropriate materials and encourages students to make observations, form hypotheses, and test solutions. . . . To answer the question about the flame, students might note the size of the jar, how long it takes for the flame to go out, and what happens if the jar has holes. . . . The teacher guides the discovery by asking leading questions: Does a candle burn longer in a larger or a smaller jar? [Larger.] What is there more of in a large, empty jar than in a small, empty jar? [Air.] What happens when you cover a fire with dirt? [It goes out.] Why? [No air.] The teacher also provides feedback about the direction activities take. Feedback must be given at the optimal moment, when students can either use it to revise their approach or take it as encouragement to continue in the direction they've chosen. (Woolfolk, 1993, p. 321)

Our constructive view of learning science also has been influenced by earlier views of school learning such as *discovery learning* (Bruner, 1960, 1966, 1971, 1990), *meaningful verbal learning* (Ausubel, 1963; Ausubel, Novak, & Hanesian, 1978), *conditions of learning* (Gagne, 1962, 1967, 1985), *generative learning* (Wittrock, 1974, 1985, 1991, 1992), and *conceptual change learning* (Posner, Strike, Hewson, & Gertzog, 1982; Strike & Posner, 1985; Strike & Posner, 1992).[1] In all of these views, teaching and learning are active processes; teachers are not viewed as robot-like transmitters of information, nor are students viewed as passive receivers waiting to record knowledge in a rote fashion. We briefly summarize some of the key ideas in these views. According to Bruner, learning is more relevant, applicable, and memorable for students if they understand the structure (ideas and relationships) of the subject matter. In order to acquire this structure, students must be active. In Bruner's view, discovery learning helps students to be active by encouraging them to think inductively, using examples to form general principles.

Like Bruner, Ausubel emphasized the structure of the subject matter and the importance of hierarchical organization. He recommended the use of Socratic questioning and *advance organizers*, or introductory materials, that support learning by activating relevant existing knowledge and connecting that knowledge to new knowledge. In contrast to Bruner, Ausubel advocated expository teaching and meaningful reception learning that encourages students to think deductively, reasoning from general principles to examples. This learning should be active, but can become rote when the student "is unwilling to put forth the necessary active effort involved in struggling with the material, looking at it from different angles, reconciling it with related and contradictory knowledge, and translating it into his own frame of reference" (Ausubel, 1963, p. 21).

Gagne, like Ausubel, believed that meaningful learning—making connections between new and existing knowledge—can occur only when the relevant existing knowledge has been activated, or brought to mind. In Gagne's view, learning should be supported by instructional events such as motivating students, communicating the learning objectives, directing students' attention, activating related knowledge, providing guidance, promoting transfer (generalization), eliciting performance, and providing feedback.

Wittrock maintained that meaningful learning involves the generation of

---

[1]The sequence in which these views are presented does not necessarily correspond to the sequence in which they were developed.

relations between new and previously acquired information. He emphasized the processes that students use to generate meaning and understanding from instruction. In his view, these processes include attention, motivation, knowledge and preconceptions, and generation. According to Wittrock (1992, p. 531), teaching involves "leading learners to use their generative processes to construct meanings and plans of action."

Posner and his colleagues believed that a student should be willing to change his or her mind through the process of *accommodation*, displacing old conceptions with new ones, when these conditions of conceptual change are present:

1. There must be dissatisfaction with existing conceptions.
2. A new conception must be intelligible.
3. A new conception must appear initially plausible.
4. A new conception should suggest the possibility of a fruitful research program. (Posner et al., 1982, p. 214)

Many strategies have been suggested for facilitating conceptual change (e.g., Anderson & Smith, 1987; Dykstra, Boyle, & Monarch, 1992; Roth, Anderson, & Smith, 1987; Smith, 1991; Smith, Blakeslee, & Anderson, 1993). For example, Roth et al. (1987) recommended these strategies: Elicit and respond to students' misconceptions, focus on students' explanations, probe after students' answers, use open-ended and closed discussions, and provide students with practice and application. Smith et al. (1993) found these conceptual change strategies to be effective when used with specially designed curriculum materials.

Our constructive view of learning science builds upon these earlier views and extends them by explaining how students can construct conceptual models of phenomena in the natural world. The construction of these conceptual models is the hallmark of science achievement. Our view further extends earlier views by providing a model of science instruction that emphasizes constructive learning and serves as a guide in planning successful science lessons. This model is presented later in this chapter, after a discussion of how students construct conceptual models.

STUDENTS' CONSTRUCTION OF CONCEPTUAL MODELS

In our view, the meaningful learning of science in schools involves actively constructing conceptual models by relating existing knowledge to new experiences (see Fig. 1.7). Studies of experts and novices in the physical and life sciences (e.g., Champagne, Gunstone, & Klopfer, 1985; Chi, Glaser, &

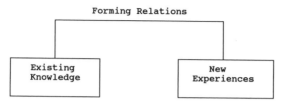

FIG. 1.7 Conceptual models are constructed by relating existing knowledge to new experiences.

Farr, 1988; Ericsson & Charness, 1994; Larkin, 1983; Schmidt & Boshuizen, 1993; Schneider, 1993) have shown that experts are experts, not just because they know more facts than novices, but because their knowledge exists in the form of related conceptual models. The construction of conceptual relations appears to enhance an expert's performance. Because the expert's knowledge is relational, it is easily stored, quickly retrieved, and successfully applied. Unfortunately, a student's knowledge is all too often learned by rote, the consequence of which is a system of knowledge that is easily forgotten and is not readily transferable to similar situations that the student may encounter.

The relations in and among conceptual models are of many kinds, including hierarchical, exemplifying, attributive, causal, correlational, temporal, additive, and adversative. It is the presence of these relations in a conceptual model that makes it meaningful to the student. For example, in a middle-school student's conceptual model of an atom, electrons (i.e., negatively charged particles) are meaningful in relation to protons (i.e., positively charged particles); both particles, in turn, are meaningful in relation to neutrons (i.e., uncharged particles). Understanding these relations enables the student to conceptually model the atom as an electrically neutral whole. Building on this related knowledge, the student can extend the model meaningfully to include an ion, a charged atom that gains a positive charge when it loses one or more electrons, or a negative charge when electrons in excess of its normal number become attached to it. In this way a concept such as *ion* becomes meaningful:

A concept can become subject to consciousness and deliberate control only when it is part of a system. . . . In the scientific concepts that the child acquires in school, the relationship to an object is mediated from the start by some other concept. . . . A superordinate concept implies the existence of a series of subordinate concepts, and it also presupposes a hierarchy of concepts at different levels of generality. . . . Thus the very notion of a scientific concept implies a certain position in relation to other concepts. (Vygotsky, 1962, pp. 92–93).

A STUDENT'S MIND: COGNITIVE ARCHITECTURE

To discuss how a student constructs conceptual models in school, it will be helpful to formulate a model of the cognitive components the student brings to bear during learning. Cognitive scientists refer to the relatively permanent framework of the mind as the *architecture of cognition*. Our specific model for learning science is consistent with more general models of cognitive architecture (e.g., Anderson, 1990; Baddeley, 1990; Britton, Glynn, & Smith, 1985; Gagne, 1985).[2]

In our *model of a student's cognitive architecture*, the perception, storage, manipulation, and recall of information are all constructive processes, not rote ones. These constructive processes are influenced by students' knowledge and experiences, but also by students' expectations, beliefs, values, and sociocultural background (Pintrich, Marx, & Boyle, 1993). As a result, no two students construct exactly the same conceptual models when they participate in a science lesson, study a science textbook, or do a laboratory activity.

Our model includes the following interactive components: *metacognition, perception, working memory*, and *long-term memory* (see Fig. 1.8). The metacognitive component represents a student's awareness of his or her own "cognitive machinery" and how the machinery works (Meichenbaum, Burland, Gruson, & Cameron, 1985). Because students differ in their metacognitive knowledge, they differ in how effectively they learn. Metacognition has an executive function. It controls the other cognitive components the student brings to bear when learning.

Visual, auditory, or tactual information is perceived and then processed in working memory, where conceptual models are formed using *science knowledge*, *science process skills*, and *basic skills* (reading, writing, and arithmetic), retrieved from long-term memory. Working memory corresponds roughly to awareness and serves as a cognitive work space. Working memory is limited in terms of how much information it can deal with at one time. Information is operated on in working memory, and the products of these operations are stored in long-term memory. Once stored, the information can be recalled into the work space to be used in subsequent operations. Long-term memory has an enormous capacity for storing categorized, hierarchically organized information.

Learning science constructively requires both science knowledge and

---

[2]This basic model of a student's cognitive architecture is intended only to introduce the concepts of metacognition, perception, working memory, and long-term memory in the context of learning science. More sophisticated cognitive architectures have been developed, known as connectionist network models, or parallel distributed processing models, that are based on parallel rather than serial processing. In these connectionist models, information is distributed over many small units rather than being located in discrete memory stores.

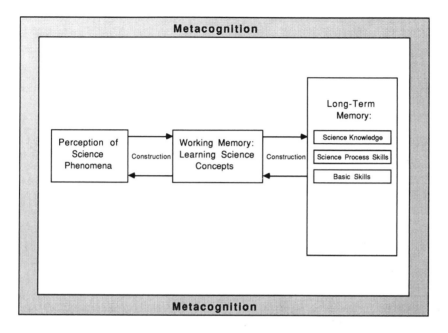

FIG. 1.8   A model of a student's cognitive architecture for learning science.

science process skills (Carey & Smith, 1993; Dunbar & Klahr, 1989; Inhelder & Piaget, 1958 ; Kuhn et al., 1988; Roth & Roychoudhury, 1993). The knowledge engages the skills that, in turn, refine the knowledge. Science knowledge includes formal theories, laws, conceptual models, principles, and facts. This is the "minds on" aspect of science learning and corresponds to what cognitive scientists call *declarative* knowledge ("knowing that"). The importance of being able to understand and explain—in clear language—the meaning of fundamental scientific concepts is a basic goal of science instruction. Scientists address this point often. For example, Erwin Schrödinger (1951, pp. 7-8) wrote of his work in quantum physics, "If you cannot—in the long run—tell everyone what you have been doing, your doing has been worthless." Along similar lines, Werner Heisenberg (1958, p. 168) wrote, "Even for the physicist the description in plain language will be a criterion of the degree of understanding that has been reached." And just a few years ago, during President Bush's term of office, the then National Science Foundation (NSF) director, Walter Massey (1989, p. 920), wrote to the President:

> I would suggest that you appoint no one as your science adviser who cannot explain to you in a language you can understand the important scientific and technological issues that will confront you. Anyone who says "It is too technical for me to explain to you" should be replaced immediately.

Science process skills are those procedures routinely performed by practicing scientists in many disciplines. This is the "hands on" aspect of science learning that corresponds to what cognitive scientists call *procedural* knowledge ("knowing how"). In the report *Project 2061: Science for All Americans* (American Association for the Advancement of Science, 1989), the science process skills were identified as computation, estimation, manipulation, observation, communication, and critical-response. Earlier compilations of science process skills distinguished between basic and integrated skills (Funk, Okey, Fiel, Jans, & Sprague, 1979; Gagne, 1967; Yap & Yeany, 1988). The basic skills are observation, classification, communication, metric measurement, prediction, and inference. The integrated skills are identifying variables, constructing a table of data, constructing a graph, describing relationships between variables, acquiring and processing data, analyzing investigations, constructing hypotheses, defining variables operationally, designing investigations, and experimenting.

The basic skills of reading, writing, and arithmetic play a vital role in achieving a constructive emphasis in the learning of science (Butler, 1991; Glynn & Muth, 1994; Holiday, 1992; Yore, 1991). These basic skills serve as conceptual tools for helping students to analyze, interpret, and communicate scientific ideas. Science activities that incorporate reading, writing, and arithmetic engage the students' minds, build on existing knowledge, and can contribute to rich, relevant contexts for learning science.

STUDENTS' KNOWLEDGE: SCIENTIFIC AND PERSONAL

In our view of constructive learning, we distinguish between *scientific knowledge* and *personal knowledge* (see Fig. 1.1). Scientific knowledge includes the current representations of natural phenomena commonly accepted by experts in the science community and introduced to students by teachers and textbook authors. These representations can take many forms, such as formal theories, laws, conceptual models, hypotheses, principles, and facts. *Scientific theories* are bodies of organized knowledge that are used to describe and explain complex phenomena and make testable predictions about them. Conceptual models are used to simplify these phenomena and make them more understandable. Scientific theories can incorporate laws, conceptual models, hypotheses, principles, and facts, but in practice these terms are not rigidly defined:

> There is no sharp general distinction among model, hypothesis, and theory. Roughly we can say that a model (whether mechanical or mathematical) is a rather limited conception to explain a particular observed phenomenon. A

hypothesis is a statement that usually can be directly or indirectly tested. A theory is a more general construction, putting together one or more models and several hypotheses to explain many effects or phenomena that previously seemed unrelated. (Rutherford, Holton, & Watson, 1975, Unit 4, p. 6)

When students are building conceptual models in science class, they are making sense of their experiences — they are constructing meaning. Students' conceptual models of natural phenomena take the form of systems that consist of related concepts and features. These systems are the result of cognitive processes that students bring to bear on their experiences. Many cognitive processes play a role here — attending, relating, forming images, organizing, and drawing analogies are among the most important (Anderson, 1990; Duit, 1991b; Glynn, 1991). As students' experience with natural phenomena grows, so too does the sophistication of their conceptual models (Anderson et al., 1990; de Kleer & Brown, 1983; Norman, 1983; White & Frederiksen, 1986). The models evolve, becoming more elaborate (see Fig. 1.9). They often are modified by adding, deleting, and modifying concepts, features, and relations. When new experiences can not be *assimilated* into existing models, then students may *accommodate* and construct radically different models (see Fig. 1.10). For example, young students who think of electricity and magnetism as two different forces must accommodate to think of electricity and magnetism as manifestations of a single force. Teachers introduce the former model when they believe that students are not developmentally ready for the latter.

Personal knowledge refers to students' own notions about natural phenomena; these notions vary in the degree to which they are consistent with scientific knowledge. *Mental models* are an important part of students' personal knowledge. Mental models are subjective and may be either identical to, similar to, or quite different from the scientifically valid *conceptual models* students are introduced to in science class. Students' personal knowledge also can include *personal facts* (e.g., Heavier objects fall faster than lighter ones) and even *personal theories*, although these rarely satisfy the criteria of scientific theories (i.e., organized knowledge that is used to describe, explain, and predict phenomena). A young child

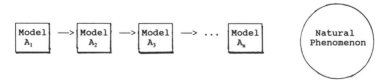

FIG. 1.9   Students' conceptual models of natural phenomena evolve, becoming more elaborate.

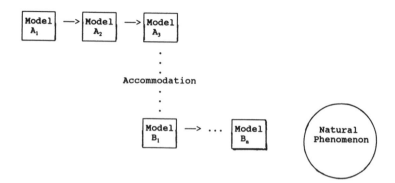

FIG. 1.10 When new experiences cannot be assimilated into existing conceptual models, then students accommodate and construct radically different models of natural phenomena.

might construct a personal theory about weather phenomena, for example. The rolling sound of thunder, according to the child, is the sound of balls rolling down an alley when the angels are bowling. When the balls pass through the clouds, the clouds are "broken" and the water in the clouds spills out. Lightning "strikes" when the angels knock down the bowling pins. And wind is caused by the angels flapping their wings.

DEVELOPMENT OF STUDENTS' KNOWLEDGE

We believe that students of all ages are predisposed to construct mental models to make sense of what they experience in the natural world around them:

> Mental models assist human reasoning in a variety of ways. They can be used as inference engines to predict the behavior of physical systems. They can also be used to produce explanations or justifications. In addition, they can serve as mnemonic devices to facilitate remembering. (Williams, Hollan, & Stevens, 1983, p. 135)

Because students experience much of the world before their schooling begins, students begin school with minds full of mental models. During the preschool years, students construct mental models for phenomena such as digestion, rain, fire, gravity, and the stars. Preschoolers construct these models based on stories they have been told, fairy tales that have been read to them, television programs they have seen, and play activities with other children. These models often are at odds with the conceptual models introduced by teachers and textbook authors. Even after schooling begins, students continue to experience more of the world outside of school than inside of it and, as a result, form mental models that may be inconsistent with the conceptual models learned at school.

In some ways, the construction of mental models by students is like the construction of conceptual models by human cultures. In fact, sometimes "ontogeny recapitulates phylogeny" and students' mental models resemble the (now invalid) conceptual models of early societies: For example, young students sometimes believe the earth is flat, cold is a thing, temperature and heat are the same, a continuous external force is necessary to keep an object moving, and moving objects stop when the force they have absorbed dissipates. Students' mental models are not, of course, always identical to the conceptual ones of early societies, but we believe the process is analogous. The advancement of scientific knowledge, in students as in societies, relies heavily on the construction of models.

CONTEXTS OF STUDENTS' KNOWLEDGE

Students' conceptual models usually are learned in school, whereas their mental models are learned in a variety of contexts such as home, church, and sports. Different models of the same phenomenon may be activated in different contexts. Language contributes significantly to these contexts in that it contains innumerable models in the form of metaphors (Lakoff & Johnson, 1980). For example, consider a physicist relaxing at home who reminds his or her children on a winter day, "Shut the door. You're letting the cold in." The home context activated an old mental model of heat, one that is reinforced by custom and linguistic metaphor (i.e., *cold* is an entity). Like many mental models, this one functions very well in simple situations, explaining its popularity. At work, however, when the physicist is solving a heat problem, the context would activate a scientifically valid conceptual model of heat (i.e., *cold* is the absence of heat).

Because mental models are reinforced continually by contexts, they are not forgotten, even when these models conflict with the conceptual models constructed later in school. Mental models and conceptual models coexist in the students' long-term memories, with situational contexts influencing which models students activate at a given time. For this reason, it is unrealistic for teachers to expect students to eliminate their mental models, replacing them with the conceptual models learned in school.[3] What is

---

[3]In our constructive view of learning, students construct and elaborate conceptual models in school by relating their knowledge and experiences. Both conceptual models and mental models are retained in students' long-term memories and are activated by contexts. In contrast, the conceptual change view suggests that students' mental models can be displaced, exchanged,

realistic is to expect students to activate the appropriate model in the appropriate context—this is a reasonable and attainable goal of science instruction. In other words, in the context of physics, we want our students to activate their conceptual models and "think like physicists." The same holds true for the other physical sciences and the life sciences. Ideally, students will learn to activate their conceptual models of physics when playing baseball, their models of chemistry when baking, their models of biology when hiking, and so forth. Teachers can encourage students to activate conceptual models in real-world contexts by bringing the natural world into the classroom and by taking the students out of the classroom. In this way, teachers will increase students' appreciation of the natural world—another goal of science instruction.

A CONSTRUCTIVE MODEL OF SCIENCE INSTRUCTION

Our constructive view of learning science has concrete implications for science instruction, even when the number of students in a class is large, lesson plans are rigid, time is short, and concepts are complex. Our view suggests a constructive model of science instruction that can serve as guide for planning science lessons and fostering the five conditions of constructive learning in Table 1.1.

In our model of science instruction, the constructive learning process interacts with all components, creating an environment that fosters *science achievement*. Students' science achievement is defined by instructional goals, and includes the learning of science knowledge and science process skills that can be applied in different contexts. The hallmark of students' science achievement is their construction of valid conceptual models.

The key components of our model of science instruction are in Table 1.3. How well these components interact determines the quality of science achievement. For example, when teachers and students are mutually constructing instructional goals, they should evaluate the prerequisite knowledge and skills needed to achieve these goals. If prerequisites are lacking, then teachers and students should revise their goals to acquire the prerequisites.

Circular patterns are used to visually represent our constructive model of science instruction because the components in it are highly interactive, with

---

or discarded. This view focuses on accommodation, and context does not play a strong role. In our view, however, all learning is contextual and much of it, if not most of it, involves assimilation. Hewson and Hewson (1992, p. 61) suggested broadening the conceptual change view because "much of what students do is learning things they didn't know by making connections to what they already know." From our perspective, this seems a step in the right direction.

TABLE 1.3
Components of a Constructive Model of Science Instruction

1. Student and teacher characteristics
2. Knowledge and skills, instructional goals, methods and strategies, and instructional resources
3. Constructive learning
4. Science achievement

decisions relating to one influencing the others (see Fig.1.11). The connections among the components are not intended to be linear or sequential. A decision that impacts on one component can, like a stone tossed in water, ripple out and impact the other components. Furthermore, the circular patterns imply that science instruction does not have rigid beginning and ending points. The sequence of instruction and instructional planning is flexible, depending on the circumstances in a given situation.

Constructive Learning

In our view, students learn science meaningfully when they *activate* their existing knowledge, *relate* it to instructional experiences, and *construct* new knowledge in the form of conceptual models. We believe that the process of relating existing knowledge to new experiences can be intrinsically motivating and that students should be encouraged to continually apply, evaluate, and revise the conceptual models they have constructed.

Teachers should guide students in the construction of conceptual models. Teachers should do this by demonstrating the constructive process for their students and prompting construction by the use of strategies.

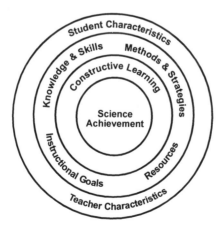

FIG. 1.11   A constructive model of science instruction.

Like playing with an Erector set, we view the process of constructing conceptual models as intrinsically motivating. Thus, students who engage their constructive process also engage their intrinsic motivation (Deci, Vallerand, Pelletier, & Ryan, 1991; Lepper & Hodell, 1989), another key process in our view of learning. We believe that intrinsic motivation can lead to positive attitudes about learning science (Koballa & Crawley, 1985) and that attitudes are an important part of students' science knowledge.

Science knowledge engages science process skills that, in turn, refine science knowledge. This circuit is broken when students are unable to construct their science knowledge. When students are unable to learn science meaningfully, they may fall back on a default strategy of rote memorization, leading to short-term, useless knowledge acquisition and poor attitudes about learning science (Glynn et al., 1991).

Teachers should encourage students to systematically apply, evaluate, and revise their conceptual models in authentic environments. An *authentic learning environment* engages students in important activities with real-world applications (e.g., a community recycling program). In such an environment, science is more than a compilation of facts; it is a way of knowing that emphasizes the application, evaluation, and revision of conceptual models.

Characteristics of Students and Teachers

These characteristics include those that are cognitive, social, and affective. An understanding of one's own and others' personal characteristics is an important aspect of metacognition. Teachers and students who understand one another are in a better position to collaborate during instruction. Moreover, this understanding can foster respect for personal and cultural diversity.

Instructional Goals

These are statements about the learning that leads to science achievement (Glynn, Muth, & Britton, 1990; Muth, Glynn, Britton, & Graves, 1988). When learning constructively, the processes the students engage in and the quality of their understanding are just as important as the product. Instructional goals will be most effective if teachers and students work together on goal construction. Students who value a goal and believe they can achieve it will work hard to do so. Instructional goals should indicate where the teachers and students are now and where they want to be in terms of science achievement.

Knowledge and Skills

Effective goals are based on the assumption that students and teachers have the prerequisite knowledge and skills to achieve those goals. By means of pretesting and structured interviews, teachers can ensure that students have the prerequisites. By means of task analyses (e.g., Wiggs & Perez, 1988), teachers can determine what those prerequisites should be.

Methods and Strategies

Constructive methods and strategies for learning science contribute to an authentic environment in which students can make sense of science and can use science to make sense of the world. An authentic learning environment doesn't just happen: Teachers and students must create it. The methods and strategies used in this environment should be adapted to students' different backgrounds and should guide students toward a genuine understanding of science. To bring about such an environment, teachers should:

- Encourage students to think metacognitively, reflecting on their own strengths and weaknesses, the processes they use, and the nature of their learning activities.
- Activate students' existing mental models by short interviews, discussions, and demonstrations of familiar phenomena and discrepant events.
- Support the process of constructing conceptual models by asking students to find relations, map concepts, and draw analogies.
- Help students to transform conceptual models into physical ones.
- Think out loud and demonstrate constructive learning and problem solving for students during science activities.
- Encourage students to represent a problem in a variety of ways including drawings, words, and mathematics.
- Have students assume the role of teachers (reciprocal teaching) and participate in cooperative learning activities.
- Employ reading, writing, discussion, and debate to engage students' interests, attitudes, and beliefs. Controversial topics, such as environmental concerns, are ideal.
- Question students, asking "who, what, when, where, why, and how." Ask students to explain both right and wrong answers. During procedures, ask students to explain what they are doing and why. Ask students to explain conceptual models, problems, and solutions in their own words. Have students supplement their explanations with drawings.
- Begin a lesson with simple concepts and problems to foster motiva-

tion. Provide opportunities for generalization to similar concepts and problems.

- Encourage students to pose their own science questions, generate hypotheses, explore alternative solutions, and practice real-world applications. Field trips can connect the classroom to the outside world.

A concrete example of a strategy that supports constructive learning is "what if" questioning (Vincent, 1993). "What if" questions asked before a lesson can activate students' existing knowledge, relate this knowledge to experiences, and intrinsically motivate students. "What if" questions asked during and after a lesson can encourage students to evaluate, revise, generalize, and apply their knowledge. In short, this strategy can foster the conditions that lead to constructive learning (see Table 1.1). In a lesson on "motion" taught to a high school class, Vincent used "what if" questions and student instructions similar to the following:

"What If" Questions

- What would happen if you fell down a hole that passed through the center of the earth to the other side?
- What would happen if the earth slowly stopped rotating on its axis over the course of a year?
- What would happen if the earth was not tilted at an angle with respect to the Sun? How would this influence weather, climate, and agriculture?

Student Instructions

- For class tomorrow, write answers to the "what if" questions. Use your imagination and think creatively!
- Tomorrow you will work in a group, brainstorming ideas, analyzing their validity, and reaching consensus on answers to the "what if" questions. Remember this is a cooperative learning activity. Have proper respect for others' opinions.
- Your group will then give a 5-minute presentation to the class, followed by comments and questions.

Instructional Resources

The implementation of methods and strategies, the development of knowledge and skills, and the realization of instructional goals are all dependent on instructional resources. Instructional resources take many forms, such as textbooks, laboratory equipment, materials for demonstrations, support personnel, library facilities, community facilities (e.g., zoos, nature parks, industries, and universities), and media (e.g., film and video). All of these resources can play an important role in the constructive learning of science.

An emerging instructional resource with great potential is the computer-based *intelligent tutoring system* (ITS). An ITS supports students' development of conceptual models in a discipline. In the area of physics, for example, there is ThinkerTools, an ITS that teaches students the basic principles of Newtonian mechanics (White, 1993). An ITS consists of various modules, one of which is the *learning environment,* defined as "that part of the system specifying or supporting the activities that the student does and the methods available to the student to do those activities" (Burton, 1988, p. 109). In order to design ITS learning environments that support constructive learning, researchers must determine exactly what expert human teachers actually do during instruction. In doing this, researchers will rely increasingly on research methods such as task analysis, structured interviews, introspection (thinking out loud), portfolios, and the systematic analysis of videotaped exemplary teaching and learning (Glynn, Law, & Gibson, 1994; Glynn et al., 1990; Wiggs & Perez, 1988).

SUMMARY

In order to help students learn science meaningfully, teachers should ensure that learning is constructive. The constructive learning of science is a dynamic process of building, organizing, and elaborating knowledge of the natural world. In our view, students learn science meaningfully when five conditions are present: (a) existing knowledge is activated, (b) existing knowledge is related to educational experiences, (c) intrinsic motivation is developed, (d) new knowledge is constructed, and (e) new knowledge is applied, evaluated, and revised.

The cornerstones of students' scientific knowledge are conceptual models. A conceptual model is a cognitive representation of a real-world process or thing. A conceptual model can be actualized in a variety of forms, such as a diagram or physical replica. Teachers and textbook authors introduce students to conceptual models in order to simplify natural phenomena, making the phenomena more understandable to students. In science instruction, several conceptual models of the same phenomenon can be valid, particularly when the developmental level of the students requires simple representations. Students, therefore, learn a progression of conceptual models.

Students vary in the nature and extent of their experiences and therefore come to science class with personal mental models that vary in the degree to which they correspond to the scientifically valid conceptual models being introduced by teachers. Students should reflect on their existing mental models when learning (constructing) conceptual models in school.

Because mental models are reinforced continually by contexts, they are not forgotten, even when these models conflict with the conceptual models constructed later in school. It is unrealistic for teachers to expect students to eliminate their mental models, replacing them with the conceptual models learned in school. What is realistic is to expect students to activate the appropriate model in the appropriate context—this is a reasonable and attainable goal of science instruction.

Our view suggests a constructive model of science instruction that can serve as guide for planning science lessons and fostering the five conditions of constructive learning. In our model, the constructive learning process interacts with all components, creating an environment that fosters science achievement. The hallmark of students' science achievement is their construction of valid conceptual models. A shortcoming in science achievement might be due to any of the following: the absence of prerequisite knowledge and skills, inappropriate goals, unsuitable methods and strategies, or inadequate instructional resources.

ACKNOWLEDGMENTS

Many of the ideas expressed here were developed in teacher in-service courses taught by the first author and supported by grants from the Georgia Eisenhower Program (Title II Higher Education) in Mathematics and Science. We appreciate the Eisenhower Program making these courses possible. The ideas expressed here do not necessarily reflect the position or policies of the Eisenhower Program.

The work reported herein also was prepared with partial support to the first author from the National Reading Research Center (NRRC) of the Universities of Georgia and Maryland. It was supported under the Educational Research and Development Centers Program (PR/Award no. 117A20007) as administered by the Office of Educational Research and Improvement, U.S. Department of Education. The findings and opinions expressed here do not necessarily reflect the position or policies of the National Reading Research Center, the Office of Educational Research and Improvement, or the U.S. Department of Education. A version of this work with implications for textbook authors was published by the first author as an NRRC Reading Research Report.

Finally, we thank Liz Doster, Tom Koballa, David Jackson, Steve Oliver, Kim Nichols, Denise Muth, Rosemarie Clark, Lloyd Rieber, Marty Carr, Michael Orey, Tom Reeves, Charles Hawkins, Tomone Takahashi, and Michael Law for their helpful comments.

REFERENCES

American Association for the Advancement of Science. (1989). *Project 2061: Science for all Americans*. Washington, DC: Author.

Anastasiow, N., Bibley, S., Leonhardt, T., & Borish, G. (1970). A comparison of guided discovery, discovery, and didactic teaching of math to kindergarten poverty children. *American Educational Research Journal, 7,* 493–510.

Anderson, C. W., & Smith, E. L. (1987). Teaching science. In V. Richardson-Koehler (Ed.), *The educator's handbook: A research perspective* (pp. 84–111). New York: Longman.

Anderson, J. R. (1989). A theory of human knowledge. *Artificial Intelligence, 40,* 313–351.

Anderson, J. R. (1990). *Cognitive psychology and its implications* (3rd ed.). New York: W. H. Freeman.

Anderson, J. R. (1993). Problem solving and learning. *American Psychologist, 48,* 35–44.

Anderson, J. R., Boyle, C. F., Corbett, A., & Lewis, M. W. (1990). Cognitive modelling and intelligent tutoring. *Artificial Intelligence, 42,* 7–49.

Ausubel, D. P. (1963). *The psychology of meaningful verbal learning*. New York: Grune & Stratton.

Ausubel, D. P., Novak, J. D., & Hanesian, H. (1978). *Educational Psychology* (2nd ed.). New York: Holt, Rinehart and Winston.

Baddeley, A. (1990). *Human memory: Theory and practice*. Boston: Allyn & Bacon.

Britton, B. K., Glynn, S. M., & Smith, J. W. (1985). Cognitive demands of processing expository text: A cognitive workbench model. In B. K. Britton & J. Black (Eds.), *Understanding expository text* (pp. 227–248). Hillsdale, NJ: Lawrence Erlbaum Associates.

Bruner, J. S. (1960). *The process of education*. New York: Vintage.

Bruner, J. S. (1966). *Toward a theory of instruction*. New York: Norton.

Bruner, J. S. (1971). *The relevance of education*. New York: Norton.

Bruner, J. S. (1990). *Acts of meaning*. Cambridge, MA: Harvard University Press.

Burton, R. R. (1988). The environment module of intelligent tutoring systems. In M. C. Polson & J. J. Richardson (Eds.), *Foundations of intelligent tutoring systems* (pp. 109–142). Hillsdale, NJ: Lawrence Erlbaum Associates.

Butler, G. (1991). Science and thinking: The write connection. *Journal of Science Teacher Education, 2,* 106–110.

Carey, S., & Smith, C. (1993). On understanding the nature of scientific knowledge. *Educational Psychologist, 28,* 235–251.

Champagne, A. B., Gunstone, R. F., & Klopfer, L. E. (1985). Instructional consequences of students' knowledge about physical phenomena. In L. H. T. West & A. L. Pines (Eds.), *Cognitive structure and conceptual change* (pp. 11–27). Orlando, FL: Academic Press.

Chandler, M. (1987). The Othello effect: Essay on the emergence and eclipse of skeptical doubt. *Human Development, 30,* 137–159.

Chi, M. T. H., Glaser, R., & Farr, M. J. (1988). *The nature of expertise*. Hillsdale, NJ: Lawrence Erlbaum Associates.

Deci, E., Vallerand, R. J., Pelletier, L. G., & Ryan, R. M. (1991). Motivation and education: The self-determination perspective. *Educational Psychologist, 26,* 325–346.

de Kleer, J., & Brown, J. S. (1983). Assumptions and ambiguities in mechanistic mental models. In D. Gentner & A. L. Stevens (Eds.), *Mental models* (pp. 155–190). Hillsdale, NJ: Lawrence Erlbaum Associates.

Duit, R. (1991a). Students conceptual frameworks: Consequences for learning science. In S. M. Glynn, R. H. Yeany, & B. K. Britton (Eds.), *The psychology of learning science* (pp. 65–85). Hillsdale, NJ: Lawrence Erlbaum Associates.

Duit, R. (1991b). On the role of analogies and metaphors in learning science. *Science Education, 75,* 649–672.

Dunbar, K., & Klahr, D. (1989). Developmental differences in scientific discovery processes. In D. Klahr & K. Kotovsky (Eds.), *Complex information processing: The impact of Herbert A. Simon* (pp. 109–143). Hillsdale, NJ: Lawrence Erlbaum Associates.

Duschl, R. A. (1990). Psychology and epistemology: Match or mismatch when applied to science education? *International Journal of Science Education, 12,* 230–243.

Dykstra, D. I., Boyle, C. F., & Monarch, I. A. (1992). Studying conceptual change in learning physics. *Science Education, 76,* 615–652.

Einstein, A. (1940). Considerations concerning the fundaments of theoretical physics. *Science, 91,* 487–492.

Ericsson, K. A., & Charness, N. (1994). Expert performance. *American Psychologist, 49,* 725–747.

Ernest, P. (1993). Constructivism, the psychology of learning, and the nature of mathematics: Some critical issues. *Science & Education, 2,* 87–93.

Funk, H. J., Okey, J. R., Fiel, R. L., Jans, H. H., & Sprague, C. S. (1979). *Learning science process skills.* Dubuque, IA: Kendall/Hunt.

Gagne, R. M. (1962). The acquisition of knowledge. *Psychological Review, 69,* 355–365.

Gagne, R. M. (1967). *Science—A process approach: Purpose, accomplishments, expectations.* Washington, DC: Commission on Science Education, Association for the Advancement of Science.

Gagne, R. M. (1985). *The conditions of learning and theory of instruction* (4th ed.). New York: Holt, Rinehart & Winston.

Gagne, R. M., & Brown, L. (1961). Some factors in the programming of conceptual learning. *Journal of Experimental Psychology, 62,* 313–321.

Gigerenzer, G. (1991). From tools to theories: A heuristic of discovery in cognitive psychology. *Psychological Review, 98,* 254–267.

Glynn, S. M. (1991). Explaining science concepts: A Teaching-with-Analogies Model. In S. M. Glynn, R. H. Yeany, & B. K. Britton (Eds.), *The psychology of learning science* (pp. 219–240). Hillsdale, NJ: Lawrence Erlbaum Associates.

Glynn, S. M., Law, M., & Gibson, N. (1994, April). *Teaching-with-Analogies: Task analyses of exemplary science teachers.* Paper presented at the meeting of the National Association for Research in Science Teaching, Anaheim, CA.

Glynn, S. M., & Muth, K. D. (1994). Reading and writing to learn science: Achieving scientific literacy. *Journal of Research in Science Teaching, 31,* 1057–1073.

Glynn, S. M., Muth, K. D., & Britton, B. K. (1990). Thinking out loud about concepts in science text: How instructional objectives work. In H. Mandl, E. De Corte, S. N. Bennett, & H. F. Friedrich (Eds.), *Learning and instruction: European research in an international context.* (Vol. 2, pp. 215–223). Oxford, England: Pergamon.

Glynn, S. M., Yeany, R. H., & Britton, B. K. (1991). A constructive view of learning science. In S. M. Glynn, R. H. Yeany, & B. K. Britton (Eds.), *The psychology of learning science* (pp. 3–19). Hillsdale, NJ: Lawrence Erlbaum Associates.

Good, R., Wandersee, J., & St. Julien, J. (1993). Cautionary notes on the appeal of the new "Isms" (constructivisms) in science education. In K. Tobin (Ed.), *The practice of constructivism in science education* (pp. 71–87). Washington, DC: AAAS Press.

Griffiths, A. K., & Preston, K. R. (1992). Grade-12 students' misconceptions relating to fundamental characteristics of atoms and molecules. *Journal of Research in Science Teaching, 29,* 611–628.

Grosslight, L., Unger, C. M., Jay, E., & Smith, C. (1991). Understanding models and their use in science: Conceptions of middle and high school students and experts. *Journal of Research in Science Teaching, 28,* 799–822.

Guba, E., & Lincoln, Y. (1989). *Fourth generation evaluation.* Beverly Hills, CA: Sage.

Heisenberg, W. (1958). *Physics and philosophy: The revolution in modern science.* New York: Harper & Row.

Hewson, P. W., & Hewson, M. G. A'B. (1992). The status of students' conceptions. In R. Duit, F. Goldberg, & H. Niedderer (Eds.), *Research in physics learning: Theoretical issues and empirical studies* (pp. 59–73). Kiel, Germany: Institute for Science Education (IPN).

Holliday, W. (1992). Helping college science students read and write: Practical research-based suggestions. *Journal of College Science Teaching, 25,* 58–60.

Inhelder, B., & Piaget, J. (1958). *The growth of logical thinking from childhood to adolescence.* New York: Basic.

Jantzen, P. G., & Michel, J. L. (1989). *Life science.* New York: Macmillan.

Kant, I. (1964). *The critique of pure reason* (K. Smith, Trans.). London: Macmillan. (Original work published 1781)

Kaplan, C. A., & Simon, H. A. (1990). In search of insight. *Cognitive Psychology, 22,* 374–419.

Kelly, G. K. (1969). Man's construction of his alternatives. In B. Maher (Ed.), *Clinical psychology and personality: The selected papers of George Kelly.* New York: Wiley. (Original paper presented 1961)

Kintsch, W. (1988). The use of knowledge in discourse processing: A construction-integration model. *Psychological Review, 95,* 163–182.

Kintsch, W. (1992). A cognitive architecture for comprehension. In H. L. Pick, P. van den Broek, & D. C. Knill (Eds.), *The study of cognition: Conceptual and methodological issues* (pp. 143–164). Washington, DC: American Psychological Association.

Kitchener, K. S., & King, P. M. (1981). Reflective judgment: Concepts of justification and their relationship to age and education. *Journal of Applied Developmental Psychology, 2,* 89–116.

Knorr-Cetina, K. D. (1981). *The manufacture of knowledge: An essay on the constructivist and contextual nature of science.* Oxford: Pergamon.

Koballa, T. R., Jr., & Crawley, F. E. (1985). The influence of attitude on science teaching and learning. *School Science and Mathematics, 85,* 222–232.

Kuhn, D., Amsel, E., & O'Loughlin, M. (1988). *The development of scientific thinking skills.* Orlando, FL: Academic Press.

Lakoff, G., & Johnson, M. (1980). *Metaphors we live by.* Chicago: University of Chicago Press.

Larkin, J. H. (1983). The role of problem representation in physics. In D. Gentner & A. L. Stevens (Eds.), *Mental models* (pp. 75–98). Hillsdale, NJ: Lawrence Erlbaum Associates.

Lawson, A. E. (1993). Constructivism taken to the absurd: A reply to Roth. *Journal of Research in Science Teaching, 30,* 805–807.

Lawson, A. E., McElrath, C. B., Burton, M S., James, B. D., Doyle, R. P., Woodward, S. L., Kellerman, L., & Snyder, J. D. (1991). Hypothetico-deductive reasoning skill and concept acquisition: Testing a constructivist hypothesis. *Journal of Research in Science Teaching, 28,* 953–970.

Ledbetter, C. E. (1993). Qualitative comparison of students' constructions of science. *Science Education, 77,* 611–624.

Lepper, M., & Hodell, M. (1989). Intrinsic motivation in the classroom. In C. Ames & R. Ames (Eds.), *Research on motivation in education* (Vol. 3, pp. 73–105). New York: Academic Press.

Levine, F. S. (1974). Concepts and models. *Education in Chemistry, 11*(3), 84–85.

Massey, W. E. (1989). Science education in the United States: What the scientific community can do. *Science, 245,* 915–921.

Meichenbaum, D., Burland, S., Gruson, L., & Cameron, R. (1985). Metacognitive assessment. In S. Yussen (Ed.), *The growth of reflection in children* (pp. 3–30). Orlando, FL: Academic Press.

Muth, K. D., Glynn, S. M., Britton, B. K., & Graves, M. (1988). "Thinking Out Loud" during text study: Attending to important ideas. *Journal of Educational Psychology, 80,* 315–318.

Newell, A. (1990). *Unified theories of cognition*. Cambridge, MA: Harvard University Press.

Norman, D. A. (1983). Some observations on mental models. In D. Gentner & A. L. Stevens (Eds.), *Mental models* (pp. 7–14). Hillsdale, NJ: Lawrence Erlbaum Associates.

Pauling, L. (1983). [Interview]. In J. C. Crimmins (Producer) & M. Jackson (Director), *The search for solutions—Modeling* [Film]. Playback Associates/Phillips Petroleum Company.

Piaget, J. (1954). *The construction of reality in the child* (M. Cook, Trans.). New York: Basic Books.

Pintrich, P. R., Marx, R. W., & Boyle, R. A. (1993). Beyond cold conceptual change: The role of motivational beliefs and classroom contextual factors in the process of conceptual change. *Review of Educational Research, 63*, 167–199.

Posner, G. J., Strike, K. A., Hewson, P. W., & Gertzog, W. A. (1982). Accommodation of a scientific conception: Toward a theory of conceptual change. *Science Education, 66*(2), 211–227.

Prawat, R. S., & Floden, R. E. (1994). Philosophical perspectives on constructivist views of learning. *Educational Psychologist, 29*, 37–48.

Roth, K., Anderson, C. W., & Smith, E. L. (1987). Curriculum materials, teacher talk, and student learning: Case studies in fifth-grade science teaching. *Journal of Curriculum Studies, 19*, 527–548.

Roth, W.-M. (1993). In the name of constructivism: Science education research and the construction of local knowledge. *Journal of Research in Science Teaching, 30*, 799–803.

Roth, W.-M., & Roychoudhury, A. (1993). The development of science process skills in authentic contexts. *Journal of Research in Science Teaching, 30*, 127–152.

Rutherford, F. J., Holton, G., & Watson, F. G. (1975). *Project physics*. New York: Holt, Rinehart & Winston.

Schmidt, H. G., & Boshuizen, H. P. A. (1993). On acquiring expertise in medicine. *Educational Psychology Review, 5*, 205–221.

Schneider, W. (1993). Domain-specific knowledge and memory performance in children. *Educational Psychological Review, 5*, 257–273.

Schrödinger, E. (1951). *Science and humanism: Physics in our time*. Cambridge: Cambridge University Press.

Smith, E. L. (1991). A conceptual change model of learning science. In S. M. Glynn, R. H. Yeany, & B. K. Britton (Eds.), *The psychology of learning science* (pp. 43–63). Hillsdale, NJ: Lawrence Erlbaum Associates.

Smith, E. L., Blakeslee, T. D., & Anderson, C. W. (1993). Teaching strategies associated with conceptual change learning in science. *Journal of Research in Science Teaching, 30*, 111–126.

Strike, K. A., & Posner, G. J. (1985). A conceptual change view of learning and understanding. In L. H. T. West & A. L. Pines (Eds.), *Cognitive structure and conceptual change* (pp. 11–27). Orlando, FL: Academic Press.

Strike, K. A., & Posner, G. J. (1992). A revisionist theory of conceptual change. In R. Duschl & R. Hamilton (Eds.), *Philosophy of science, cognitive psychology, and educational theory and practice* (pp. 147–176). Albany, NY: SUNY Press.

Vincent, F. C. (1993). What if . . .? Questions that stimulate classroom discussion. *Science Teacher, 60*(5), 30–31.

von Glasersfeld, E. (1992). A constructivist's view of learning and teaching. In R. Duit, F. Goldberg, & H. Niedderer (Eds.), *Research in physics learning: Theoretical issues and empirical studies* (pp. 29–39). Kiel, Germany: Institute for Science Education (IPN).

Vygotsky, L. S. (1962). *Thought and language*. New York: Wiley.

White, B. (1993). ThinkerTools: Causal models, conceptual change, and science education. *Cognition and Instruction, 10*(1), 1–100.

White, B. Y., & Frederiksen, J. R. (1986). *Progressions of qualitative models as a foundation for intelligent learning environments* (Report No. 81–1502). Cambridge, MA: BBN

Laboratories.

Wiggs, C. L., & Perez, R. S. (1988). The use of knowledge acquisition in instructional design. *Computers in Human Behavior, 4*, 257–274.

Williams, M. D., Hollan, J. D., & Stevens, A. L. (1983). Human reasoning about a simple physical system. In D. Gentner & A. L. Stevens (Eds.), *Mental models* (pp. 131–153). Hillsdale, NJ: Lawrence Erlbaum Associates.

Wittrock, M. C. (1974). Learning as a generative process. *Educational Psychologist, 11*, 87–95.

Wittrock, M. C. (1985). Learning science by generating new conceptions from old ideas. In L. H. T. West & A. L. Pines (Eds.), *Cognitive structure and conceptual change* (pp. 11–27). Orlando, FL: Academic Press.

Wittrock, M. C. (1991). Generative teaching of comprehension. *Elementary School Journal, 92*, 167–182.

Wittrock, M. C. (1992). Generative learning processes of the brain. *Educational Psychologist, 27*, 531–541.

Woolfolk, A. E. (1993). *Educational psychology* (5th ed). Boston: Allyn & Bacon.

Yap, K. C., & Yeany, R. H. (1988). Validation of hierarchical relationships among Piagetian cognitive modes and integrated science process skills for different cognitive reasoning levels. *Journal of Research in Science Teaching, 25*, 247–281.

Yore, L. D. (1991). Secondary science teachers' attitudes toward and beliefs about science reading and science textbooks. *Journal of Research in Science Teaching, 28*, 55–72.

2 Constructivism and the Learning of Science

Robert E. Yager
University of Iowa

Ernst von Glasersfeld (1992) viewed constructivism as a way of thinking about learning; specifically he saw it as a useful model that should never be offered as "truth." Describing the Constructivist Learning Model can be a most useful effort to stimulate science teachers and others to ponder their teaching practices as they relate to student learning (Yager, 1991a). Focusing on learning and evidence that has occurred can influence teaching much more directly than focusing on a new scope and sequence of concepts that a new leadership group promotes to improve the curriculum. Yet many science educators and funding agencies continue to focus on curriculum frameworks that they expect teachers to use in new ways. It seems clear, however, that such new ways to use instructional materials will not be found without concentrating on instruction per se — instruction that is based on what we know about human learning.

Certainly the emphasis for research in science education for the past decade has been on "cognitive science." When National Science Foundation (NSF) funding for science education was restored in 1983, learning psychologists were quick to emphasize that new correctives to resolve the science education problems should be based on the best possible research. These leaders were successful with urging a transfer of major funding designated for science education reform to the psychology directorate, to the alarm and disdain of many science education researchers. Somehow, using dollars earmarked for research in cognitive science had more appeal than using dollars designated to promote reform in science education. After all, the cognitive scientists were experts in the area of learning.

For the past decade there was much concern about the failure of typical science teaching that seemed to focus on transferring information from instructor to students. It was assumed that nearly all students could learn what curriculum guides, textbooks, and teachers defined as important science concepts. What was needed was a better understanding of how humans learned, so that important information could be transferred more efficiently and effectively to students. With NSF funding achieved, the cognitive scientists proceeded to study the few success stories arising from typical K–12 classrooms. These few were those who were interested and talented enough to pursue science majors in college. It was assumed that studying the problem-solving abilities of the best students could define ways of gaining better performances on the part of the less interested and talented. After all, the reports of the misconceptions and erroneous views on the part of large numbers of high school graduates were frequent and attracted universal support for correctives. Finding out how the best student attained appropriate concepts and views could help in getting more students to achieve in similar ways.

After gaining financial support totaling several million dollars, the cognitive science researchers identified college students who had elected physics as an undergraduate major (as perhaps the most successful high school graduates). Later, other college students were studied, including extensive work with engineering students, a group about which great concerns regarding collegiate programs were being raised by industries employing new engineers (Mestre & Lochhead, 1990).

Instead of finding answers to questions about how the most successful students learned for use in helping less successful students learn, reports emerged that there were major deficiencies with the most successful students. The majority of physics majors (85%) could not solve real-world problems in which the concepts, laws, theories, and skills they were using in college classes could be used in new contexts. In studies of engineering students 90% of the undergraduate students could not apply the concepts and processes to new problems. Instead of determining how learning occurred in the most successful students—the original aim—it was found that very few of them could do more than repeat concepts and follow directions in the laboratory. Furthermore, it was discovered that 85% of the typical class activities were verification of phenomena already described. It was as if Feynman's description of the deplorable conditions for teaching science in Brazil were universally true in the United States (Feynman, 1985).

The results provided by cognitive researchers produced new questions about learning. Instead of finding answers to questions about learning from the most successful students, it was found that successful students were not really successful. They had the same explanations of natural phenomena as their less successful peers. Their knowledge was limited to situations where they had only to repeat ideas and to perform skills as provided by instruction. Apparently the most successful learners of science are like actors and actresses — they speak well and perform well — even with conviction and with interest; however, they really know little and can not perform without instructions and an instructor.

When cognitive scientists investigated the source of inaccurate explanations, they found that they invariably arise from some direct experiences and some personal interpretations that were created by the person — often in a nonschool situation.

The emerging results from the cognitive science research caused many to review again the philosophy and the research findings from academicians who called themselves constructivists. This was a natural step because the actual conceptions held by the best students arose from their own experiences and from personally constructed meaning. There is little evidence that meaning can be transferred directly to learners unless learners engage themselves in a thought process — often initiated by a problem or discrepant event.

Today's research in science education has been shifting from being concerned with teachers to one equally or more concerned with students. With emphasis on the learner, we see that learning is an active process occurring within and influenced by the learner as much as by the instructor and the school. From this perspective, learning outcomes do not depend on what the teacher presents. Rather, they are an interactive result of what information is encountered and how the student processes it based on perceived notions and existing personal knowledge. All learning is dependent on language and communication. Table 2.1 illustrates how communication might occur as constructivist practices are used in classrooms.

Ernst von Glasersfeld (1988a) claimed that the existence of objective knowledge and the possibility of communicating that knowledge by means of language have traditionally been taken for granted by educators. During the last three decades, faith in objective scientific knowledge has served as the unquestioned basis for most of the teaching in K–12 schools and higher education. The traditional epistemological paradigm is now being turned upside down. Yet in most situations, teacher preparation and staff development programs continue as though nothing new has happened and as if the quest for never-changing objective truths were completely possible to fulfill. Recent developments in cognitive science have deprived these presuppositions of their former plausibility. It is important that all educators know of these developments if changes and reforms based on them are to have impact.

Giambattista Vico, an Italian philosopher, is credited with first proposing constructivism in 1710. One of Vico's basic ideas nearly three centuries ago was that persons can know nothing but the cognitive structures they themselves have put together. "To know" means "to know how to make."

TABLE 2.1
Constructivist Grid for Student Engagement

Who	Problems	Responses	Results
Individual student	Identifying problem	Suggesting possible explanations	Self-analysis
Pairs of students	1. Comparison of ideas 2. Resulting questions	Agreeing on approach to problem(s)	Two person agreement
Small Group review	1. Consider different interpretations 2. Achieve consensus	1. Consider different responses 2. Achieve consensus	Small group consensus
Whole class (local community)	1. Discussion 2. Identify varying views	Acts to gain consensus	Whole class agreement
Science community	Comparison of class views vs. those of scientists	Explaining difference between class views vs. those of scientists	Consensus/new problems/actions

He substantiated this notion by arguing that one knows a thing only when one can explain it. Such explanations are for others to see, to understand, and to use.

Indeed, constructivists do not consider knowledge to be an objective representation of an observer-independent world. For them, knowledge refers to conceptual structures that persons consider viable. Constructivists are like pragmatists, in that they do not accept the idea of truth as a direct correspondence to reality. Modern science does not give us truth; it offers a way for us to interpret events of nature and to cope with the world. The context in which humans need information and skills seems to be more important than the concepts and process skills teachers or textbooks include in their lessons for students.

A human being's experience always includes and is strongly influenced by the social interaction with other humans. One can only know what one has constructed oneself, but such learning always takes place in a social context. Even when one seems to think, to identify issues, and to propose responses, language is used in accomplishing each. The use of a schema always involves the expectation of a result. On an abstract level, we often turn expectation into a prediction. If we grant that others are capable of planning, this means we believe others can have schemas — perhaps even the ones that have worked well for us. Then if a particular prediction we have made turns out to be corroborated by what another person does, this adds a second level of viability to our schema, which in turn strengthens the experiential reality we have constructed.

Many cognitive psychologists believe that American pedagogy has been dominated by the behavioristic model. In the behaviorist approach to teaching and learning, the teacher's task consists of providing a set of stimuli and reinforcements that are likely to get students to emit an appropriate response. If the goal is to get students to replicate a certain behavior, this method works well, but if understanding, interpretation, synthesis, and the ability to use information in new situations is our goal in education, a behaviorist approach is not successful. Because there is no place in the model for understanding, it is not surprising that behaviorist training rarely produces the desired behaviors.

From communication theory we have learned that neither words nor sounds carry meanings in themselves. And yet, traditionally we see many science teachers convinced that the first step to learning science is to learn its special vocabulary—often by rote. From a constructivist point of view, then, this means the language users must individually construct meanings of words, sentences, and stories. This construction does not always need to proceed entirely from scratch. Once a child has learned a certain amount of vocabulary and has some idea of the rules of combining words and phrases, these patterns can be used to speed up the process of communication. From a constructivist perspective, however, the use of language per se in teaching cannot be a means of transferring information. The language must have meaning, and not be a source for it. We use language to cope with our environment, to help us make sense of our world, to communicate how we can use the meaning formulated.

Von Glasersfeld argued that instead of presupposing that knowledge has to be a representation of what exists, we instead think of knowledge as a mapping of what turns out to be feasible, given human experience. He suggested that if we were to adopt this view, profound changes in the way we teach our children would result (von Glasersfeld, 1988b). It would force educators to separate more clearly goals of teaching from goals of learning. Curriculum materials would be designed more effectively, and teachers would realize that rote learning and repeated practice are not likely to generate real understanding and useful knowledge. Teachers would also understand that knowledge cannot simply be transferred by means of words without first obtaining an agreement about meaning and some experiential base. Explaining a problem will not lead to understanding unless the learning has an internal scheme that maps onto what a person is hearing. Learning is the product of self-organization and reorganization. Knowledge is not acquired passively. Constructivist teachers of science promote group learning, where two or three students discuss approaches to a given problem with little or no interference from the teacher. What happens to, and with, such small groups of students can be used as a whole class arrives at consensus regarding the various small group analyses.

Insofar as learning and knowledge are instrumental in establishing and maintaining the student's equilibrium, they are adaptive. Once this way of thinking takes hold, teachers change their views of problems and solutions. It is no longer possible to cling to the notion that a given problem has only one solution. It is also difficult to justify conceptions of right and wrong answers. Constructivist teachers would rather explore how students see the problem and why their paths toward solutions seem promising to them. Constructivist teachers help students connect their own prior experiences to the current situation. In typical situations, science students seldom see anything they study in science classes as having any relevance or applicability in their own lives. Some specific strategies used by constructivist teachers include:

- Encourage and accept student autonomy, initiation, and leadership.
- Allow student thinking to drive lessons (this means shifting content and instructional strategy based on student responses).
- Ask students to elaborate on their responses.
- Allow wait time after asking questions.
- Encourage students to interact with each other and with the teacher.
- Ask thoughtful, open-ended questions.
- Encourage students to reflect on experiences and predict future outcomes.
- Ask students to articulate their theories about concepts before presenting the important concepts and encouraging note-taking.
- Look for students' alternative conceptions and design lessons to address any of these conceptions which do not represent those held by scientists.
- Encourage students to connect ideas to phenomena in their daily lives.

Some examples of constructivist teaching practices can be seen in observing science classrooms of the leaders in the Iowa Chautauqua Program (Blunck & Yager, 1990) and the Iowa Scope, Sequence, and Coordination (SS&C) Project (Aldridge, 1989; Yager, 1991b). Following are descriptions of teacher strategies used in science classrooms that illustrate constructivist practices. In both instances the major aim is to encourage the use of the Science/Technology/Society (STS) approach to science teaching. All of the features of STS teaching are congruent with those elaborated as examples of constructivist practices.

EAST UNION SCHOOL, SCOTT HOEGH

Tony, an eighth-grade student, came to science class with a problem. The problem he had was that his family was unable to drink their tap water. I asked him what the problem was. He replied that there was a concern about the number of nitrates. The water must now be hauled in at great expense. Tony then asked, "What is a nitrate and why is it harmful? Are there other chemicals in the water that could be harmful?"

Tony's interest in water caused me to start a module "Raindrops Keep Falling On My Head." All the modules in my science course use constructivist and STS philosophies.

We began the class with Tony's problem, no more water because of the high level of nitrates. Several students told Tony they had the same problem and the same questions. Jesse had a different problem: His water was too high in *E. coli*. Shawna asked, "I have soft water, what's that?" The onslaught of student-generated questions had begun.

The class then discussed water. We brainstormed questions the students had. Here are a few examples: What are nitrates? How do nitrates get into the water? Can eighth graders test for nitrates? What is *E. coli*? How does *E. coli* get into the water? What is pH? Can eighth graders test for pH? What is hard and soft water? What is carbonated water? How can we filter water? Should everyone drink bottled water?

"How can we find the answers to these questions?" I asked. The students generated a list of possible resources. A few examples were library, parents, farmers, Culligan person, conservationist, water treatment plant, and sewage plant.

The class decided to divide into groups to answer their questions. The groups were to research and report the results back to the class. As they began their research, more questions arose. For example, when one group was researching carbonated water, they wondered why soft drinks went flat or lost their fizz.

Several interesting things came about from the students' research:

1. Several groups contacted resources outside the school. One of the resources, the county conservationist, came to class as a guest speaker.
2. One group brought in a carbonation machine they had at home and demonstrated and gave samples, plain and flavored. They were able to answer why their soft drinks go flat.
3. Another group obtained sample testing kits from the county conservationist and students' water was tested in class. Testing of pH and nitrates was accomplished.

4. The group with *E. coli* was able to obtain petri dishes from the local junior college.
5. A contest was developed to filter water. Students polluted the water with many substances and challenged the class groups to filter out as much as possible, using only natural substances.

One can see how a unit in the classroom can be changed from the page-by-page textbook study into an exciting, challenging constructivist approach. The eighth grade science students learned a lot of practical and other relevant information about water and science concepts. When assessed following the module, students were able to demonstrate that they learned a great deal. Both low and high achievers excelled in all assessments.

Tony's thoughtful, open-ended question was answered, as well as the many other questions that developed from other students. The students found the answers through many different avenues. This is just one example of a constructivist classroom . . . it works!

ST. JOHN'S SCHOOL, JANICE CONOVER

Constructivist teaching is both something that comes about naturally and something that can be improved. My best example of constructivist teaching is that of building bridges. I didn't choose this topic. My sixth grade class was working on a natural disasters unit when a student wanted to know what would happen if there were an earthquake at the New Madrid fault (Missouri) and it reached Burlington. As the students were discussing what might happen, someone asked about the new cable-span bridge being built across the Mississippi River. Would it collapse? Would it be washed away? How are bridges constructed? What makes them seem to defy gravity? Other questions came, and I decided to latch onto the moment.

We brainstormed ways to find the answers to our questions; we divided into groups to do research. The students still had control of the ideas and activities, as well as the direction they were going. The consensus of the class was to have someone talk to us who was working on the new bridge; it was also suggested that we try to construct our own bridges using specific materials decided on by the class. They set up the criteria, the procedure, and the assessment.

Using this example, the students had complete ownership. After all the building was done, we tested it. Then we discussed why some bridges held the weight and some didn't. Using the new information students had gleaned from each other, they went back and modified their designs for another trial.

The students used each other as sounding boards for ideas and tested the ideas to see if they really worked. For their conclusion, the students discussed why they believe the new bridge would withstand an earthquake and how and why the design for the new bridge was most appropriate.

The students learned an incredible amount about forces, simple machines, water flow, bridge building materials, and the effects of the environment. All of these things needed to be covered to some extent during the year, yet by letting the students take ownership, they learned even more than I could have hoped. The real-world context helped do what was expected in the class.

BURTON R. JONES JUNIOR HIGH SCHOOL, CURT JEFFRYES

Once a teacher in the classroom adopts constructivist thinking it becomes the guidepost of the classroom experience for the students and the instructor. Preassessment, direction of study, student experiences (i.e., experiments and research projects), cooperative learning situations, unit/ module assessment, and subsequent follow-up instruction all become centered around the meanings students have constructed.

The first effect that constructivism had on my teaching was a shift from the specific instruction of "data bits" to focusing on larger pictures that included patterns and cycles. Some specific examples are:

1. Instead of teaching students about animal classification with all of its specific terminology, I would become more concerned about the picture students had of animals and how they are interconnected with the world in which we live.
2. Instead of teaching students about the water cycle, carbon cycle, nitrogen cycle, photosynthesis, and conservation of matter and energy individually, I would encourage the students to make connections between each of them and how they are interrelated.
3. Instead of teaching students about different forms of energy such as heat, electricity, light, nuclear, sound, chemical, and mechanical, I would try to have the students explore the law of conservation of matter and energy as it applies to heating their homes, driving cars, and issues involved with our energy use (i.e., pollution and greenhouse effect).

The reason for this shift was based on my need to see what kind of models and theories (or in my words, "pictures") the students had about the natural world in which live. These "pictures" then become the guiding influence for instruction in my classroom.

The evidence of constructivist practice in my classroom shows first in preassessment. Rather than giving a pencil-paper pretest that examines students' grasp of concepts and applications, I usually will ask the students a series of questions that allow them to explain the pictures they have constructed about the world. Examples of these questions include:

1. What do you know about animals?
2. What do animals need in order to survive?
3. What would cause an animal to die and/or become extinct?
4. What happens to animals when they die?
5. How are animals alike? . . . different?
6. Are animals important to have around? . . . Should we try to save animals that are almost gone?
7. What relationship does man have to animals?

Questions such as these allow the students to show the "pictures" they have constructed about animals, causes of extinction, and man's relationship to them (cause and effect) and to each other. The questioning process itself is often dictated by the directions the students' answers lead me. It is important that this questioning not create closure and that it be accepting of all student responses.

This form of preassessment is usually accomplished in classroom discussion and a written reaction in the form of a log/journal entry. (I use both written and oral to insure that I hear from all students and to accommodate different student strengths.) On occasion, this preassessment is accomplished by having the students create a scenario to role play. The scenario may come in the form of discrepant events.

These activities give me a clear view of the "pictures" students have drawn about animals and usually point out the gaps in their understandings or misconceptions they have formed. This style of preassessment also dictates from where learning situations will start. I no longer assume that students "know absolutely nothing" or that students should already know this because they had it in fifth grade. The starting point of instruction is a reaction to the "pictures" that the students bring into the classroom.

This student centeredness dictates flexibility in planning and instruction. I use the preassessment to help me in focusing students' directions of study and the hands-on activities that the students will develop/experience. In being a constructivist, I know that real learning will only take place if the students are involved in planning the direction of study and the development of activities. The students must do the work of learning.

As a constructivist teacher, assessment becomes the focus for instruction. The need to assess student progress becomes a daily ritual so that I can see how their "pictures" are forming or changing. Constructivist teaching also lends itself to more nontraditional forms of assessment. Standard multiple choice tests do not give a complete view of where the student is. These are some of the ways I monitor or assess student learning:

1. Class discussion — allows me to see where the class is as a whole.
2. Student questions — the types of questions asked show growth, or lack of it, in construction of new ideas.
3. Student interview — Individual questions to the student can show level of construction or understanding.
4. Log/journal entry — Reading students' thoughts gives insight on level of construction.
5. Task completion — The completion of an activity or project and the types of conclusions students form give evidence of the level of construction.
6. Objective tests — This more traditional form of assessment can still give valuable information regarding how students are constructing ideas.

Some of the assessments I use to monitor students are very informal. The class discussion, student questions, student interviews, and log/journal entries are guideposts for me in my role as a teacher. They clearly and quickly give immediate feedback on the progress of the students as they are constructing new ideas or modifying old ones. These simple assessments also identify when students' "pictures" are flawed or marred with misconceptions. These types of assessments can be used in a more formal assessment picture. Because assessment in my class is ongoing and daily in one form or another, reteaching or remediation is also ongoing.

Being a constructivist teacher has changed my professional life. Teaching is not necessarily easier, but certainly full of change and challenge. Endless repetition has been replaced with endless variety.

CLINTON HIGH SCHOOL, DAN BOYD

The Scientific Process Module typifies the constructivist approach to teaching. Utilizing a constructivist approach has allowed me to focus on the information the students bring with them into the classroom. Preassessment of the students' knowledge helped me formulate a plan for starting the module. The students were asked about the typical components found in the scientific process using the Self Report Knowledge Inventory (SRKI) and by responding to the question, "Is there a set procedure for the scientific method?" Students' previous science training often leaves them with the misconception that there is only one way that the scientific process occurs. Preassessment helps to identify misconceptions.

Students were asked to work in groups of four to discuss their understanding of the concepts related to the scientific process. The group interaction allowed the students the opportunity to discuss their interpretation of how the scientific process is conducted in the scientific arena. Each group was asked to explain its understanding of the process. This gave the student groups a chance to elaborate on their responses as they interacted with each other and with the teacher. Some students were able to interview scientists, engineers, and others in the community who had studied and/or who practice "science."

The small group setting is a realistic model for the way scientists work. The teacher benefits from working with the small group as the teacher can identify students' misconceptions and use them as a guideline for developing lessons that deal with misconceptions.

During the next class period the students address components of the scientific process. Students contribute the components that they find to be the most significant by writing them on overhead transparencies to be shared with the class. Students generally begin to identify that the rigid sequence they had learned previously is just one way that the scientific process may occur.

During the next two class sessions the student groups set out to design a scientific process based on the contents of a bag of plain M&M's. The students were asked to devise a process that would lead them to use the contents of the bag of M&M's using the concepts previously discussed as well as their prior experiences to articulate their ideas within the group. The student groups pursued a number of approaches to determine more about the actual contents of the bag. Most groups based their process around the number of M&M's of each color in the bag: red, green, yellow, light brown, and dark brown. A few groups related the number of colors in each bag to the total number in the bag, whereas others utilized information from the other groups in the class to determine the average number of each color.

The student groups designed the method that they wanted to pursue and assigned specific roles to each member of the group. This helped the students to gain a better understanding of the methods scientists use as they work together towards a common goal.

Upon gathering data the students shared their processes and results with the whole class. The students were asked to identify the components of the scientific process that they felt were applicable. Using this consensus approach the students were able to distinguish between the scientific process that they had learned previously from textbooks and their current perceptions. The once rigid step-by-step sequence that they believed all scientists followed was now identified as a process that shares common components but that lacks the rigid sequence. Postassessment confirmed this new understanding of the scientific process. The students were constructivist as they had constructed a meaning of scientific processes more similar to that demonstrated in realistic settings.

PHILIPSBURG JUNIOR HIGH SCHOOL, PETER VERONESI

I asked my students what is wrong with the stream in our town. I waited quite a while for each to think about any responses they had and asked one to record the responses on the board.

Most felt that the pollution was due to the coal mines but had no idea about the acid conditions in the stream. After a few moments of general responses, students got into groups and discussed the reasons for the pollution in the stream. It enabled us to explore the concepts of acids and bases.

With this example, as a teacher I am finding out about a number of things. First, the subject being discussed, a local stream, is something with which each student is familiar. Perhaps in a traditional classroom students would be immediately "told" about hydronium ions or hydroxide ions and then asked to take notes. By ascertaining the students' conceptions, I had a good understanding of how best to proceed.

Second, the use of wait time is apparent. Wait time has been shown to increase understanding in students (Rowe, 1986). Adequate wait time enables students to process the question, formulate a good thought, and, for those who may normally refuse to answer a question, provides needed time to respond meaningfully. Too often we have a false sense of security about the understanding our students have about many concepts. There are students who are always volunteering information and who enjoy participating. These students usually have the correct answers as well. As time progresses, those students who are behind gradually get farther behind and never catch up. Wait time enables many more students to respond to questions.

Third, I used cooperative learning to get students discussing the problem of the stream themselves. Students are more likely to believe their peers than any other source. Students, indeed all people, learn from debates and arguments. When a problem is posed with which they are familiar and about which they can argue or debate, they will discuss it in their own language and come to consensus at a level with which they are most comfortable. These ideas can then be shared with the entire class for approval or disapproval. During such times, a teacher is able to spend time with each group, making observations and assessing the progress of each group. Group learning also provides time for formal alternative assessment.

Each member in the group may be assigned a different responsibility. For example, one may be discussion leader, another could be a recorder, and another could be the communicator with the rest of the class. These tasks would be changed for each topic being discussed, and the overall achievement of the group would be based on all members. Each "job" could be assessed by the teacher as well as the group members in a way that is truly authentic.

Students have been trained to listen to the teacher because "The Teacher Knows All!" It is perhaps the easiest thing in the world to "tell" students things because "we" know them to be true. Therefore, we automatically presume students should know what we know, regardless of the fact that it may have taken 30 or 40 years to acquire this knowledge! Students in our educational system have been trained to sit passively, for the most part, and to be quiet "acceptors of knowledge." This is the *tabula rasa* view of education. Luckily, this view is fading in light of constructivism.

DENISON MIDDLE SCHOOL, JERRY PETERMAN

During each unit I get students to share their interests with me; my teaching is patterned by the majority of their ideas. We were studying about rocks a few weeks ago and one student came up to me and said she was interested in learning about birthstones. Before I could say anything, she informed me that another teacher in the building was going to call the local jeweler that evening. A light went on in my head and I proceeded to ask her some questions. I first asked her why she asked someone else to get the information for her. Her response was that she never really gave it a thought. I then asked if she had ever spoken on a phone before. "Of course," she said, smiling. I told her to write down some questions that she thought were pertinent to ask the jeweler. When she had completed them, we practiced a short while to build her confidence. She then took the phone into the hallway to make the call. I guess I was most impressed with the way her face lit up with excitement!

This teacher valued the student's thought and enabled her to gain autonomy of a situation by allowing her to make the phone call. In this way she was able to be responsible for her own learning.

Constructivist practices are apparent in this teacher's dialogue. He used a student's idea to function as a learning experience for her. The student was much more focused on rocks and minerals after the phone call with the jeweler. With her questions to the jeweler, she obtained a great deal of new information. There was opportunity to share this information with the rest of the class, perhaps taking the class in a different direction.

A key ingredient to constructivism is the way in which student experience is used. Such experience is a cherished commodity and is extremely important for real learning to occur. The student referred to here was interested in birthstones. Although it is not stated, one could infer that she was recently given one or had discussed them with a friend. Any number of stories would be acceptable. The main issue at hand is that when her interest was attended to, she immediately responded in a positive way and solved a problem herself.

It is necessary for teachers to be responsive to their students' ideas. This particular teacher gives us a clear understanding of what listening really means.

JEFFERSON ELEMENTARY, GEORGENA MILLER

I came to science class wearing my "pop can jewelry." I heard giggles and questions like "why are you wearing those?" After a while student questions became more elaborate and a few hit on the idea of recycling.

I had 100% participation and the excitement level was very high. They all were curious as to why I had a costume made of garbage! I used the Self Report Knowledge Inventory (SRKI) to try to find out how much each student knew about recycling and exactly "what" they knew. We concluded by talking about ways they might know about sorting garbage. Many related ways in which they recycle at home.

Focusing student attention with a motivating event increases their natural curiosity. Wearing a costume made of garbage created an atmosphere for learning about recycling. Almost instantly students began to generate questions for this teacher, and she was able to observe and take note of the conceptions that students had. Students formulate and ask questions based on their past experiences. A key component of constructivism is student questioning. In this example, the teacher had nothing to do with the way in which her students phrased the questions. Her students were able to be autonomous with their questions and were free to ask anything they wished.

Preassessment was evidenced by the SRKI. The conceptions each student had about recycling were obtained with the SRKI. Teachers who take the time to find out what their students know are able to design lessons that are understood by a larger majority of the student population. When students realize that their ideas are important, they will feel more at ease in discussing their thoughts and feelings with each other and the teacher.

FOWLER SCHOOL, LAWRENCE KELLERMAN

The students came into the classroom one morning quite angry. That very morning the principal had announced no more skateboards were to be allowed on the school grounds, and the four or five boys in this first period class who were skateboarders felt that was unfair.

In our initial discussions that morning all the students decided the topic of skateboards would be a good one to study, so we immediately decided to brainstorm all the related issues. Such issues/topics as safety, recreation, fun, exercise, laws, popularity, friction, speed, dangerous, money, and expertise were shouted out.

The class knew what to do next. Students decided to write down a number of questions that might be answered as they explored the topics they had just brainstormed and were soon in cooperative work groups writing questions to study. Those questions were submitted to me to be reviewed and possible connections were made for the next day's class. By the following day I was able to identify five distinct areas of study to submit for student approval. After some discussion the students agreed these were appropriate for the questions they had handed in.

I then asked the entire group a series of questions designed to elicit their knowledge about the potential study areas. The students' prior conceptions in several of the areas were noted for several reasons. They were used to define the range of potential resources. They were also empowered to facilitate instruction as students researched and studied the areas they chose.

JACKSON MIDDLE SCHOOL, BECKY LEWIS

My science students and I designed a mock space shuttle mission based on a similar idea in *Science Scope*. It proved to be one of the most exciting experience of the year and fostered a very positive attitude toward science in every one of my 150 students. Living in the Houston area less than one hour from NASA, my students were naturally curious about what it would be like to travel in space. They had certain ideas of their own about what space travel was like, but most of their conceptions came from watching science fiction shows. My goal for this activity was not only to have students change some previous conceptions they had about space travel, but also for them to become problem solvers and to discover for themselves the real kinds of problems that astronauts have to deal with in space.

Training for the "mission" came mainly from activities called *Life in Space* prepared by NASA, as well as articles students found in the library. Through hands-on activities as well as library research, students found out some of the problems with which space travelers were confronted. However, it was not until the actual "flight" that students really experienced these problems and had to figure out how to deal with them.

The space shuttle itself was a small storage room in the school that was fairly close to the science rooms, yet somewhat isolated from the main-stream of activity. A large floor-to-ceiling mural of the space shuttle was painted on white paper and attached to the outside of the room. This was definitely a group effort and involved the art teacher, the janitor, a parent volunteer, and, of course, the students who directed the project and knew exactly how it should look. The end results gave students the feeling that they were really entering the shuttle when they entered the room.

The layout for the room was based on information students found out during their "preflight training." The flight deck had a student-designed control panel made by special education students, and was equipped with the school's walkie-talkies that students borrowed from the office. The aft crew station had a computer on loan from one of the classrooms, set up to run a database program on satellites. The galley was located in a small closet and was stocked with dehydrated food containers, food trays, and three-quarter-sized eating utensils collected by students. A menu binder containing 18 different menus was prepared by students during the training phase and incorporated food that would be feasible to eat in space.

A life-size model of the salad machine that NASA was in the process of developing was located to the right of the galley. Students read about the device in *Odyssey* and *Science Scope*, designed their own version, and succeeded in convincing parents to build it according to their specifications. It was interesting to see how the final design emerged. It was a combination of ideas from many different students and underwent much revision and improvement before the final idea was agreed on. Tomatoes, onions, peppers, lettuce, carrots, and radishes for the salad machine were donated by the local food store, and the beans were leftovers collected from a previous class project. Like NASA's model, the students grew their plants in water and they found that plastic soda bottles served the same purpose as NASA's more sophisticated containers.

Students equipped the shuttle with a Shuttle Orbiter Medical System (SOMS) that contained a stethoscope, forehead thermometer, bandages, and "medication" for insomnia, motion sickness, and the common cold, ailments they found out might confront astronauts in space. The walls of the shuttle were decorated with satellite pictures, a map of the universe, a cartoon depicting astronaut humor, and charts describing general directions for the tasks to be carried out during the actual flight, as well as job descriptions for each member of the crew. A cassette player located in the aft crew section played *Seeker's Journey* by Andreas Vollenweider to add to the mood of being in space.

The actual flight itself involved eight students at each time for each 45-minute flight. The anticipation of each crew when it was their day to "fly" was simply amazing. The attendance rate was great, and one student who was really quite sick and couldn't come to school had her mother call to make sure she would get another opportunity to participate. Students selected their own crews, and each one had a specific job to complete during the 45-minute flight. Students wore badges to indicate their role, and they could refer to the wall chart if they forgot what their responsibility was or if a controversy arose about who was to do what.

When students entered the room on the day of their flight, they were on their own. This was probably harder for me to handle than for them, but I kept the faith! The students' only communication with the outside world was by walkie-talkie. Various activities had to be carried out during the flight, from taking health data and recording calorie consumption to launching a satellite (actually a boiled egg) by using a hand-made robotic arm. In order to accomplish all the tasks, cooperation was essential. Students were on their own and had to decide how they would use their time. It astonished me that every crew really wanted a successful flight and that this was serious business to them.

The students not only enjoyed the activity, but learned much more than I expected. They found out that teamwork was essential to a successful flight and that a small room can seem even smaller when you are stuck in it with seven other people for 45 minutes. They did encounter problems they had not anticipated, but they figured them out on their own. From this experience came many thought-provoking questions from students. They reflected on their experience and related it to what actual space travel must be like. These students were not honors students, nor would they be considered at all well-behaved in a traditional setting. However, in this situation they took their role as astronauts seriously and behaved accordingly. I was very pleased with the result of this activity, and more importantly, the students themselves were pleased with themselves; they had ownership of this project.

DISCUSSION

Constructivism is an idea that is nearly 300 years old, with literally thousands of research reports to support its validity and to develop it as a useful theory of learning. Basic to constructivism is the necessity for every human to put together thoughts, interpretations, and explanations that are personal constructs for him or herself. Knowing means being able to do something with information—that is, something more than verbalizing meaningless phrases or performing tasks by mimicry. The reports of teachers utilizing constructivist practices provide specific examples of the approach.

Learning as evidenced by giving definitions or by duplicating certain skills purportedly used by practicing scientists has been accomplished by behaviorist tactics. Unfortunately, extensive research conducted during the past decade has shown pretty clearly that most (85–90%) of the most successful students in elementary, middle, and high school classrooms taught in such a manner cannot use the information or the skills that they seem to know in classrooms and laboratories. They cannot use science information or skills in any real-world setting in solving problems. Under-graduate college students majoring in science (i.e., the most successful and interested high school graduates) are like actors and actresses—only seeming to know, but doing so with feeling and gusto.

As persons construct their own meaning, many factors contribute. The constructions of individuals are often not solitary acts. Peers contribute, and so can teachers. Unfortunately, they contribute by suggesting situations where the first constructed explanations illustrate the shortcomings of an initial conception (an explanation offered by an individual). Written materials can also assist by engaging students in real activities.

Constructivism suggests that there is more to learning and teaching than exposing would-be learners to basic science concepts and process skills. The context (i.e., the situation) is perhaps more important than any particular concept or process generally advanced to define what is to be taught and what we hope is learned.

Constructivism suggests the fallacy of teaching and learning being accomplished by acts of transmission. Meaning is not passed from one human to another (i.e., teacher to student or textbook to student). Instead, teachers must seek out what students seem to know about given situations and then confront them via peers, events, or alternative constructions that challenge the original construction. It is only when students (or any humans) are confronted with situations that do not fit the individually constructed explanations that more accurate constructions can be developed by a person.

How can science teachers move to constructivist approaches? It may not be a significant shift from existing practice, but rather a reorganization with new emphases. In fact, many exemplary teachers instinctively use many procedures that illustrate constructivist practices. Some of these include:

- Seeking out and using student questions and ideas to guide lessons and whole instructional units.
- Accepting and encouraging student initiation of ideas.
- Promoting student leadership, collaboration, location of informa-tion, and taking actions as a result of the learning process.
- Using student thinking, experience, and interest to drive lessons (this means frequently altering teachers' plans).
- Encouraging the use of alternative sources of information from both written materials and live "experts."

- Using open-ended questions.
- Encouraging students to elaborate on their questions and their responses.
- Encouraging students to test their own ideas, for example, answering their questions, making guesses as to causes, and predicting of certain consequences.
- Encouraging students to challenge each other's conceptualizations and ideas.
- Utilizing cooperative learning strategies that emphasize collaboration, respect individuality, and use division of labor tactics.
- Encouraging adequate time for reflection and analysis.
- Respecting and using all ideas that students generate.
- Encouraging self-analysis, collection of real evidence to support ideas, and reformulation of ideas in light of new experiences and evidence.

The degree that a teacher allows students to construct their own meaning will vary for teachers, individual students, and particular classrooms. School policies may also dictate the extent to which teachers can utilize constructivist approaches.

Ten points are offered to characterize science classrooms where constructivist practices can work best. Teachers can monitor their own use of constructivist practices with this 10-point self-assessment tool by responding either "seldom," "sometimes," or "often" to each point. They can also note their changes in teaching over periods of time.

- Utilize student identification of problems with local interest and impact as organizers for the course.
- Involve students in seeking information that can be applied in solving real-life problems.
- Use local resources (human and material) as original sources of information that can be used in problem resolution.
- Extend learning beyond the class period, the classroom, the school.
- Make frequent references of science/technology occupations — especially those used as sources of information.
- Focus on the impact of science and technology on each individual student.
- View science content *not* as information that exists merely for students to master for tests.
- Deemphasize process skills as the "special" skills that should be learned because they are used by practicing scientists.
- Provide opportunities for students to perform in citizenship roles as they attempt to resolve issues they have identified.

- Demonstrate that current science and technology impact the lives of all currently and will impact them in the future.

Constructivism represents a useful model for indicating how learning occurs. It is an active process that occurs in the brain of each person. The process includes forming explanations of natural phenomena. Many of these conceptions are not backed with much real evidence for their validity. But once an individual offers his or her personal explanation for a given phenomena, it remains useful and a part of that person's "knowing." The job of the teacher is to help the student expand and/or alter the concept to account for new evidence and/or observations that render the original conception as inadequate.

Constructivism demands classrooms and teachers quite unlike traditional ones if real learning is to occur. It also demands different instructional materials to facilitate real learning. These materials include real people as well as original sources of written materials. Textbooks as organizers for lessons and teaching units are seldom used.

THE RESULTS WITH CONSTRUCTIVIST TEACHING

Iowa teachers like those cited here have also collected much valuable information concerning their successes with constructivist practices. Most cited are leaders in the Iowa Chautauqua Program, an in-service education program enrolling 250 new teachers each year and utilizing 50 experienced lead teachers as part of the staff team. The list that follows illustrates the nature of the program.

1. A 2-week leadership conference for 25 of the most successful teachers from previous years who want to become a part of the instructional team for future workshops.
2. A 3-week summer workshop at each new site for 30 new teachers electing to try constructivist practices and strategies; the workshop provides experience with such practices where the teachers are the students. Time is provided to plan a 5-day constructivist unit to be used with students in the fall.
3. Use of 5-day STS unit in the classrooms of all summer participants during September or early October.
4. A 2½-day fall short course for 30–50 teachers (including the 30 enrolled during the summer); the focus is on developing a month-long module where constructivist practices are used along with an extensive assessment plan.

5. An interim communication with central staff, lead teachers, and fellow participants, including a newsletter, special memoranda, monthly telephone contacts, and school/classroom visits.
6. A 2½-day spring short course for the same 30–50 teachers who participated in the fall; this session focuses on reports by participants on their experiences with constructivist teaching and the results of the assessment program.

Fifteen lead teachers have participated in several experiments where they taught one section of students with constructivist practices and a contrast section from a regular textbook. Six goal and assessment domains are recognized as a means of utilizing constructivist practices and assessing their success when compared to student performance in regular textbook sections. The domains include:

Concept Domain (mastering basic content constructs).
Process Domain (learning the skills scientists use in sciencing).
Creativity Domain (improving quantity and quality of questions, explanations, and test for the validity of personally generated explanations).
Attitudinal Domain (developing more positive feelings concerning the usefulness of science, science study, science teachers, and science careers).
Applications and Connections Domain (using concepts and processes in new situations).
World View Domain (formulating an accurate picture of the nature of science and technology).

The following results have been attained after several studies of Chautauqua Lead Teachers teaching a section of science with constructivist practices compared with a section where the textbook was the primary organizer. In all cases, the students in the constructivist environment displayed significantly more positive attitudes and more growth in the domains. Specific generalizations include:

1. Students in classes taught with a constructivist approach learn more science concepts when compared to students in classes taught with a textbook-oriented approach.
2. Students in classes taught with a constructivist approach develop science process skills significantly better than did students in classes taught with a textbook-oriented approach.
3. Students in classes taught with a constructivist approach are able to apply more science concepts and principles when compared to students in classes taught with a textbook-oriented approach.

4. Students in classes taught with a constructivist approach are able to develop more science creativity skills when compared to students in classes taught with a textbook-oriented approach.
5. Students in classes taught with a constructivist approach develop more positive attitudes toward science when compared to students in classes taught with a textbook-oriented approach.
6. Students in classes taught with a constructivist approach gain improved more in their understanding of the nature of science when compared to students in classes taught with a textbook-oriented approach.
7. Students in classes taught with a constructivist approach possess more accurate perceptions concerning science careers than do students in classes taught with a textbook-oriented approach.

CONCLUSION

Constructivist behaviors in teachers produce students in K–12 classrooms who more nearly match desired learning outcomes. Students understand the nature of science better and have more accurate and realistic views of science careers. But most importantly, students in constructivist classrooms: (a) demonstrate a superior understanding of basic science concepts, (b) use and understand basic processes of science better, (c) can apply science concepts and processes in new situations, (d) have more positive attitudes of science, science study, and science teachers, (e) develop better creativity skills including questioning, proposing solutions, and predicting consequences, and (f) have more complete views of the nature of science. In short, many of the most perplexing problems of science education are resolved when teachers use constructivist procedures.

Questions remain concerning the ability of all teachers to use such techniques and what 13 years of student experiences in constructivist classrooms might produce. The indications are exciting; the potential for real reform has never been greater.

REFERENCES

Aldridge, B. G. (1989, January/February). Essential changes in secondary science: Scope, sequence, and coordination. *NSTA Reports!*, pp. 1, 4–5.

Blunck, S. M., & Yager, R. E. (1990). The Iowa Chautauqua Program: A model for improving science in the elementary school. *Journal of Elementary Science Education, 2*(2), 3–9.

Feynman, R. P. (1985). *Surely you're joking, Mr. Feynman.* New York: Bantam.

Mestre, J. P., & Lochhead, J. (1990). *Academic preparation in science: Teaching for transition from high school to college.* New York: College Entrance Examination Board.

Rowe, M. B. (1986). Wait time: Slowing down may be a way of speeding up! *Journal of Teacher Education, 37*(1), 43-50.

Vico, G. (1858). *De antiquissima Italorum sapientia*. Naples, Italy: Stamperia dé Classici Latini. (Original work published 1710)

von Glasersfeld, E. (1988a, July-August). *Environment and communication*. Paper presented at the ICME-6, Budapest, Hungary.

von Glasersfeld, E. (1988b). *Cognition, construction of knowledge, and teaching*. Washington, DC: National Science Foundation.

von Glasersfeld, E. (1992). Questions and answers about radical constructivism. In M. K. Pearsall (Ed.), *Scope, sequence, and coordination of secondary school science: Volume II: Relevant research* (p. 169). Washington, DC: National Science Teachers Association.

Yager, R. E. (1991a). The constructivist learning model: Towards real reform in science education. *The Science Teacher, 58*(6), 52-57.

Yager, R. E. (1991b). SS&C initiates nationwide reform. *SS&C IOWA UPDATE, 1*(1), 1.

3 Children's Attitudes Toward Learning Science

Thomas R. Koballa, Jr.
University of Georgia

Terrell, a fifth grader, is talking with his parents about the events of today's science lesson:

> It started out *real bad* because we watched a *stupid* egg squeeze into a bottle, and then Ms. Wilson made us do it. Vernard, Mike, and Patricia were in my group. Vernard is one of my *best friends*, but I *don't like* Mike because he picks on Patricia. She has red hair and freckles, you know.
>
> Things *got better* after Ms. Wilson made Mike go stand out in the hall. I held the rolled-up piece of paper for Patricia to light. It was a little *scary* holding that flaming paper. I felt a *lot better* when I shoved it into the bottle and Vernard put the egg on top. It was *fun* to watch the egg sort of dance on top and then squirt into the bottle, I guess because we were doing it and not watching Ms. Wilson. The *fun* didn't last long, however. Ms. Wilson handed out a *dumb* worksheet full of questions. I *hate* that ditto paper; it smells real *bad*. The first five questions were *easy*, but the others were *super hard*. I could *care less* about how to get that egg out of the bottle.

As his account of the science lesson suggests, it's not just what Terrell knows about how air pressure causes the egg to enter and exit the bottle, but also how he feels about the experience that will influence his future choices and goals. Terrell, other students like him, and his teacher probably are not conscious of the extent to which affective concerns play a role in their learning environment. The feelings or emotions that one has about the natural world are at the center of affective learning in science (Simpson, Koballa, Oliver, & Crawley, 1994). Affective learning in science involves the

59

learning of attitudes and values about science and the development of students' personal and emotional growth.

Affective learning is of interest to both teachers and researchers because it is an outcome of science instruction that has implications far beyond the immediate classroom experience (Rutherford & Ahlgren, 1990). Unfortunately, efforts to clarify affective objectives and to deliberately introduce affective learning into the elementary science curriculum have not been particularly easy (Raizen et al., 1989). Affective objectives are the planned outcomes of affective learning. Some teachers see affective objectives as irrelevant or unattainable, whereas other teachers want to attain them, but find that their efforts to do so erode over time. According to Ringness (1975), this erosion occurs because the attainment of affective objectives is a slow process and because these objectives are hard to evaluate. Philosophical, political, and legal embranglements often accompany teachers' attempts to evaluate and grade pupils' affective achievement. Teachers do not want their instruction to be perceived as indoctrination.

Despite the complexity of the task, the promotion of favorable feelings toward science, scientists, and science learning remains an important goal of science education (Bybee et al., 1989). To achieve this goal, educators need to consider the feelings that are wittingly and unwittingly fostered in the context of elementary school science.

The purpose of this chapter is to describe the affective domain in science education, paying particular attention to science learning in the elementary grades. In this regard, attention is directed to two areas: the findings of science education research in the affective domain, and new approaches for understanding how affect influences science-related behaviors. Much of the discussion focuses on attitudes, because attitude theory integrates the themes of cognition and motivation (Eagly & Chaiken, 1993) and because attitudes have been given far more attention by science educators over the years than any other construct in the affective domain (Simpson et al., 1994).

AFFECTIVE RESEARCH IN SCIENCE EDUCATION

The complexity of the learning process makes it difficult to study in its entirely. Thus, psychologists and educators classify human learning into three domains: cognitive, psychomotor, and affective (e.g., Bloom, 1976). Classifying learning in this way simplifies its description and facilitates its evaluation. Science in the elementary grades involves behaviors from all three domains. Activities that may be loosely described as thinking, such as remembering, analyzing, and evaluating, are considered within the cognitive domain. Science skills such as reading a thermometer, building a bird house, and operating a pulley system are largely concerned with psycho-motor learning. Expressions of feeling, emotion, or degree of acceptance regarding science are included within the affective domain. Interestingly, no action is solely cognitive, psychomotor, or affective. For example, it would be unlikely for a person to build a bird house without giving some thought to the matter and without having some feeling for birds. Each domain includes facets of the other two, but the more dominant aspect of any act may be identified (Ringness, 1975).

Historical Background

The inspiration for attitude research in science education originated from John Dewey's philosophy of science education. In the inaugural issue of *General Science Quarterly*, which later came to be called *Science Education*, Dewey (1916) underscored the need for teaching scientific attitudes in the elementary grades as an important aspect of educating reflective thinkers. Of interest to Dewey were the attitudes of intellectual integrity, observation, interest in testing opinions and beliefs, and open-mindedness. He believed that science education should be about the business of developing "a certain mental attitude," rather than communicating "a fixed body of information, or . . . preparing a small number of persons for the further specialized pursuit of some particular science" (Dewey, 1934, p. 3).

Efforts to translate Dewey's thoughts about scientific attitudes into practice were numerous. An early attempt by Weller (1933) was her development of a true–false attitude scale to determine if scientific attitudes could be taught in the elementary grades. "Finding a four leaf clover brings good luck" and "To go to sleep while looking at the moon causes nightmares" are two items that appeared on her scale (Weller, 1933, p. 93). More recently, some researchers labored at defining the elements of scientific attitude and developing scales to measure them (Baumel & Berger, 1965; Davis, 1934; Koslow & Nay, 1976), whereas others worked at determining the effects of instructional interventions on scientific attitudes (Charen, 1966; Scott, 1940).

Research on students' attitudes toward science, scientists, and science learning appeared in the science education literature in the 1960s (e.g., Schwirian, 1968; Vitrogen, 1967; Weinstock, 1967). The inspiration for this research did not originate from Dewey's philosophy of education, but from the literature of the social sciences, primarily psychology. Major influences seemed to be Thurstone (1928) and Likert's (1932) pioneering work on attitude measurement and popular notions about attitude and its relation-ship to behavior (e.g., Festinger, 1957; Sherif, Sherif, & Nebergall, 1965), although these influences were rarely acknowledged in the research reports. *Attitude* was presented as a person's general evaluation of an object, where the object was typically identified as science or related to science. Attitudes toward science were distinguished from scientific attitudes by Aiken and Aiken (1969), and later by Klopfer (1976) and others (Laforgia, 1988; Shrigley, 1983) to help clarify the differences between these two similarly named concepts. Today, "the term attitude toward science . . . refer[s] to a general and enduring positive or negative feeling about science [and] should not be confused with scientific attitude, which may be more aptly labeled scientific attributes" (Koballa & Crawley, 1985, p. 223). The label *scientific attributes* stems from the notion that scientific attitudes embody the characteristics or attributes of scientists that are considered desirable in students.

Over time it became increasingly evident to teachers and researchers that even though students are knowledgeable about the modes of thinking that characterize scientific attitudes, they "may be quite unwilling to adopt them as their own" (Schibeci, 1984, p. 27). According to Schibeci (1984), this means that children may hold favorable or unfavorable personal attitudes toward these scientific attitudes. Although scientific attitudes remain fixed as science curriculum objectives (Gauld, 1982), students' attitudes toward science and the related topics of attitudes toward science learning and attitudes toward scientists became the foci of researchers' attention.

The study of science attitudes proliferated during the 1970s and 1980s as teachers, curriculum developers, and researchers began to recognize the important role played by attitudes in science learning. Attitudes were considered both facilitators and products of the cognitive learning process. Early efforts focused on documenting student attitudes and their relationship to science achievement; later, theoretical models from the social and behavioral sciences began to guide the research. Essentially, the investigations focused on three issues summarized by Simpson et al. (1994, p. 216) as three questions: "(1) What is the magnitude of science related affect in school students? (2) What changes in attitudes can be detected in response to research treatments or changes in school science practices? (3) What relationships can be supported between attitude and school-science related behaviors?" It is to these issues that we now turn. These questions are answered, in part, in reviews by Gardner (1975), Schibeci (1984), Blosser (1984), and Simpson et al. (1994). These reviews provide a wealth of information about the study of attitudes pertinent to the elementary grades. But before turning our attention to the findings highlighted in these reviews, it is important that something be said about the attitude instruments developed for use with children. The instruments take many forms, and vary in terms of their psychometric complexity. Some of the more popular instruments are described in Table 3.1. Satisfactory reliability for these instruments has been reported by developers and users, but the validity of these instruments has not been well documented. Whether or not the

TABLE 3.1
Summary Data for Sample Attitude Instruments

Developers and Instrument Focus	Instrument Format	Sample Items
The Ayers and Price (1975) instrument assesses fourth to eighth grade students' attitudes toward science.	Projective instrument of sentence fragments and objective questions with four response options, ranging from "never" to "always."	We study science in school because . . . Do you like the science experiments you do in school?
Chambers' (1983) instrument measures elementary grade students' attitudes toward scientists.	Draw a scientist on a blank sheet of paper.	Picture of scientist compared to criteria for standard image: lab coat, eye glasses, symbols of research and knowledge, etc.
Hadden and Johnstone (1982) constructed a scale to assess 10-year-old Scottish students' science attitudes.	Semi-structured interview, seven-point semantic differential scale and five-point Likert scales, ranging from "strongly agree" to "strongly disagree."	What does 'scientist' mean to you? Studying science is . . . interesting-dull, exciting-boring. Doing science experiments in school is boring.
Haladyna and Thomas' (1979) instrument measures children's attitudes toward science and other school subjects.	Visual arrays of happy, neutral, and sad faces.	What face do you wear . . . when it is school time? when science is over?
The Harvey and Edwards (1980) survey assesses the attitudes toward physical science and biological science of 9- to 12-year-old students.	Visual arrays of five circles that increase in size from left to right, with the smallest labeled "dislike" and the largest labeled "like."	Items were not included in the report.
Lowery's (in Hofman, 1977) instrument measures fourth grade students' attitudes toward science, the scientific process, and scientists.	Word association, picture interpretation, and sentence completion.	Words: science, experiment, and scientist; pictures: images of science, experiments in progress and scientists. Sentence completion items were not presented in the report.
Perroin's (1966) instrument was designed to measure fourth to eighth grade students' attitudes toward science as a school subject.	Projective items consisting of sentence fragments and questions with four response options, ranging from "never" to "always."	We study science in school because . . . Do you like the science experiments you do in school?
Shrigley's (1972) scale measures sixth grade students' attitudes toward science, science content, and handling science equipment.	Five-point Likert scale, ranging from "strongly agree" to "strongly disagree."	I dislike science. I feel like a scientist as I work with the equipment.

measures actually reveal childrens' science attitudes remains a concern (Schibeci & Sorensen, 1983).

Children's Attitudes Toward Science

Despite the problems associated with attitude instruments, what they reveal provides us with the best available information about children's attitudes toward science. According to several authors (Hodson & Freeman, 1983; Lovell & White, 1958), attitudes toward science tend to be established at an early age, and children enter secondary school with attitudes toward science that are well formulated. Based on their review of research on scientific arousal, Ormerod and Duckworth (1975) put the period of 8 to 13 years as the critical stage in which a child's attitude toward science can be influenced.

The findings of several assessments indicated that although 9-year-olds feel quite positive about science, attitude scores drop as students progress through the grades (Ayers & Price, 1975; Johnson, 1981; Mullis & Jenkins, 1988). Observers attribute these attitude changes to science teaching (Johnson, 1981; Simpson et al., 1994), because young children and adolescents infrequently associate science with encounters outside of school. Science teaching where a textbook is central and experiments are few results in less favorable attitudes toward science. However, Johnson (1981) pointed out that students may be unable to separate their attitudes toward science from their attitudes toward school. Thus, the declines witnessed may indeed reflect children's growing disenchantment with school rather than with science.

Children's drawings reveal much about their perceptions of scientists and the work that scientists do. A stereotypic image of a scientist as a man with lab coat, eyeglasses, and beard (see Fig. 3.1) appears frequently in children's drawings (Chambers, 1983; Krause, 1976; Schibeci & Sorensen, 1983). Sometimes children's drawings of scientists include women, science equipment, and activities (see Fig. 3.2 and 3.3), and symbols of science products, such as a scientist saying "Eureka, I've discovered the formula!" Alternative images of scientists and the scientific enterprise were found to develop concurrently with children's standard image of scientists (Chambers, 1983). The children's alternative images highlight the perceptions of mythical, diabolic, and secretive aspects of scientists' work.

Attitude, Achievement, and Behavior

Johnson (1981, p. 39) believed that children's attitudes toward science are important for several reasons. "Attitudes help shape achievement, determine whether students will want to take unrequired science courses, and encourage or discourage students to pursue science-related careers." But, does research corroborate Johnson's beliefs about how attitudes are related to achievement and science-related behaviors?

FIG. 3.1 A boy depicts a scientist as bearded man, with eyeglasses and a pocket protector for pens.

FIG. 3.2 A girl depicts a scientist as a woman in a lab coat, with eyeglasses, and science equipment and books.

Studies that investigated the relationship between science attitudes and achievement report mixed findings. Over 130,000 elementary students were represented in Willson's (1983) meta-analysis. He reported an average correlation of .17 between the two variables at the elementary level, a relationship that he described as "quite low." Research reviews by Gardner (1975) and Schibeci (1984) provided little confirmation of a substantial attitude-achievement relationship from the elementary grades through college. The majority of the studies looking for a relationship between

FIG. 3.3   A second girl depicts a scientist as a man unearthing fossils with a shovel.

attitude and achievement reviewed by Gardner found either no relationship or a negative relationship. Of the studies reviewed by Schibeci, several reported a positive attitude-achievement relationship with correlations averaged between .3 and .5, whereas others reported no relationships. Rennie and Punch (1991) suggested that the narrow interpretation of attitude applied in most studies is likely responsible for the weak relationships found between attitude and achievement. Unfortunately, most research tends to corroborate Fraser's (1982) position that no evidence exists for the assumption that achievement scores can be enhanced by improving attitudes. Thus, teachers should not expect students with favorable attitudes toward science to be high science achievers.

The relationship between attitude and such science-related behaviors as choosing to enroll in elective science courses and prepare for science careers have not been studied in the elementary grades. These relationships have been traditionally studied during the high school and college years when decisions of life-long importance are often made by students. Studies involving older students are discussed here because the conclusions they offer may be applicable when working with children. Shrigley (1990, p. 97) concluded from a review of studies that looked at the relationship between attitude and behavior that "Science attitude scales can be expected to predict science-related behavior," but only under certain conditions. The conditions identified by Shrigley are:

- When attitude and the behavior of interest are measured at the same level of specificity.
- When social context and individual differences, including cognitive ones, are considered.
- When the person's intention regarding the behavior is known.

These conditions suggest that instead of using only a measure of science attitude to predict children's participation in a school science fair, a researcher should measure attitude toward science fair participation, assess the social context of the action, and gather information about children's intentions to participate. When these conditions were operationalized by Crawley and Koballa (1992), they found that Hispanic-American students' enrollment in high school chemistry could be predicted with accuracy. Similar results are expected for student career choices. Each of Shrigley's three conditions is addressed in Ajzen and Fishbein's (1980) theory of reasoned action, which is discussed later in this chapter.

Attitudes and Gender

A conclusion reached in a number of studies of the relationship between gender and attitudes toward science is that girls have less positive attitudes toward science than boys, with these differences becoming more pronounced by ages 13 and 17 (Johnson, 1981; Mullis & Jenkins, 1988; Shrigley, 1972; Simpson & Oliver, 1990). Other studies suggest that the attitudes of boys and girls differ depending on whether the biological or the physical sciences are considered. Nine- to 12-year-old girls were less interested in physical sciences and more interested in biological sciences than boys of the same age (Harvey & Edwards, 1980).

Both physiological and sociological functions have been examined to explain these findings. More credence is given to the sociological factors because it seems that they can be influenced (Campbell & Connolly, 1987; Thomas, 1986). The different experiences with science, particularly physical science, provided for males and females and cultural expectations placed on girls by parents and teachers are among the most frequently given sociological reasons for why girls have less positive attitudes toward science than boys (Campbell, 1991).

Attitudes and Socioeconomic Status

Fleming and Malone's (1983) meta-analysis revealed no significant relationship between socioeconomic status and science attitudes among elementary school students. Furthermore, their study showed that African-American students' attitudes toward science are less positive than the attitudes of their Anglo-American counterparts during the elementary grades, but that the trend is reversed by the time students reach high school. The results may be misleading, however, because the findings of several studies included in the meta-analysis are suspected of being confounded by students' socioeconomic status. This contention is supported by Johnson's (1981) report of the 1977 National Assessment of Educational Progress results that revealed no significant difference between Anglo- and African-American 9- and 13-year-olds in their attitudes toward science.

Attitudes and Instruction

Advocates of activity-oriented science instruction at the elementary level emphasize the development of favorable attitudes toward science as one of its merits. The results of some research studies seem to support this claim (Johnson & Ryan, 1974; Kyle, Bonnstetter, & Gadsden, 1988; Lowery, 1967, Simmons & Esler, 1972; Wideen, 1975; Story & Brown, 1979). Yet other investigators reported that children who participated in activity-oriented science programs displayed attitudes that were no better than the attitudes reported by children who were not program participants (Allen, 1972; Krockover & Malcolm, 1978; Vanek & Montean, 1977). Despite the conflicting findings, the favorable effects of activity-oriented instruction on children's attitudes toward science are generally accepted. This acceptance is particularly strong when activity-oriented instruction includes opportunities for children to discuss and reflect on what is taught (Tippins & Koballa, 1991).

Empirical Research on Children's Attitudes: Conclusions

In general, the research tells us that children's attitudes toward science appear to become less positive as they progress through the elementary grades, and become even less positive as students move onto middle school and high school. Gender seems to play an important role in how students feel about science, with girls preferring the biological sciences over the physical sciences. The influence of socioeconomic and instructional factors on attitudes is minimal at best. Explanations for such low correlations have been offered by Krynowsky (1988) and Simpson et al. (1994). Paramount among these explanations is the dearth of clarity associated with concept of attitude. This conceptual uncertainty has greatly hindered science educators' efforts to assess and improve attitudes. Acknowledging this problem, Krynowsky urged researchers to base their work on theoretical foundations that can guide the development of assessment instruments, as well as strategies that will improve and maintain favorable attitudes toward science.

THEORETICAL MODEL FOR ATTITUDE RESEARCH

There are few efforts to base attitude research on theoretical models in the science education literature. One such effort, launched by Shrigley in the late 1970s, has spanned more than a decade and has produced some rather informative results. The research legacy of social psychologist Carl Hovland (Hovland, Janis, & Kelley, 1953) served as the foundation for much of the work that focused on the identification and testing of variables that drive attitude change. Along the way, attention was also directed to the psychometrics of attitude assessment.

Guided by the work of Hovland, the study of persuasion became the thrust of the research. Persuasion is the act of "encouraging someone to *choose* to make a change in beliefs, attitudes, and/or behaviors" (Reardon, 1991, p. 12). No matter what approach or strategy is utilized, according to Petty and Cacioppo (1981), persuasion is the vehicle for all belief, attitude and behavior change. And when operationalized via Hovland's model, persuasion looks a lot like classroom instruction. In the science classroom, the teacher as the message source and students as the message receivers function as active agents in the persuasive process (Koballa, 1992; Koballa & Warden, 1992). Students construct their own meanings from the messages presented by the teacher, often by negotiating meaning with their classmates (Wheatley, 1993).

The research program guided by Shrigley studied mainly the science-related attitudes and behaviors of teachers and high school students (see Shrigley & Koballa, 1992). Nevertheless, the research led to several conclusions that have implications for the study of attitudes at the elementary level. One conclusion is that a speaker who is perceived to be trustworthy and an expert on the topic will be more persuasive than one who is not. Another is that attitudes can be changed in as little as 30 minutes when the persuasive message is designed to address the audiences' salient beliefs. A third is that anecdotal messages and messages that present both sides of an issue are more persuasive than those that contain statistical, data-summary information and that present only one side of an issue. Other conclusions germane to attitude study at the elementary level are that positive shifts in attitudes are not related to science achievement gains, message acceptance is not affected by the recipient's self-esteem or intelligence, and videotaped and audio-taped messages are no more convincing than printed ones.

A COGNITIVE REVOLUTION SHAPES ATTITUDE RESEARCH

Attitudes have both affective and cognitive components. However, much of the attitude research, due to its heavy reliance on intuition and dated theoretical foundations, tends to focus on the feelings for or against something without considering the accompanying intellectualization. Munby (1990) noted this weakness in describing a tension he detected in science attitude research. The tension is closely tied to the use of two dichotomies that both use the term cognition. One is the cognitive-affective dichotomy that, according to Munby, presents the misleading idea that affect need be separated from cognition. He claimed that this dichotomy helps us to sort out and make sense of the complex concepts associated with the affective domain of learning, but it tends to cause us to view affective responses as not arising from cognitive structures. In short, Munby recommended the abandonment of theoretical approaches that dichotomize *affective* and *cognitive*.

The other dichotomy that Munby described is an epistemological one: cognitive and behavioral. The behaviorist view of attitude is characterized by correlational studies that seek relationships between attitude and other variables like achievement and gender, and intervention studies where little attention is paid to what might have caused attitude changes, if any occurred. It is this behaviorist view that seems to have directed most of the research reviewed in the preceding sections of this chapter. Munby claimed that research guided by this orientation "steers us away from asking questions about mental functioning" (p. 378). Viewing affective responses as mental states encourages research that focuses on cognitive aspects of affect. Studies that are guided by this orientation can benefit from recent advances in the study of cognition.

Like Shrigley's research program, the focus for attitude studies guided by the cognitive revolution was not centered in the elementary grades. Secondary students and preservice teachers were chosen as research subjects due mainly to their ability to communicate their feelings verbally and on paper. However, the research findings and recommendations are important because they suggest how the science-related attitudes of elementary school children might be assessed, improved, and maintained.

Constructivism

Novak (1977) and Driver and Easley (1978) are credited with introducing science educators to the cognitive revolution via constructivist philosophy (Cobern, 1993). The constructivist movement was identified by Yeany (1991) as having important consequences for science education research due to its power to function as a unifying theme. As an epistemological view of learning, constructivism's influence is well known in studies of students' alternative notions of science concepts. Science education research guided by constructivism attends to the actual content of the learner's conceptions, and has been advanced recently by the realization that science learning must be considered from the cognitive as well as the sociocultural milieu of the pupil.

Constructivism, according to Cobern (1993, p. 53), paints a picture of an individual as a "knowing being who constructs knowledge that is personally meaningful." Kelly (1955), the architect of personal construct theory, envisioned constructs as analogous to meter sticks with positive and negative ends and operating much like bipolar adjective scales. They are useful in "measuring the meaning of objects, actions, and contexts" (Reardon, 1991, p. 14). Given relevant encounters, constructs increase in number and complexity, and thereby enable people to make inferences and generate predictions about events in which they participate or witness. In essence, constructivism has caused science education researchers to focus more on how pupils interpret reality and the complexities of the learning processes in which they engage.

Attitude research is science education has not been bypassed by the constructivist movement. Introduction came via Greenwald's (1968) cognitive response theory in the early 1980s (see Petty, Ostrom, & Brock, 1981). More recent influences include Fishbein and Ajzen's (1975; Ajzen & Fishbein, 1980) theory of reasoned action, its recent corollary, Ajzen's (1985) theory of planned behavior, and Petty and Cacioppo's (1986) elaboration likelihood model of persuasion. Science education studies that have made use of these models are few, but growing in number (see Black, 1990; Crawley & Koballa, 1994; Warden, 1991).

Theories of Reasoned Action and Planned Behavior

An interest in dealing with the weak link often reported between attitude and behavior prompted science educators to carefully examine the work of Fishbein and Ajzen (1975; Ajzen & Fishbein, 1980). Fishbein and Ajzen argued that the relationship between attitude and behavior is mediated by two concerns. One is the degree of correspondence that exists among four elements that delineate the behavior. To assure correspondence, they recommended that attitude measures match the behavior in terms of action, target, context, and time. The second concern deals with other variables that should be measured along with attitude. The two additional variables recommended in addition to attitude are subjective norm and perceived behavioral control. *Subjective norm* is the perceived social encouragement or discouragement to perform the behavior, and *perceived behavioral control* is the perceived resources and opportunities that make performing the behavior possible or impossible. Perceived behavioral control is the center piece of Ajzen's (1985, 1989) theory of planned behavior, which extends the theory of reasoned action to account for the performance of behaviors that are not under the person's total control. Individual attitude, subjective norm, and perceived behavioral control scores are combined to produce a behavioral intention score. This score is considered to be the best predictor of behavior. The relationships among the theoretical variables are shown in Fig. 3.4.

Several science education studies involving middle and high school students have tested the tenets of the theories of reasoned action and planned behavior (Black, 1990; Crawley, 1990; Crawley & Coe, 1990; Koballa, 1988, 1989; Warden, 1991). Research findings revealed that attitude, subjective norm, and perceived behavioral control are determinants of science-related behavioral intentions and that from their combination, behavioral intention and, in turn, behavior may be accurately predicted.

An added strength of the Ajzen and Fishbein theories is that they provide direction for the development of persuasive messages. Persuasion is considered to be mediated by cognitive processing and is contemplated in light of expectancy-value formulations of attitude, subjective norm, and perceived behavioral control. The expectancy-value formulation for attitude was initially presented by Fishbein (1963) to illustrate the association between attitude toward an object and beliefs about the same object. "In the

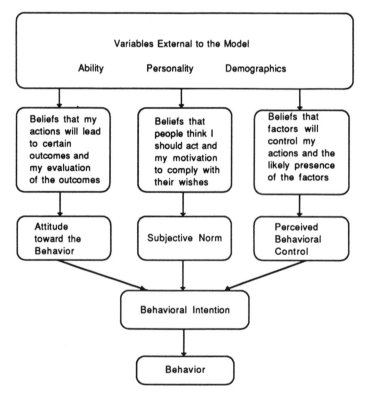

FIG. 3.4   Theory of planned behavior. Adapted from Ajzen and Fishbein (1980).

language of the expectancy-value theorem," according to Crawley and Koballa (1994, p. 37), "a person's attitude toward any object is a function of the beliefs the person holds about the object and the implicit evaluative responses associated with those beliefs." Following from the expectancy-value theorem, subjective norm and perceived behavioral control are viewed as linear combinations of salient beliefs (cognition), with each belief weighted by its importance (evaluation). These expectancy-value linkages reflect the cognitive processing that occurs before decision making (Crawley & Koballa, 1994).

Because the constructivist position is essentially a cognitive-developmental one (O'Keefe, 1980), it is of little surprise that the concept of belief and its evaluation are central to persuasion. Cobern (1993) contended that changing students' ideas about science and the ways in which they act on their ideas is difficult because doing so involves changing beliefs. From the constructivist perspective, "there is no unambiguous ontological distinction between knowledge and belief," because they "both represent what one has reason to believe is true" (Cobern, 1993, p. 62). Thus, key to persuasion are the specific beliefs that a message recipient holds about the results of performing the behavior and the evaluation of those beliefs. Recent studies (Black, 1990; Crawley & Black, 1992; Crawley & Koballa, 1992; Warden, 1991) indicate that persuasive messages designed to address message recipients' salient beliefs and the evaluation of those beliefs are more effective than are messages that contain information initially considered persuasive by the message developers.

Message design and instrument development that follow from the work of Fishbein and Ajzen have a common point of origin. Both begin with data collected from the target audience about the behavior of interest. Pupils' beliefs about the behavior are probed using a set of questions:

- What do you see as the personal advantages and disadvantages of performing the behavior?
- Who are the people who approve or disapprove of your performing he behavior?
- Why do you think they approve or disapprove?
- What things could occur to make it easier or more difficult for you to perform the behavior?

Responses are analyzed to identify the most often mentioned outcomes, referents, and control factors. These are considered modal salient beliefs and are used in designing scale items and message arguments (see Crawley & Koballa, 1994).

Items used to assess the model constructs of behavioral intention, attitude, subjective norm, and perceived behavioral control follow a standard format where only the description of the behavior is altered to match the intended purpose. These constructs are measured by seven-point, sematic-differential scales, the format of which was described by Ajzen and Fishbein (1980) and Ajzen (1985). Beliefs and evaluations that function as the antecedents of attitude, subjective norm, and perceived behavioral control are also measured using sematic-differential scales, but each belief statement and its corresponding evaluation statement are constructed from responses gathered using the questions identified above. Items that might appear on an instrument used to study children's elective participation in a science fair are presented here:

Attitude

Belief: Building a science fair project helps me learn more about science

always __(a)__ __(b)__ __(c)__ __(d)__ __(e)__ __(f)__ __(g)__ never
                                don't know

Evaluation: My learning more about science is

good __(a)__ __(b)__ __(c)__ __(d)__ __(e)__ __(f)__ __(g)__ bad
                                don't know

Subjective Norm

Belief: My parents/guardians think I should build a science fair project.

always __(a)__ __(b)__ __(c)__ __(d)__ __(e)__ __(f)__ __(g)__ never
                                don't know

Evaluation: I do what my parents/guardians think I should do.

always __(a)__ __(b)__ __(c)__ __(d)__ __(e)__ __(f)__ __(g)__ never
                                don't know

Perceived Behavioral Control

Belief: Playing soccer after school would keep me from building a science fair project.

always __(a)__ __(b)__ __(c)__ __(d)__ __(e)__ __(f)__ __(g)__ never
                                don't know

Evaluation: Playing soccer when I should be building a science fair project is

good __(a)__ __(b)__ __(c)__ __(d)__ __(e)__ __(f)__ __(g)__ bad
                                don't know

Designing a persuasive message involves using the beliefs to construct arguments that are supportive of the desired behavior. Building on the work of Stutman and Newell (1984), Crawley and Koballa (1994) recommended that beliefs supportive of the desired behavior be reinforced and that nonsupportive beliefs be downplayed or, if possible, discredited. In addition, the relationship between each supportive belief and its evaluation should be strengthened, whereas each nonsupportive belief should be disassociated from its evaluation. When writing arguments that make use of these recommendations, multiple sources of information should be considered. More information about how these recommendations may be operationalized in message construction is available from Ajzen and Fishbein (1980).

Elaboration Likelihood Model

Petty and Cacioppo's model of persuasion extended the work of Hovland and Fishbein and Ajzen by offering a "constructivist-based explanation for why not all people are persuaded, and why, even when persuasion is successful, sometimes its influence . . . endures and at other times it fades" (Shrigley & Koballa, 1992, pp. 18–19). The model states that the thoughts an individual personally constructs about information received determine the extent to which beliefs and, in turn, attitudes are changed and maintained. Most notably, the model has caused science educators to direct more attention toward the recipient of a persuasive message, the student, and away from the message's source, the teacher, and the multitude of variables associated with the persuasive context, such as the recipients' gender and intelligence and whether both sides of an issue are presented in a persuasive message. The result is that the passive receiver metaphor — an individual accepting of all that is proffered in a message — has given way to one of a cognitively active recipient.

The Elaboration Likelihood Model proposed two types of information processing strategies. The strategies relate incoming information to ideas about the topic of the message already within a recipient's memory and result in an evaluative judgment that determines the effectiveness of the persuasive appeal. One processing strategy, called the *central route*, involves detailed scrutiny of message content and message-relevant thinking. The recipient who follows this route carefully listens to, scrutinizes, and elaborates on the message, constructs beliefs and attitudes, and decides on actions based on information incoming from the message as well as from long-term memory (Greenwald, 1968). One's use of the central route requires ability and motivation to process incoming information.

In the second processing strategy, the *peripheral route*, the recipient does not scrutinize and elaborate upon the message arguments, but reflects on heuristics and cues associated with the message. Demanding less cognitive energy than the central route, use of the peripheral route is increased when motivation and ability to process information abate. As might be expected, attitudes changed via the peripheral route are susceptible to counterpersuasion and tend to be short-lived (Petty & Cacioppo, 1986). Given the relationships between type of information processing and attitude and behavior change, Shrigley and Koballa (1992) urged science educators to design persuasive messages that are both motivating to and understandable by the target audience in order to encourage central route processing.

Special care must be taken when considering the use of the model to design messages to engage children in central route processing. Sophisticated persuasive messages, wherein the recipient is asked to take the perspective of others, may be ineffective with children because of their inability to do so while engaged in information processing (Clark & Delia, 1976). Moreover, Kahneman and Tversky's (1984) choice-framing research suggests that persuasion is less effective when arguments describe the gains associated with engaging in a certain behavior than when they detail the lost benefits and opportunities for not doing so. Putting this research in practice, teachers would be wise to tell children about the potential losses associated with not engaging in science-related reading rather than the benefits of doing so.

Current and Future Direction in Attitude Research

Attitude research in science education has been shaped by social psychology. Shrigley (1978) introduced science educators to the schools of thought on attitude change that had been investigated by social psychologists since the 1950s. He chose to investigate Hovland's learning theory model of persuasion. The model is summarized in the five-part statement: *who says what to whom how with what effect*. For more than a decade, science educators used the statement as a template to isolate variables whose affects on attitude change could be tested (see Shrigley & Koballa, 1992). The findings of nearly a dozen studies conducted during the 1970s and 1980s yielded details about variables that affect the success of persuasive messages once constructed, but said very little about what arguments should be included in a persuasive message and how thoughts generated when listening to a persuasive message affect beliefs, attitudes, and subsequent behaviors (Crawley & Koballa, 1994).

Emerging from the shadow of Hovland's five-part statement, today's attitude research in science education centers on the message recipient—the person who may or may not attend to, comprehend, and yield to a persuasive message (Simpson et al., 1994). The shift in attention away from message context and toward the content of persuasive messages is due to the reconceptualizing of persuasion as self-persuasion, brought about by the models proposed by Ajzen and Fishbein (1980), Petty and Cacioppo (1986), and others (Eagly & Chaiken, 1993). Message recipients are no longer thought to just listen and memorize the arguments presented by the messenger, but to listen, elaborate, and generate their own beliefs and attitudes in response to message arguments (Eagly & Chaiken, 1993). Transitional studies that helped move attitude research in science education toward reliance on cognitive psychology include Koballa (1985) and Beisel's (1988) tests of message recipients' cognitive elaborations and Stead (1985) and Crawley and Coe's (1990) construction of belief-based measures of behavioral intention.

Guided by the cognitive revolution, attitude researchers in science education are investigating radically new questions such as, "How can combinatorial models proposed by the Theories of Reasoned Action and Planned Behavior being used to assess attitude-behavioral relations?" and "How can the cognition and motivational themes integrated in attitude theory be applied to the construction of persuasive messages?" Investigating behaviors that vary from students' enrollment in elective high school science courses to teachers' use of investigative instructional strategies, researchers have confirmed the role of attitude, subjective norm, and perceived behavioral control as antecedents of science-related behavioral intentions (Coleman, Koballa, & Crawley, 1992; Crawley, 1990; Krynowsky, 1988; Myeong & Crawley, 1993; Ray, 1989). The focus of other studies is the relationship among the three antecedents of behavioral intention, the beliefs that underlie the three antecedents, and the effectiveness of persuasive messages based on the salient beliefs of message recipients (Crawley & Koballa, 1994; Koballa & Chen, 1993). The cognitive and motivational elements of the Elaboration Likelihood Model have served to interpret the outcomes of studies in social psychology, but a model variable has been manipulated in few science education study. When studying the interaction of recipient motivation and ability to process message arguments on intention change, Warden (1991) found that, under certain conditions, increased motivation to process message arguments leads to long-term change.

Attitude research in science education has only begun to reap the benefits of the cognitive revolution. The theoretical models from social psychology and the findings of recent science education research provide an archetype for effective persuasive messages and ways of interpreting the operation of persuasive messages. Attitude research in science education is moving toward congruence with Munby's (1990) call for abandoning approaches that dichotomize affect and cognition and focusing on questions that highlight the learner's mental functioning. Questions likely to drive future attitude research in science education center on issues of message design and message operation; these questions highlight the message recipient—the learner whose mental elaborates are the key to persuasion. Many of the questions lend themselves to investigation using the same methods of naturalistic inquiry employed by science educators studying the role of social negotiation in learning (Wheatley, 1993) and the culturally based beliefs brought to the science classroom by teachers and their students (Cobern, 1993). The questions posed here are emerging as key ones for researchers whose focus is science learning in the elementary grades:

- How can information be collected from children about what arguments should be included in a persuasive message? What are the unique strengths of individual interviews, focus group discussions, and open-ended questionnaires for collecting information on children's arguments?
- What form should psychometric scales take to assess the antecedents of children's science-related behaviors? How should naturalistic inquiry be used to investigate children's science-related behaviors and their antecedents?
- What kinds of persuasive messages will work best with children? How are children persuaded by messages that are computer-based, text-based, videotaped, and audio-taped? Are children more easily persuaded by interactions that do not involve verbal exchanges?
- How can messages and situations be designed to encourage children to carefully scrutinize and elaborate on message arguments?

CONCLUSIONS

Terrell's discussion with his parents presented at the beginning of this chapter revealed that feelings play an important part in science learning. Feelings like those expressed by Terrell have been explored through attitude research in science education. Consistent with the goal of this chapter, research findings related to the science attitudes of children and emerging research approaches were discussed.

The research findings that have been amassed over the decades provide us with a few tentative answers to questions about: (a) how children's attitudes can be measured, (b) how their attitudes may be favorably influenced, and (c) what variables are related to children's science attitudes. It is known that children have rather favorable attitudes toward science, boys' attitudes toward science are generally more favorable than girls' attitudes, girls prefer the biological sciences over the physical sciences, and instruction crafted to address children's science-related beliefs can influence their science attitudes.

In addition, much has been learned about the power of theory-based research. Through the efforts of a cadre of science educators who based their work on Hovland's model of persuasion, it is known that attitudes can be changed quickly, that a credible source and an anecdotal message facilitate persuasion, and that attitude gains do not guarantee knowledge gains. These research findings have implications for how to improve elementary school children's attitudes toward science. Researchers are attending increasingly to the cognitive functioning that occurs as attitudes are developed and changed.

Research that focuses on children's science attitudes should be guided by theoretical models like those introduced by Fishbein and Ajzen and Petty and Cacioppo. Science educators' use of the theories of reasoned action and planned behavior (Ajzen, 1985; Ajzen & Fishbein, 1980) has resulted in the development of both assessment instruments and belief-based persuasive messages. The theories of reasoned action and planned behavior have helped researchers to better understand the relationship between attitude and behavior and to realize the need for collecting multiple types of data to accurately predict behavior. Petty and Cacioppo's (1986) Elaboration Likelihood Model of persuasion has enabled science educators to begin to explain how children are affected by persuasive messages. Future research on children's science attitudes will no doubt benefit from the new thinking brought about by the cognitive revolution.

ACKNOWLEDGMENTS

I thank David Gunter, Kimberly McCoy, and Stephanie Smith for their drawings of scientists.

REFERENCES

Aiken, L. R., & Aiken, D. R. (1969). Recent research on attitudes concerning science. *Science Education, 53*, 295–305.

Ajzen, I. (1985). From intentions to actions: A theory of planned behavior. In J. Kuhl & J. Beckman (Eds.), *Action control: From cognition to behavior* (pp. 11–39). New York: Springer-Verlag.

Ajzen, I. (1989). Attitude structure and behavior. In A. R. Pratkanis, S. J. Breckler, & A. G. Greenwald (Eds.), *Attitude structure and function* (pp. 241–274). Hillsdale, NJ: Lawrence Erlbaum Associates.

Ajzen, I., & Fishbein, M. (1980). *Understanding attitudes and predicting social behavior.* Englewood Cliffs, NJ: Prentice-Hall.

Allen, L. R. (1972). An evaluation of children's performance on certain cognitive, affective, and motivational aspects of the interaction unit of the science curriculum improvement study elementary science program. *Journal of Research in Science Teaching, 9*, 167–173.

Ayers, J. B., & Price, C. O. (1975). Children's attitudes toward science. *School Science and Mathematics, 75*, 311–318.

Baumel, H. B., & Berger, J. J. (1965). An attempt to measure scientific attitudes. *Science Education, 49*, 267–269.

Beisel, R. W. (1988). The effect of central versus peripheral cognitive responses on the science attitudes of preservice elementary and early childhood teachers. *Dissertation Abstracts International, 48*, 2574A.

Black, C. B. (1990). Effects of student and parental messages on Hispanic students' intention to enroll in high school chemistry: An application of the theory of planned behavior and the elaboration likelihood model of persuasion. *Dissertation Abstracts International, 52*, 124A.

Bloom, B. S. (1976). *Human characteristics and school learning.* New York: McGraw-Hill.

Blosser, P. E. (1984). *Attitude research in science education.* Columbus, OH: ERIC Clearinghouse for Science, Mathematics and Environmental Education.

Bybee, R. W., Buchwald, C. E., Crissman, S., Heil, D. R., Kuerbis, P. J., Matsumoto, C., & McInerney, J. D. (1989). *Science and technology education for the elementary years: Frameworks for curriculum and instruction.* Washington, DC: National Center for Improving Science Education.

Campbell, J. R. (1991). The roots of gender inequity in technical areas. *Journal of Research in Science Teaching, 28*, 251–264.

Campbell, J. R., & Connolly, C. (1987). Deciphering the effects of socialization. *Journal of Educational Equity and Leadership, 7*, 208–222.

Chambers, D. W. (1983). Stereotypic images of the scientist: The draw-a-scientist test. *Science Education, 67*, 255–265.

Charen, G. (1966). Laboratory methods build attitudes. *Science Education, 50*, 54–57.

Clark, R. A., & Delia, J. G. (1976). The development of functional persuasive skills in childhood and early adolescence. *Child Development, 47*, 1008–1014.

Cobern, W. W. (1993). Contextual constructivism: The impact of culture on the learning and teaching of science. In K. G. Tobin (Ed.), *The practice of constructivism in science education* (pp. 51–69). Washington, DC: American Association for the Advancement of Science.

Coleman, D. C., Koballa, T. R., Jr., & Crawley, F. E. (1992). TLTG interactive videodisc physical science program: Interest results of the 1988–89 field test. *Journal of Educational Multimedia and Hypermedia, 1*, 223–234.

Crawley, F. E. (1990). Intentions of science teachers to use investigative teaching methods: A test of the theory of planned behavior. *Journal of Research in Science Teaching, 27*, 685–697.

Crawley, F. E., & Black, C. B. (1992). Causal modeling of secondary science students' intentions to enroll in physics. *Journal of Research in Science Teaching, 29*, 585–599.

Crawley, F. E., & Coe, A. E. (1990). Determinants of middle school students' intention to enroll in a high school science course: An application of the theory of reasoned action. *Journal of Research in Science Teaching, 27*, 461–476.

Crawley, F. E., & Koballa, T. R., Jr. (1992). Hispanic-American students' attitudes toward enrolling in high school chemistry: A study of planned behavior and belief-based change. *Hispanic Journal of Behavioral Sciences, 14*, 469–486.

Crawley, F. E., & Koballa, T. R., Jr. (1994). Attitude research in science education: Contemporary models and methods. *Science Education, 78*, 36–57.

Davis, I. C. (1934). Measurement of scientific attitude. *Science Education, 19*, 117–122.

Dewey, J. (1916). Methods of science teaching. *General Science Quarterly, 1*, 3–9.

Dewey, J. (1934). The supreme intellectual obligation. *Science Education, 18*, 1–4.

Driver, R., & Easley, J. (1978). Pupils and paradigms: A review of literature related to concept development in adolescent science students. *Studies in Science Education, 5*, 61–84.

Eagley, A. H., & Chaiken, S. (1993). *The psychology of attitudes.* Fort Worth, TX: Harcourt Brace Jovanovich.

Festinger, L. (1957). *A theory of cognitive dissonance.* Stanford, CA: Stanford University Press.

Fishbein, M. (1963). An investigation of the relationships between beliefs about an objects and attitude toward that object. *Human Relations, 16*, 233–240.

Fishbein, M. & Ajzen, I. (1975). *Beliefs, attitudes, intention and behavior. An introduction to theory and research.* Reading, MA: Addison-Wesley.

Fleming, M. L., & Malone, M. R. (1983). The relationship of student characteristics and student performance as viewed by meta-analysis research. *Journal of Research in Science Teaching, 20*, 481–495.

Fraser, B. (1982). How strongly are attitude and achievement related? *School Science Review, 63*, 557–559.

Gardner, P. L. (1975). Attitudes to science: A review. *Studies in Science Education, 2*, 1–41.

Gauld, C. F. (1982). The scientific attitude and science education: A critical appraisal. *Science Education, 66*, 109–121.

Greenwald, A. (1968). Cognitive learning: Cognitive response to persuasion, and attitude change. In A. Greenwald, T. Brock, & T. Ostrom (Eds.), *Psychological foundations of attitudes* (pp. 147–170). New York: Academic Press.

Hadden, R. A., & Johnstone, A. H. (1982). Primary school pupils' attitudes toward science: The years of formation. *European Journal of Science Education, 4*, 397–407.

Haladyna, T., Thomas, G. (1979). The attitudes of elementary school children toward school and subject matter. *Journal of Experimental Education, 48*, 18–23.

Harvey, T. J., & Edwards, P. (1980). Children's expectations and realisations of science. *British Journal of Educational Psychology, 50*, 74–76.

Hodson, D., & Freeman, P. (1983). The effect of primary science on interest in science: some research problems. *Research in Science and Technological Education, 1*, 109–118.

Hofman, H. H. (1977). An assessment of eight-year old children's attitudes toward science. *School Science and Mathematics, 77*, 662–670.

Hovland, C. I., Janis, I. L, & Kelley, H. H. (1953). *Communication and persuasion.* New Haven, CN: Yale University Press.

Johnson, R. T. (1981). What research says: Children's attitudes toward science. *Science and Children, 18*, 39–41.

Johnson, R. T., & Ryan, F. L. (1974). Inquiry and the development of positive attitudes. *Science Education, 58*, 51–56.

Kahneman, D., & Tversky, A. (1984). Choice, values, and frames. *American psychologist, 39*, 341–350.

Kelley, G. A. (1955). *The psychology of personal constructs.* New York: Norton.

Klopfer, L. E. (1976). A structure of the affective domain in relation to science education. *Science Education, 60*, 299–312.

Koballa, T. R., Jr. (1985). The effect of cognitive response on the attitudes of preservice elementary teachers toward energy conservation. *Journal of Research in Science Teaching, 22*, 555–564.

Koballa, T. R., Jr. (1988). The determinants of female junior high school students' intentions to enroll in elective physical science courses in high school: Testing the applicability of the theory of reasoned action. *Journal of Research in Science Teaching, 25*, 479–492.

Koballa, T. R., Jr. (1989). Using salient beliefs in designing a persuasive message about teaching energy conservation practices to children. *Science Education, 73*, 547–567.

Koballa, T. R., Jr. (1992). Persuasion and attitude change in science education. *Journal of Research in Science Education, 29*, 63–80.

Koballa, T. R., & Chen, C. S. (1993). Influencing Chinese prospective elementary teachers' decisions about teaching about the environment. *Journal of Elementary Science Education,* *5*(1), 27–49.

Koballa, T. R., Jr., & Crawley, F. E. (1985). The influence of attitude on science teaching and learning. *School Science and Mathematics, 85,* 222–232.

Koballa, T. R., Jr., & Warden, M. A. (1992). Changing and measuring attitudes in the science classroom. In F. Lawrenz (Ed.) *Research matters . . . to the science teacher: NARST monograph* (pp. 56–68). Manhattan, KS: National Association for Research in Science Teaching.

Koslow, M. J., &, Nay, M. A. (1976). An approach to measure scientific attitudes. *Science Education, 60,* 147–172.

Krause, J. P. (1977). How children "see" scientists. *Science and Children, 14,* 9–10.

Krockover, G. H., & Malcolm, M. D. (1978). The effects of the science curriculum improvement study upon a child's attitude toward science. *School Science and Mathematics, 78,* 575–584.

Krynowsky, B. A. (1988). Problems in assessing student attitude in science education: A partial solution. *Science Education, 72,* 575–584.

Kyle, W. C, Jr., Bonnstetter, R. J., & Gadsden, T., Jr. (1988). An implementation study: An analysis of elementary students' and teachers' attitudes toward science in process-approach vs. traditional science classes. *Journal of Research in Science Teaching, 25,* 103–120.

Laforgia, J. (1988). The affective domain related to science education and its evaluation. *Science Education, 72,* 407–421.

Likert, R. (1932). A technique for the measurement of attitudes. *Archives of Psychology, 140,* 1–55.

Lovell, K., & White, G. E. (1958). Some influences affecting choice of subjects in school and training college. *British Journal of Educational Psychology, 28,* 15–24.

Lowery, L. F. (1967). An experimental investigation into the attitudes toward science of fifth grade students toward science. *School Science and Mathematics, 67,* 569–597.

Mullis, I. V., & Jenkins, L. B. (1988). *The science report card: Elements of risk and recovery.* Princeton, NJ: Educational Testing Service.

Munby, H. (1990). Attitude: invited commentary. *Science Education, 74,* 377–381.

Myeong, J. O., & Crawley, F. E. (1993). Predicting and understanding Korean high school students' science track choice: Testing the theory of reasoned action by structural equation modeling. *Journal of Research in Science Teaching, 30,* 381–400.

Novak, J. D. (1977). *A theory of education.* Ithaca, NY: Cornell University Press.

O'Keefe, D. J. (1980). The relationship of attitudes and behavior: A constructivist analysis. In D. Cushman & R. McPhee (Eds.), *Message-attitude-behavior relationship* (pp. 117–148). New York: Academic Press.

Ormerod, M. B., & Duckworth, D. (1975). *Pupils' attitudes to science: A review of research.* Berkshire: NFER Publishing.

Perroin, A. F. (1966). Children's attitudes toward elementary science. *Science Education, 50,* 214–218.

Petty, R. E., & Cacioppo, J. T. (1981). *Attitudes and persuasion: Classic and contemporary approaches.* Dubuque, IA: Brown.

Petty, R. E., & Cacioppo, J. T. (1986). *Communication and persuasion: Central and peripheral routes to attitude change.* New York: Springer-Verlag.

Petty, R. E., Ostrom T. M., & Brock, T. C. (1981). Historical foundations of the cognitive response approach to attitudes and persuasion. In R. E. Petty, T. M. Ostrom, & T. C. Brock (Eds.), *Cognitive responses in persuasion* (pp. 5–29). Hillsdale, NJ: Lawrence Erlbaum Associates.

Raizen, S. A., Baron, J. B., Champagne, A. B., Haertel, E., Mullis, I. V., & Oakes, J. (1989). *Assessment in elementary school science education.* Washington, DC: National Center for

Improving Science Education.

Ray, B. D. (1989). The determinants of grade three to eight students' intentions to engage in laboratory and nonlaboratory science learning behaviors. *Journal of Research in Science Teaching, 28*, 147-161.

Reardon, K. K. (1991). *Persuasion in practice.* Newbury Park, CA: Sage.

Rennie, L. J., & Punch, K. F. (1991). The relationship between affect and achievement in science. *Journal of Research in Science Teaching, 28*, 193-209.

Ringness, T. A. (1975). *The affective domain in education.* Boston: Little, Brown.

Rutherford, F. J., & Ahlgren, A. (1990). *Science for all Americans.* New York: Oxford University Press.

Schibeci, R. (1984). Attitudes to science: An update. *Studies in Science Education, 11*, 26-59.

Schibeci, R., & Sorenson, I. (1983). Elementary school children's perceptions of scientists. *School Science and Mathematics, 83*, 14-20.

Schwirian, P. M. (1968). On measuring attitudes toward science. *Science Education, 52*, 172-175.

Scott, W. F. (1940). A study in teaching scientific method and attitude in junior high school. *Science Education, 24*, 30-35.

Sherif, C. W., Sherif, M., & Nebergall, R. E. (1965). *Attitude and attitude change. The social judgment-involvement approach.* Philadelphia: W. B. Saunders.

Shrigley, R. L. (1972). Sex differences and its implications on attitude and achievement in elementary school science. *School Science and Mathematics, 72*, 633-638.

Shrigley, R. L. (1978). The persuasive communication model: A theoretical approach for attitude change in science education. *Journal of Research in Science Teaching, 15*, 335-341.

Shrigley, R. L. (1983). The attitude concept and science teaching. *Science Education, 67*, 425-442.

Shrigley, R. L. (1990). Attitude and behavior are correlates. *Journal of Research in Science Teaching, 27*, 97-113.

Shrigley, R. L., & Koballa, T. R., Jr. (1992). A decade of attitude research based on Hovland's learning theory model. *Science Education, 76*, 17-42.

Simmons, J., & Esler, W. (1972). Investigating the attitudes toward science fostered by the process approach program. *School Science and Mathematics, 72*, 633-638.

Simpson, R. D., Koballa, T. R., Jr., Oliver, J. S., & Crawley, F. E. (1994). Research on the affective dimension of science learning. In D. Gabel (Ed.), *Handbook of research on science teaching and learning* (pp. 211-234). New York: Macmillan.

Simpson, R. D., & Oliver, J. S. (1990). A summary of major influences on attitude toward achievement in science among adolescent students. *Science Education, 74*, 1-18.

Stead, K. (1985). An exploration, using Ajzen and Fishbein's theory of reasoned action, of students' intentions to study or not to study science. In R. P. Tisher (Ed.), *Research in science education* (vol. 15, pp. 76-85). (ERIC Document Reproduction Service No. ED 267 974)

Story, L. E., & Brown, I. D. (1979). Investigation of children's attitudes toward science fostered by a field-based science methods course. *Science Education, 63*, 649-654.

Stutman, R. K., & Newell, S. E. (1984). Beliefs versus values: Salient beliefs in designing a persuasive message. *Western Journal of Speech Communication, 48*, 362-372.

Thomas, G. E. (1986). Cultivating the interest of women and minorities in high school mathematics and science. *Science Education, 70*, 31-43.

Thurstone, L. L. (1928). Attitudes can be measured. *American Journal of Sociology, 33*, 529-554.

Tippins, D. J., & Koballa, T. R., Jr. (1991). Elementary science education: Looking toward the future. *Journal of Elementary Science Education, 3*, 23-39.

Vanek, E. P., & Montean, J. J. (1977). The effect of two science programs (ESS and Laidlaw) on student classification skills, science achievement, and attitudes. *Journal of Research in*

Science Teaching, 14, 57–62.

Vitrogen, D. A. (1967). Origins of the criteria of a generalized attitude toward science. *Science Education,* 51, 175–186.

Warden, M. A. (1991). The effect of two videotaped persuasive messages on 7th grade science students' intentions to perform an AIDS-related laboratory behavior. *Dissertation Abstracts International, 52,* 126A.

Weinstock, H. (1967). Differentiating socio-philosophical attitudes toward science from problems pertinent to science teaching. *Science Education, 51,* 243–245.

Weller, F. (1933). Attitudes and skills in elementary science. *Science Education, 17,* 90–97.

Wheatley, G. H. (1993). The role of negotiation in mathematics learning. In K. G. Tobin (Ed.), *The practice of constructivism in science education* (pp. 121–134). Washington, DC: American Association for the Advancement of Science.

Wideen, M. F. (1975). Comparison of student outcomes for science—A process approach and traditional science teaching for third, fourth, fifth, and sixth grade classes: A product evaluation. *Journal of Research in Science Teaching, 12,* 31–39.

Willson, V. L. (1983). A meta-analysis of the relationship between science achievement and science attitude. *Journal of Research in Science Teaching, 20,* 839–850.

Yeany, R. H. (1991, June). A unifying theme in science education? *NARST News, 33,* 1, 3.

Students' Beliefs About Epistemology, Science, and Classroom Learning: A Question of Fit

4

Kenneth Tobin
Florida State University

Deborah J. Tippins
University of Georgia

Karl S. Hook
Florida State University

> I think the role of the learner is to always be learning, even from your classmates. The teacher is a learner, but the learner can also be a teacher. In other words, the roles aren't set in stone. The learner is sometimes the teacher and the teacher is sometimes the learner. There should be no defined roles as to who should be the teacher or the learner all the time. People should be encouraged to take on the roles that they might not normally do. Some of my teachers consider themselves as teachers only. But I have some that say maybe there's something they can learn from me. These teachers encourage us to teach others. I think our teacher is very open-minded and sees himself as a learner too. (Jenny, Grade 8 student)

This excerpt from an interview with Jenny suggests that the reform agenda in science education is well underway at her school. Her words exemplify the spirit of so many reports that have called for the restructuring of science education. However, Jenny is but one student. How do her beliefs about learning and teaching compare to those of her classmates? How do they compare to the beliefs and practices of her teacher? And is Jenny a satisfied learner in her science classroom? These are among the questions posed in this study of teacher and student beliefs and the reform of science teaching and learning.

For a number of years, calls for reform of science teaching and learning have been persistent (National Commission on Excellence in Education, 1983; National Council of Teachers of Mathematics, 1989; National Science Teachers Association, 1983, 1989; Weiss, 1987). Despite legislation and incentives to improve the quality of science learning, the evidence suggests that, on a systemic level, changes are not discernible (e.g., Dana, 1992).

That is not to say that individual teachers have not been successful in maintaining classrooms that are ideal for learning science (e.g., Tobin & Fraser, 1987). However, there is evidence that some teachers, who have a strong commitment to improving the quality of their teaching, make changes, accomplish some successes, and then revert to their former practices (e.g., Briscoe, 1991). Tobin, Tippins, and Hook (1994) indicated that beliefs, which act as referents for actions, can explain what teachers do in their classrooms and what ought to be done in particular circumstances. For example, beliefs about the nature of knowledge and knowing, and beliefs about power and control, can provide a basis for actions in a vast array of situations. If teachers are to change their actions and sustain those changes, it seems as if the referents for acting in given situations need to change. However, Roth and Roychoudhury (1993, 1994) described how the epistemological beliefs of students resulted in diverse sets of perceptions of the classroom learning environment. Even though the teacher in their study had developed a set of goals and had structured learning activities accordingly, students acted in the classroom in agreement with their own goals and referents for action. Students with a perspective that was essentially objectivist in nature looked for correct answers and used resources, such as the teacher and the textbook, as if they were reservoirs of knowledge. The actions of this group of students, often a significant majority of the class, acted as a force toward the maintenance of traditional practices. These studies suggest that sociocultural factors play a significant role in shaping the science curriculum.

PURPOSE

In an endeavor to build a mosaic of understanding about curriculum change, the study discussed in this chapter focuses on the roles and actions of students in relation to teaching and the science curriculum. In particular, the study investigates the extent to which students' beliefs about epistemology, the nature of science, and teaching and learning relate to their perceptions of the learning environment and academic performance in science. In addition, the extent to which there is a fit between the preferred and experienced learning environments of students was investigated, as well as the degree of fit of teacher and student perceptions of the learning environment. We expected to find significant differences between teacher and student perceptions of the learning environment and between the environments preferred and experienced by students. Furthermore, within the student data we expected to find considerable variation in experienced and preferred environments.

RATIONALE

Studies that have adopted a constructivist perspective on learning and teaching often focus on the learning of individuals in isolation from the cultural milieu in which the roles of teachers and learners, and the goals they seek, have a negotiated set of meanings. In addition, significant aspects of the educational process, such as curriculum, are often conceptualized in ways that are separate from the culture in which curricular acts are inextricably embedded. In this sense, research is decontextualized from the lives of the teachers and students it aims to understand. Paradoxically, in the instances mentioned, the constructivist assumptions that underpin the theoretical frame for the study of learning are often not applied to the milieu in which learning occurs. The reason for this is often one of focus and parsimony. No group of researchers can study everything at once. Accordingly, we focus our studies on what is of paramount interest to us. For example, those with an interest in misconceptions in science honed in on the sense making of individuals, but in many cases failed to examine those so-called misconceptions in a larger sociocultural sense. This individualistic and often mentalistic focus has allowed some to claim that constructivists have an "anything goes" attitude to the curriculum. That is, the curriculum should allow students to learn whatever they happen to learn and retain extant understandings as long as they are personally viable. The anything-goes assertion misrepresents the constructivist position on knowledge and knowing.

The constructivist perspective we employ in this chapter regards all knowledge as personally constructed and socially mediated within a culture. Individuals are unable to extricate themselves from the cultures in which they live their lives and give meanings to experiences. All meanings are saturated with the knowledge that exists within a culture. Based on this belief we have examined teaching and the manner in which teachers represent what they know as they teach from a sociocultural perspective. A particular interest of ours has been to make sense of what teachers do in their classrooms, how they learn, and how they implement and sustain curriculum change. Our view of curriculum has been influenced by many scholars including Grundy (1987) and Beyer and Apple (1988). We are therefore sensitive to the desirability of examining curricular events from a sociocultural perspective. Thus, we have examined teaching in relation to learning of students, even though our primary interest has been in the learning of teachers and the representation of teacher knowledge in action. As our studies have progressed, it has become an increasing priority to look more closely at the beliefs of students and the manner in which student beliefs mediate curricular processes.

This study represents our first serious attempt to examine the science curriculum in terms of student and teacher beliefs. The study regards beliefs as actions that are deemed personally viable in the social contexts in which they are to occur. Thus, we are concerned with beliefs in relation to goals, and the extent to which the actions of participants in a classroom are compatible. Because our previous research has explored teacher beliefs about knowledge and knowing, power and control, and learning, we extended our questions of teachers to include students and then examined the extent of the fit between individual's sets of beliefs.

PROCEDURES OF THE STUDY

The study described in this chapter is a component of research on teaching and learning that commenced in Australia in 1984 and has continued in the United States for the past 5 years in middle school science classes taught by Karl, the teacher involved in this study (e.g., Tippins, Tobin, & Hook, 1993a, 1993b). An interpretive methodology that incorporated a constructivist perspective (Guba & Lincoln, 1989) was utilized in the study. One of the main goals of the study was to construct a set of assertions for which the amount of supporting data far outweighs the amount of nonsupporting data (Erickson, 1986; Lincoln & Guba, 1985). These assertions would be valuable to teachers and researchers who are collaboratively engaged in reforming the science curriculum. Drawing on our understanding of constructivism, a second goal was to identify relationships between teachers, students, and other aspects of the learning environment that previously had remained invisible.

Participants and Classroom Context

Karl has participated as a teacher researcher in these classroom-oriented studies for the past 5 years. Research conducted during this period has resulted in a number of papers that have explored relationships between teacher beliefs and classroom actions in the context of middle and high school science (e.g., Tippins, Tobin, & Hook, 1993a, 1993b). Classroom observations undertaken in Karl's science classrooms continued throughout this period, including the several weeks leading up to the writing of this chapter. The class on which we focused this particular study consisted of 25 Grade 8 learners, 13 males and 12 females, who were students in an "integrated science" course that met for 2-hour time blocks every other day. From a constructivist perspective, these 25 students entered the science classroom shaped by ideology and culture, bringing with them personal sets of beliefs that had been culturally validated. They also brought to the classroom images of themselves as students. During the most recent observation phase, students completed a study of optics, began to study static electricity, and constructed concept maps to demonstrate their learning.

Data Sources and Data Framing

In this chapter we adopt a constructivist view of research in that data are not seen as existing independently of knowers. Accordingly, instead of *data collecting*, which implies that data exist independently of researchers and can be collected objectively to match a given reality, we prefer the term *data framing*, which acknowledges the significance of the researchers' beliefs. Throughout this chapter we have made our constructivist beliefs explicit because of the close relationship between data framing, interpretation, and the personal theories and values we use as referents (Guba & Lincoln, 1989; Roth & Roychoudhury, 1994).

The primary data sources in the study were two questionnaires, interviews with two students (Lisa and Jenny) and the teacher (Karl), and classroom observations. Lisa and Jenny are pseudonyms for the student participants in the study. Karl Hook is the actual name of the teacher. These data sources allowed for triangulation of data and for the inclusion of thick descriptions in this report of what we learned.

The Classroom Environment Scale (CES) was developed for use in studies such as this one by an international group of science educators that included Barry Fraser, the leading international scholar in the field of research on classroom learning environments. The CES consists of 25 items that provide measures of student perceptions and preferences for particular features of the classroom learning environment. Each item was developed with constructivism as a referent for thinking about teaching and learning science. The items are associated with five dimensions: participation, autonomy, relevance, commitment, and disruption. Each of the dimensions is measured by five items except for the disruption scale, which is measured by four items. A final item that provides a measure of the self-esteem of students is seen as important because it provides an indication of the extent to which respondents perceive themselves as being constructed as important by others and how they would prefer to be constructed. The 25 items were written in such a way that students would respond in terms of their personal learning environment on two Likert scales; one scale enabled respondents to indicate the experienced frequency of occurrence of an event and the second to indicate the respondent's preferred frequency of occurrence. A sample of items from the survey are contained in Table 4.1.

Participation, autonomy, relevance, commitment, and disruption were selected as scales for inclusion in the CES because of their salience for learning in the classes in which we conduct our research. The scales were

TABLE 4.1
Sample of the Items from the Classroom Environment Survey

1. I ask other students about their ideas.
2. I decide how to solve problems.
3. The teacher asks me about what I have learned in the past.
4. I am interested in the lessons.
5. Other students make it hard for me to learn.
6. I talk with other students about solving problems.
7. The teacher shows the correct way to do problems.
8. I see the importance of what I learn.
9. I am willing to learn.
10. The teacher starts class on time.

grounded in the sense that they had emerged as important categories in our previous research. The participation dimension contains five items associated with the opportunities students have for interacting with others. From a constructivist point of view, students who perceive they have more opportunities to participate are likely to enjoy a better learning environment than those who perceive they have fewer opportunities to participate. Autonomy was thought to be an important feature of learning. Students with opportunities to assume responsibility for their own learning might make more sense of their experiences. If learning is viewed as a social process of making sense of experience in terms of what is already known, then the relevance of the curriculum to the experiences and knowledge of individuals is an important feature of a learning environment. The greater the experienced relevance of activities, the better the learning environment. Commitment to learning is an important aspect of learning. No matter what a teacher might do to enhance learning, it is important for learners to have a high level of commitment to learning. Finally, the extent of the disruption to the learning of students is regarded as a significant negative factor associated with today's classrooms. Teacher or student actions can disrupt the learning of others. The higher the experienced disruption, the less desirable the learning environment.

Two forms of the CES were administered. The student form was administered to students and the teacher form was completed by the teacher. Karl cooperated by completing the form twice. On the first occasion he completed the questionnaire from his perspective. That is, what is represented in the responses to the questionnaire are his beliefs about what he experienced to happen in the class and what he would prefer to happen. He then completed the questionnaire in the way he would expect a typical student from his class to complete it. On this occasion his responses represent his beliefs about student perceptions and preferences.

A questionnaire entitled Views About Science (VAS) was administered to the class along with the classroom environment questionnaire. VAS consists of 26 assertions to which students agree or disagree on a four-point scale of strongly agree, agree, disagree, strongly disagree. Eleven assertions concerned epistemology and the nature of science, nine assertions involved the learning of science, four assertions were associated with the balance between teacher and student control in the classroom, and two assertions related the teacher's role to the provision to students of correct answers and correct approaches to problem solving. Karl also completed VAS, simulating what he believed to be the responses of a typical student in his class. His intention was to represent his beliefs about the way a typical student in his class would complete this questionnaire. A sample of items from VAS is included in Table 4.2.

The two students selected as informants in this study were extreme cases neither of whom was, from the teacher's perspective, a prominent member of the class. Lisa is a Caucasian female who completed the VAS questionnaire in a way that was typical of students in the class. Lisa was described by Karl as a D student who "wants to be told what to do and how to do it and to get the grade. Learning is not the major goal." In contrast, Jenny, who was described by Karl as a B student and a quiet "loner," is a Caucasian female who completed the questionnaire very much like a radical constructivist, and whose profile of responses to the CES differed from the class average profile to a greater extent than any other student. Responses to the questionnaires were used as a framework for promoting discussion. The focus of interviews was to obtain more data in relation to the assertions as they were emerging.

Interviews with Karl were conducted regularly over a period of 5 years; however, the excerpts used in this chapter were from interviews conducted in the past year. Field notes from members of the research team were used to provide a context for interpreting data created from the interviews and questionnaires.

TABLE 4.2
Sample of Assertions from the Views About Science Survey

1. Science is a search for truth.
4. Scientific knowledge is always correct.
6. Scientific knowledge is verified by experiment.
7. Scientific knowledge exists only in the minds of people.
14. I prefer to learn science by doing experiments.
15. I learn about science by discussing what I know with others in my class.
19. I learn very little science when I work in small group situations.
22. My science teacher should tell the correct answers to science problems.
23. My science teacher should show me how to get right answers to science problems.
26. My science teacher should take charge of the class.

Analyses and Interpretations

A response profile was computed for each student for each scale of the CES (i.e., participation, autonomy, relevance, commitment, disruption) as the mean of the scores of the constituent items for each scale. Accordingly, the minimum score for each scale is 1 and the maximum is 5. An average was then computed for each scale for the class.

For each student a score profile was computed from responses to the assertions on the VAS. The scores for each item were used qualitatively and quantitatively to describe individual's beliefs about the nature of science, its truth value, and its independence of human existence; the social dimensions of scientific knowledge; learning of science; power distribution between teacher and students in science classrooms; and the teacher's role in relation to the provision of correct answers and procedures. Although these dimensions can be regarded as scales for which average scores per item can be calculated, this was not done for this study.

We began the study with a general perspective that student beliefs would be referents for their classroom actions and the manner in which they conceptualized the roles for participants in the classroom (i.e., the teacher and students). We also discussed the question of epistemological fit. It was apparent from the research of Roth and Roychoudhury (1994) that the epistemological beliefs of students were mainly objectivist in character. Thus, we felt that, given the significance of sociocultural dimensions of classrooms, the beliefs of students would lead to actions that might conflict with the preferences of teachers, such as Karl, who were wanting to establish environments built from a platform of constructivist oriented beliefs. Our decision to develop and use the questionnaires was based on these a priori beliefs, which were grounded in our earlier research and studies of our colleagues. Accordingly, framing and analyses of data were constrained by an a priori assertion that the extent to which the learning environment was perceived as productive was associated with the degree of fit between the beliefs and associated actions of the teacher and students.

ALTERNATIVE BELIEFS ABOUT
LEARNING ENVIRONMENTS

It's hard for me to ask other students about their ideas, because we usually don't have time to turn to the other person and ask their ideas. We're involved in other types of participation, which is usually focused on the teacher and involves taking notes. . . . I would spend less time taking notes and more time on how my peers understand the lesson and how they make sense of what the teacher is saying. I think science in this class is really relevant. Because everything we do in here we apply it to our daily lives. Like why the microwave works and why the drier pops. During our optics unit we learned why the sky is red during sunset and sunrise and it was relevant to me because I actually saw a sunset. . . . I probably wouldn't have chosen to study optics, but now it is a lot more relevant than it was before. (Jenny)

This section of the chapter discusses what we learned from the study in terms of epistemology and the nature of science, the learning environment, the social dimensions of learning science, and power relationships in the classroom.

Teacher and Student Epistemologies and Beliefs about the Nature of Science

It's not a search for truth—it's a search for understanding. It's not like, somebody came into this room and said there's some truths and there's some lies. It's trying to understand things. This is different from a search for truth. A search for truth is trying to disprove something. Most science isn't trying to disprove something. I think science starts out as trying to understand things rather than disprove them. (Jenny)

The data suggest to us that the beliefs of the teacher in relation to epistemology and the nature of science do not fit with those of the majority of the class. Although Karl has begun to make sense of knowledge and the nature of science in terms of constructivism, most students in the class appear to have an objectivist orientation. Karl's beliefs are constructivist in nature and he uses them as a basis for making sense of his teaching roles. Examples of these beliefs are provided:

I do believe that there is truth out there, and it's our role to find it. That's what scientists do. Scientists go out to try to find the truth. Whether they are doing that, whether they are finding the truth or not, that's another story. But that's the role of scientists, to find the truth. . . . Instead of saying "this is truth," say, "this is what I see." You have your personal objectivity, but you cannot impose that on someone else. This is my impression, my perspective of it. . . . We can never really be sure if we have the truth. And what is the truth? We can all raise the truth but will we ever really notice the truth? When it comes to science you really can't teach truth at all. You can talk about best accepted theories but there's really no guarantee that this is the way it's always going to be or the way it is universally. So when you teach you have to keep reinforcing it to the kids that this is the best postulate at the time. . . . People always will interpret the truth differently. Unless you have something that everyone can agree on, like when technology provides a reading. People are not always going to agree on what that measurement is telling us. . . . It's real uncomfortable not having that truth. Not having something you can count on. (Karl)

The extent of the fit between Karl's epistemological beliefs and those of the majority of students is not close; however, a few individuals demonstrated through their responses to the VAS questionnaire that they held views that might be described as constructivist in nature. Most students expressed very different beliefs to those of Karl. Students agreed with the assertions that science is a search for truth, that scientific knowledge exists whether or not there are people to know it, that scientific knowledge does not exist only in the minds of people, and that scientific knowledge exists in books. This vector of beliefs suggests that most students have an objectivist perspective on knowledge. Their responses to assertions about the teacher's role in the classroom, with respect to telling correct answers to problems and showing them how to do problems, is also consistent with the view that knowledge exists independently of knowers and can be learned as truths. Students agreed that their science teacher should tell the correct answers and show them how to get the correct answers to science problems. This outcome is consistent with the findings of Roth and Roychoudhury (1994, p. 12), who investigated the nature of epistemological commitments of 42 students from Grades 10 and 11 and reported: "When directly asked about the nature of scientific knowledge, its truth value, and its independence from human existence, a large number of students responded with views which are commensurate with an objectivist epistemology."

Responses to other assertions on the VAS suggest that students believe that scientific knowledge changes over time, getting closer to the truth as time goes by. Most students also believe that scientific knowledge is not always correct; however, as Lisa's interview suggests, this might be a statement about the fallibility of scientists rather than a belief about the nature of knowledge.

> Sometimes knowledge is not correct because they didn't do the experiment right. They might not have mixed the chemicals right. They might be mixed up wrong. And then the scientists may not be good scientists. They don't know what is right or wrong. If you take a bad scientist, for example, then scientific knowledge might not be correct. (Lisa)

The social dimensions of knowledge were apparent in the students' beliefs in that they agreed with the assertion that scientific knowledge is verified by experiment, scientists decide what scientific knowledge is correct, scientists often disagree about scientific knowledge, and scientific knowledge is not the same throughout the world. Roth and Roychoudhury (1994, p. 15) also noted, "A considerable number of students hold views commensurable with a constructivist-relativist position when they talked about the presuppositions of, and social influence on, scientific knowledge."

Typical of the students who answered the questionnaires with an objectivist orientation was Lisa, who agreed that science was a search for truth, that scientific truth changes with time, that scientific knowledge gets closer to the truth as time goes by, and that scientific knowledge exists whether or not there are people to know it. An interview with Lisa provided insights into the way most students thought about knowing, the nature of science, and teaching and learning.

> You go out and kill an animal and then you dissect it to see what is inside. When you find out what's inside, then you've found out the truth. It means you go out there and find the truth of something you're looking for. (Lisa)

> [Scientific knowledge is] the stuff that you know . . . that you learn from people and books. Like encyclopedias and science books. You can learn this scientific knowledge from science books and other people. . . . [Science is] a type of study about people, animals, medicine, biology. It studies the atmosphere, it shows how the earth rotates and how many plants we have. Science is always a study because it's hard and difficult to understand. If something is very hard to understand, like light waves and stuff, then it is science. (Lisa)

> You find something better, like a new medicine. Or you find something different that's connected to new things. It changes by putting different pieces of information together. Like in an experiment and then testing it to see if its true. Right now some diseases we don't have a cure for like AIDS and cancer. But if we find more money to study these, then we would find a cure. Most things we will find the truth for when we have enough money. (Lisa)

Jenny's beliefs about science, as represented in her responses to the assertions on the VAS, are constructivist in their orientation. Two examples of her beliefs are evident in the following excerpts from interviews.

> I see knowledge like when you experiment you're always trying to learn more. Knowledge never stops, especially in science. Scientific knowledge is a category all of its own. Although you can sometimes understand scientific knowledge from history, they're basically never related. I don't think scientific knowledge is always in books. The stuff that is in the books is not knowledge as we know it today. It can't be applied to things today. (Jenny)

> They have to devote time to understand it. You can't just pass over science and think you will know it. You must want to know it and get yourself into it, and in some cases live it. . . . I think to know science it has to be more hands-on than books. You need to talk to your classmates, see what they think and feel about science. You need to understand how your classmates understand science in order to make more sense of it for yourself. (Jenny)

The Social Context of Learning Science

[The ideal environment is] everybody getting along well, listening to others' ideas, sharing their ideas. Everybody working together on hands-on activities. A teacher that has high expectations of each of us. And a big modern equipped lab. Lots and lots of independence in our learning. That means class time to work on stuff and do experiments that are relevant to our learning. (Jenny)

An examination of the means in Table 4.3 reveals several interesting trends. At the class level students prefer the environment to be such that the practices represented in the questionnaire occur about once a lesson, with the exception of the items associated with disruption to learning, which should occur less than once a month. The perceptions of what happens in class suggest that these expectations are not quite met. A crude way of examining the data in Table 4.3 is to compare class means in relation to standard deviations. The standard deviation of a set of numbers is a measure of the dispersion of those numbers. If the numbers are normally distributed, more than 68% of the sample will lie within one standard deviation either side of the mean and approximately 96% of the sample will lie within two standard deviations either side of the mean. Accordingly, it is informative to compare an individual's deviation from a class mean to the standard deviation of the scores of class members. The effect size, which is the discrepancy between the preferred and the experienced learning environments compared to the standard deviation of the experienced, varies from 0.17 (autonomy) to 0.83 (relevance). Although an effect size of almost 1 is of statistical importance, it seems to have little practical importance in this case because of the magnitude of the mean and the relatively small standard deviation. The class data suggest that the fit between the vector representing the preferred learning environment and that representing the experienced learning environment is quite good, and that, on the average,

TABLE 4.3
Mean Scores for the Survey on Experienced and Preferred
Classroom Environments

Scale	Class		Karl		Lisa		Jenny	
	Exp.	Pref.	Exp.	Pref.	Exp.	Pref.	Exp.	Pref.
Participation	3.4 (1.0)	3.8 (0.9)	2.4	5.0	3.6	3.4	3.6	5.0
Autonomy	3.9 (0.6)	4.0 (0.7)	3.0	4.6	2.4	2.2	4.0	4.2
Relevance	3.5 (0.6)	4.0 (0.7)	3.2	5.0	2.8	3.4	4.0	4.8
Commitment	4.0 (0.7)	4.5 (0.6)	2.8	5.0	3.8	4.8	3.6	5.0
Disruption	2.3 (0.8)	1.7 (0.7)	2.8	1.3	4.3	4.3	2.3	1.0

Note. Standard deviations are shown in parentheses for class-level data.

the learning environment is conducive to learning, at least as far as the dimensions measured in this questionnaire are concerned.

Although the standard deviations are relatively small compared to the means, an inspection of the data for each student reveals that some students are quite discrepant from the mean. For example, three students have scores that are more than two standard deviations below the mean of the participation scale; seven students have scores that are more than one standard deviation below the mean for autonomy; only one student has a score that is more than one standard deviation below the mean for relevance; four are more than one standard deviation below the mean on commitment; and three students were more than one standard deviation above the mean for the disruption to learning scale.

In terms of his perceptions of students, Karl has rated each scale at a low level, particularly participation and commitment. In relation to the class mean, Karl perceives the classroom environment to be about a standard deviation below the mean for student perceptions of participation, more than a standard deviation below the mean for autonomy, a half a standard deviation below the mean for relevance, almost two standard deviations below the mean for commitment, and more than a half a standard deviation above the mean for disruption. This is an unusual result compared to traditional learning environment studies (Fraser, 1990). There are several plausible reasons for Karl's jaundiced view of the classroom environment, but perhaps the most likely is Karl's frustration in being unable to attain a higher level of success in implementing his vision after so many years of attempting reform. Karl's preferred classroom environment was more favorable than the class mean on every scale. The lack of fit between Karl's perceptions and his preferences is distinctive. In every case, he would prefer the class to be more conducive to learning. It is possible that Karl has become more sensitized to those who do not conform to his vision, and those who do conform are not as apparent to him.

Lisa's self-esteem was about where she wanted it to be. She indicated that students realized she was important about once per lesson and she preferred to be recognized as such more than once per lesson. Lisa perceives few opportunities to be autonomous and would prefer even fewer. These beliefs are consistent with her beliefs about Karl's role as a resource for providing her with correct answers and procedures for obtaining those answers. In addition, her beliefs about autonomy are consistent with her beliefs about knowledge being out there to be learned as truths. The other significant perception of Lisa's is that she is frequently disrupted from learning. This belief is consistent with our field notes, an interview with Lisa, and Karl's observation that she engages in social discourse frequently. Furthermore, Lisa does not enjoy participating in science and would prefer to participate less than she does at the present time. This belief is most likely related to her lack of success in science and her perception that it is difficult to learn. In relation to the class mean, Lisa perceives about the same level of participation and commitment. However, significant differences occur in Lisa's experienced levels of autonomy (2½ standard deviations below the mean), relevance (more than a standard deviation below the mean), and disruption (2½ standard deviations above the mean). Lisa's preferences were discrepant from the class mean in all cases. She preferred less participation (approximately half a standard deviation), less autonomy (2½ standard deviations), less relevance (approximately a standard deviation), more commitment (half a standard deviation), and more disruption (more than three standard deviations). The largest discrepancies between preferred and experienced for Lisa are for relevance and commitment. Lisa would like the relevance of the science content to be greater, and for her commitment also to be higher.

Compared to Lisa, Jenny perceives greater autonomy, more relevance of the content, and fewer disruptions to learning. Jenny perceives the classroom environment in much the same way as her peers in terms of participation, autonomy, and disruption. Her perceptions are significantly different from the class mean in the case of relevance (almost a standard deviation above the mean) and commitment (more than a half a standard deviation below the mean). Jenny would prefer the classroom environment to be improved on every scale. Most significant is her preference to participate to a greater extent and to display a greater commitment to learning. There are two aspects to this set of responses. First, her vision is an ideal that is not easily attained in Karl's class at the present time, largely due to the actions of other students. Second, because Jenny is not assertive with respect to her own learning, she might not feel committed to engage in public interactions. This interpretation has some support in light of Jenny's indication that students do not often regard her as being important. Jenny perceives herself to be unimportant in the eyes of her peers but would like to be perceived as important. A difference of three scale points on this item is a signal that she might experience some difficulty in participating to the extent she would like in social settings. Given this belief and a preference to be regarded by her peers as important, Jenny might well be inclined to sit back and not engage to a great extent in the types of activities that are prescribed. Significant discrepancies between the experienced and preferred classroom environment on three scales are regarded as potentially problematic for Jenny, and for Karl in terms of his role in mediating Jenny's learning.

The social dimensions of knowledge were evident in students' beliefs about how they might best learn science and their roles in the learning process. Students indicated a preference for learning science by doing experiments, not by reading books. They also endorsed the importance to learning of listening to the teacher but did not agree that more lectures should occur. The questionnaire responses indicate that students were in support of the significance to learning science of working in groups, listening to others, disagreeing, discussing what is already known, and connecting what is known to what is to be learned. Lisa emphasized the importance to her learning of Karl and other resources such as textbooks. Distinct differences were seen in the beliefs about the teacher's preferred role in relation to the science learning of the students. Lisa, who believed that knowledge existed within sources such as a teacher, held beliefs that were consistent with that epistemological belief. For example, she felt strongly that Karl should make it possible for her to know the correct answers to science problems and the most appropriate way to solve problems.

> Some of the problems we had to do just didn't make much sense. And I asked my friends to help me but they couldn't. I asked [Mr. Hook] to help but he said no. You've got to figure it out. I didn't understand it. I like it when the teacher shows how to work out the problems. I feel really down when he doesn't give us the answers. I feel like I really missed the answer and he won't tell you. I feel down because I know I will miss it on a test. . . . I think he [Mr. Hook] knows all the answers. He just wants us to work it out. He wants us to work it out for ourselves not to go to him for help all the time. I see why he wants us to do that, but it just makes me feel really down, to feel like I don't know the answers. (Lisa)

> I should listen while the teacher is explaining something. I might need to know it on a test. The teacher should be explaining things that he likes and what he wants us to spend time on. He should not spend time on something he doesn't like or doesn't think is important. What he explains might be in the textbook, and then you can look it up and study it. Some of the projects he gives out, like our optics scrapbook. Some of the things [Mr. Hook] said I didn't understand, but when we did the optics scrapbook, that helped me understand. . . . If you have questions or don't understand, he'll explain it to you in a different way. Sometimes in class we start activities, and then [Mr. Hook] has time to come and sit and explain things to me in a different way that helps me learn. But that happens very little. (Lisa)

Lisa's beliefs about the nature of science suggest that science is a body of knowledge that exists out there to be learned. She does not view science as personally constructed, through her own efforts, usually involving language. The following excerpt from an interview provides a clear example of how Lisa perceives the value of her own talk.

> . . . in my own life I talk and talk and talk. And in science you can't talk. It's mostly just listening or doing activities that you don't choose to do. I like to

talk, but not necessarily about science. I would rather talk about what I did on the weekend. I don't like science, except that I do like reports. But I don't like to do experiments. I like to write reports because it's all right there in the encyclopedia. (Lisa)

The relationship between understanding science and the desire to participate is shown in an excerpt from an interview with Lisa.

If I have a question then I look at the picture or diagram and read the paragraph below it. That way I can understand better. I learn science by working on a project someone gives me. Last year we had to do an individual science investigation. We had to do the research and do experiments with it. I found a lot on plants and animals and did experiments to see how they worked. I think I learned more science doing that. . . . I want to participate more, but I don't understand science. I participate a lot in my math class because I understand. [Science] is hard, it's hard for me to answer any questions. And when you raise your hand to say you don't understand you feel weird, like something is bad or wrong that you don't understand. I really feel left out almost all of the time. But about two-thirds of the class don't understand. (Lisa)

Lisa's belief that science is hard and her failure to relate understanding to her own efforts seem to interact to place her in a position with respect to learning science that is relatively disempowered. The solutions to her problems seem to lie elsewhere. This idea is reminscent of Lisa having an external locus of control (Rowe, 1974; Tobin & Capie, 1982). Although Lisa perceives Karl to have a significant role in assisting her to learn science, Jenny emphasizes her own role in relation to Karl and emphasizes the point that teachers can sometimes be difficult to read. She noted:

We have a teacher who has much higher expectations than any other teacher we've had before. He really expects us to put our best foot forward, and sometimes we're not sure which one that is. . . . Mr. Hook explains well and has very high expectations for us to learn ourself. Sometimes he does hands-on activities that are fun and help us learn. When we do a big project we have a lot of stuff we do. We have to do a lot of reading and use a lot of resources. We have to know our subject inside out to do our projects and that helps us learn. (Jenny)

Throughout this study Jenny consistently maintained a belief that she learns best through interacting with her peers, making sense of what the teacher says, and being overtly involved in learning:

A lot of things we don't understand, but when we actually do them, we understand better. Like today, static electricity, it will help us understand the concepts better with our static electricity demonstrations. . . . He actually promotes team activities and working in groups. It's easier to get ideas from people about what might improve your project. And once you get to know the people in your group they'll give you their constructive criticism and opinion to help you learn. Peer criticism and teacher criticism are a bit different. Your peers' criticisms are easier to understand because they're on a different level, you don't tend to feel threatened. The teacher's criticism tends to be on a higher level and more in depth than peer criticism. When I say higher level, I mean higher level of thinking. It's like your peers talk the language that you talk, but some teachers don't talk that language. [Mr. Hook] talks our language sometimes, but when he's talking science he sometimes goes over our heads and we have to turn to our peers for a translation. (Jenny)

Karl's beliefs about learning reflect his epistemological beliefs and beliefs based on his experience as a teacher and a student. His beliefs are somewhat at odds with those of Lisa and most others in the class. However, as was the case in earlier sections of this chapter, Karl has similar beliefs to Jenny. The social aspects of learning are evident in Karl's comments about groups and in an embedded way, in his comments about his own role and the use of resources such as textbooks:

How I feel that students learn is that there are different types of experiences — you can experience it by doing it, you can experience it several ways. But I've found that if students don't have first hand knowledge of it they are not really learning. For a couple of reasons. One is they doubt it if they just hear it. They hear a side of it but they don't believe it until they actually do some kind of a demonstration or do something themselves. But, . . . learning is the ability to use something in a variety of situations. If it's just an isolated bit, I really don't think that's learning. That's just a different way of memorizing. But, to be able to take something and apply it to several different aspects of their life, I think that's learning. And so, for example, if they just read about something in a book without experiencing it themselves, that's not learning. Or if you just do an experiment and a situation similar to that comes up again and you can't transfer it, that's not learning. So, in order to learn, you've got to experience it. But then also be able to transfer it to other situations. (Karl)

A comparison of the life in classrooms that is encapsulated in the excerpts given and the quantitative view provided in the previous section suggests a significant difference in Karl's constructions of the experienced and preferred classroom environment. Insights into the feelings Karl has about the discrepancy are seen in the following excerpts from an interview:

Teaching science to my middle school students is very stressful. I am wanting students to accept greater responsibility for their own learning but they don't want to do it. When an observer walks into the classroom they should see the students engaged in a variety of activities. There should be so much activity that the room looks chaotic. Some students would be at lab stations conducting investigations and others would be at their seats doing the same. Some students would be in groups of two to six students involved in conversation, while others are on the phone, working on the computer, or reading books. In fact, not all of these students would be in the room. Some would be in the library, others in another classroom, and still others would be off campus. The observer would not be able to identify the teacher right off because he would be nestled amongst the students in conversation or observing one of the activities going on.

I arrange them in groups for several reasons. One is a practical reason. When you are doing experiments and things you need less equipment. Another one is that while they are doing it they can talk to each other about it. They can share, they can get ideas from each other. Because when something neat happens you want someone there to experience it with you. So you have somebody to share the task with, to bounce ideas off of. And I still believe that students learn best by talking to people. But this is a hard vision to achieve. Many of the students want me to feed them knowledge. They want me to tell them the correct ways to solve problems, tell them if their answers are correct, and decide what the learning activities will be. The students want me to control the pace of the lessons and take charge of the class. Although students prefer to learn science by doing experiments they do not see the value of other students as learning resources, nor the purpose of speaking to peers about their work or listening to one another to improve learning. Interactions with peers are usually seen as meeting their social needs. The attitudes of students make it difficult for me to implement the curriculum as I would prefer. For six or seven years they've been taught and have learned this one system and they succeed in this one system. Now here's a guy who has a whole different system that is the opposite of what they do and so they are resistant to it. Even though it's best in the long run for them, and I can see it might be better for them in the long run, there's conflict between us right now. . . . There's the conflicts, the clash between the students and I. Because I have a different belief than they have, and it's a totally new experience for them, it's causing me stress. . . . Then their attitude toward science is going down too because of this change. So their attitudes towards the class, attitudes toward learning about science, attitudes toward concepts, are all just negative for them in the short term. I am not sure how it affects them in the long term because we have not seen long term effects. (Karl)

Power Relationships

I think we have a lot of autonomy and independence to learn in this classroom. A lot of our learning is done on our own time and in our own environment. I think we should have more autonomy than we do have now. I think we can teach ourselves better sometimes than teachers can teach us. We learn our own way. . . . I'd like to do hands-on things and take notes. I like to repeat and go over things several times, and that is uncommon in this class. (Jenny)

Responses to the four assertions from the VAS that relate to the distribution of power between the teacher and students suggest that in some circumstances students believe they should have more power and in others the teacher should have control of the curriculum. Students agreed they should have more autonomy to choose what to learn in science. However, they agreed that the science teacher should control the pace of lessons and take charge of the class. Students did not agree that the science teacher should closely follow the textbook. This might reflect a belief that the teacher, not a textbook, should decide what is the most appropriate science content to be studied. Lisa saw the need for teacher control in terms of her belief that the teacher had the knowledge which had to be transferred to learners. In other situations Lisa wanted "a lot of freedom. I don't want to do any work. The only work I want to do is reports. That's easiest and that's what we did last year." Lisa commented:

> I think the teacher should be in control 90 percent of the class. The kids have to learn it but the teacher doesn't have to teach it. It's all in the textbook. He just has to say read this — I want it due Monday. The stuff that he wants you to know is in the book and the book might explain it better than the teacher. Students should only have control over how loud they get. Because if they act up while the teacher is explaining something it's their own fault if they don't get it. (Lisa)

In contrast, Jenny, who demonstrated a constructivist orientation to both her responses on the questionnaires and in the interviews, emphasized the importance of a balance of power in classrooms. She explained how it was important for the teacher to have control in certain situations and for students to have greater control over what was to be learned and the pace of learning:

> The teacher should have most of the control, but the students should have some say. The teacher is the ultimate leader, but the class needs other leaders besides the teacher. I think sometimes students know better then the teacher how long things take. Also, students should be able to study more what they're interested in. So students should be able to have more say in what they're interested in. But that's usually not the case. I think it should be about 70/30. The students should have some noticeable control over their learning, but not as much as the teacher. . . Right now we have about 85/15. We have a little less control than we'd like. But we have enough control so that most of us are pretty comfortable with the class. [Jenny]

Karl's beliefs about control were context dependent and informed by a range of knowledge. The following excerpt provides insights into Karl's beliefs about control:

> I've got a range of control. There's times when, like the police captain or the prison warden, I want them all listening, sitting there, and focusing on one thing. Students have very little control there. If they choose not to listen they can put their heads on the desk, but they don't get a chance to get up and goof around. . . . I guess it depends on my agenda, because even in the time when they get to walk in and choose what they want to do, I'm in control because I'm the one that chose what they are going to do for that period of time. And again, they feel that they like that because they say that I have a perception when they are getting off task and not doing science. I can sense when that is and I pull them together to give them a focus. And when I feel that I can trust them I let them go, and that way I prove my trust. When I think the students can do something without hurting someone else or the equipment, then I give them more control. It's important for the students to learn to choose their own focus—to set priorities. If someone always sets the priorities for the students I don't think they learn. (Karl)

Karl went on to use the metaphor of an air traffic controller to describe his role as a controller of students in particular situations:

> When you're directing a discussion, it might not be like a warden. More of an air traffic controller when you're directing the discussion around the room. But it's a warden too, because that's the chance, the students don't have the chance to get up out of their seats because it might disrupt the discussion. Another aspect is students' behavior. If they are very rowdy and there's a chance that something might happen. They are damaging the equipment or themselves. Then it's time to settle down, relax, take a deep breath. I'm going to be in control now. (Karl)

The next excerpt suggests that Karl sees student actions as constraints to implementing his vision of what the science curriculum could be like:

> I want to believe that students should be in control of their learning. And I want to believe that student time in the classroom belongs to them. But in my image, I see the students being on task, happily learning, doing whatever it takes to learn more. But in reality, they come in and they see that ability to make their own decisions. And they sit down, socialize, chase each other around the room or whatever, and I think there's a problem there. That they don't see the same image of the classroom that I do, that is, that they come in and they're active learners. They see it as a teacher who's going to come in the room and not take control and not be an authority figure. Possibly a week

teacher who they'll take advantage of. And so I have this image of them learning and if they don't choose to learn in that mode then I take control and get them in line.

CONCLUSIONS

Students like Jenny are in a minority in Karl's class, and, we suspect, in most science classes. However, it is clear that in comparison to Lisa, Jenny's views of what science learning ought to be like are similar to Karl's and the quality of her learning environment seems more conducive to the types of learning advocated in reports calling for reform and that underlie Karl's approaches to teaching science. Lisa's beliefs and her practices in the science classroom are closer to those of most students in her class. Although she perceives the learning environment to be close to what she would prefer, her experienced and preferred learning environments are significantly discrepant from Jenny's experienced and preferred environments. According to Karl, he was continually challenged by students like Lisa who preferred traditional "knowledge transmission" approaches to teaching. As Karl perceived the classroom environment, students like Lisa were preeminent and students like Jenny were almost invisible. His beliefs and associated practices were responsive to the majority, often to the detriment of Jenny and the few others who held similar beliefs about epistemology and the nature of science, the learning environment, the social dimensions of learning science, and power relationships. The questions we are left with relate to the challenges Karl faces in becoming more responsive to students like Jenny and whether or not students like Lisa can be educated to become more like Jenny.

What does Lisa do in her science classes? Our field notes and interviews with Karl indicate that she is not overtly involved to a great extent. She sits back and watches others get involved and when she has the chance she engages in social discussions. Her interviews indicate that she sees science as difficult and her efforts are directed toward getting a passing grade, remembering correct answers and procedures for getting correct answers. Figuring things out and making sense were not a part of Lisa's vocabulary as she explained about life in her science class. Her actions are consistent with what we understand to be salient beliefs associated with her learning environment. If her actions are to change, we believe it will be necessary for her to come to understand teacher and learner roles in relation to knowing and learning in fundamentally different ways. This study provides no insights into how such changes in beliefs might be facilitated. However, from what we believe about learning, it will be necessary for any changes to be grounded in what Lisa currently believes and does. If she is to change it will be necessary for her to be reflective in relation to her beliefs and actions. Presently, this is not a significant component of Karl's agenda. His goals relate mainly to the learning of science content, although he also spends time in assisting students to work in cooperative groups and to use techniques such as concept mapping to facilitate learning. If Karl were to include among his goals some that relate to learners getting a better understanding of the processes of learning and knowing, it is interesting to ponder whether or not the community at large would regard these as legitimate components of a science program. Based on this study, we feel that such a focus is not only legitimate, but essential. Unless students have an understanding of the roles of teachers and students in relation to the goals of science, it seems unlikely that the reform agenda will progress as planned. It is not sufficient for teachers alone to build understandings about the roles of themselves and students and then attempt to steer students to new ways of learning and knowing.

Teacher educators need to seriously consider the sociocultural dimensions of changing a curriculum. It is not sufficient to focus on teachers; as Karl would attest, unless the students cooperate in building shared visions for the implemented curriculum, the forces favoring maintenance of the status quo are difficult to withstand. We see additional studies on the beliefs of students in relation to their involvement in the curriculum as a priority to be undertaken as a precursor to understanding the factors associated with the sustaining of reform. Although we have only just begun to understand how the beliefs of students might relate to the implemented curriculum, it is essential to probe other areas as well. Other priorities are associated with building new understandings about the roles of administrators, parents, and the community.

As we leave this chapter, we finish as we began — with Jenny. We are left with a feeling of awe at her grasp of teaching and learning. According to Karl, Jenny is a loner who rarely speaks out in class and prefers to speak to him at the front of the class. She is a B student who never stands out in the class. However, Karl noted that she has high expectations and provides lots of detail when she responds to questions. Is this the same Jenny whom we have watched and spoken with? We think not. Jenny, as she constructs herself, is an active learner, a person with a vision of science and science learning that is just within her grasp. But as she is constructed by Karl, she is a loner with some personal problems. This is a problem for Jenny. Perhaps she is constrained by the way Karl has constructed her, and these constraints might be deleterious to her learning and attitude toward science. Unfortunately, we will not know the end to this story. Tomorrow Jenny leaves for a new school and a new chapter in her science education.

I think there should be a lot of class and teacher participation. I like it when everybody gives their opinions and are honest and open and share their ideas.

I learn better with people because they give me outlooks on things I've never seen before. And it's a lot easier to learn with someone else because you learn together and teach each other. . . . I think hands-on stuff helps me to do science better. Like testing acid rain, doing experiments. It's easier to grasp a concept by doing it rather than having a teacher or book in front of me saying that's the way it is. Because I want to ask, why is it that way? Can you show me? If you're doing an experiment you can apply your basic understanding to what you're doing. Like, I see this is how the wave travels in optics. It's a lot easier to understand relationships. It's the application part that makes it easier to understand for me. (Jenny)

REFERENCES

Beyer, L. E., & Apple, M. W. (1988). Values and politics in the curriculum. In L. E. Beyer & M. W. Apple (Eds.), *The curriculum: Problems, politics, and possibilities* (pp. 3–16). Albany, NY: State University of New York Press.

Briscoe, C. (1991). *Cognitive frameworks and classroom practices: A case study of teacher learning and change.* Unpublished doctoral dissertation, Florida State University, Tallahassee.

Dana, T. M. (1992). *Achieving comprehensive curriculum reform: An analysis of the implementation of a mathematics and science education policy.* Unpublished doctoral dissertation, Florida State University, Tallahassee.

Erickson, F. (1986). Qualitative methods in research on teaching. In M. C. Wittrock (Ed). *Handbook of research on teaching* (3rd ed., pp. 119–161). New York: Macmillan.

Fraser, B. J. (1990). Students' perceptions of their classroom environments. In K. Tobin, J. B. Kahle, & B. J. Fraser (Eds,), *Windows into science classrooms: Problems associated with higher-level cognitive learning* (pp. 199–221). Basingstoke, Hampshire: Falmer Press.

Grundy, S. (1987). *Curriculum: Product or praxis?* London: Falmer Press.

Guba, E., & Lincoln, Y. S. (1989). *Fourth generation evaluation.* Beverly Hills, CA: Sage.

Lincoln, Y. S., & Guba, E. (1985). *Naturalistic inquiry.* Beverly Hills, CA: Sage.

National Commission on Excellence in Education. (1983). *A nation at risk: The imperative for educational reform.* Washington, DC: U.S. Department of Education.

National Council of Teachers of Mathematics. (1989). *Curriculum and evaluation standards for school mathematics.* Reston, VA: NCTM.

National Science Teachers Association. (1983). Recommended standards for the preparation and certification of teachers of science at the elementary and middle/junior high school levels. *Science and Children, 21* 65–70.

National Science Teachers Association. (1989). *Essential changes in secondary science: Scope, sequence and coordination.* Washington, DC: NSTA.

Roth, W. M., & Roychoudhury, A. (1993). About knowing and learning physics: The perspectives of four students. *International Journal of Science Education, 15,* 27–44.

Roth, W. M., & Roychoudhury, A. (1994). Physics student' epistemologies and views about knowing and learning. *Journal of Research in Science Teaching, 31*(1), 5–30.

Rowe, M. B. (1974). Relation of wait time and rewards to the development of language, logic and fate control: Part II — Rewards. *Journal of Research in Science Teaching, 11,,* 291–308.

Tippins, D. J., Tobin, K., & Hook, K. (1993a). Dealing with dilemmas of laboratory science: Making sense of safety from a constructivist perspective. *International Journal of Science Education, 15*(1), 45–49.

Tippins, D., Tobin, K., & Hook, K. (1993b). Constructivist perspectives on the ethical dimensions of teaching. *Journal of Moral Education, 22*(3), 221–240.

Tobin, K., & Capie, W. (1982). Relationships between classroom process variables and middle school science achievement. *Journal of Educational Psychology, 74*, 441–454.

Tobin, K., & Fraser, B. J. (1987). *Exemplary practice in science and mathematics education.* Perth, Australia: Curtin University of Technology.

Tobin, K., Tippins, D. J., & Hook, K. S. (1994). Referents for changing a science curriculum: A case study of one teacher's change in beliefs. *Science & Education, 3*(3), 245–264.

Weiss, I. S. (1987). *Report of the 1985–1986 National Survey of Science and Mathematics Education.* Washington, DC: National Science Foundation.

II | Conceptual Development in Science Domains

Jean Piaget demonstrated that students in different levels of cognitive development see the world differently. The students in any science class differ greatly both in their level of cognitive development and in their conceptual knowledge. Science teachers who understand these differences can respond more effectively to students' individual needs. In recent years, science education researchers have built upon Piaget's earlier work and explored students' conceptual development in biology, chemistry, earth science, astronomy, and physics. The chapters in Part II highlight this research and its implications for instruction.

5 Children's Biological Ideas: Knowledge About Ecology, Inheritance, and Evolution

Colin Wood-Robinson
University of Leeds, England

Most children have an intrinsic interest in the living world. They develop their own ideas about the workings of plants and animals. They have their own theories about how they reproduce their kind, how they interact with each other and their environment, and how they have come to be the way they are. They form theories without regard to much of the teaching they experience in the context of formal schooling. Children gain this knowledge from a wide variety of sources including their own firsthand experience, the conversations they have with their parents and other adults, their discussions with other children, and from watching television and reading magazines. Onto this rich background is superimposed what they learn from their teachers from preschool to high school. All of these sources of knowledge and understanding interact as students construct their own views of plant and animal functioning and their interrelationships in the living world.

As teachers we are therefore only one component in the total learning experience of each student. If we are to have the maximum effect on our classes we must be aware of "what the learner already knows" so that we can use this to help our students construct ideas that are similar to those of scientists. There is evidence to suggest that formal instruction may have little effect on children's understanding of the physical and biological world in which they live (Engel Clough, Driver, & Wood-Robinson, 1987). This may be precisely because we, as teachers, have not spent the time to ascertain what our students already understand about the world before we embark on a course of instruction in school. Indeed, Simpson and Arnold (1982) suggested that the presence of prior ideas that students bring to their science classes may actually interfere with their acquisition of scientifically acceptable concepts. Driver, Leach, Scott, and Wood-Robinson (1994) recently reviewed some of the implications of research into children's ideas for the planning of the science curriculum.

What is known about children's understanding of the biological world? Over the last three decades there has been a progressive increase in research activity focusing on children's understanding of a wide spectrum of science concepts. Much of this has concentrated on young people's understanding of the physical world. But Wandersee, Mintzes, and Arnaudin (1989) analyzed over a hundred papers concerned with the learner's view of various aspects of biology, and Carmichael et al. (1990) listed over twice that number of papers concerned with children's biological ideas. There is therefore much we can now say about the biological ideas that children bring to the school classroom. Mintzes, Trowbridge, Arnaudin, and Wandersee (1991) summarized children's ideas in the fields of animal classification, the functioning of the cardiovascular system, and photosynthesis. Wood-Robinson (1991) drew together what is known about children's views on the functioning of plants. This chapter considers what we know about children's ideas related to three central and all-pervading aspects of biology—ecology, inheritance, and evolution.

The very word *ecology* may have a completely different meaning to children and to the general public compared with that held by professional biologists. To the biologist, ecology is the study of plants and animals, and their interrelationships, in their natural environment. But in recent years the word has come to be associated with "green" issues and with studies of ways in which the human species alters the environment in a whole variety of ways, from pollution to overfishing and from deforestation to intensive farming. This dual or multiple use of the word *ecology* is illustrative of a widespread problem that is encountered, but all too often ignored, in the teaching of science. Many of the terms used by scientists have everyday meanings that are quite different from the scientific meanings. *Animal, energy, food, nervous, power, pressure, respire, sexual,* and *work* are just a few of the terms that have quite different meanings to the scientist compared with what they convey to that mythical "person in the street." Notice that in some of these (such as animal and sexual) the everyday meaning is much more restrictive than the scientific meaning. Thus, *animal* is often taken to mean a furry, four-legged creature (i.e., a mammal), rather than the far broader scientific meaning, which would include worms, insects, fish, birds and much else besides. Similarly, *sexual* has everyday connotations related to humans and is not normally thought of in relation to flowering plants, let alone algae and mosses. In contrast to this, the term *food* has a far narrower, more specific meaning to the scientist than it does in its everyday use. To the scientist it means "organic material that can be broken down in cellular respiration." The everyday meaning of anything solid taken into the body of an animal or any inorganic nutrients taken in through the roots of a plant is a far broader concept. Yet other terms, such as *nervous* or *pressure*, are simply used in quite different ways by the scientist and members of the general public. This phenomenon of different meanings is not peculiar to science. It is at the very heart of our use of language. (Notice the use of the word *heart* in this context!) But it is a particular problem for science teachers who are trying to use language to convey an understanding of concepts in a very precise way.

ECOLOGY

Near the start of their formal biological education, students may be introduced to feeding relationships in an environment through the use of diagrams incorporating food chains and food webs such as that shown in Fig. 5.1. However, even these apparently simple ways of depicting trophic

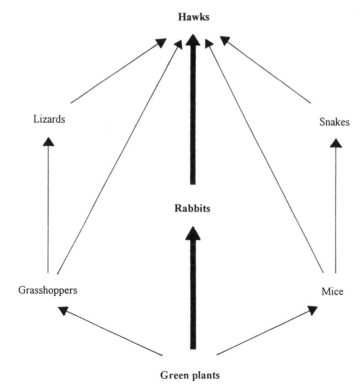

FIG. 5.1.   A food web. A single food chain is shown in bold type.

relationships have their problems. Senior (1983) showed that students aged 15 were not comfortable with the arrow notation commonly used in school science and hence may fail to understand the underlying principles of the relationship. This finding has recently been confirmed by Hind (1992), who found that the arrow is frequently taken to symbolize action. Hence students would be unlikely to grasp "rabbits → hawks" as meaning the direction in which matter and energy pass through a feeding relationship. Instead they would symbolize the relationship as "hawks → rabbits," meaning that hawks actively feed upon the rabbits. Schollum (1983) suggested that lines rather than arrows be used to link organisms in diagrams showing feeding relationships. As teachers, perhaps we should concentrate initially on building up an understanding of the feeding relationships involved without resorting to food chain or food web diagrams. Only when these ideas are understood should we then proceed to symbolize the relationships. Even at this point we should be careful to explain precisely to what the symbolism refers. It refers to the flow of energy—or the passage of food—through the group of organisms.

In a detailed study of students' understanding of food webs, Griffiths and Grant (1985) identified five major misconceptions among students aged 15–16. The first of these suggested that almost all (95%) of the students interpreted food webs in terms of a food chain. Thus, when asked to predict the effect of a sudden change in the population of one organism on that of another organism in the same web, they only considered changes along one chain and failed to realize that the change could be passed along several pathways in the web. Brumby (1982) found that biology students, even at the university level, encountered similar problems. The second view, which was found in 16% of Griffiths and Grant's sample, was that a change in one population will only affect another population if the two are directly related as predator and prey. If the populations of organisms were "further apart" in the web than a simple predator/prey relationship, students thought that one population could not influence another. Thus these students again failed to appreciate the complex interactions existing in a food web in which any change has its effects on the populations of all the other organisms in the web.

A third misconception, found in almost a fifth of the sample, was that a population depicted higher in a food chain within a web is a predator on the populations of all the organisms located below it in the chain. The fourth and fifth misconceptions, identified by Griffiths and Grant in small proportions of their sample, were that changes in the size of a prey population would have no effect on the population of its predator, and that if the size of one population in the web is altered, all other populations are altered in the same way. Thus an increase in the population of one organism is seen as increasing the populations of all the other organisms in the web.

A further aspect of the populations of organisms within an ecosystem concerns the reasons why the population of a given organism is the size that it is. Adeniyi (1985) worked with Nigerian students aged 13–15 and found that many of them argued that the reason why there were more herbivores than carnivores in a community was either that people keep and breed herbivores (but not carnivores) or that herbivores produce more young at a time. Many students also thought that populations of herbivores were large in number in order to satisfy the food requirements of their predators. This finding, illustrating teleological reasoning, was confirmed by Leach, Driver, Scott, and Wood-Robinson (1992, in press-b). Thus one student, when asked to explain the relative population sizes of various organisms in a community, argued: "I think there will be a lot of insects because that is what most of the creatures eat."

Leach et al. also found anthropomorphic explanations common, such as the population of a particular organism being large because that organism "liked" the habitat under consideration. During a lesson in which the students had documented the uneven distribution of an alga around the trunk of a tree, one student stated to the teacher: "Miss, we discovered that . . . if it had light on it, it grew better, but if it were heat, then it weren't; so it just wants the light of the sun not the heat."

A key aspect of any environment is the way in which matter is cycled through the biological components of that environment (the producers, the primary consumers, and their predators) and is eventually made available to the producers once again through the action of decomposers. These events are summarized in Fig. 5.2. Central to this idea of cycling is the concept of the conservation of matter. Thus the matter taken in by any organism either is transformed into new tissue within that organism through growth, or is returned to the environment through respiration or excretion. Even that which is used for growth is eventually returned to the environment through other organisms that feed on it, or by decomposers. However, it is quite clear from the work of Sequeira and Freitas (1986), Smith and Anderson (1986), and Leach et al. (1992, in press-a) that most children do not perceive matter as being cycled through organisms and returned to the environment in this way. Indeed, they may not even think of matter as being conserved in this context.

It is well known that most students, and indeed many adults, think of plants as taking in all their food from the soil (see, e.g., Bell, 1985; Mintzes et al., 1991; Wood-Robinson, 1991). They either ignore the intake of atmospheric carbon dioxide, or do not conceive it possible that plants can actually synthesize food from inorganic precursors such as gases, which are often thought of as being without mass (see Brook, Driver, & Hind, 1989) This is perhaps understandable, as food is usually viewed in human terms as something solid that is taken in from the outside. Barker and Carr (1989)

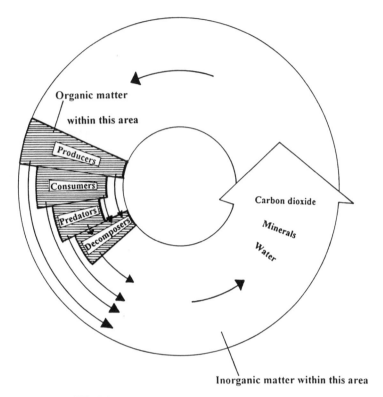

Organic matter

within this area

Producers

Consumers

Predators

Decomposers

Carbon dioxide

Minerals

Water

Inorganic matter within this area

FIG. 5.2.   The cycling of matter within ecosystems.

suggested that our approach to teaching plant nutrition overemphasizes the importance of starch as food, and Barker (1986) put forward an alternative approach centered on plant growth. Perhaps as teachers we should stress the importance of plants using inorganic precursors to contruct plant tissue and reduce our emphasis on plants "making their own food."

We also find that animal growth is not seen by many students as the transformation of food into animal tissue. Smith and Anderson (1986) suggested that many students aged 12 hold one of two views about animal growth. In the first of these, students think of food as being converted into waste materials and then eliminated from the body. They view this process as being essential to life, but do not see the food as being utilized in any other way. In the second view, students think of the food as being "used up" during growth—possibly in being converted to energy—but do not think of the food as contributing to the matter that makes up the consumer's body. In apparent contradiction to this, Leach et al. (1992, in press-a) found that a large number of students (40% at age 7, rising to over 80% at age 14) maintained that food is the main source of matter for animal growth.

However, even at the age of 16 years, very few understood that food is chemically transformed into body matter during growth.

Another aspect of children's ways of considering the living world is found throughout much of the research literature. There are many reports that students do not seek a physical explanation for many aspects of the functioning of plants and animals. Instead, they seem to adopt a naturalistic approach and accept that things "just happen." Thus growth is seen as an inherent characteristic of plants and animals and no explanation as to the mechanism of growth is put forward. "They just grow."

The process of decay illustrates another aspect of the cycling of matter and its conservation within ecosystems. As we have seen, a scientific explanation of the decay of plants and animals involves the release by decomposers of matter from the bodies of the plants and animals (and their excretory products) into the soil and the atmosphere. Some of this material is also used to form the bodies of the decomposing organisms themselves, but they too eventually die and the matter from their bodies is hence also returned to the atmosphere and the soil.

Many students do not view decay in this way. Sequiera and Freitas (1986) examined the views of decay held by students aged 8–13. Very few pupils grasped the concept of organic matter (in dead plant and animal tissue) being converted during decomposition to inorganic matter in the soil and the atmosphere. Large numbers of students thought of the organic matter as partially or totally disappearing during the decomposition process. Smith and Anderson (1986) found that many children (aged 12) held one of two naive views of the process of decay. The first sees decay as a spontaneous process leading to the formation of minerals or soil, but not as involving any other organisms, such as decomposers. The process is seen as "just happening" without the intervention of any causal agency. The second view is one of decay being an inevitable process that enriches the soil in some way and that takes place simply as a function of time, but once again does not involve any other organisms.

Leach et al. (1992, in press-a) investigated views of decay among students aged from 5 to 16. Two contexts were used as stimuli for this work. In the first, children were presented with a photograph of a decaying apple beneath a tree. In the second they were shown a time-lapse videorecording of a bowl of fruit rotting. Some of the students in the youngest age group (aged 5–7) appeared to have no experience at all of the phenomenon of decay, but by the age of 8–9 all pupils were familiar with the process.

About half of the 5–7 year olds made some suggestions as to what had caused the decay. These suggestions often centered on the belief that it is the very nature of fruit to decay if left for a long period of time, although some did suggest visible causal organisms such as insects. About 10% of the children suggested "germs" as a cause of decay. By the age of 11 a larger proportion (75%) gave some explanation about why the apple had decayed, with a larger number mentioning germs or bacteria as causal organisms. Some suggested physical factors, such as sunlight or air as causing decay. By the age of 12–14 almost all students offered some explanation as to the cause of decay, with over half mentioning microorganisms without prompting. The findings were similar at age 15–16, with an even greater proportion mentioning microorganisms.

Very few of the youngest children were able to make any prediction about the fate of the matter that comprised the fruit after decay had taken place. Those who did suggested that the total amount of matter would get less as decay proceeded. By the age of 11 all children were familiar with decay and used words like *rot*, *moldy*, and *decay* to describe the process that they had observed. About half the children of this age made some prediction about the fate of matter after decay—mostly to say that some matter would enter the soil. But none suggested that the total amount of matter would remain the same. The following conversation between the research interviewer and a group of students aged 13–14 years, who had watched the time-lapse videorecording showing rotting fruit, illustrates this point:

Interviewer: "You know we were talking about stuff getting smaller yesterday—you saw it on the video—why do you think the stuff was going to get smaller?"

Pupil 1: "It were all eaten inside . . ."

Interviewer: "What ate it?"

Pupil 1: "The maggots and decomposers."

Interviewer: "I see, and at the end of the video, I know it's impossible, but just supposing, if we could collect together all the stuff that hadn't been eaten and the stuff that had, and get it all back together, do you think it would have the same amount of stuff there?"

Pupil 2: "No! A bit of it'd have disintegrated."

Interviewer: "Just gone altogether?"

Pupil 2: "Yeh!"

Even by the age of 15–16 very few thought that matter must be conserved in the process of decay, and these could not explain how conservation would take place.

Another important aspect of the feeding interrelationships within an ecosystem is the way in which energy flows through the system. This is summarized in Fig. 5.3. There is evidence that students rarely conceive of

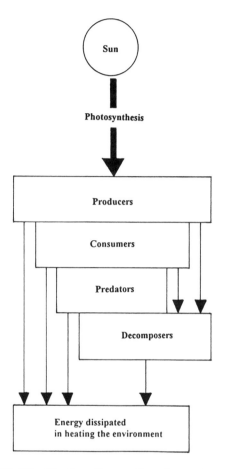

FIG. 5.3.   The flow of energy through ecosystems.

energy flow through ecosystems in this way (see Leach et al., 1992). Indeed, there is frequently little distinction made between food, energy, and matter, which may be seen to be interconvertable. Thus, food may be seen as being "converted into energy" and used up in the process, thus providing further evidence that students fail to apply the concept of conservation of matter in this context. Carr (1987) and Wood-Robinson (1986) both suggested that students may get a quite different concept of energy in the biology classroom compared with what they acquire in physics lessons. In the physical sciences, teaching tends to emphasize the first law of thermodynamics (the conservation of energy) through the consideration of a number of examples of energy transformation in which the energy is transformed quite rapidly. In biological systems the energy transformation may be relatively slow (in respiration for example) and there may be greater emphasis on the second law of thermodynamics — although this is rarely made explicit.

Finally, the concept of *habitat* has not received much attention from researchers, except in the context of an organism's adaptation to its habitat. This is considered later during the discussion of students' understanding of evolution.

INHERITANCE

Students understanding of inheritance has been investigated by a number of workers. This work has been reviewed by Wood-Robinson (1994). Deadman and Kelly (1978), working with students aged 14–15, and Brumby (1979), who used university students, found that both groups recognized the existence of intraspecific variation but failed to understand its origin in genetic mutation. It is therefore perhaps understandable that there is widespread confusion among students between the concept of inherited changes in populations of organisms over time and that of noninherited changes that take place within the lifespan of an organism (e.g., Brumby, 1979; Kargbo, Hobbs, & Erikson, 1980). The accepted scientific view is that most changes in an organism that take place in its own lifetime (such as the increase in red blood cells in humans in response to temporary residence at high altitude, or the temporary darkening of human skin following exposure to prolonged sunlight) normally have no effect on the organism's genetic makeup and hence cannot be passed on to the next generation. However, changes brought about as a result of genetic mutation (such as the occurrence of the melanic form of the moth *Biston betularia*, or the occurrence of albinism in many species of animal) are inherited by the descendants of the mutant form. Kargbo et al. found that a belief in the inheritance of acquired characteristics was widespread among their sample of students aged 6–14. This was even true when they were presented with quite bizarre scenarios such as questions about the offspring of a dog that had become lame as a result of an accident. Many of the students thought that the puppies of such a dog would also be lame.

This lack of distinction between a change at the individual level and one that alters the genetic makeup of that individual's germ cells is parallelled in the findings of Albaladejo and Lucas (1988), who investigated the understandings of "mutation" demonstrated by Catalan students (aged 14–18) in Barcelona. It is clear from this work that students associated mutation with the idea of change. But it is equally clear that any permanent biological changes (e.g., the physiological and anatomical changes associated with puberty in humans) were interpreted as mutations by many students. If these two types of changes are regarded by students as being similar, then it is not surprising that many accept the idea of acquired characteristics being inherited.

In a detailed investigation involving over 80 individual interviews, Engel Clough and Wood-Robinson (1985a) found similar beliefs were widespread among students aged 12–16. These students had not yet experienced any significant formal teaching about inheritance. Their beliefs must therefore be due to their general experience of inheritance patterns in humans and pet animals, and to ideas gained from television programs, books, magazines, peers, and adults.

Thus, when presented with a hypothetical question about whether the offspring of mice from which a scientist had chopped the tails would or would not have tails, 19% of the sample maintained that the baby mice would lack tails. As one 12-year-old put it: "I think you would get babies with chopped-off tails . . . because both the mice [i.e., the parents] haven't got tails to start with, and when they mate you'd expect to get babies with chopped off tails."

In a related question that referred to athletes who had trained hard and become good runners, in spite of not being naturally proficient, 13% thought that their descendants would also be good runners. But when it came to a third task related to gardeners developing calluses on their hands, only two students though that this feature would be inherited.

When asked to explain their views, very few of those students who had correctly maintained that these acquired characteristics are not inherited based their argument on the lack of genetic change in the organism being considered. Most (44–65%, depending on the context) argued that the characteristic was not inherited because it was simply "unnatural." Thus, one 12-year-old maintained that the babies born to mice with chopped-off tails would have normal tails "because it's not natural, nature didn't make it happen." Less than a third of the students used an explanation based on a lack of genetic change to account for their belief that the offspring of the tailless mice would have normal tails. This proportion fell to only 17% and 13% in the contexts of the questions based on the athletes and the gardeners.

An interesting additional dimension to the belief in the inheritance of acquired characteristics was exposed by Engel Clough and Wood-Robinson (1985a) when they asked the students about the effect of time and the passage of many generations on the expected results. In the contexts of the mice tails and the athletes' running ability, almost half the students who had maintained that these characteristics would not be inherited by the next generation thought that they would be if the treatment was continued over several generations. For example, one 14-year-old gave the following prediction:

I think you would probably have ones with . . . after a time it might end up that babies don't have tails, if he [the scientist] keeps repeating it . . . it probably would happen, it's hard to say how many generations . . . well, probably after four or five generations, they might start to have no tails.

Okeke and Wood-Robinson (1980), Kargbo et al. (1980), and Engel Clough and Wood-Robinson (1985a) all examined different aspects of the mechanism of inheritance of intraspecific variation. Okeke and Wood-Robinson reported that 40% of their sample of Nigerian pupils, aged 16–18, did not believe that plants were capable of sexual reproduction. This may be related to the view found in 17% of Engel Clough and Wood-Robinson's sample suggesting that intraspecific variation did not exist in plants. Kargbo et al. found that even the youngest of the students they interviewed (aged 6) had their own theories to explain inheritance. They correctly maintained that the coloring of puppies was derived from their parents. But they believed that the mother dog had a greater influence than the father over the color of her offspring. When questioned about the causes of the height of individual humans, many students thought that the parent of the same gender was the major factor in determining this characteristic.

Engel Clough and Wood-Robinson also probed understanding of the origins of intraspecific variation in the context of the coloring of dogs and were able to confirm that most of their students recognized the importance of both parents. However, half their sample made no mention whatsoever of any genetic entity. Only 40% referred to genetic material passed on at fertilization, with a small proportion of these extending this to an explanation based on the chemical structure of the genes, or chromosomes carrying information that is translated by the cells. The language in which the students expressed their explanations varied considerably, from the everyday vocabulary of the 12-year-old who said, "Well, say take these two [photographs of dogs] for example . . . that one might have more of its mother's look . . . that might look more like the mother and that might look more like the father," to that of the 14-year-old who explained:

Yes, each parent contributes something to the makeup of its children and, of course, each parent has different coloring to begin with, so if you combine the genes of the two parents you get a sort of mixture which won't be exactly the same as either of the parents. That's how you get the differences.

The equality of the contributions of the two parents to the genotype of their offspring is an idea that many students seem not to grasp. In some respects this idea seems to run counter to everyday experience. Many individual humans may appear more like one parent than the other, and it is thus tempting to believe that their inherited characteristics are derived more from that parent. Engel Clough and Wood-Robinson documented numerous examples of students who clearly believed in the unequal contribution of the two parents in the genotype of their offspring. Thus, when called on to explain the identical appearance of monozygotic twins, a 16-year-old maintained that it was derived from the mother through the egg, but not from the father: "Usually only one sperm'll get through but sometimes two do get through, then you end up with twins . . . I expect it's because it's one egg [that they look alike]."

Five percent of the students interviewed believed that the resemblance of offspring to their parents was due to some form of "likeness" being transferred from the mother to the embryo during development and that this therefore ensured that the maternal influence is larger than the paternal contribution. There was also a widespread belief that some characteristics are inherited from one parent whereas other features come from the other. Thus one 14-year-old, in discussing the tailless mice task, said: "Well they'll take after the father without a tail . . . I suppose it could have something passed down from the mother — you know if the mother had exceptionally large ears!"

Many students clearly believed that the mother's contribution was either greater than the father's, or, in some cases, was the only inherited contribution received by the offspring. Less commonly, some students thought that the father's contribution was the greater. Thus in explaining the tailless mouse task, two students said, "I think it depends on the mother's side . . . well from both, but mainly from the mother" (14-year-old student) and "the father passed more . . . I can't think what they're called . . . to some of his mouses . . . the mother . . . maybe a little bit, but . ." (12-year-old student). This belief in the unequal contribution of the two parents was also reported by Kargbo et al. (1980).

It has also been found that many students believe that all the sperm and egg cells that are released at the same time give rise to identical phenotypes. A 16-year-old, in Engel Clough and Wood-Robinson's (1985a) sample, tentatively explained the fact that monozygotic twins are identical, whereas a brother and sister merely have a family resemblance, in the following way:

> Student: "I don't know, perhaps all the . . . of the whole lot of sperm that swims towards the egg all carry the same ingredients for a person, I don't know . . ."
>
> Interviewer: "I see. Well how then do you explain the fact that the brother and sister don't look the same?"
>
> Student: "No, but with them, they obviously would have been born with years between them so. . ."

The concepts of dominance and recessiveness and the distinction between a gene and an allele give rise to considerable confusion among students of all ages (and also among teachers and textbook writers!). Thus students may think that a given allele may be dominant over another in one offspring, but the situation may be reversed in another offspring. A student interviewed in Engel Clough and Wood-Robinson's sample maintained that "The genes from the tailless mouse — parent — would be dominant in some of the offspring and recessive in the others which will have tails," whereas another said, "Sometimes his genes were predominant in the baby mice who were born without tails, in others his mate's genes were predominant when the mouse born had a tail."

Note that both these students use the term *gene*, which they have probably picked up outside of science or biology classes. In both cases *allele* would have been the more appropriate term, but this is not a word usually used in everyday talk about inheritance. Indeed, teachers may try and simplify their explanations of inheritance by avoiding the term *allele*. It is better to use the term because the concept of an allele, as one of a number of alternative forms of a gene, is essential to a proper understanding of genetics. There is also a widespread belief that an allele is either dominant or recessive per se. In reality an allele can only be dominant over another allele. A useful teaching analogy here is to liken the concepts of dominance and recessiveness to those of *longer* and *shorter* when referring to pieces of string. Thus one piece of string is only longer (or shorter) in relation to another piece of string. A piece of string cannot be longer (or shorter) per se. Thus the word *dominant* (or *recessive*) should never be applied to an allele without reference to a second allele. Clearly the terms *dominant* and *recessive* can never be applied to genes, but only to alleles in relation to other alleles.

This discussion emphasizes the importance of precision in the language used in teaching genetics. This precision, and the necessary distinction between words such as *gene* and *allele*, and between *chromatid* and *chromosome*, was identified by Longden (1982) as a prime cause of the comprehension difficulties experienced by his sample of students, aged 17–18, who had undergone formal instruction in genetics.

Pearson and Hughes (1988a, 1988b) have carried out a detailed analysis of the genetic terms in texts used by students (aged 16–19) in the schools of Britain and a number of countries in the Commonwealth. This analysis points to the widespread misuse of genetic terminology by textbook writers. This problem clearly exacerbates the misunderstandings demonstrated by students. Two professional geneticists, Radford and Baumberg (1987), drew up a glossary of terms for teaching genetics, and it would be advisable for teachers to consult this before embarking on teaching the topic. However, even geneticists may not be consistent in their correct use of language and terminology. For example, the frequently used term *gene frequency* displays a misuse of the term *gene*. *Allele frequency* is really what this concept should be called. If professional scientists, textbook writers, and teachers use language in a confusing way, it is not surprising if our students end up confused!

EVOLUTION

Evolution is one of the cornerstones of modern biology. It forms the "conceptual spectacles" through which many areas of biology, such as classification and structure/function relationships, are viewed. It is also a popular subject with the media and with elementary school teachers who have their young students use library and other resources to investigate past forms of life on the earth. What then are the ideas on evolution acquired by our students before they reach high school?

Wood-Robinson (1994) has reviewed research into young people's understanding of evolution. One of the earliest studies of students' ideas about evolution has already been referred to and was carried out by Deadman and Kelly (1978), who interviewed over 50 boys aged 11–16 years. All the students were aware of evolution as a phenomenon, although many regarded it as a series of disconnected events affecting specific examples of animals that lived in the past. In explaining why evolution had occurred, most students used either naturalistic explanations that referred to animals' "needs" or "wants" or based their explanation on animals responding to a change in the environment, such as the Ice Age. Often the overall process of evolution was explained in naturalistic ("it just happened"), teleological ("it happened because it was needed"), or Lamarckian terms ("repeated use resulted in change"). Similar explanations were also offered to explain adaptation. Only a few of the boys appeared to have a concept of adaptation, which they expressed as "an aspect of the process of change instead of just the end-product of a process of change" (p. 10). A few of the older boys appreciated intraspecific selection and its effects on the characteristics of a species, but most students regarded selection as causing some species to become extinct while others survived.

Engel Clough and Wood-Robinson (1985b) interviewed students (aged 11–16) about their understanding of adaptation in relation to two situations. The first asked them to explain the occurrence, in a forest, of dark-colored caterpillars on dark backgrounds and light-colored caterpillars on light backgrounds. The second probed the students' understanding as to how the arctic fox had come to have a thick coat of fur, which was important in its survival in cold conditions. Only about 10% of the students gave scientifically acceptable explanations, although understandably these were often given in everyday language, as the students had not yet received any formal instruction on the subject. An excellent example of such an explanation was given by a 12-year-old student:

> Well possibly there were some foxes with thin coats and some foxes with slightly thicker coats, but the foxes with thin coats would have frozen to death and the foxes with slightly thicker coats may have survived long enough to have more offspring with thick and thin coats, and the thin ones would die out, so the thicker-coated ones would survive more so they eventually ended up with very thick coats.

A slightly larger proportion of students explained the adaptations in terms of a conscious and deliberate response to a need created by environmental change. Thus another 12-year-old explained the adaptation of the arctic fox like this: "When it turned all cold the foxes fought to keep themselves alive and gradually they began to grow thicker coats until they were able to survive properly . . . yes, they were sort of determined to stay alive." A 14-year-old said of the caterpillars, "Well the caterpillars would have to get lighter as well . . . well the caterpillars would be aware that their environment is changing and then they'd try to change by changing the pigment of their skin."

Another common approach to adaptation, found especially in response to the caterpillar problem, suggests that animals self-consciously seek out an environment that favors their physical characteristics. This is illustrated by the following quotation: "On another tree — they'd move on another dark tree. 'Cos they'd find out now that more are being killed off and the ones who are left say 'Well, its growing moss and it's getting a lot paler, so we might as well move.' "

Most students have difficulty in distinguishing between adaptation at the individual level and that which alters populations of organisms. This is perhaps to be expected as professional biologists, including teachers, use the same word *adaptation* to describe both kinds of change. We thus refer to a person "adapting" to life at high altitude by producing additional red blood cells, or to life in a sunny climate by becoming tanned and hence protecting the lower layers of the skin from radiation. We also use the word *adaptation* in the evolutionary sense implied by the tasks on the arctic fox and the caterpillars just discussed. Perhaps we as teachers need to be more careful in defining precisely in what context we are referring to the word. Perhaps we need to coin another word so that we can distinguish more clearly between adaptation at the individual and at the population levels.

An interesting finding from Deadman and Kelly's (1978) work was that all the students interviewed thought of evolution solely in terms of animals. Although given ample opportunity for doing so, no student mentioned plants in an evolutionary context. As we have seen, Engel Clough and

Wood-Robinson's (1985b) work drew only on animal examples in considering both adaptation and inheritance. The classical work on inheritance undertaken by Gregor Mendel a century and a half ago was, of course, concerned with plant inheritance, and this is doubtless often referred to with students. But an underlying message for teaching is that we should ensure that we do not neglect plants, as well as animals, when considering evolution.

Anthropomorphic and Teleological Reasoning in Students' Explanations

Anthropomorphic explanations involve human attributes being ascribed to nonhuman organisms. Thus explanations that suggest that plants "know that they need to grow toward the light" or that "an insect deliberately selects an appropriately colored background on which to rest because they know that birds would not see it" both incorporate an anthropomorphic viewpoint. Teleological explanations draw on the view that developments are due to the purpose or design that is served by them. Thus the view that "the arctic fox has developed thick fur in order to protect itself against the cold" is a teleological explanation. There is clearly a sense in which teleology is a particular example of anthropomorphism.

A number of workers have drawn attention to the way students use teleological and anthropomorphic explanations to account for biological phenomena, and this has already been referred to in discussing Engel Clough and Wood-Robinson's (1985b) work on adaptation. As an example, the following explanation of the distribution of dark and light caterpillars on dark and light trees illustrates an anthropomorphic viewpoint: "They knew they'd got to change and it'll have took a long time, but gradually they started to get darker and darker" [16-year-old student].

Leach et al. (1992, in press-b) found that many students explained the relative abundance in an ecosystem of producers compared with primary consumers in terms of the needs of consumers for a supply of food.

Jungwirth (1975) discussed the use of anthropomorphic and teleological metaphors in textbooks and demonstrated that such explanations are not uncommon — even in books aimed at university students. The British zoologist and television broadcaster David Attenborough, whose programs, such as "Life on Earth," have had a world-wide audience, frequently draws on teleological explanations in his commentaries, and such popular (and convincing) accounts of adaptation may well influence the way in which students perceive the situation. Tamir and Zohar (1991) have reviewed the acceptance of such reasoning by 15- to 17-year-old Israeli students across a number of biological areas. Their findings confirm that both anthropomorphic and teleological statements are accepted by many students as explanations of biological events. Thus over 80% of their (albeit small) sample ($n = 28$) accepted anthropomorphic explanations: 29% believed that plants really "wished," "tried," or "strived," and 62% believed that animals demonstrated these characteristics. Almost all their sample accepted teleological or partially teleological explanations as well.

One of the difficulties facing us as teachers is that explanations that avoid teleology and anthropomorphism are often more tortuous and difficult for students to understand. We may therefore be tempted to slip into a form of "anthropomorphic or teleological shorthand" that we ourselves recognize as being scientifically unacceptable. But our students may accept our explanation at its face value and hence genuinely adopt an anthropomorphic view. As teachers we must therefore think more carefully about the metaphors and explanations we use so that we avoid unknowingly sowing the seeds of such misunderstandings.

The theme of this chapter has been that our students often have well-formed ideas about and explanations for the biological world around them. They have frequently acquired these ideas and explanations from their own observations and experiences and from informal sources. These views of the world are often in conflict with those that are accepted by the scientific community. If we are to make our teaching effective we must be more aware of these viewpoints so that we can move our students away from them and toward more acceptable scientific explanations. We must therefore create opportunities for students to reveal their ideas to each other and to us as their teachers. We can then put their ideas to the test and challenge them in ways that lead our students toward the acceptance of scientific explanations. It is important, however, that this takes place in a nonthreatening classroom or laboratory environment. Students will certainly not reveal their views of the world in an atmosphere in which they are likely to be ridiculed as naive and ill informed. Much of the research reported on here has been carried out in the context of individual interviews in which the interviewer makes it clear that the views of the student are of interest and value. Such one-to-one contact is only rarely possible for the busy teacher who has a whole class to contend with. But strategies can be devised that do help us to get a better feel for our students ideas. Pencil and paper tasks that are devised to probe ideas before teaching, as oppose to checking progress after teaching, are one possibility. Group activities, in which students share their ideas with their peers before presenting them to the class as a whole, are another possibility. In this way the group's spokesperson is presenting the group's ideas rather than the spokesperson's own. Hence the views are made less personal to the individual who put them forward. The creation of a poster or the designing of an investigation to test an idea are two other ways in which a group can work together in a nonthreatening way and reveal "what the learner already knows."

REFERENCES

Adeniyi, E. O. (1985). Misconceptions of selected ecological concepts held by some Nigerian students. *Journal of Biological Education, 19*(4), 311-316.

Albaladejo, C., & Lucas, A. M. (1988). Pupils' meanings for "mutation." *Journal of Biological Education, 22*(3), 215-219.

Barker, M. (1986). *Where does the wood come from? An introduction to photosynthesis for third and fourth formers.* Hamilton, New Zealand: Centre for Science and Mathematics Education Research, University of Waikato.

Barker, M., & Carr, M. (1989). Photosynthesis—Can our pupils see the wood for the trees? *Journal of Biological Education, 23*(1), 41-44.

Bell, B. (1985). Students' ideas about plant nutrition: What are they? *Journal of Biological Education, 19*(3), 213-218.

Brook, A., Driver, R., & Hind, D. (1989). *Progression in science: The development of pupils' understanding of physical characteristics of air across the age range 5-16 years.* Leeds, England: Children's Learning in Science Project, Centre for Studies in Science and Mathematics Education, University of Leeds.

Brumby, M. (1979). Problems in learning the concept of natural selection. *Journal of Biological Education, 13*(2), 119-122.

Brumby, M. (1982). Students' perceptions of the concept of life. *Science Education, 66*(4), 613-622.

Carmichael, P., Driver, R., Holding, B., Phillips, I., Twigger, D., & Watts, M. (1990). *Research on children's conceptions in science: A bibliography.* Leeds, England: Children's Learning in Science Research Group, Centre for Studies in Science and Mathematics Education, University of Leeds.

Carr, M. (1987). The matter of energy. *Research in Science Education, 17*, 31-37.

Deadman, J. A., & Kelly, P. J. (1978). What do secondary school boys understand about evolution and heredity before they are taught the topics? *Journal of Biological Education, 12*(1), 7-15.

Driver, R., Leach, J., Scott, P., & Wood-Robinson, C. (1994). Young people's understanding of science concepts: Implications of cross-age studies for curriculum planning. *Studies in Science Education, 24*, 75-100.

Engel Clough, E., Driver, R., & Wood-Robinson, C. (1987). How do children's scientific ideas change over time? *School Science Review, 69*(247), 255-267.

Engel Clough, E., & Wood-Robinson, C. (1985a). Children's understanding of inheritance. *Journal of Biological Education, 19*(4), 304-310.

Engel Clough, E., & Wood-Robinson, C. (1985b). How secondary students interpret instances of biological adaptation. *Journal of Biological Education, 19*(2), 125-130.

Griffiths, A. K., & Grant, B. A. C. (1985). High school students' understanding of food webs: Identification of a learning hierarchy and related misconceptions. *Journal of Research in Science Teaching, 22*(5), 421-436.

Hind, A. (1992). *Children's understanding of food chains and the implications for teaching strategies.* Unpublished paper, University of Leeds.

Jungwirth, E. (1975). Preconceived adaptation and inverted evolution: A case study of distorted concept formation in high school biology. *Australian Science Teaching Journal, 21*, 95-100.

Kargbo, D. B., Hobbs, E. D., & Erikson, G. L. (1980). Children's belief about inherited characteristics. *Journal of Biological Education, 14*(2), 137-146.

Leach, J., Driver, R., Scott, P., & Wood-Robinson, C. (1992). *Progression in understanding of ecological concepts by pupils aged 5-16.* Leeds, England: Children's Learning in Science Research Group, Centre for Studies in Science and Mathematics Education, University of

Leeds.

Leach, J., Driver, R., Scott, P., & Wood-Robinson, C. (In press-a). Children's ideas about ecology 2: Ideas found in children aged 5–16 about the cycling of matter. *International Journal of Science Education.*

Leach, J., Driver, R., Scott, P., & Wood-Robinson, C. (In press-b). Children's ideas about ecology 3: Ideas found in children aged 5–16 about the interdependency of organisms. *International Journal of Science Education.*

Longden, B. (1982). Genetics — Are there inherent learning difficulties? *Journal of Biological Education, 16*(2), 135–140.

Mintzes, J. J., Trowbridge, J. E., Arnaudin, M. W., & Wandersee, J. H. (1991). Children's biology: studies on conceptual development in the life sciences. In S. M. Glynn, R. H. Yeanx, & B. K. Britton, (Eds.), *The psychology of learning science.* (pp. 179–202). Hillsdale, NJ: Lawrence Erlbaum Associates.

Okeke, E. A. C., & Wood-Robinson, C. (1980). A study of Nigerian pupils' understanding of selected biological concepts. *Journal of Biological Education, 14*(4), 329–338.

Pearson, J. T., & Hughes, W. J. (1988a). Problems with the use of terminology in genetics education: 1, A literature review and classification scheme. *Journal of Biological Education, 22*(3), 178–182.

Pearson, J. T., & Hughes, W. J. (1988b). Problems with the use of terminology in genetics education: 2, Some examples from published materials and suggestions for rectifying the problem. *Journal of Biological Education, 22*(4), 267–274.

Radford, A., & Baumberg, S. (1987). A glossary of terms for teaching genetics. *Journal of Biological Education, 21*(2), 127–135.

Schollum, B. W. (1983). Arrows in science diagrams: Help or hindrance to pupils? *Research in Science Education, 13*, 45–49.

Senior, R. A. (1983). *Pupils' understanding of some aspects of interdependency at age 15.* Unpublished MEd. dissertation, University of Leeds, England.

Sequiera, M., & Freitas, M. (1986). *Death and decomposition of living organisms: Children's alternative frameworks.* Toulouse, France: Association of Teacher Education in Europe.

Simpson, M., & Arnold, B. (1982). The inappropriate use of subsumers in biology learning. *European Journal of Science Education, 4*(2), 173–184.

Smith, E. L., & Anderson, C. W. (1986). *Alternative student conceptions of matter cycling in ecosystems.* Paper presented to the Annual Meeting of the National Association for Research in Science Teaching, San Francisco.

Tamir, P. & Zohar, A. (1991). Anthropomorphism and teleology in reasoning about biological phenomena. *Science Education, 75*(1), 57–68.

Wandersee, J. H., Mintzes, J. J., & Arnaudin, M. W. (1989). Biology from the learner's viewpoint: A content analysis of the research literature. *School Science and Mathematics. 89*(8), 654–668.

Wood-Robinson, C. (1986). Energy — A biologist's viewpoint. In R. Driver, & R. Millar, (Eds.), *Energy matters* (pp. 53–57). Leeds, England: Centre for Studies in Science and Mathematics Education, University of Leeds.

Wood-Robinson, C. (1991). Young people's ideas about plants. *Studies in Science Education, 19*, 119–135.

Wood-Robinson, C. (1994). Young people's ideas about inheritance and evolution. *Studies in Science Education, 24*, 29–47.

6 Conceptual Development of Basic Ideas in Chemistry

Ruth Stavy
Tel Aviv University, Israel

Matter is one of the fundamental concepts in science in general, and is the main object of the study of chemistry in particular. Everyday life provides children with countless opportunities for interacting with a variety of materials, and observing their properties and the changes they undergo. Thus, every child presumably develops some intuitive ideas about matter.

In this chapter, I describe studies conducted by my colleagues and myself aimed at determining what kind of knowledge about matter is developed through out-of-school experience, and the course of the development of this knowledge with age and instruction. In addition, the effects of different factors on children's responses is described. These factors include content-related ones such as the nature of the physical system, the perceptual input, and so forth, and learner-related ones such as age and/or instruction.

We first look at the concept of matter and its place in the curriculum, and then present some findings related to elementary and junior high school children's declarative knowledge (conceptions, beliefs, and images) about matter and its properties. These findings were obtained (a) by directly asking children what they thought matter was, whether they thought different items (including air) were matter or not, and what they thought a gas was, and (b) from children's verbal explanations accompanying their answers to problems related to matter.

Finally, we present findings that relate to children's ability to solve problems (their operative knowledge) regarding the conservation of weight in different transformations (especially from visible to nonvisible form), the awareness of the reversibility of the process of change of state, and the substantial nature of gases (the weight of a system after a gas was added or removed from it). The relationship between these two types of knowledge is discussed. The information described in this chapter regarding the development of ideas about matter in children is used to recommend a rationalized sequence and method of teaching.

As stated earlier, matter is one of the fundamental concepts in science in general, and the main object of the study of chemistry in particular. The problem of deciding on the boundaries of materiality has occupied scientists as well as philosophers throughout the history of science and philosophy (McMullin, 1978; Toulmin & Goodfield, 1962). The distinction between matter and nonmatter (a physical agent like heat or magnetism, but with no mass) was accepted only toward the middle of the 19th century. Earlier, no clear criteria existed and therefore air, steam, fire, and heat, which are not considered matter according to the modern definition, were considered as matter. Even today, however, the boundaries of materiality are not very sharp and clear. For instance, after many years of discussions about the nature of light, the idea emerged that it (and some other small particles) has a dual nature. In some instances its behavior is better understood in terms of waves, and in other cases it is better understood in terms of particles. However, in the junior high school science curriculum, matter is explicitly or implicitly treated as anything that occupies space and has mass (or weight).

Aristotelian doctrine, widely accepted for many centuries, strictly differentiated between matter and weight. Weight was conceived as an accidental property of matter resulting from two opposing forces of heaviness and lightness (Meyerson, 1962). It was regarded as a property like color or temperature. The existence of weightless matter (e.g., caloric, phlogiston, and ether) was commonly accepted. This ancient perception of matter has changed during the course of history due to empirical research on the macroscopic level (such as that of Lavoisier) and theoretical considerations on the microscopic level (such as the particulate theory of matter). Matter is a highly abstract concept. The perceptual elements on which it is built are not always very salient, and the variance within matter is very great. Solids and liquids are concrete forms of matter that have attributes visibly demonstrable to children. Gases are abstract forms of matter that have no visible attributes available to children. It is therefore possible for them to relate to gas as matter only if they know the criteria that define matter. In addition, children have access to a very limited number of gases in their everyday life, and therefore their knowledge of gases prior to instruction is poor.

The law of the conservation of matter is one of the most basic laws of science. It is one of a set of known conservation laws. Many scientists (e.g., Arons, 1977) regard the conservation laws as empirical laws that state that for a given system of objects there exist measurable quantities whose total amount does not change. The laws determine the conditions in which each quantity is conserved. Different ideas concerning the conservation of matter have been raised throughout the history of science, and the problem of conservation of matter has occupied scientists at different times. Children do not have direct empirical experiences that would lead them to the laws of conservation.

Concepts related to matter, change of state, and conservation of matter are usually taught in junior high school in conjunction with the particulate theory of matter and are treated as a means to teach the latter. At the same time, the physical attributes of each of the three states of matter — solid, liquid, and gas — as well as the process of change of state are usually described, and the properties and behavior of matter are explained, in terms of the particulate theory of matter.

CHILDREN'S DECLARATIVE KNOWLEDGE ABOUT MATTER AND ITS PROPERTIES

We obtained children's declarative knowledge about matter (a) by directly asking them about matter in general and about the abstract form of matter, gas, and (b) from their verbal explanations to problems related to matter and to problems related to gas.

Knowledge Obtained by Directly Asking Children to Define Concepts

Matter

It is evident from our studies that matter for many children is something they can see and grasp. It is preferably solid and inanimate. How is this notion of matter reflected in their behavior?

When children were directly asked to explain what they thought matter was (Stavy, 1991a), they (especially the younger ones, up to age 10, fifth grade) tended to explain by giving typical examples or by describing function and not by defining properties. Their responses indicate that the mental model they have with regard to matter is associated very strongly with either moldable or useful solid materials such as plasticine, clay, cement, or iron. This model persists until the seventh grade. From the age of 8 (third grade) on, children start also to think of matter in terms of structure ["matter is something that is made (or built or constructed) of things"] or properties (specific properties such as hardness, tangibility, color, etc., or properties related to the form of matter such as solid, powder, etc.). Only about 10% of the seventh-grade students (having studied a chapter on the structure of matter) related to the properties of weight and/or volume that are relevant in a scientific context.

When children were asked to classify different items — solids (iron, wood, ice, cotton wool, iron spring, sugar, flour, $KMnO_4$, soil), liquids (milk, mercury, water), gas (air), biological materials (flower, human body, meat), phenomena associated with matter (fire, electricity, wind, smell), and nonmatter (heat, light, shadow) — into matter and nonmatter, it was found that young children's concept of matter is, on the one hand, underextended. Their concept does not include some solids (e.g., soil, ice, cotton wool), most liquids (e.g., water, milk) and biological materials (e.g., meat), and gas. On the other hand, the children's concept is overextended, including some phenomena associated with matter and nonmatter items. Similar results were obtained by Andersson (1989) in Sweden.

During development and instruction, there is a gradual shift in the classification pattern toward a more scientific one (e.g., from 60% correct classifications of solids in the first grade to 90% in the eighth, from 40% correct classifications of liquids at the first grade to 85% in the eighth, and from 5% correct classifications of gases in the first grade to 55% in the eighth; see Fig. 6.1), but it seems that this shift is not associated with a parallel shift in the nature of explanation or definition of the term *matter*. The improvement in explaining matter in terms of the properties of weight or volume lags behind the ability to classify items into matter and nonmatter. A similar phenomenon of improvement in the ability to classify

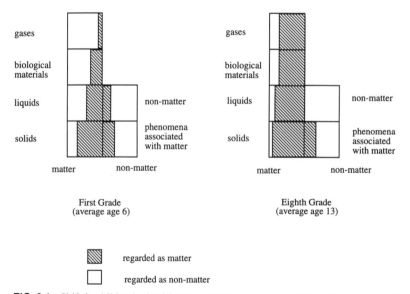

FIG. 6.1   Shift in children's classification of different groups of items into matter and nonmatter.

without parallel improvement in defining ability also was observed with regard to the concepts *solid* and *liquid* (Stavy, 1994; Stavy & Stachel, 1985). This phenomenon may suggest the preexistence of implicit knowledge about matter, which directs the classification activity before the ability to explicitly express it is acquired.

Gas

As has been shown, matter is grasped by many children as a concrete solid object, whereas most of them — at all grade levels — do not regard a gas (air) as material. Because a gas is an abstract form of matter, relating to it as material requires using the criteria that define matter. It is therefore interesting to find out how children conceive of gases. Childrens' conceptions of the other states of matter (solid and liquid) are discussed elsewhere (e.g., Stavy, 1994; Stavy & Stachel, 1985).

As was expected, young children between ages 9 and 11 (Grades 4 to 6, prior to learning the chapter about the structure of matter) do not develop the concept of gas spontaneously (Stavy, 1988b), as can be seen in Table 6.1. When directly asked what a gas is, these students tended to verbally explain by means of typical examples such as cooking gas, gas in carbonated drinks, air, tear gas, laughing gas, poisonous gas, and so on. These students

TABLE 6.1
Children's Definitions of the Term *Gas* (Percent)

	Grade					
Definition	*4*	*5*	*6*	*7*	*8*	*9*
By *example*, such as:	*85*	*80*	*65*	*35*	—	—
Cooking gas	40	20	35	—	—	—
Gas in light drinks	35	15	25	—	—	—
Air	5	40	20	35	—	—
Steam	—	10	—	—	—	—
Others (tear gas, poisonous gas, laughing gas, etc.)	10	5	—	—	—	—
As a *form of matter* relating to:	—	*20*	*20*	*45*	*75*	*35*
Properties	—	10	10	25	5	—
State of matter	—	10	10	20	70	35
By means of the *particulate theory of matter* relating to:	—	—	—	—	*25*[a]	*80*[b]
Distance between particles	—	—	—	—	25	70
Motion of particles	—	—	—	—	10	20
Arrangement of particles	—	—	—	—	5	5
Attraction forces between particles	—	—	—	—	5	5
Not known or irrelevant	15	—	—	—	—	—

Note. The figures are computed on the basis of the total number of answers for each age group.

[a]Students in this age group preferred the use of the term *atoms*.

[b]Students in this age group preferred the use of the term *molecules* or *particles*.

have no general idea of gas and are unaware of the properties or attributes common to gases (volume, mass, fluidity, compressibility, etc.). Their knowledge as displayed in the examples is mainly functional, such as, "gas is the thing that warms the pot," or "the thing from which you can make soda water." Seventh and eighth grade students (12–13 years old) tended to define gas as a form of matter. They refer to common properties of gases: "materials that spread, lighter or heavier than air; some can be seen, others can't," "a kind of material in nature, colorless, tasteless, looks transparent and has smell," or "gas has volume." Some of them relate to gas as one of the states of matter: "another form of matter" or "gas is one of the states of matter, it has very small specific weight, it is compressible and intangible." Most probably this type of definition develops as a consequence of learning about the structure of matter in the seventh grade.

It is interesting to note that, although students study about gas as a form of matter in the seventh grade, only 45% of seventh grade students use this type of definition in the seventh grade, immediately after learning, and 35% of them still use definitions by means of example. Only after a delay of a year, in the eighth grade, do most of the students use this type of definition. It seems that many students need a long period of time to incorporate and assimilate the new idea that gas is material. The use of this type of definition declines in the ninth grade, when students prefer to define gas by means of the particulate theory of matter. Definitions by means of particles were given only by eighth- and ninth-grade students. Most of the students in both grades referred to the distance between particles, for example, "a substance in which the distances between the atoms are large." Here again, in spite of recent instruction on the particulate theory of matter, none of the seventh grade students defined gas by means of the particulate theory of matter. Only 25% of the eighth grade students and most of the ninth graders did so. A gap of 2 years exists between the time students are taught the particulate theory of matter and the time they spontaneously apply it to define the term *gas*. It seems that the process of acquiring this new knowledge is very slow and continuous. Students first use the idea that gas is a form of matter (a macroscopic description), and only later do they adequately understand the particulate theory of matter and use it to explain the gaseous state (a microscopic theoretical interpretation).

A further point of interest is that although only 25% of students in Grade 9 defined the concepts of solid and liquid by means of the particulate theory of matter (Stavy, 1988a, 1994) and about 15% of them explained the process of change of state by means of this theory (Stavy, 1990a), the majority of ninth grade students did use it with regard to the concept of gas. This becomes readily understandable on the basis of students' intuitive knowledge about solids and liquids. Students believe that solid is something hard and that liquid is something that pours like water (Stavy, 1994; Stavy

& Stachel, 1985). These ideas strongly suggest that matter is continuous. The newly taught idea that both solids and liquids are built of small discrete particles is counterintuitive. In other words, students' strong intuitive knowledge with regard to solids and liquids may be said to compete with the new ideas taught in school. On the other hand, students' ideas about gas (something intangible and shapeless that spreads) are not counterintuitive to the particulate theory of matter, and thus students tend to use it more when explaining gas. It seems that it is easier to accept formal theoretical explanations when they do not run counter to preexisting intuitive ideas. Although the majority of students at the ninth grade used terms from the particulate theory to explain the gaseous state, their understanding of this theory was very fragmentary. As mentioned earlier, many of them did not apply it when explaining what solids and liquids are (Stavy, 1990a, 1994) and failed to understand important aspects of this theory (Gabel, Samuel, & Hunn, 1987; Krajcik, 1991; Novick, & Nussbaum, 1978; Osborne & Schollum, 1983). Least assimilated were the following aspects of the particulate theory: empty space, motion, and interaction between particles. In many cases students retained their continuous model of matter even though they appeared to be holding a particulate model of matter simultaneously.

Knowledge Obtained From Children's Verbal Explanations Accompanying Their Answers to Problems

Matter

Children conceive of matter as:

A. Concrete Solid Object. This conception is supported by data obtained from children's verbal explanations of their answers to different conservation of matter problems. When presented with iodine sublimation in a closed test tube, a number of fourth- and fifth-grade children explained that "the color in the test tube is from the *matter* that was there before" or "there is no *matter*, only purple color; the crystal was heated and the *matter* disappeared," or "gas cannot be turned back into *matter*." The purple gas that filled the test tube is not seen as matter by these children. When presented with evaporation of acetone in a closed test tube, some reactions were "the water of the acetone disappeared, the material and even the smell remain stuck to the walls of the test tube." Liquid or water is presented as nonmatter.

B. A Material Core and Nonmaterial Properties Such as Color, Smell, Flammability, or Weight (Heaviness). This is evident from childrens' (Grades 4 to 6) explanations of the process of evaporation of acetone in a closed test tube: "the acetone disappeared but the smell remained" or, in the case of iodine, "there is no matter, only color." Piaget and Inhelder (1974) and Inditzky (1988) found a similar conception, at a younger age, of the property of sweetness of sugar dissolved in water ("the sugar disappears, the sweetness remains"). Stavy and Stachel (1985a) found that young children believe that a melted candle loses its property of flammability.

C. Not Necessarily a Solid, but Some Perceptual Evidence for Its Existence Is Necessary. Matter ceases to exist when the evidence disappears. The existence of matter is therefore not conceived as permanent. The colored iodine gas, for instance, is perceived as matter, whereas the colorless acetone gas is not: "There is matter because there is color." The presence of color aided children (Grades 4 to 6) to believe that there was material in the test tube even though it was in a gaseous state. Apparently, the visual property of color provides much stronger evidence of the existence of matter than does smell. This is similar to the finding of Piaget (1969) regarding the existence of air. Piaget found that young children believe in the existence of air only when it moves. Sere (1985) also found that students (ages 11–12) believed that gas exists either when it moves, when they can feel the pressure it is exerting, or when it can be seen.

D. Weightless. Children do not regard weight as an intrinsic property of matter. When presented with change of state, children believe that weight can change with the state of matter. It seems that children construct a set of intuitive rules or propositions regarding the correlation between weight of matter and its state. The following rules were found in the case of melting candle wax: (a) The liquid weighs more than the solid, (b) the liquid has no weight, (c) the liquid weighs less than the solid, and (d) the weight of the liquid is equal to the weight of the solid from which it was formed. These rules progress with age from the first through to the fourth. Similar rules were found regarding the process of dissolving sugar in water (which children may perceive as melting): (a) Sugar/water solution is heavier than the total weight of sugar and water, (b) the dissolved sugar has no weight, (c) the weight of the sugar/water solution is smaller than the total weight of sugar and water, and (d) the weight of the sugar/water solution is equal to the sum of the respective weights of the sugar and water. In the case of evaporation or sublimation, (a) gas has no weight, (b) gas always weighs less than solid or liquid, and (c) the weight of gas is equal to the weight of the solid or liquid from which it was formed.

All these rules stem from children's intuitions regarding the "lightness" and "heaviness" of matter (or groups of materials), which is an intensive quantity or property. The children refer to the intensive quantity (density) instead of the extensive quantity (weight) about which they were asked. It is possible to explain this behavior as follows. The major change in all these processes is in the state of matter, which is expressed as a change in density. Probably, children are affected by the changing dimension of the task and regard it as the significant dimension of the problem. Apparently, the term *weight* is connected in the children's cognitive systems with "specific weight" and "absolute weight" (and probably also with other weight aspects, such as swings, balance scales, free fall, etc.). These terms are not sufficiently defined, and as long as this remains the case, the children can use them according to the specific characteristic of the situation.

E. Particulate.   A particulate conception of matter in young children, prior to the learning about the structure of matter in school, was reported by Piaget and Inhelder (1974) and by Inditzky (1988), with regard to the process of dissolution. Piaget and Inhelder found that children (ages 6–8) explained that when sugar was dissolved in water, it disintegrated into very small bits or particles. Inditzky, too, found some evidence for such a conception in young children. It is interesting to note that only 24% of the seventh-grade students, after studying about the particulate theory of matter, used particles to explain the process of dissolution (Inditzky, 1988). Only 15% of the eighth- and ninth-grade students, after studying the particulate nature of matter, explained the process of change of state in terms of the particulate theory; however, some of them claimed that dense particles are heavier than rare ones. They had, in fact, adapted the particulate theory to their own conception according to which solids, for example, weigh more than gases. It seems that most young children do not spontaneously develop a particulate conception of matter. Moreover, even though they have learned it in school, the particulate theory is not internalized and does not become useful for most of the students when solving conservation of matter problems.

Gas

In addition to the already mentioned conception that gas has no weight or that gas is always lighter than the solid or liquid from which it was formed, some children believe that gas is an agency of lightness. According to this idea, adding gas to a system decreases the weight of the system because "gas adds lightness," or conversely, when gas escapes from a system its weight increases. For example, about 15% of fourth- to sixth-grade students think that the weight of a cup of soda water increases as the carbon dioxide leaves the water (Stavy, 1988b), and about 50% of eighth- and ninth-grade students believe that the weight of a test tube containing clear lime water decreases when exhaled air is bubbled into it and a precipitate of calcium carbonate is formed (the process is explained to the students: carbon dioxide from the exhaled air reacts with calcium ions to give a precipitate; Stavy, Eisen, & Yaakobi, 1987).

To sum up, it seems that children's conceptions of matter are similar in some aspects to those of historical scientists. This similarity, of course, does not suggest that young children of the present comprehend the meaning of matter as did the august ancient philosophers. Yet it is possible that both young children and ancient philosophers based their understanding of matter on common intuitive primary images whose origin is in immediate sensual experience in the physical world.

CHILDREN'S OPERATIVE KNOWLEDGE RELATED TO CONSERVATION OF MATTER

In this section we describe children's ability to solve two groups of conservation of matter problems: (a) problems related to the conservation of weight in change of state processes, and (b) problems related to the weight of a system after gas was added or removed from it.

The development of children's understanding of conservation of matter was first studied by Piaget, according to whom quantitative conservation takes place at the concrete operational stage (ages 7–11) when children develop the following logical operations: compensation, reversibility, identity, and additivity (Piaget & Inhelder, 1974). It has been found, however, that children can solve certain conservation of matter tasks without being able to solve others (e.g., Lovell & Ogilvie, 1961–1962; Stavy & Stachel, 1985b; Uzigris, 1964). It is of interest to find out how children respond to the two types of conservation of matter problems mentioned and to understand the factors that affect their performance.

Problems Related to Processes of Change in the State of Matter

Conservation of Weight in Different Types of Transformations of Matter

When children are presented with conservation of weight problems that involve change of state, the children's responses are different. It seems that the ability to conserve weight depends on the nature of the transformation (Stavy, 1990a, 1990b). It is first expressed in the case of the simple change of translocation (e.g., plasticine deformation), then in the change of state from solid to liquid (e.g., melting of ice), and finally in the change from liquid to gas (e.g., evaporation of acetone; see Fig. 6.2).

Figure 6.2 indicates that in the case of the placticine deformation task,

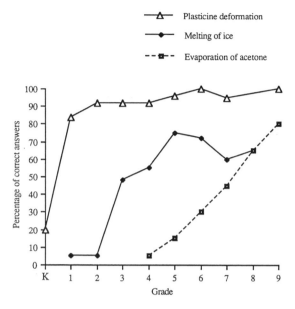

FIG. 6.2   Percentage of correct answers for different conservation of weight tasks, by grade.

20% of kindergarten children — and from first grade on practically all children — conserved weight. Children who succeeded in the task used identity explanations ("it is the same plasticine"), reversibility ("the ball can be changed back"), compensation ("There are more pieces, but they are smaller"), and additivity ("nothing was added or subtracted"). This means that from Grade 1 children have the logical system to deal with at least one type of conservation problems (translocation; e.g., plasticine deformation). However, when they are presented with a problem that involves transformation from solid to liquid — melting of ice (see Fig. 6.2) or melting of candle (Stavy & Stachel, 1985b) — their responses are different. Hardly any of the younger children in Grades 1 and 2 conserve the weight of the melted ice. Thereafter, the percentage of success gradually increases and reaches a maximum of about 70% in the fifth grade. The evaporation of acetone shows a linear rise from 0% to 80% success from the fourth grade to the ninth. The majority of students who did not correctly answer the melting of ice task believed that water is heavier than ice ("because ice floats on water") or that water has no weight. Few of the younger ones thought that ice is heavier than water ("because ice is harder than water"). With regard to the evaporation of acetone, the younger students tended to believe that gas has no weight, whereas the older ones thought that the liquid is heavier than the gas. The development of conservation of weight in the process of dissolving sugar in water, and expansion of water by heat, are very similar to the development of conservation in the melting of ice task (Fig. 6.3). The younger students who did not respond correctly to the sugar/water task believed the sugar/water solution to be heavier than the sum of the weights of the sugar and water because "sugar is heavy and makes the water heavier." The older ones tended to believe the sugar/water solution to be lighter than the sum of the weights of the sugar and water because "the sugar becomes smaller until it disappears." In the expansion of water task, the majority of students thought that the hot water is heavier because its volume expanded. But few of the older students (Grades 8 and 9) thought that "cold water is always heavier," and some even explained that the density of cold water is greater (Megged, 1978).

It can be concluded that children's responses to essentially similar conservation of weight problems are affected by the nature of the transformation. The different types of transformations (translocation, melting, evaporation) are perceptually different, and it may very well be that children therefore react differently to them. Moreover, children react in a similar way to different transformations that are perceptually similar (e.g., melting and dissolving).

The Effect of Perceptual Input on the Children's Conservation of Weight

In order to better understand the role of perceptual input in students' responses to conservation of weight problems, children's responses to

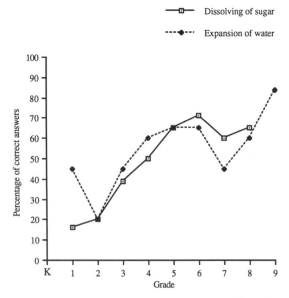

FIG. 6.3 Percentage of correct answers for the conversation of weight in the dissolving of sugar and expansion of water tasks, by grade.

essentially identical conservation of weight problems, such as in the process of evaporation of acetone and in the process of evaporation (or sublimation) of iodine, were compared. The iodine, as opposed to the acetone, has color and can be seen in its vapor state. It turns out that many more fourth to seventh grade students conserved the weight of the iodine than the acetone (the acetone task was first given). Students in this age group who conserved the weight of iodine and not that of acetone were clearly responding to the fact that they could see the material. They explained their answers with statements similar to those given for the conservation of weight of plasticine: "The crystal breaks up so it is exactly the same thing," or "the same thing that was in the crystal is in the test tube." From the seventh grade on, students begin to regard weight conservation of iodine in the same fashion as they regard that of acetone: "Only the state of matter was changed," or "nothing was added or subtracted." A few students referred to particles and said, "The particles only got farther apart."

Apparently, specific perceptual input from the task affects students' judgments. Beginning in the seventh grade, the effect of perceptual input disappears and the percentages of success in the two different tasks become parallel. One can assume that at this age all conservation of weight tasks involving changes of state are represented in the same way. This may indicate the beginning of formal conservation.

In the case of melting, however, two essentially similar problems – one relating to the melting of ice and the other to the melting of candle wax – show similar developmental curves. The developmental curve of success for the sugar/water task, the expansion of water task, and the evaporation of iodine task are similar to these. All these tasks are perceptually similar: They are concrete and involve changes in the volume or in the organization of visible matter. Apparently, students relate to all of them in a similar way.

Conservation of Weight and Reversibility

The understanding of reversibility was not found to be a prerequisite for the capability of weight conservation. There were cases in which students conserved weight without understanding the reversibility of the process (melted candle and iodine sublimation) and (rare) cases in which they grasped the reversibility of the process but did not conserve weight. It turns out that the two developmental curves of success in the reversibility tasks (namely, the evaporation of acetone and the sublimation of iodine) are very similar (see Fig. 6.4).

The curves are linear and have a sharp rise around age 12, that is, the seventh grade. At age 14 a drop appears that is different for each of the tasks, apparently because of oversophistication and attention to technical details regarding the reversibility of the process. These facts suggest that children represent the reversibility tasks related to the change of state from

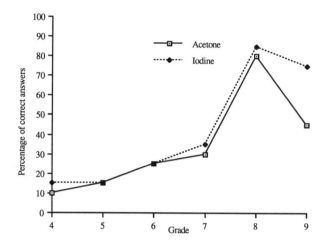

FIG. 6.4   Percentage of correct answers for the reversibility of evaporation tasks, by
grade.

liquid to gas in the same way and are not affected by perceptual elements of
the tasks. It is possible that the understanding of the reversibility of the
process, which emerges at age 12, is a result of school learning and/or due
to the development of formal thinking. The reversibility curve is almost
identical to that of the conservation of weight in the acetone evaporation
task, which is the most difficult of the tasks presented here. It is therefore
possible that there is some correlation between students' understanding of
reversibility and their capability to conserve weight in cases in which there
are no supporting perceptual elements, or at ages when these elements do
not function as supporting entities (formal conservation). The developmental curve of success in the reversibility of melting candle wax also
develops gradually from kindergarten up until age 14 (see Fig. 6.5). This
curve precedes that of reversibility of evaporation by approximately 4 years.

   In the case of melting ice, the majority of children between ages 6 and 14
understand the reversibility of the process, although many of them do not
conserve weight in this case. It is possible that children of these ages do not
have a general conception of the reversibility of the melting process, but
that they judge each case specifically, on the basis of their life experiences.

Problems Related to the Weight of a System After Adding/Removing Gas

Students were presented with two essentially similar tasks, each involving
the release of gas from a system. One system consisted of a cup of soda
water, and the students were asked about the weight of the soda water

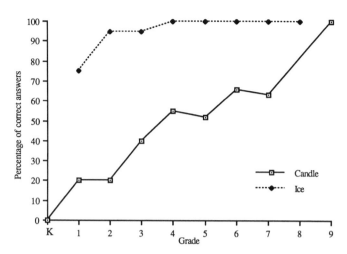

FIG. 6.5 Percentage of correct answers for the reversibility of melting tasks, by grade.

before and after it went flat. The second system consisted of a CO_2 cartridge (a very popular apparatus for making soft drinks in Israel). The students were asked about the weight of the cartridge before and after using it to prepare soda water. Figure 6.6 shows the percentage of children who gave correct responses to the two tasks. Most of the younger students (in the fourth to sixth grades) gave incorrect responses to the soda water task. Only from the seventh grade onward did the majority of the students answer the soda water question correctly, most probably as a consequence of studying "The Structure of Matter." The curve of success in this task is similar to that in the weight conservation of evaporating acetone task, but it is steeper with a sharper increase between sixth- and seventh-grade students. The explanation for correct answers was usually that "the bubbles (or gas, or air) also have weight." Incorrect answers to this question divided into two types. One reflected the already mentioned belief that gas has no weight and therefore the weight of the system should not change as a result of the release of the gas. The second reflected another previously mentioned belief characteristic of the lower grades (4–6) that gas adds lightness, and therefore, the weight of the system should increase as a result of the release of the gas.

Figure 6.6 also describes the percentage of children who answered the CO_2 cartridge problem correctly. The developmental curve here is similar in shape to that of the soda water task, but the number of students who answered correctly is much higher (by approximately 50%). The most common incorrect answer was that the weight of the CO_2 cartridge before and after releasing the gas remained constant. The students explained this by arguing that "air (or gas) weighs nothing." Correct answers were explained by saying "The cartridge was full, now it is empty" or "air (or gas

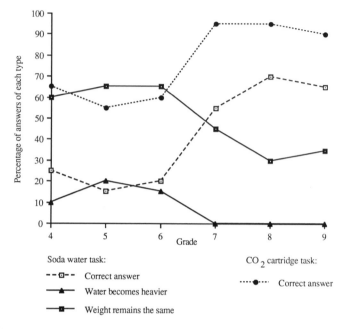

FIG. 6.6   Percentage of children who gave different types of answers to the soda-water task and a CO_2 cartridge task according to age group.

or CO_2) also has weight." A possible explanation for the high percentage of correct answers for this task, as opposed to the previous one, is that the students did not see the gas escape from the cartridge; they only saw the cartridge, and therefore their thinking was not muddled by ideas to the effect that "gas has no weight" or that "gas adds lightness." The students did not refer to the gas as such, but rather to matter in the general sense, by stating that matter was used or taken out of a container.

One problem involving the addition of gas to a system was presented to eighth and ninth grade students. They were shown two test tubes filled with the same volume of clear lime water. It was ascertained that the students knew that the initial weight of the two test tubes was the same. Exhaled air was bubbled into one of the tubes and the process was explained. (Carbon dioxide from exhaled air reacts with calcium ions to give a precipitate.) Students were asked whether the weight of the two test tubes was the same or different, and, if there was a difference, which was heavier. Only about 50% of the students understood that when carbon dioxide gas reacts with calcium ions in solution, the weight of the liquid increases (Stavy et al., 1987) (see Table 6.2). These results are similar to those described earlier (related to the soda water task) and suggest that students' ability to conserve the weight of gas when it is added or removed from a system is limited to certain situations only (when the gas is not concretely shown) rather than

TABLE 6.2
Students' Answers to the Questions About Gas as a Substance
(in Percentages)

	Weight		
	Heavier	Same	Lighter
Eighth grade ($n = 18$)	61.2	38.8	–
Ninth grade ($n = 15$)	40.0	46.6	13.3
Eighth and ninth grades ($n = 33$)	51.5	42.4	6.06

being generalized. It seems that children's scientific knowledge can be either supported or inhibited by perceptual factors.

INTERACTION BETWEEN DECLARATIVE AND OPERATIVE KNOWLEDGE

So far we have described children's declarative and operative knowledge relating to matter and changes of state. In this section we discuss the interaction between these two types of knowledge.

Most of the tasks testing students' operative knowledge are formally identical. Matter undergoes a transformation and a student is asked to compare weight. It has been shown that children can solve certain conservation tasks without being able to solve others, and that children's responses improve with age, although not necessarily in a linear fashion. The other group of tasks that were used to test students' operative knowledge involved addition or removal of substance (gas) from a system. In this case, too, students' performance changed according to task.

It is of interest to find out what the factors are that affect students' performance in these groups of tasks.

The most important of these seems to be the existence in the student's cognitive system of an intuitive, experience-based system of declarative knowledge associated with weight and state of matter. This sometimes inappropriate knowledge, in the form of laws or propositions that relate weight to state of matter, competes with the existing, relevant, and logical operative knowledge about the problem-solving mechanism. The dominant declarative knowledge, at a given moment, overcomes all other bits of knowledge.

The more dominant knowledge with regard to the problem will drive children in their solution to the problem. So even if the appropriate knowledge exists in the cognitive system, it is not always expressed in the actual solution. For instance, half of the children above age 7 conserved weight in the melted candle task by using logical additivity justifications, whereas the other half used their intuitive knowledge according to which a solid candle was heavier. But all children responded correctly to the weight conservation task with the plasticine. In the case of plasticine, at this age, the competing, inappropriate declarative knowledge characteristic of younger children is already weakened and thus cannot compete with the relevant logical operations. This may explain the high degree of success in this task. In the case of the candle, two bits of knowledge of about equal strength are probably used.

Among the children ages 8 to 9 the knowledge that the solid candle is heavier becomes more dominant, probably as the result of experience in the physical world and the successful use of this knowledge in solving other types of problems (solids usually have higher specific weights than the corresponding liquids). So the percentage of success drops and then rises again in the sixth and seventh grades when the knowledge that solids are heavier than liquids is channeled to relevant problems and no longer competes with the operative knowledge relevant to conservation. This process of finding the boundaries within which one's knowledge is applicable may lead one to identify (even unconsciously) a problem and relate to it according to its type or category (even if the response is incorrect). In such a case, the person's response will not be affected by irrelevant perceptual information and the solution will deal with the type and essence of the problem, generating a more formal or abstract response.

It seems that learning in the seventh grade about the states of matter and the particulate theory of matter can also strengthen the knowledge that solids are heavier than liquids and that liquids are heavier than gases. This may explain the drop in performance observed in the seventh grade with regard to certain tasks (see Fig. 6.2–6.4).

In addition, the different bits of knowledge may get temporary support from immediate perceptual inputs of the task — verbal, visual, or those that relate to the dynamic aspects of the changing dimensions of the task. For example, visual elements such as having color may support the appropriate logical apparatus so that the child will conserve weight during the process of evaporation of iodine but not in the evaporation of acetone. The supportive effect of such visual elements may be due to the lowering of the amount of information that the child must keep in its working memory: The child sees the substance and does not have to remember it was there before. Another example relates to the effect of the changing dimensions of the task. It seems that the child's cognitive system is affected by the changing dimension of the task (e.g., density change during change of state) and regards it as the significant dimension in the problem. The child then applies knowledge that is relevant to this dimension.

In sum, the different types of knowledge in the cognitive systems of children regarding certain physical entities — sometimes including the appropriate one—compete with one another. This is a dynamic competition between the different knowledge systems in which the more dominant prevails. In our case, children had the operative knowledge necessary to solve the conservation of weight problems, but instead they used irrelevant knowledge, which at certain ages or situations is quite dominant. It should be added that this inappropriate knowledge may be appropriate for other situations or problems.

The interplay between the different knowledge systems is an ongoing process through which children gradually learn the boundaries within which their knowledge is applicable. It is possible that the expansion of knowledge starts with instances of immediate perceptual input that offer positive reinforcement for correct knowledge, and from these instances is transferred by analogy to other cases.

EDUCATIONAL IMPLICATIONS

This chapter described how children construct basic concepts and ideas in chemistry related to matter and to change of state, and how different factors related to children (age, formal school teaching) and to the content (e.g., perceptual input from the task) affect this process.

Knowledge about the rate and sequence of this process and about its specific pitfalls might assist us, as teachers and curriculum developers, in creating more appropriate learning situations that will support students in elementary and junior high school in improving their construction of these concepts and ideas.

This can be achieved first by attending to problematic concepts or ideas, then by choosing more suitable examples to represent them together with a more sensible timing and sequencing for teaching them, and finally by using more appropriate specific teaching strategies.

Paying Attention

Often in the course of science teaching we tend not to pay enough attention to the very basic and fundamental concepts or ideas. As they are so basic, they seem self-evident to us. This chapter shows that this is not the case. It is true that many of these basic concepts are used in everyday life and language and develop spontaneously, but this common, everyday meaning does not necessarily coincide with the scientific one. Because these concepts are so very basic, leaving them unattended may result in difficulties in understanding any advanced concept or idea in the same subject-matter area, or in other related ones. As this chapter shows, matter for many children is something they can see and grasp. It is preferably solid and inanimate. Children also have difficulty in differentiating between matter and the phenomena it supports. It seems that there is no point in teaching the particulate nature of matter when students don't know what we mean by matter and don't believe that gas, for example, is material. Nor is there a point in teaching biological concepts related to photosynthesis, nutrition, and so forth when students don't regard biological objects as material. Attendance to the concept of matter may include presenting examples and nonexamples, classifying items according to this concept and looking for common defining attributes. It is suggested to start with items that students regard as matter (e.g., solids) and to look for their common features (mass or weight, if students have not been introduced to the concept of mass and volume). Then one could proceed to items students usually do not regard as matter (liquids, biological materials, and gases) by testing whether they possess the common features. One should also discuss nonmaterial items that students regard as matter, trying to show these don't agree with the common features.

Choosing Examples

When teaching science, it is common to present new concepts with the most typical examples instead of those with the strongest perceptual features. For instance, when teaching about gases, the examples of oxygen, nitrogen, carbon dioxide, ammonia, and so forth are given but not those of iodine, bromine, chlorine, or nitrogen oxide, which are colored. The opposite is also true—in cases in which the typical exemplars have strong perceptual attributes, other examples are not usually given. For instance, when teaching about liquids, the common examples of water, drinks, oil, and so forth are normally given, but this is not augmented with examples of viscous liquids or powders. Thus, nothing is added to the students' existing intuitive knowledge. It is therefore suggested that psychologically appropriate examples for presenting new concepts should be introduced.

Timing and Sequence

In general, the present chapter suggests that instruction should follow the natural sequence and pace of students' learning. Moreover, enough time should be allowed for ideas to be incorporated and understood. When a new phenomenon, term, law, or theory is taught, one should try to begin with an example that provides maximal perceptual reinforcement for correct intuitive knowledge. For example, in weight conservation in the process of evaporation one should start (at an appropriate age) with a colored material (such as iodine) in order to reinforce the existing intuitive knowledge, namely, that weight is conserved in this case. Only then should one proceed by analogy to cases with reduced perceptual reinforcements, for instance, colorless substances with smell and then colorless matter without smell.

We suggest that instruction in the conservation of weight should be done according to the following sequence:

1. Conservation in translocation — crumbling a lump of solid into powder.
2. Conservation during melting, dissolving, and in change of volume (of solids and liquids) during heating (or cooling).
3. Evaporation or sublimation (to be started with materials that have clearly visible properties in the gaseous state), and changes of volume of gas (heating/cooling or changing pressure).
4. Chemical reactions that do not involve the evolution or absorption of gases.
5. Chemical reactions in which gas is evolved or absorbed.

In all these transformations, the reversibility of the process must be regarded.

Another example involves the concept of gas. It was found that students first acquire the knowledge about the substantial nature of gases, then they develop the general idea of gas as a form of matter, and in the last stage they take in the particulate theory of matter. It seems logical to follow this sequence and to allow enough time for the new ideas to be incorporated and understood.

A third example relates to children's conception of matter. It was found that an intuitive notion that matter is particulate is evoked in children by presenting them with the process of dissolving of solid in liquid. This finding may indicate that teaching about the particulate nature of matter should take off from treating processes of dissolving, and then be further elaborated.

Specific Teaching Strategies

Two specific strategies for teaching conservation of weight during evaporation are described here. Both of them exploit the situation in which children can solve one weight conservation task (e.g., iodine) and cannot solve another (acetone). One involves teaching by analogy (see also Clement, 1987) and the second teaching by conflict (see also Stavy & Berkovitz, 1980). This situation in which students give contradicting judgments about externally different but essentially similar tasks enables us to use the intuitively correct knowledge related to the one (iodine task) in order to teach conservation of weight in the other (acetone task). This could be achieved by first presenting children with the iodine task to activate and support their correct intuitive knowledge, only then to present them with the acetone task, stressing the similarity between the tasks. Trying this strategy with fifth and sixth grade children resulted in significant improvement in children's ability to solve the acetone task (Stavy, 1991b). (Percent of success in the acetone conservation of weight task was 13% when first presented and 44% when presented after the iodine task.)

The same situation can also be used for conflict training. A conflict is generated by producing successively contradictory judgments about essentially similar tasks. At the same time, the child is made aware that the two tasks are essentially similar but that their responses are different. The child is then asked whether he or she would like to change responses. Trying this strategy with fifth- and sixth-grade students also resulted in significant improvement in children's ability to solve the acetone task (Cohen, 1992; Stavy & Cohen 1989). Percent of success in the acetone task increased from 0% before children were presented with the conflict to 45% immediately after and 50% at 1 month later — for this study we chose only children who answered the iodine task correctly but did not succeed in the acetone one.

There is a profound difference between conflict training and teaching by analogy. In conflict training, students have the opportunity to make their ideas explicit; they are made aware of the analogy between the tasks, of the contradiction in their judgments, of the need to resolve this contradiction, and of the learning process. But this teaching strategy may in certain instances result in students' loss of self-confidence and can sometimes cause regression; that is, students may change from the correct to the incorrect conception. In teaching by analogy, students do not explicitly express their alternative ideas; they are not made aware either of the conflict or of the learning process. They are told only that the tasks are similar. (The learning takes place without the students' awareness.) From the students' point of view, there were no misconceptions and no learning took place; they have intuitively come to understand both situations. Moreover, there is no danger of students losing their self-confidence or of regressing to incorrect judgements. From the teacher's point of view, no special teaching technique is required; the learning is directed by the choice of an appropriate starting situation or example. The result of this type of learning is actually stretching the limits of application of an analogous, intuitive idea to new situations.

REFERENCES

Andersson, B. (1989). *Pupils' conceptions of matter and its transformations (ages 12–16)*. In P. L. Lijnse, P. Licht, W. DeVos, & A. J. Waarlo (Eds.), *Relating macroscopic phenomena to microscopic particles: A central problem in secondary science education* (pp. 12–35). Utrecht, The Netherlands: CD-β Press.

Arons, A. (1977). *The various language.* New York: Oxford University Press.

Clement, J. (1987). Overcoming student's misconceptions in physics. In. J. Novak (Ed.), *Proceedings of Second International Seminar: Misconceptions and educational strategies in science and mathematics III* (pp. 84–97). Ithaca, NY: Cornell University.

Cohen, M. (1992). *The effect of conflict training and teaching by analogy on children's understanding of conservation of matter.* Unpublished master's thesis, School of Education, Tel Aviv University, Tel Aviv, Israel.

Gabel, D. L., Samuel, K. V., & Hunn, D. (1987). Understanding the particulate nature of matter. *Journal of Chemical Education, 64,* 695–697.

Inditzky, R. (1988). *The development of understanding of the particulate nature of matter among 7–13 year old children.* Unpublished master's thesis, School of Education, Tel Aviv University, Tel Aviv, Israel.

Krajcik, J. S. (1991). Developing students' understanding of chemical concepts. In S. M. Glynn, R. H. Yeany, & B. K. Britton (Eds.), *The psychology of learning science* (pp. 219–240). Hillsdale, NJ: Lawrence Erlbaum Associates.

Lovell, K., & Ogilvie, E. (1961-1962). A study of the conservation of weight in the junior school child. *British Journal of Educational Psychology, 31,* 138–144.

McMullin, E., (1978). *The concept of matter in modern philosophy.* Notre Dame, IN: University of Notre Dame Press.

Megged, C. (1978). *The development of the concept of density in children from ages 6-16.* Unpublished master's thesis, School of Education, Tel Aviv University, Tel Aviv, Israel.

Meyerson, E. (1962). *Identity and reality.* New York: Dover.

Novick, S., & Nussbaum, J. (1978). Junior high school pupils' understanding of the particulate nature of matter: An interview study. *Science Education, 62,* 273–282.

Osborne, R., & Schollum, B. (1983). Coping in chemistry. *Australian Science Teacher Journal, 29,* 13–24.

Piaget, J. (1969). *The child's conception of physical causality.* Totowa, NJ: Littfield, Adams. (Original work published 1927)

Piaget, J., & Inhelder, B. (1974). *The child's construction of quantity.* London: Routledge and Kegan Paul. (Original work published 1941)

Sere, M. G. (1985). The gaseous state. In R. Driver, E. Guesne & A. Tiberghien (Eds.), *Children's ideas in science* (pp. 105–123). Milton Keynes, England: Open University Press.

Stavy, R. (1988a). *The impact of instructional programs on the understanding of the concepts solid and liquid by junior high school students.* Unpublished manuscript, School of Education, Tel Aviv University, Tel Aviv, Israel.

Stavy, R. (1988b). Children's conception of gas. *International Journal of Science Education, 10,* 553–566.

Stavy, R. (1990a) Children's conceptions of changes in the state of matter: From liquid (or solid) to gas. *Journal of Research in Science Teaching, 27,* 247–266.

Stavy, R. (1990b). Pupils' problems in understanding conservation of matter. *International Journal of Science Education, 12,* 501–512.

Stavy, R. (1991a). Children's ideas about matter. *School Science and Mathematics, 9,* 240–244.

Stavy, R. (1991b). Using analogy to overcome misconceptions about conservation of matter. *Journal of Research in Science Teaching, 28,* 305–313.

Stavy, R. (1994). States of matter — Pedagogical sequence and teaching strategies based on cognitive research. In P. Fensham, R. Gunstone, & R. White (Eds.), *The content of science* (pp. 221–236). London: Falmer Press.

Stavy, R., & Berkovitz, B. (1980). Cognitive conflict as a basis for teaching quantitative aspects of the concept of temperature. *Science Education, 64,* 679–692.

Stavy, R., & Cohen, M. (1989). Overcoming student's misconceptions about conservation of matter by conflict training and by analogical reasoning. *Proceedings of the Second Jerusalem Convention on Education,* Hebrew University of Jerusalem

Stavy, R., Eisen, Y., & Yaakobi, D. (1987). How students aged 13–15 understand photosynthesis. *International Journal of Science Education, 9*, 105–115.

Stavy, R., & Stachel, D. (1985a). Children's ideas about solid and liquid. *European Journal of Science Education, 7*, 407–421.

Stavy, R., & Stachel, D. (1985b). Children's conception of changes in the state of matter: From solid to liquid. *Archives de Psychologie, 53*, 331–344.

Toulmin, S., & Goodfield, J. (1962). *The architecture of matter*. London: Hutchinson.

Uzigris, I. C. (1964). Situational generality of conversation. *Child Development, 35*, 831–841.

7 Children's Understanding of Astronomy and the Earth Sciences

John Baxter
St. Lukes College, Exeter University, England

One of the most compelling images depicting the birth of humankind's modern understanding of the universe features a medieval monk pulling back the sphere of primary perception to reveal the cosmos that lay hidden behind these initial ideas (Fig. 7.1). The monk's view, although dangerously controversial at the time,[1] has permeated almost all cultures over the past 400 years and it is now commonly assumed that children and adults draw back the same sphere-like veil to gain a similar perspective. But over the past decade there has been a growing body of evidence that throws doubt on the assumption that children and scientifically naive adults form post-Copernican notions about planet Earth in space (see Durant, Evans, & Thomas, 1989). Research shows that pupils frequently come to their lessons having constructed their own explanations for many of the easily observed astronomical events, and that these children's notions or "alternative frameworks" (Driver, 1983) are at variance with accepted views, often persisting into adulthood.

The work of Nussbaum and Novak (1976) and Sneider and Pulos (1983) showed that children's ideas about planet Earth in space and the gravitational field develop from a naive flat Earth notion through a series of phases to the accepted view. These phases cut across cultural boundaries; Mali and Howe (1979) and Klein (1982) identified similar notions and phases of development in children from a number of different cultural backgrounds.

---

[1]This woodcut is not what it is often claimed to be. It is pure art nouveau, first published by Camille Flammarion in 1888 (see Gingerich, 1988).

FIG. 7.1   A medieval view of the cosmos.

Research into children's ideas about other science areas — for example, evaporation (Russell, Harlen, & Wall, 1989) and sound (Linder & Erickson, 1989) — shows that pupils frequently construct their own explanations for many of the fundamental concepts of the science curriculum. This growing body of data on pupils' alternative frameworks has given rise to the *constructivist* or *alternative conceptions* movement, ACM (Gilbert & Swift, 1985). The principal axiom of the ACM is that a child's alternative framework is analogous to a scientific theory and will only be exchanged when it is challenged and fails to hold good in the light of new evidence.

Millar (1989) claimed that the ACM has brought science education research into the classroom, but research into alternative frameworks usually involves lengthy interviews with pupils to uncover their particular notions. Limited time and large numbers of pupils in each class preclude this as a commonly practiced classroom activity, and, as with so much science education research, the transition from research data to classroom practice is not always clear.

If research into alternative frameworks is to influence teaching strategies, it needs to be more than an inventory of pupils' ideas; it needs to inform teachers about trends in the progression of these ideas, to demonstrate ways in which pupils defend their notions when they are challenged, and to give examples on how children's alternative frameworks can become the central focus of a teaching strategy.

With these aims as the primary target, the author set up a research program into alternative frameworks about astronomy. This was recently undertaken in Great Britain. Astronomy was selected for two principal reasons. First, almost all children have some experience of the easily observed astronomical events and, in all probability, have constructed their own explanations for these changes long before they enter school. Second, there was a need to promote the more widespread teaching of astronomy in schools.

COLLECTING PUPILS' IDEAS ABOUT THE EASILY OBSERVED ASTRONOMICAL EVENTS

In this research program, children's theories about four astronomical domains were investigated:

1. Planet earth in space and the gravitational field.
2. Day and night.
3. Phases of the moon.
4. The seasons.

The sample of pupils between 9 and 16 years old was taken from pupils attending a comprehensive school in a semirural area of southwest England and its four feeder primary schools. At the time of the survey the schools did not feature astronomy in their science curriculum.

A two-phase process of data collection was used. First, 20 pupils between 9 and 16 years old were interviewed individually about their theories concerning the four domains. The sample covered the full range of abilities (based on their teachers' judgments) and included five pupils from each of the age groups 9-10, 11-12, 13-14, and 15-16, including equal numbers of boys and girls. The interviews were audiotaped and transcribed and records of pupils' drawings were kept. Second, the commonly occurring conceptions were used to construct an astronomy conceptual survey instrument. This comprised a series of statements with supporting diagrams based on the drawings produced by the interviewees. Pupils responded to the statements and their accompanying diagrams by placing a mark on the face that best represented their view (Hearty & Beall, 1984); see the example in Fig. 7.2. This instrument was administered to a representative sample of 48 boys and 52 girls from the same four age groups as the interviewees.

Results of the Survey

For clarity of presentation, the results from the original interview for each domain investigated are followed by the results obtained using the as-

Spoken statement

" It gets dark at night because the moon covers the sun."

FIG. 7.2   Example of question in the survey instrument.

tronomy conceptual instrument for that particular domain. The commonly occurring notions are represented diagrammatically and are followed by prevalence diagrams showing the percentage frequency of pupils who hold these notions.

Planet Earth and Gravity.   Children surveyed by interview and through the conceptual survey instrument were all presented with the same situation. They were asked to imagine that they had taken off from planet Earth in a space rocket and after they had been traveling away from Earth for a day they looked out of the window toward Earth. They were then asked to draw how they thought Earth would look.

After completing their drawing they were asked to draw in some people to show where they could live, then some clouds followed by showing rain falling from the clouds. As Fig. 7.3 shows, the drawings fell into four distinct notions and closely resemble those first proposed by Nussbaum (1979).

The first notion (common with younger children) represents planet Earth as a flat surface or saucer shaped, bearing a remarkable resemblance to the world view of the ancient Babylonians, Egyptians, and early Greeks (see Koestler, 1959). The older children almost always represented Earth as a sphere; however, it was common for them to draw in people and clouds on the "top half" or northern hemisphere only. A "prevalence diagram" shows

Notion 1

Earth shaped more like a saucer.

Notion 2

Earth sphere shaped but idea of
up and down still persists.
People only live on the upper
half.

Notion 3

Earth sphere shaped. People living all
over the surface but the idea of up and
down still persists.

Notion 4

Correct view. People living all over
the earth and 'down' towards the
center of the earth.

FIG. 7.3   Pupils' notions about planet Earth and gravity.

the percentage of pupils holding particular notions at certain ages (see Fig.
7.4). Notion 3 was the one most commonly held (the notion with the
widest block). This representation shows a round Earth, with people living
all over the surface, but with their heads facing the north pole; rain is shown
falling "down" from the northern hemisphere. Very few children repre-

Notions

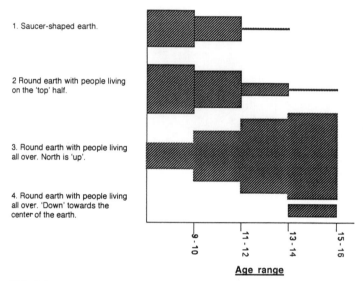

1. Saucer-shaped earth.

2 Round earth with people living on the 'top' half.

3. Round earth with people living all over. North is 'up'.

4. Round earth with people living all over. 'Down' towards the center of the earth.

9 - 10   11 - 12   13 - 14   15 - 16

Age range

FIG. 7.4   The prevalence of pupils' notions about planet Earth and gravity.

sented planet Earth as a sphere with people living all over the surface, their feet pointing toward the center, and rain falling toward the center of the earth (see Fig. 7.3, notion 4).

Although, as the prevalence diagram Fig. 7.4 shows, a belief in the more naive notions of a saucer-shaped Earth or a round Earth with people living on the top half only declined with age, it is notable how few pupils — even in the older age ranges — subscribed to the accepted notion. This suggests that a Newtonian view of gravity does not feature in most pupils' thinking, an observation supported by the studies of Watts and Zylbersztajn (1981) and Preece (1985).

Day and Night.   Interviewees were asked to explain why they thought it gets dark at night. They were able to explain their idea through drawings or by using polystyrene spheres. Their explanations gave rise to six distinct diagrams (see Fig. 7.5).

As with children's notions about planet Earth in space, a belief in the more naive notion of near and familiar objects causing the phenomenon declines with age, but the number of older pupils who explain day and night using a construct other than the earth spinning on its axes in front of a fixed sun is relatively high (see Fig. 7.6).

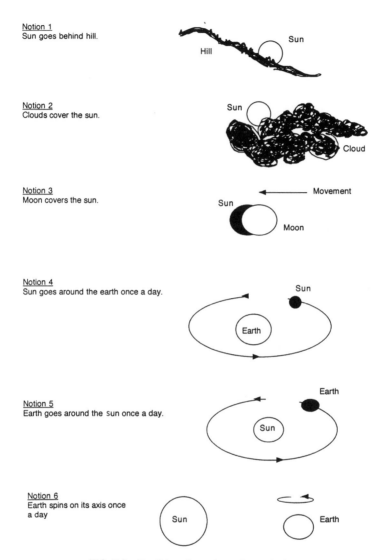

Notion 1
Sun goes behind hill.

Hill   Sun

Notion 2
Clouds cover the sun.

Sun

Cloud

Notion 3
Moon covers the sun.

Movement

Sun

Moon

Notion 4
Sun goes around the earth once a day.

Sun

Earth

Notion 5
Earth goes around the sun once a day.

Earth

Sun

Notion 6
Earth spins on its axis once a day

Sun   Earth

FIG. 7.5   Pupils' notions about day and night.

Phases of the Moon.   All pupils interviewed were aware that the moon changes shape, but few were able to relate any patterns to these changes. The more naive explanations for the apparent changes in the moon's shape bore a resemblance to pupils' explanation for day and night, namely, that near and familiar objects were the cause of the phenomena (see Fig. 7.7).

As the percentage prevalence diagram shows, the most popular notion —

Notions

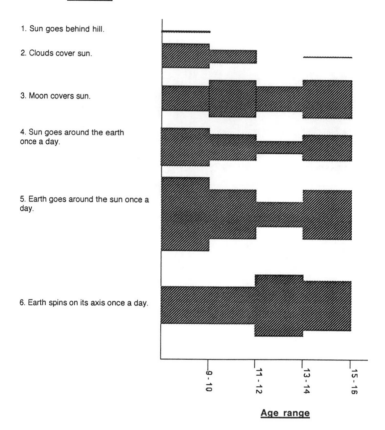

1. Sun goes behind hill.

2. Clouds cover sun.

3. Moon covers sun.

4. Sun goes around the earth once a day.

5. Earth goes around the sun once a day.

6. Earth spins on its axis once a day.

9 - 10   11 - 12   13 - 14   15 - 16

Age range

FIG. 7.6   The prevalence of pupils' notions about day and night.

and one that, increased with age — was of the earth casting its shadow on the moon, thus giving rise to its changes in shape (see Fig. 7.8).

The Seasons.   Interviewees were asked to explain what caused it to be cold during the winter. Again pupils explained their ideas using drawings or polystyrene spheres. Their responses fell into six distinct notions, with the idea of the sun being further away during the winter the most popular explanation (see Fig. 7.9).

Once again, two notable features emerge from this survey, namely, that the younger children use near and familiar objects to explain the phenomenon, and a small percentage of older pupils explain the event by using the accepted notion (see Fig.7.10).

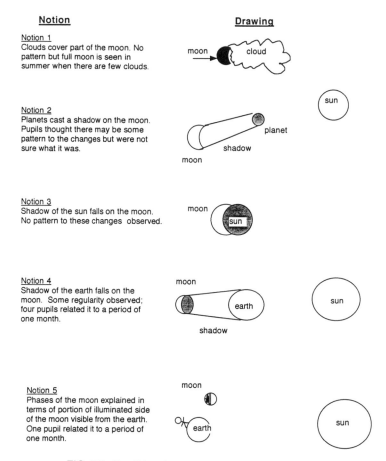

FIG. 7.7   Pupils' notions about the phases of the moon.

Discussion

Although the ideas children use to explain the easily observed astronomical events vary from one context to another, a number of conceptual developmental phases in the pupils' explanations can be identified. These phases are shown in Fig. 7.11.

The data from this research shows how children's early notions tend to be based on observable features of near and familiar objects; however, although these early notions tend to be used less frequently by older children, they are often exchanged for another alternative framework, one that involves a higher level of spatial awareness.

Although the results of this survey show a reduction in the more naive views as age increases, misconceptions still persist in many pupils up to 16

Notions

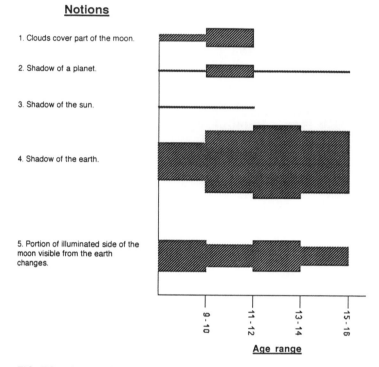

1. Clouds cover part of the moon.

2. Shadow of a planet.

3. Shadow of the sun.

4. Shadow of the earth.

5. Portion of illuminated side of the moon visible from the earth changes.

9 - 10   11 - 12   13 - 14   15 - 16

Age range

FIG. 7.8   The prevalence of pupils' notions about the phases of the moon.

years of age. This finding supports the claim that many alternative frameworks persist into adulthood, a view supported by the research of Durant et al. (1989), which indicated that a large proportion of the general public in Great Britain are confused about many scientific notions, including the motion of the earth around the sun.

It appears that misconceptions about basic astronomy are not peculiar to Great Britain; a survey carried out in France by Acker and Pecker (1988) showed that about 33% of the public still believed that the sun orbits the earth. Similarly naive notions have been observed in America by Sadler and Luzader (1988). Seemingly, medieval notions about planet Earth in space and a geocentric universe are alive and well in the way people construct their own explanations for basic astronomical events.

MISCONCEPTIONS ABOUT THE EARTH SCIENCES

Research into children's misconceptions about the earth sciences is less well documented than the misconceptions about astronomy. However, the

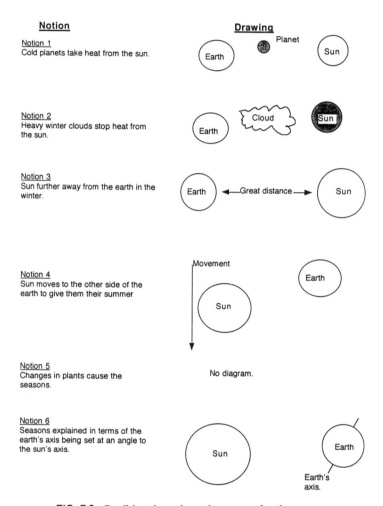

FIG. 7.9   Pupils' notions about the reasons for the seasons.

available literature demonstrates that—as with astronomy—pupils come into their lessons holding a number of misconceptions about our planet Earth. Philips (1991) reported on children who think that Earth is supported in space by resting on something, and that we live on the flat middle of the sphere. He went on to report about college students who think that all rivers flow "down" from north to south (consistent with the north being "up" notion mentioned earlier in this chapter).

Preliminary surveys carried out in Great Britain by the author support the findings of Phillips. It appears to be quite common for children to think that the inside of the earth is hollow and that it is possible to walk around

Notions

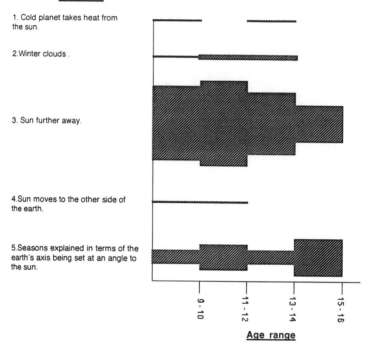

1. Cold planet takes heat from the sun.

2. Winter clouds .

3. Sun further away.

4. Sun moves to the other side of the earth.

5. Seasons explained in terms of the earth's axis being set at an angle to the sun.

9 - 10   11 - 12   13 - 14   15 - 16

Age range

FIG. 7.10   The prevalence of pupils' notions about the reasons for the seasons.

quite freely inside the earth. Other children think that the earth is molten apart from a thin crust around the outside.

Children's ideas about the formation of mountains appear to offer a rich source of alternative notions. The following diagrams and explanations were obtained from a group of 11- to 12-year-old pupils in response to the question, "How do you think the mountains were formed?"

James claimed that in the beginning the Earth was flat like a smooth ball and that the streams eroded the valleys leaving the high ground as mountains (see Fig. 7.12). Ten percent of the 20 pupils taking part in these preliminary interviews subscribed to an idea similar to that given by James.

Nigel, along with 4% of the sample, thought that rocks falling from the sky formed the mountains (see Fig. 7.13).

Some pupils' explanations revealed a mix between science topics taught to them and their own explanations for the formation of the mountains. Steven combined his understanding of the water cycle—one of the topics recently studied during his science course—with his own explanation for the formation of the mountains (see Fig. 7.14). Ideas like Steven's offer a

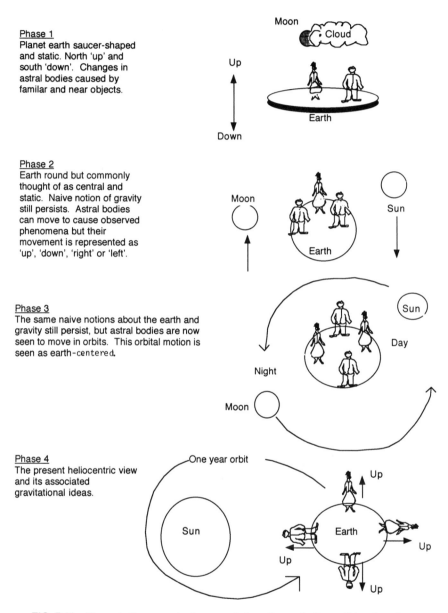

Phase 1
Planet earth saucer-shaped and static. North 'up' and south 'down'. Changes in astral bodies caused by familar and near objects.

Phase 2
Earth round but commonly thought of as central and static. Naive notion of gravity still persists. Astral bodies can move to cause observed phenomena but their movement is represented as 'up', 'down', 'right' or 'left'.

Phase 3
The same naive notions about the earth and gravity still persist, but astral bodies are now seen to move in orbits. This orbital motion is seen as earth-centered.

Phase 4
The present heliocentric view and its associated gravitational ideas.

FIG. 7.11   Phases in the conceptual representations that underlie pupils' explanations.

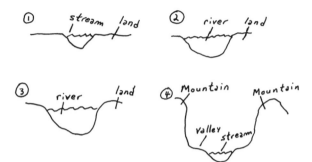

FIG. 7.12   James's explanation: "I think that planet Earth was once flat without mountains and streams eroded the land to make gullies and valleys."

FIG. 7.13   Nigel's explanation: "I reckon the mountains got there when rocks fell from the sky."

creative springboard for the design of experiments through which pupils can test their ideas.

USING ALTERNATIVE FRAMEWORKS IN THE CLASSROOM

During the early part of the 20th century, there was a growing recognition by educators that science is a practical activity; subsequently, there was an increase in the amount of practical laboratory work carried on during school science lessons. But the activities undertaken by pupils were little

FIG. 7.14   Steven thought that as water evaporated from the sea to form clouds, tiny particles of rock, which had become dissolved in the sea, were lifted into the clouds along with the evaporated water. When the rain falls the particles of rock are returned to the land where they build up into mountain ranges.

more than routine exercises that had lost the educational value of real experiments and had evolved into arid, repetitive activities. The widespread introduction of general science during the 1930s led to the rejection of a great deal of this repetitive practical work, and by the 1960s the activities performed in school often had their roots in the common experiences of the children (Kerr, 1963).

Since the 1960s there has been a further increase in the amount of practical work carried on during science lessons, which is introduced to be illustrative or to provide confirmatory evidence for the presented theories (Driver, 1986). This strategy assumes either that children come into their lessons as empty pots and can be filled with the "right bits" of knowledge, or that they will discard their own ideas when presented with the accepted view by the teacher—a fact that Gilbert, Osbourne, and Fensham (1982) and Solomon (1983) showed does not necessarily happen. When science is presented in this way, children frequently form hybrid notions, a mix between their original ideas and those presented by the teacher, or the students function in two domains, that of their everyday experiences and that of the school laboratory, with different ideas in each domain.

The alternative conception movement offers a valuable and productive alternative, where many of the traditional illustrative or confirmatory "practicals" are replaced by activities that encourage pupils to put forward their own viewpoint and enable them to test alternative theories. If we accept the view that learning involves pupils in a process of conceptual change, then a knowledge of the initial conceptions they bring with them into lessons becomes important, as it provides a basis for the design of teaching materials that address these ideas. Such initial conceptions form a starting point from which pupils can test their ideas and modify them should they not hold good in the light of new evidence.

There are two levels at which the ACM can influence and enhance classroom practice:

Level 1. The teacher's awareness can be developed of the commonly occurring alternative frameworks for the particular topic being introduced. This can be achieved by including a summary chart of research data in the teachers' guide to a topic (see, e.g., Baxter & Sage, 1990). Teachers can then organize their teaching around the presentation of evidence to show that these commonly occurring alternative frameworks do not hold good when challenged.

Level 2. During a level 2 approach, pupils identify their own particular explanation for the topic being studied and then put their notion to the test to discover if it holds good, thus following the scientific process depicted in Fig. 7.15.

Using a Level 2 Approach to Challenge Pupils' Notions About the Seasons

The examples of pupils' responses given in this section were obtained from a group of average ability pupils attending a comprehensive school in the southwest of England. In this school astronomy is covered during two 35-minute periods for 6 weeks and forms a part of the modular science course.

During the early stages of the astronomy module, pupils are introduced

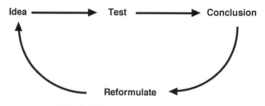

FIG. 7.15   The scientific process.

to the idea that scientific theories are always undergoing change. Examples are taken from early notions of planet Earth in space from a time when the most highly respected thinkers believed that the earth was saucer-shaped (see Draper, 1875/1970). With reference to examples from history, pupils are made to feel more comfortable about identifying and articulating their own notions when they discover that their ideas, although incorrect in the light of scientific advancement, were once popular views.

Examples of pupils' responses using a level 2 ACM approach were obtained during a typical lesson. The discussions with pupils were brief and more closely represent the discussions that take place during the course of a normal science lesson.

Pupils were first asked to draw and write about what they think causes the seasons to change. They did this in silence. Each pupil then made and used the model of the seasons (see Fig. 7.16) to challenge their ideas. If their original ideas did not hold good, they were asked to write about how they had to change their thinking.

As expected, most pupils thought that the earth moves away from the sun during the winter, although many of the other alternative frameworks reported in the first part of this chapter were identified too. For most pupils, the idea that the earth is slightly further away from the sun during the northern hemisphere winter was such a contradiction of their everyday sensory experience that it tended to dominate their discussions. The following short case studies of three pupils — Richard, Linda, and Anthony — make this point, and also demonstrate that conceptual change is often resisted.

Richard. In this interview the teacher (T) is asking Richard (R) about his work on the seasons. See Fig. 7.17 for Richard's diagram.

T: Richard, what did you say was the cause of the seasons; can you explain your drawing?

R: Well, it's this part of Earth facing the sun. When it is, it's summer.

T: OK., what about winter then?

R: Well it's the same only this part [R points to the other side of Earth] that turns and they get summer.

T: Why do you think it's colder here? [T points to part of Earth not facing the sun.]

R: That's 'cause it's further away from the sun there.

T: Did you have to change your idea after using the model?

R: Yes. The nearer the sun is to the earth it's winter.

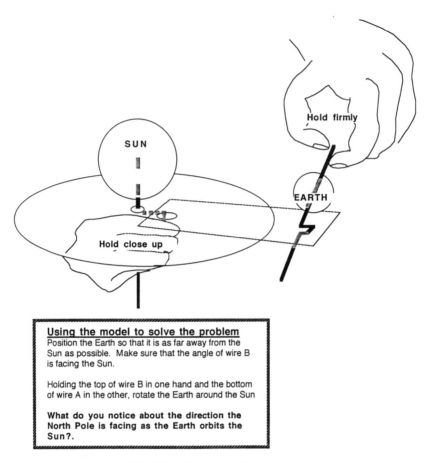

FIG. 7.16   The model of the seasons.

T: But you have written something here about the angle of the earth's axis. Does it make any difference?

R: Yes, it turns us away in the winter when we are closer.

Richard, like many pupils, was so taken with this challenge to his own sensory experience about distance and heat, that he was unable to integrate information. Richard forgot about the cause of day and night (he had worked on this information previously and understood this). His diagram shows the earth taking 1 year to spin on its axis. This is a common feature of pupils' alternative frameworks on astronomy: One notion contradicts another.

Linda. Linda's diagram (see Fig. 7.18) is very similar to Richard's; it is difficult to see how she can explain both the seasons and the cause of day

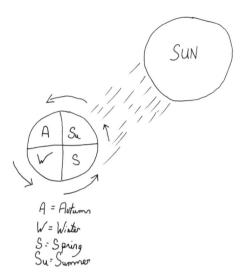

A = Autumn
W = Winter
S = Spring
Su = Summer

FIG. 7.17 Richard's ideas. Original explanation: "When part of the earth is facing the sun this is summer. The part of the earth furthest away is the winter. The parts that are left are spring and autumn. The parts are really quarters."

Idea change: "Angle of the earth to the sun. The nearer the sun is to the earth it is winter and vice versa."

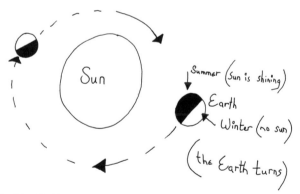

FIG. 7.18 Linda's ideas. **Original explanation:** "We get seasons because the earth orbits around the sun. When the earth is orbiting the sun it turns. The seasons are caused because the earth at times is not facing the sun (winter). Other times it is facing the sun (summer)."

Idea change: "The seasons are caused by the angle of the sun. Summer is when the earth is furthest from the sun. Winter is when the earth is closets to the sun but we are facing the opposite way to the sun."

173

and night. After using the model, she places an emphasis on the earth being closer to the sun during the winter. She has also retained something of her original idea in as far as she still retains the "facing the opposite way" part of her explanation. Linda, like many pupils, will go to considerable lengths to interpret new evidence in a way that supports her original notions.

Anthony.   Anthony is very protective about his original idea, claiming that he was "almost right." The part played by the moon in his first idea is clearly wrong, but he chooses to use the gentle phrase "I think I was wrong." He has either not noticed (which is unlikely, as their teacher circulated around the group drawing pupils' attention to the angle of the earth's axis) or refuses to acknowledge the importance of the angle of the earth's axis to the plane of its orbit. His attempts to protect his original idea are noticeable in the short interview carried out just after he had written about how his idea had changed. (Fig. 7.19).

T: Anthony, did you have to change your idea about the cause of the seasons?

A: Well a bit, but not much, I got it almost right.

T: What bit of your thinking did you have to change?

A: Well it was that bit about the moon . . . but I didn't say it was the reason, just it may be.

T: Use your model to show me how we get the different seasons.

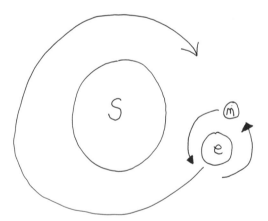

FIG. 7.19 Anthony's ideas. **Original explanation:** "The seasons change because we move around the sun, when that changes the weather from hot or to cold when we move around the sun. Or it probably gets colder if the moon gets in front of us as well."
  Idea change: "My thinking was almost right, when I said the earth orbits the sun and the seasons change accordingly but I think I was wrong about the moon getting in between the earth and the sun."

A: [Picks up the model and orbits the earth around the sun.]Well it's like I said, the earth orbits the sun and we get the seasons.

T: Where will the earth be when it's winter north of the equator?

A: Places the earth in the correct position with the angle of inclination directed away from the sun.]It's winter now.

T: What's special about this position; what makes it winter?

A: The earth has gone around to here, and here is where winter is.

T: OK, what makes it winter here [takes model and moves earth to northern hemisphere summer position] and not here?

A: It can't be winter there cause we're facing the sun.

T: What makes us face the sun?

A: Well it's this angle here [points to the wire axis].

T: Can you now tell me how we get the seasons, but this time mention the angle.

A: We go around the sun like I said and we get winter here 'cause we're angled away from the sun. And when we get to there it's summer and we're facing the sun. This is where summer is and this is where winter is [he orbits the earth around the sun while saying this].

The evidence from these brief case studies suggests that pupils, like many scientists, attempt to interpret their results so that they support their original ideas. Those pupils who attempt to protect their original ideas appear to be faced with a crisis (like scientists during the demise of Ptolemaic cosmology), and like scientists appear to resist changes in theoretical structure (Donnelly, 1986). Paradigm shifts appear to be difficult experiences for both scientists and pupils.

Pupils' explanations for one astronomical phenomenon often are in contradiction with their explanations for another, related phenomenon. This fact can be put to good use by teachers. For example, after pupils have given their explanations for the cause of the seasons, they can be asked if their explanations will work in the light of what they know about the cause of day and night. For many pupils, this question will help them to revise updating their original explanations.

The results of this research show that when pupils revise their original notions, they may well pass through one or more stages before believing in the accepted view. Perhaps teachers should plan instructional sequences so that pupils can gradually move toward a theory without requiring them to reach clear-cut conclusions along the way (Nussbaum, 1989). Such an approach resembles how science has progressed in the past. For example,

Herakleides of Portus (4 BC) proposed an intermediate model of our solar system in which Mercury and Venus orbited the sun, all three of which — according to his model — were in orbit around Earth (Koestler, 1959). Even the Copernican system was an intermediate model, later being revised to incorporate elliptical orbits. Progress in science is a stage-like process, often taking many years to change from one paradigm to another. Perhaps teachers are unrealistic in expecting pupils during one science lesson to make the same conceptual leaps that the world's finest scientists took years to achieve.

By adopting a teaching strategy in which our pupils are given an opportunity to challenge their own explanations, much of the astronomical ignorance that appears to pass into adulthood can be avoided. Pupils can emerge from their pre-Copernican world view just like the scientific community did. Teachers can symbolically recarve Flammarion's woodcut by helping pupils pull back their own sphere-like veil to catch a glimpse of the real universe that lies beyond their primary perception.

REFERENCES

Acker, A., & Pecker, J. C. (1988). Public misconceptions about astronomy. In J. M. Pasachoff & J. R. Percy (Eds.), *The teaching of astronomy* (pp. 229-238). Cambridge: Cambridge University Press.

Baxter, J.,& Sage, J.(1990) *Earth in space*. Bristol: Resources for Learning Development Unit.

Donnelly, J. (1986). The work of popper and Kuhn on the nature of science. In J. Brown, A. Cooper, A. Horton, F. Toats, & D. Zeldin (Eds.), *Science in schools* (pp. 224-235). Milton Keynes, England: Open University Press.

Draper, J. W. (1970). *History of the conflict between religion and science*. Farnborough, England: Gregg International. (Original work published 1875)

Driver, R. (1983). *The pupil as scientist*. Milton Keynes, England: Open University Press.

Driver, R. (1986). From theory to practice. In J. Brown, A. Cooper, A. Horton, F. Toats, & D. Zeldin (Eds.), *Science in schools* (pp. 268-278). Milton Keynes, England: Open University Press.

Durant, J. R., Evans, G. A., & Thomas, G. P. (1989). The public understanding of science. *Nature, 340*, 11-14.

Gilbert, J, K, Osbourne, J., & Fensham, P. (1982). Children's science and its consequences for teaching. *Science Education, 66*, 623-633.

Gilbert, J. K., & Swift, D. J. (1985). Towards a Lakatosian analysis of the Piagetian and alternative conceptions research programmes. *Science Education, 69*, 681-696.

Gingerich, O. (1988). The use of history in the teaching of astronomy. In J. M. Pasachoff & J. R. Percy (Eds.), *The teaching of astronomy* (pp. 39-44). Cambridge: Cambridge University Press.

Hearty, H., & Beall, D. (1984). Towards the development of a children's science curiosity measure. *Journal of Research in Science Teaching, 21*, 425-436.

Kerr, J. F. (1963). *Practical work in school science*. Leicester, England: Leicester University Press.

Klein, C. A. (1982). Children's concepts of the sun: A cross cultural study. *Science Education, 65*, 95-107.

Koestler, A. (1959). *The sleepwalkers*. London: Hutchinson.

Linder, C. J., & Erickson, G. L. (1989). A study of tertiary physics students' conceptualisations of sound. *International Journal of Science Education, 11*, 491–501.

Mali, G. B., & Howe, A. (1979). Development of Earth and gravity concepts among Nepali children. *Science Education, 63*, 685–691.

Millar, R. (1989). Constructive criticisms. *International Journal of Science Education, 11*, 587–596.

Nussbaum, J., (1979). Children's conceptions of the earth as a cosmic body: A cross age study. *Science Education, 63*, 83–93.

Nussbaum, J. (1989). Classroom conceptual change: Philosophical perspectives. *International Journal of Science Education, 11*, 481–490.

Nussbaum, J., & Novak, J. D. (1976). An assessment of children's concepts of the earth using structured interviews. *Science Education, 60*, 535–550.

Philips, W. C. (1991). Earth science misconceptions. *Science Teacher, 58*(2), 21–23.

Preece, P. F. W. (1985). Children's ideas about the Earth and gravity. In P. Preece & D. Clish (Eds.), *The teaching of astronomy* (pp. 67–73). Exeter: University of Exeter.

Russell, T., Harlen, W., & Wall, D. (1989). Children's ideas about evaporation. *International Journal of Science Education, 11*, 566–576.

Sadler, P. M., & Luzader, W. M. (1988). Science teaching through its astronomical roots. In J. M. Pasachoff & J. R. Percy (Eds.), *The teaching of astronomy* (pp. 257–276). Cambridge: Cambridge University Press.

Sneider, C., & Pulos, S. (1983). Children's cosmographies: Understanding the Earth's shape and gravity. *Science Education, 63*, 205–221.

Solomon, J. (1983). Learning about energy: How pupils think in two domains. *European Journal of Science Education, 5*, 49–59.

Watts, D. M., & Zylbersztajn, A. (1981). A survey of some children's ideas about force. *Physics Education, 16*, 360–365.

8 Conceptual Development in Physics: Students' Understanding of Heat

Sofia Kesidou
American Association for the Advancement of Science

Reinders Duit
IPN, University of Kiel, Germany

Shawn M. Glynn
University of Georgia

It is so easy for students to confuse heat and temperature. After all, as the temperature of an object increases, so does the amount of energy it contains. Unfortunately, many students mistakenly believe that one object possesses more heat, or more energy, than another simply because its temperature is higher. A bowl of boiling chicken soup is hotter than a large pot of warm soup; however, the pot could melt more ice than the bowl. Many students, even students exposed to demonstrations of the chicken soup sort, do not generalize from their experience and form principles of thermodynamics. Many students do not understand relatively abstract principles such as the following: Different substances that have the same mass, are at the same initial temperature, and cool down by the same number of degrees, release different amounts of heat. For example, at the same temperature, 1 kg of boiling water can melt more than 30 times more ice than 1 kg of gold.

In this chapter, we discuss how students develop an understanding of a fundamentally important physics concept—heat. First, we discuss the accepted, scientific view of heat and related concepts—a view that teachers want their students to adopt. Next, we discuss how perspectives about the concept of *heat* evolved during the history of science. A brief review of these concepts sets the stage for an understanding of the various conceptions, or *alternative frameworks*, that students have about heat. Often these alternative frameworks are quite different from the accepted, scientific view, and often these frameworks are very resistant to the teachers' efforts to change them.

In our view, in order to teach heat meaningfully, teachers should help students to unfold and develop the undifferentiated view of heat that most students have. Teachers should help students to differentiate heat from related concepts, such as temperature, energy, and entropy (see Fig. 8.1).

A SCIENTIFIC FRAMEWORK FOR HEAT

A scientific framework for heat includes related concepts, such as temperature and internal energy. These concepts should be differentiated in the students' minds as prerequisites for a meaningful understanding of heat (Zemansky, 1970). These concepts are briefly reviewed here, as background for a discussion of students' alternative frameworks. According to Hewitt (1987):

> **Temperature** is a measure of the motion of the molecules or atoms within a substance; more specifically, it is a measure of the *average* kinetic energy of the molecules or atoms in a substance. Temperature is not a measure of the *total* kinetic energy of the particles within a substance. (p. 301)

> The energy that is transferred from one object to another because of a temperature difference between the objects is called **heat**. It is common—but incorrect—to think of matter as *containing* heat. Heat flows from one thing to another; it is the energy that is being transferred. Once heat has been transferred to an object or substance, it ceases to be heat. It becomes . . . *internal energy*. (p. 302)

> In addition to the kinetic energy of jostling molecules or atoms in a substance, there is energy in other forms. There is potential energy due to the forces between molecules or atoms. There is also kinetic energy due to movements of atoms within molecules. The grand total of all energies inside a substance is called **internal energy**. A substance does not contain heat—it contains internal energy.

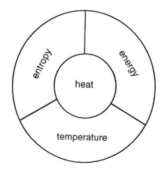

FIG. 8.1.   Heat and related concepts.

> **Heat** is the internal energy transferred from one body to another by virtue of a temperature difference. The quantity of heat involved in such a transfer is measured by some change — such as the change in temperature of a known amount of water that absorbs the heat. (p. 304)

So, heat is the energy that flows from one system to another, if there are system temperature differences, whereas internal energy is the total energy in a system. It is important that students distinguish correctly between heat and internal energy. The reason is the following. The temperature of a system (e.g., a piece of metal) may be raised by bringing it into contact with another system of higher temperature. Then heat flows from the hotter to the colder system. But the temperature of the system may also be raised by other processes, such as by friction (rubbing the metal). Temperature decrease of a system likewise may be due to heat flow to a colder system or due to other mechanical or chemical processes. Heat is used solely to indicate energy flow due to temperature differences: therefore, it is a "process" energy form, not a "storage" energy form. Heat is not stored in a system. The heat energy that flows into a system may leave it in another form.

Energy is an *extensive* quantity, whereas temperature is an *intensive* quantity (Falk & Ruppel, 1976). If two portions of water that have the same temperature are poured together, the total internal energy is the sum of the internal energies of the two portions before pouring them together, but the temperature stays the same. Extensive quantities, in general, may be viewed as analogous to substances; it makes sense to speak of amounts of these quantities. It is also correct to view them as amounts being contained in a system, or amounts being transported from one system to another. Intensive quantities, in contrast, may not be viewed as analogous to substances. Although it makes sense to ask "how much" for extensive quantities, it only makes sense to ask "how strong" or "how high" for intensive quantities.

The Laws of Thermodynamics

There are three basic laws of the physics framework of heat. They focus on the basic concepts presented in Fig. 8.1.

Thermal Equilibrium Law. This law is also called the *zeroth law of thermodynamics*. It states that temperature differences even out if bodies are in thermal contact and if there are no other interactions involved that cause new temperature differences somewhere. If a piece of hot metal is put into cold water, after a while the metal and the water will have the same temperature. Furthermore, if this temperature is different from the temperature of the surroundings, after some further time the temperatures of the surroundings, the metal, and the water will be the same.

The First Law.   This is the principle of energy conservation. It states in its general form that energy may not be created out of nothing nor vanish into nothing. In a closed system, the internal energy is constant, whatever happens in this system.

The Second Law.   The second law has to do with the entropy concept. Entropy is a measure of the distribution of energy in a system. In a closed system, entropy increases whenever a process is running. The second law states that all processes that are running, in reality, can proceed on their own (i.e., without another process involved) only in one direction. All real processes, in this sense, are irreversible—they do not go backward on their own. Temperature differences always equalize. Heat always flows from a hot to a cold body and never the other way around.

THE HISTORY OF HEAT AND RELATED CONCEPTS

There is an evolution of the heat concept throughout the history of science. We focus our discussion on the past 400 years, with special attention given to the development of the concepts presented in Fig. 8.1.

In the 17th century, many different types of thermometer were designed. Some devices were built in ancient times, for instance, by the famous Heron of Alexandria in about 130 AD, but they were not used in a systematic way to investigate heat phenomena. Such a research program was carried out in the 17th century, however, in the Academia del Cimento (Academy of Experiments) in Florence. The most eminent scientists and mathematicians of that time were involved in investigating heat phenomena and in constructing theories of heat. Wiser and Carey (1983), who analyzed the struggle of these "experimenters," concluded that they worked mainly with an undifferentiated heat concept and did not distinguish between intensive and extensive variables. The notion of what we now call *thermal equilibrium* was also missing. McKie and Heathcote (1935) noted that heat, until the middle of the 18th century, was viewed as a quality with only one measure, its intensity.

In the 18th century a clear distinction between the intensive variable *temperature* and an extensive variable *heat* was developed. Joseph Black's (1728–1799) experiments of mixing materials of different temperatures played a key role in this distinction. Black's theoretical considerations were based on a "substance" model of heat that was predominant in science from the 18th century to the middle of the 19th century:

> Many inventors in the eighteenth and nineteenth centuries . . . regarded heat as a thin, invisible substance that could be used over and over again to do work without being used up itself. (Rutherford, Holton, & Watson, 1975, Unit 3, p. 40)

In the 19th century, the undifferentiated conception of heat evolved when Sadi Carnot (1796-1832) added the entropy concept to the differentiation between heat and temperature in 1824. About 25 years later, his ideas were further developed by Rudolf Clausius (1822-1888) and Lord Kelvin (1824-1907).

In the 18th century and in the first part of the 19th century, when the substance model was the dominating and generally accepted view of heat, a "particle" model of heat was being developed (Arons, 1965; Brush, 1988). According to Rutherford et al. (1975):

> During the 1840's, many scientists recognized that heat is not a substance, but a form of energy which can be converted into other forms. . . . James Prescott Joule and Rudolf Clausius . . . reasoned that the "heat energy" of a substance is simply the kinetic energy of its atoms and molecules. . . . This idea is largely correct. It forms the basis of the *kinetic-molecular theory of heat.* (Unit 3, p. 69)

> In order to emphasize that our model is a theoretical one, we will use the word "particle" instead of "atom" or "molecule." There is now no doubt that atoms and molecules exist and have their own definite properties. The particles in the kinetic theory model, on the other hand, are idealized and imaginary. We imagine such objects as perfectly elastic spheres, whose supposed properties are hopefully similar to those of actual atoms and molecules. (Unit 3, p. 71)

A paradigm shift toward the particle model of heat and away from the substance model took place during the 19th century. The lessons on heat that are taught in schools today are generally consistent with the particle model and the kinetic-molecular theory of heat. Hewitt (1987), for example, introduced his chapter on "Temperature and Heat" in the following way:

> All matter—whether solid, liquid, or gas—is composed of continually jiggling molecules or atoms. By virtue of this energetic motion, the molecules or atoms in matter possess kinetic energy. The average kinetic energy of the individual particles is directly related to a property you can sense: how hot something is. Whenever something becomes warmer, the kinetic energy of its particles increases. (p. 300)

STUDENTS' UNDERSTANDING OF HEAT PHENOMENA

Keeping in mind the key components of the concept of heat and the historical development of these components, we turn our attention now to research studies on students' understanding of heat phenomena. Students bring diverse frames of reference into their science classes. These frames of reference are called alternative frameworks when they differ from accepted scientific views.

Students' Alternative Frameworks About Heat and Temperature

Students' difficulties in differentiating heat and temperature have been explored in a number of studies with students ages 10–20 years old (Kesidou & Duit, 1993; Lewis & Linn, 1994; Rosenquist, Popp, & McDermott, 1982; Stavy & Berkovitz, 1980; Tiberghien, 1983; Wiser, 1986; Wiser, Kipman, & Halkiadakis, 1988). Typically, students were interviewed to probe their meanings of *heat* and *temperature* and the difference between these two terms. In most cases, students used the two terms interchangeably. Students viewed temperature as a synonym of heat, as the measure of heat, or as a unifying term for hot and cold (Erickson, 1985; Kesidou & Duit, 1993; Tiberghien, 1983).

Many students do not use accurate frameworks to explain heat phenomena, even after several years of physics instruction. In a physicist's framework, a clear distinction is made between heat as an extensive quantity and temperature as an intensive quantity. Students, on the other hand, often do not make this distinction. Heat is frequently viewed by students either as an "intensity," with temperature the measure of this intensity, or as an "extensity," with temperature the measure of the amount of heat.

Students' difficulties in differentiating between heat and temperature are not due simply to difficulties in terminology—that is, students do not merely use the term *heat* instead of the term *temperature* and vice versa. Rather, students' interpretations of heat phenomena reveal that the students incorrectly explain such phenomena with only one concept, heat. Furthermore, students may incorrectly view heat in three ways: (a) heat as intensity, (b) heat as a partly extensive quantity and temperature as the amount of heat, and (c) heat as an extensive quantity and temperature as the measure of the amount of heat per unit volume or mass. We now discuss these three ways, or frameworks, of incorrectly interpreting heat exchange phenomena.

Heat as Intensity.   Students with this framework incorrectly think of heat as an intensive quantity, and temperature as the measure of the heat intensity. They have no concept of the "amount of heat." They never talk about heat as an extensive quantity: For example, they never speak of "more" heat or "amount of heat" in the extensive sense. Further, they do not connect the quantity of heat with mass. When solving heat problems, students with a "heat as intensity" framework base their solutions solely on temperature. For example, in an interview study with 34 students, ages 15 and 16, who had received instruction in elementary thermodynamics, Kesidou and Duit (1993) asked the students if a cup of coffee and the surrounding room (both were at the same temperature) had the same or different heat. As noted earlier, from the physicist's point of view, it is incorrect to talk about the amount of heat contained in a body. We used the word *heat* in our investigations in an "open" way (i.e., not necessarily in the physicist's way) because we wanted to find out about students' understanding of this word. More than half of the students answered that the cup of coffee and the surrounding room had the same heat. A typical student in this group, gave this explanation: "They have the same heat, the heat which is present everywhere."

Kesidou and Duit further asked the students to explain the situation in Fig. 8.2. Based on the information that the alcohol reaches the temperature of 30°C in 2 minutes and the water in 4 minutes, students were expected to infer correctly that the water had received more heat and stored more energy (although it is at the same temperature as the alcohol). Forty-four percent of the students incorrectly responded that both liquids had received and stored the same heat or energy; they interpreted the situation in terms of "heat applied to the liquid" and not "heat amounts transferred from the burner to the liquid." According to the students, because the temperature of the burners was the same, the heat applied was the same and, in consequence, the heat (or some students said "energy") received and stored by the liquids was the same.

Similar results have been reported by Wiser (1986). Wiser asked ninth-grade American students to predict and explain the following situation:

Suppose we have two pieces of steel. The first piece is twice as large as the other piece. Both pieces of steel are heated on identical hot plates for a minute. Do the pieces of steel have the same or different temperature?

The majority of students ignored the volume of the pieces of steel entirely, predicting incorrectly that the two pieces would reach the same temperature because they received the "same heat."

FIG. 8.2. Suppose equal amounts of water and alcohol at 20°C are heated with two identical burners. After 2 minutes the temperature of the alcohol is 30°C; the water has this temperature after 4 minutes. Has one of the liquids received more heat? Has it received more energy? Has one of the liquids stored more heat? Has one of the liquids stored more energy?

It should be noted that students' intuitive notion of heat as intensity may be reinforced by their everyday experiences. For example, everyday language suggests that heat has intensity, or "hotness." Further, sources of heat (e.g., stoves and ovens) are often marked in degrees, which may lead some students to believe that these sources apply heat of certain degrees rather than deliver units of heat.

Heat as a Partly Extensive Quantity and Temperature as the Amount of Heat.   Students with this framework know that heat has extensive aspects; however, they still do not differentiate between heat and temperature. They incorrectly think that temperature measures the amount of heat or energy. This belief prevents them from reasoning in terms of the extensity of heat in certain situations.

In the Kesidou and Duit study with the 15- to 16-year-old students described previously, students were invited to explain temperature equalization processes. The students thinking within the "heat as a partly extensive quantity" framework thought the sum of the temperatures of the bodies in the beginning of the process would be the same as the sum of the temperatures of the bodies at the end of the process. For example, one student argued it was impossible that at the end of a thermal interaction of a metal piece of 80°C and water of 20°C, the water could be 29°C and the metal piece 15°C:

> Student: It is not possible, because the rest of the heat is lost, and that cannot happen.
>
> Investigator: What do you mean?
>
> Student: I mean the metal piece was in the beginning at 80°C and the water at 20°C, together 100°C, and here the degrees are missing, it is only 44°C.

When asked if a cup of coffee and the room surrounding it (both at the same temperature) had the same or different heat, these students responded that the coffee and the room had the same heat because they had the same temperature. But their language indicated that they did not actually view heat as intensity in this context. Rather, their responses could be explained by their view of temperature as the measure of the amount of heat in a body: When the temperatures of the bodies are the same, the amounts of heat in the bodies must be the same as well.

During the interview, some students noticed the contradiction between their view of heat as an extensive quantity and their belief that temperature measured heat. For example, thinking through the water-and-alcohol situation in Fig. 8.2 encouraged students to rethink their conception about temperature as the measure of heat. Students with an extensive notion of heat typically had little difficulty correctly recognizing that the water received more heat than the alcohol; however, they could not accept that the water had actually stored more heat or energy than the alcohol, because both liquids had the same temperature at the end of the process. Some students realized there was a discrepancy between their initial conception of heat as an extensive quantity and their notion of temperature as the measure of heat (or energy), but could not resolve this conflict. A typical comment was:

> I said before temperature is the unit for heat. When I say the temperatures (of the water and alcohol) are equal, then there should be equal amounts of heat energy in both after the heating. However, water received more energy than alcohol. It's a problem, on the one side more energy, here more . . . I don't know. I don't have a solution at the moment.

Other students resolved this conflict by believing that a part of the heat given off by the alcohol burner was lost in the environment.

Heat as an Extensive Quantity and Temperature as the Measure of the Amount of Heat per Unit Volume or Mass.   Students with this framework correctly view heat as an extensive quantity and incorrectly view temperature as the amount of heat per unit volume or mass. Thus, this framework is close to the physicist's where the differentiation between an extensive quantity (heat) and an intensive quantity (temperature) is concerned. Although students using this framework think of temperature as an intensive concept, to them it is still not a concept clearly differentiated from heat. It may be viewed as an intermediate concept that enables the students to make correct predictions about thermal interactions between bodies of different volume (or mass) and the same material; however, it does not enable students to make correct predictions in cases where the interacting bodies are of different materials.

Students' Alternative Frameworks About Heat and Energy

It is a well-known outcome of research into students' understanding of the energy concept that, even after instruction, many students are unable to interpret phenomena in terms of energy transformation, energy conservation, and heat dissipation (Brook & Driver, 1984; Duit, 1982; Kesidou & Duit, 1993). In general, students realize that heat and energy are closely related. In the Kesidou and Duit (1993) study, half of the students used the word "energy" when they explained the meaning of heat; however, most of these did not view energy as physicists do. Some students viewed energy as an intensive quantity and had only a vague notion of the transformation of kinetic energy (or, more generally, mechanical energy) to heat energy.

Kesidou and Duit asked students to explain the phenomenon of a pendulum's oscillations "dying out." Students were first asked to generally explain the phenomenon in their own words. Then the students were asked more specific questions:

> Can you explain what happened using the word *energy*? Does the pendulum have more, less, or the same energy as in the beginning of the process? Where is the energy now? Did it disappear?

Only 41% of the students correctly recognized that energy was transferred from the pendulum to the surroundings. Most of these students thought energy was transferred in the form of air movement, whereas the others thought it was transferred in the form of heat.

Some students did not recognize that heat was involved in the process. This is not surprising, given that students often do not recognize temperature changes that are not perceptually obvious. For example, Brook and Driver (1986) asked 13- to 14-year-old students what happens to the energy when an object falls on a foam pad. A number of students responded that the energy was "wasted" in heat, reciting what they had recently been taught. However, these students did not believe that the foam would get even slightly hotter, indicating that the students had no real understanding of what they had learned.

The students in the Kesidou and Duit (1993) study, who did recognize that heating took place during the process, did not necessarily link it with the loss of energy of the pendulum during an energy transformation. The heating was seen simply as an outcome of friction involved in the process. This response is consistent with the more general student behavior to favor explanations of phenomena that imply a causal sequence, that is, to offer as explanations accounts that describe sequences of events over time, rather than energy compensations (Brook & Driver, 1984).

Many of the students in the Kesidou and Duit study believed that "energy was not lost" or that "energy was conserved" during the process; however, their explanations varied widely, and in many cases were in contradiction with the concept of energy conservation. For example, some students thought energy was not lost because energy had brought about an effect; it was used to overcome the forces of gravity and air resistance. Other students expressed *qualitative* ideas about energy conservation. They thought energy was conserved in the sense that at the end of the process there was some energy involved, namely, heat. However, this did not mean to the students that energy was quantitatively conserved; they did not realize that the energy of the pendulum decreased and the energy of the surroundings increased exactly by the same amount. On the contrary, some of the students' responses indicated that they thought the energy was reduced during the process. Students' difficulties in interpreting the energy changes in the phenomenon presented in terms of energy conservation were at least partly due to students' lack of differentiation between heat and temperature. Students had difficulty understanding that the total amount of energy is the same when heat diffuses. These findings suggest that the differentiation of heat as an extensive quantity and temperature as an intensive quantity is a prerequisite to understanding the quantification of heat energy and energy conservation.

Students' Alternative Frameworks About Heat and Particles

The results of several studies on students' understanding of heat indicate students do not spontaneously give explanations of heat, temperature, and thermal phenomena in terms of the particle model. Moreover, few students appear to understand the molecular basis of heat transfer even after instruction (Kesidou & Duit, 1993; Wiser, 1986).

Several studies have documented that students tend to inappropriately transfer qualities from the macroscopic to the microscopic world (Andersson, 1990; Rennstrom, 1987). For example, students incorrectly believe that upon heating a substance, its particles may melt or expand (Brook, Briggs, Bell, & Driver, 1984). In the study with 15- to 16-year-old students, Kesidou and Duit (1993) found that students attributed macroscopic properties to microscopic particles. For example, some students explained that some substances are easier to heat than others by attributing the property of inertia to the particles of the substance. According to these students, some particles (typically of gases) have less inertia, and thus require less heat to be set into motion than other particles (typically of solids). Other students explained the heating of a body in this way. Particles rub against one another and thus become warmer. Finally, some students appeared to hold the idea that heat makes particles hotter and heat is transferred from one particle to the other in the process of heat conduction.

A further idea expressed by the students was that the particles do not continue to move but slow down and eventually stop. They explained this by indicating that the particles do not have enough space to oscillate or that "inertia" slows the particles down. It is important to note that the students' idea that particles slow down by themselves implies that energy is lost during this process.

Students' Alternative Frameworks About Thermal Equilibrium

In order to understand thermal equilibrium from the physicist's point of view, students should first view thermal phenomena as thermal interactions. Second, students should identify the systems that take part in the thermal interaction; for example, students should take into account, when appropriate, the ambient air. Third, students should recognize that energy is transferred between the bodies in contact and that a temperature difference is a necessary condition for such a transfer to occur. Unfortunately, many students do not do these things and, as a result, they do not acquire a valid understanding of thermal equilibrium.

Thermal Interactions and Equilibrium. Students often think objects cool down and/or release heat spontaneously, that is, without being in contact with an object of lower temperature (Kesidou, 1990; Wiser, 1986). In a study of 13- to 14-year-old students, Millar and Arnold (1992) found a large proportion of the students viewed the cooling down of an object as a natural phenomenon. They thought the cessation of heating was, by itself, sufficient to cause the temperature of an object to fall. Furthermore, a large number of these students did not recognize that while cooling down, the object was losing heat to the environment.

Further evidence that students often fail to view thermal processes as interactions comes from the finding that students view temperature changes in a body solely in terms of the properties of this body. The students do not consider the properties and the state (temperature) of the bodies with which it is in contact. For example, different materials placed for several hours in an oven of 60°C are at different temperatures, in the opinion of some students (Lewis, 1991; Tiberghien, 1985). According to these students, flour is less than 60°C because "flour does not heat up very much," metallic objects are more than 60°C because "metal heats up faster," and water is at 60°C because "it takes the temperature from the surroundings." Even after instruction, some students have difficulties giving up their naive notion that some substances (e.g., flour, sugar, and air) cannot heat up.

The difficulties students have thinking of heat exchange phenomena as interactions lead to difficulties in understanding the concept of thermal equilibrium from the physicist's point of view. The students' notion of the spontaneous release of heat is inconsistent with the notion of a temperature difference being the cause of heat transfer. For example, Kesidou and Duit (1993) asked 15- to 16-year-old students to react to the situation in Fig. 8.3. Surprisingly, some students thought the metal piece would cool down "by itself," although it was isolated from the environment, and that the heat released would warm up the water:

Yes. [Such a process is possible.] Namely, I think that metal can absorb heat quicker than the water, so it can cool down quicker than the water. And the heat energy must go somewhere, and if it is isolated from the environment, it therefore would go into the water.

The students' notion that temperature changes in a body depend exclusively on the properties of this body and not on the properties and the state (temperature) of the bodies with which it is in contact is inconsistent with the scientific principle that temperature differences equalize. In actuality, no matter how fast heat energy flows or how much heat energy is exchanged, the exchange will stop when the two materials reach the same temperature. In contrast, students often think that heat absorption depends exclusively on the substance that is absorbing heat: Some materials absorb more heat, or absorb heat more quickly, than others, in all circumstances (Tiberghien, 1985; Wiser, 1986). Furthermore, students often think that faster heat absorption leads to greater heat absorption, and as a result to higher temperatures (Lewis, 1991).

Students' Conceptions of Temperature Equalization. When objects at different temperatures come in contact, students typically predict that the warmer object will cool down and the cooler will heat up; however, temperature equalization is not always, for students, a general principle that governs all thermal phenomena. In some cases, students may think that a temperature difference may remain at the end of the thermal process, or that a temperature difference may occur by itself out of the temperature equalization state.

When several objects are for a long time in the same environment they eventually reach the same temperature. Students, however, may have difficulties recognizing the equalization of temperatures in such situations. As noted before, this is partly due to the students' notion that temperature changes depend exclusively on the nature of the substances involved. In addition, students' difficulties are compounded by the difference in sensa-

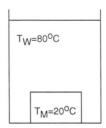

FIG. 8.3.   A metal piece at 20°C is placed into water at 80°C. The system is isolated from the environment. The temperatures first equalize at 73°C, and then the water heats up at 76°C while the metal piece cools down at 50°C. Can such a process occur? Why or why not?

tion generated by touching good conductors (e.g., metals) and good insulators (e.g., wood) that are in the same environment. Students' difficulties persist even after relevant instruction, such as a demonstration that the temperatures of metal and wood in the same environment, measured by the same thermometers, are the same (Lewis, 1991; Tomasini & Balandi, 1987). Students try very hard to make sense of such demonstrations on the basis of their ideas. In the metal-and-wood example, some students interpreted the demonstration in the following way: They viewed the environment as an external agent that forces the objects to take its temperature, but, in the words of one student, "they keep having one of their own because I can feel them different when I touch them" (Tomasini & Balandi, 1987).

During individual interviews, Kesidou and Duit (1993) explored whether 15- to 16-year-old students thought a temperature difference may occur by itself out of the temperature equalization state. Over half the students were of the opinion that, under certain circumstances, such a process may occur. Most students justified these beliefs by pointing to the different materials of the bodies that were part of the thermal interaction. The explanations of why different materials were influential were: (a) the ease with which heat enters or leaves different material varies, (b) different materials attract or retain heat differently, and (c) the particles of the materials have different properties, for example, they are closer to each other or they have different inertia or speed. Some students thought the process of temperature change may continue in the same direction even after temperature equalization, due to "heat inertia." They drew an analogy with the oscillations of mechanical bodies.

Although students often predict that temperature differences equalize and do not occur by themselves, their explanations of this fact take different forms. As discussed earlier, physicists explain thermal equilibrium with two distinct quantities, an extensive quantity (heat) and an intensive quantity (temperature). Heat is transferred from places of higher temperature to places of lower temperature until temperature equalization occurs. Students often do not understand this differentiation and, for this reason, their explanations of equilibrium differ from that of the scientific view. Instead, thermal equilibrium is interpreted by students on the basis of intuitive principles.

UNDERSTANDING HEAT SCIENTIFICALLY

When new information is presented to students, several outcomes may occur. First, students may just accumulate the information, without integrating it into their existing frameworks; they may just add new words, such as *specific heat*, *conductors*, or *insulators*, without changing their explanations of heat phenomena (Tiberghien, 1985). Second, the information may not make sense within the students' frameworks, in which case the students may ignore it. Third, students may distort contradictory information to make it fit into their frameworks. This process often results in misconceptions.

A "constructivist" view of learning sheds light on how students' alternative frameworks guide, and even determine, the learning process. These frameworks guide the learning that occurs during in-class experiments, lectures, discussions, and textbook reading. Students are usually satisfied with their alternative frameworks. Their everyday, intuitive heat frameworks consist of a network of ideas that allow the students to make sense of many phenomena they routinely encounter. Instruction, therefore, has to convince students that the accepted scientific frameworks are more powerful than their alternative ones.

Guiding Students Toward Scientific Understanding

Some studies have attempted to guide students toward a scientific understanding of heat, temperature, and the difference between these concepts. For example, Stavy and Berkovitz (1980) found that 10-year-old students had little difficulty predicting what happens when two cups of cold water are poured together—the water stays cold, said the students. But when asked what happens when a cup of water of 20°C is poured together with a cup of water of 10°C, some students incorrectly predicted the water would be 30°C, and others, 10°C. Stavy and Berkovitz suggested these incorrect responses arise from a conflict between two representational systems for temperature, the intuitive (qualitative) and the quantitative. These researchers successfully employed a "training by conflict" strategy to make students aware of discrepancies between their qualitative-intuitive system and the quantitative-numerical system.

Watson and Konicek (1990) had little success in guiding students toward a scientific understanding of heat. They asked students to observe the readings of thermometers placed inside sweaters, hats, and a rolled-up rug. Students predicted that the readings would be higher than outside because these materials "give heat." Remarkably, the unexpected outcome did not convince students that their alternative frameworks were wrong. The students rationalized that a longer measuring time is necessary or that, in some way, cold air came in from outside. After the thermometers stayed in the materials overnight and were protected against cold air coming in, the readings remained the same. The students again were surprised, but still did not change their alternative frameworks.

Experiments and demonstrations whose results challenge students' frameworks should play an important role in instruction. These experiments and demonstrations generally will be effective, however, only after students have already differentiated the key conceptions surrounding the phenomena in question. For example, Wiser (1986) reports on ninth grade students' understanding of heat phenomena after a teaching intervention designed to help students differentiate between heat and temperature, develop a relation between heat and mass, and develop the notion of specific heat. Two "thermal laws" were at the center of the instruction:

1. If the same amount of heat is given to different masses of the same substance, the temperature rise is greater in the smaller mass.
2. It takes different amounts of heat to raise the temperature of equal amounts of different substances by the same amount of degrees (a fact captured by the concept of specific heat).

During Wiser's intervention, students conducted several experiments, the results of which were in contradiction with their conceptions. After the intervention, many students learned there is a difference between heat and temperature, but few were willing to give up the notion that temperature measures heat. Some students ended up being confused and thinking a larger beaker with water has more heat and is hotter than a smaller beaker of the same temperature. Others thought there are two measures of heat, its intensity (or degree) and its amount. Although this conception may be seen as some progress toward the scientific conception, in some cases it leads students to erroneous predictions. For example, students recognized a smaller piece of steel would be hotter than a larger piece of steel given the same amount of heat. However, they thought the smaller piece would cause a higher temperature increase than the larger piece when placed into a beaker of water because "it released hotter heat."

Students in Wiser's study had difficulties assimilating the idea "if the same amount of heat is given to different masses of the same substance, the temperature rise is greater in the smaller mass." They interpreted "amount of heat" as heat intensity and argued that if the heat is the same, then the temperature has to be the same. As a result, the students concluded from the law that "larger masses absorb more heat or have more heat" (which made sense within their framework), but ignored the second part of the law, "larger masses take more heat to increase the temperature by the same number of degrees" (which did not make sense within their framework).

The Wiser findings indicate that guiding students from their everyday conceptions to accepted scientific conceptions is a difficult and lengthy process. In particular, even providing students with experiences to encourage them to develop their frameworks about heat and temperature may not be sufficient. Experiences may not help, if they are not interpreted in the intended way. Students should be provided with a new framework that is intelligible to them and that helps them to understand and integrate both classroom and everyday experiences.

Based on the premise that integrated understanding results from providing students with an appropriate model of the phenomena under study, Linn and Songer (1991) developed and tested a 13-week thermodynamics curriculum for eighth grade students. Students actively predicted outcomes, reconciled results, and used a qualitative heat-flow model of thermodynamics to integrate their experimental results. The instruction contributed to a more elaborate differentiation between heat and temperature and understanding of the variables influencing heating and cooling (see also Lewis, 1991). Only a few students, however, generalized their understanding of heat and temperature to naturally occurring phenomena. Most students maintained that such phenomena were governed by different principles. Apparently, to change students' thinking, students need not only familiarity with an accepted scientific view, but also a reason to replace their current alternative frameworks with the scientific view.

SUMMARY AND CONCLUSIONS

In the introduction of this chapter, we suggested that understanding the scientific concept of heat may be viewed as a process of unfolding and differentiating the related concepts of *energy, temperature,* and *entropy.* We have viewed students' everyday concepts of heat, and their conceptual development, from the vantage point of the historical development of these concepts. Our students' difficulties are reminiscent of difficulties experienced by researchers in the history of science. For example, both the experimenters of the 17th century and the students today lacked a differentiation of heat and temperature, and an "interaction view" of heating and cooling processes. The unfolding and differentiation of our students' conceptions, like those in the history of science, are complex processes because the conceptions involved are closely interrelated. Understanding of temperature equalization, for instance, requires at least initial differentiation of heat and temperature, but this differentiation also requires an understanding of temperature equalization.

The results of newly designed teaching and learning approaches show, in our view, that this unfolding and differentiation can occur more effectively than it does in "traditional" approaches. All too often in traditional teaching, heat concepts and processes are mistakenly considered as simple and self-evident by some teachers. It is taken for granted, for instance, that students have the idea of temperature equalization — but many students do not. Therefore, new instructional approaches should address this issue explicitly. For example, teachers should ask students to measure the temperatures of bodies of different materials in the same room. Many students will be surprised to find the same thermometer readings for a piece of metal and a piece of wood. Because students often think different rules apply to different objects in warm environments, cold environments, and at room temperature, the temperature equalization idea should be tested in different surroundings. Students' ability to explain the perceived warmth of materials may come later as they combine their evolving concepts of heat flow, rate of heat flow, and thermal equilibrium (see Lewis, 1991). Empirical evidence alone usually will not convince students that their preconceptions (alternative frameworks) are not valuable in certain contexts. The scientific view also has to be provided by the teacher, and it is the teacher's task to promote this view, that is, to explain to the students why the scientific view is the most useful.

Teachers sometimes take for granted that students view cooling and heating as thermal interaction processes, but many students do not. Challenging demonstrations are called for to alter the students' views (Lehman, 1988). For example, one hot cup of coffee is put into a closed box, the other not. Temperatures of the coffee and the surrounding air are measured. In the box the temperature of the air increases markedly in comparison to the air around the nonboxed cup. Thermal interaction and thermal equilibrium are key concepts in students' understanding of the scientific view of heat; these concepts form the basis needed for meaningful learning and conceptual development in elementary thermodynamics.

In conclusion, it will help in teaching physics concepts, such as heat, if we keep the students' alternative frameworks in mind. We should not forget that teachers and students often view the same phenomena from very different perspectives.

REFERENCES

Andersson, B. (1990). Pupils' conceptions of matter and its transformations (age 12–16). *Studies in Science Education, 18*, 53–85.

Arons, A. (1965). *Development of concepts of physics*. Reading, MA: Addison-Wesley.

Brook, A., Briggs, H., Bell, B., & Driver, R. (1984). *Aspects of secondary students' understanding of heat: Summary report*. Leeds, England: University of Leeds, Centre for Studies in Science and Mathematics Education.

Brook, A., & Driver, R. (1984). *Aspects of secondary students' understanding of energy: Full report*. Leeds, England: Centre for Studies in Science and Mathematics Education.

Brook, A., & Driver, R. (1986). *The construction of meaning and conceptual change in classroom settings: Case studies on energy*. Leeds, England: Centre for Studies in Science and Mathematics Education.

Brush, S. (1988). *The history of modern science: A guide to the second scientific revolution, 1800–1950*. Ames, IA: Iowa State University Press.

Duit, R. (1982). Students' notions about the energy concept—Before and after instruction. In

W. Jung, H. Pfundt, & C. von. Rhoeneck (Eds.), *Problems concerning students' represen-tation of physics and chemistry knowledge: Proceedings of an international workshop* (pp. 268–319). Ludwigsburg: Paedagogische Hochschule.

Erickson, G. (1985). Heat and temperature. An overview of pupils' ideas. In R. Driver, E. Guesne, & A. Tiberghien (Eds.), *Children's ideas in science* (pp. 55–66). Philadelphia: Open University Press.

Falk, G., & Ruppel, W. (1976). *Energie und Entropie* [Energy and entropy]. Berlin: Springer Verlag.

Hewitt, P. G. (1987). *Conceptual physics.* Menlo Park, CA: Addison-Wesley.

Kesidou, S. (1990). *Schuelervorstellungen zur Irreversibilitaet.* Kiel, Germany: Institute for Science Education (IPN).

Kesidou, S., & Duit, R. (1993). Students' conceptions of the second law of thermodynamics. An interpretive study. *Journal of Research on Science Teaching, 30,* 85–106.

Lehman, J. H. (1988). Cool it: Activities with liquid nitrogen can stimulate bracing physics discussions. *Science Teacher, 55,* 29–33.

Lewis, E. L. (1991, April). *The development of understanding in elementary thermodynamics.* Paper presented at the Annual Meeting of the American Educational Research Association, Chicago.

Lewis, E. L., & Linn, M. C. (1994). Heat energy and temperature concepts of adolescents, adults, and experts: Implications for curricular improvements. *Journal of Research in Science Teaching, 31,* 657–677.

Linn, M., & Songer, N. B. (1991). Teaching thermodynamics to middle school students: What are appropriate cognitive demands? *Journal of Research in Science Teaching, 28,* 885–918.

McKie, D., & Heathcote, N. (1935). *The discovery of specific and latent heats.* London: Edward Arnold.

Millar, R., & Arnold, M. (1992). *Developing an analogy for the teaching of thermal equilibrium.* Unpublished working paper. York: Department of Educational Studies, University of York.

Rennstrom, L. (1987). Pupils' conceptions of matter. A phenomenographic approach. In J. Novak (Ed.), *Proceedings of the 2. international seminar "Misconceptions and Educational Strategies in Science and Mathematics"* (Vol. 3, pp. 400–415). Ithaca, NY: Cornell University.

Rosenquist, M., Popp, B., & McDermott, L. (1982, June). *Helping students overcome conceptual difficulties with heat and temperature.* Paper presented at the meeting of the American Association of Physics Teachers, Ashland.

Rutherford, F. J., Holton, G., & Watson, F. G. (1975). *Project physics.* New York: Holt, Rinehart and Winston.

Stavy, R., & Berkovitz, B. (1980). Cognitive conflict as a basis for teaching quantitative aspects of the concept of temperature. *Science Education, 64,* 679–692.

Tiberghien, A. (1983). Critical review on the research aimed at elucidating the sense that the notions heat and temperature have for students aged 10 to 16 years. *Proceedings of the first international workshop: Research on physics education* (pp. 73–90). Paris: Editions du CNRS.

Tiberghien, A. (1985). Heat and temperature. The development of ideas with teaching. In R. Driver, E. Guesne, & A. Tiberghien (Eds.), *Children's ideas in science* (pp. 66–84). Philadelphia: Open University Press.

Tomasini, G., & Balandi, P. (1987). *Teaching strategies and children's science: An experiment on teaching "hot and cold."* Bologna, Italy: University of Bologna, Physics Department.

Watson, B., & Konicek, R. (1990). Teaching for conceptual change: Confronting children's experience. *Phi Delta Kappan, 71,* 680–685.

Wiser, M. (1986). *The differentiation of heat and temperature: An evaluation of the effect of microcomputer teaching on students' misconceptions* (Technical Report). Cambridge, MA:

Harvard Graduate School of Education.

Wiser, M., & Carey, S. (1983). When heat and temperature were one. In D. Gentner & A. Stevens (Eds.), *Mental models* (pp. 267–297). Hillsdale, NJ: Lawrence Erlbaum Associates.

Wiser, M., Kipman, D., & Halkiadakis, L. (1988). *Can models foster conceptual change? The case of heat and temperature* (Technical Report). Cambridge, MA: Harvard Graduate School of Education.

Zemansky, M. (1970). The use and misuse of the word "heat" in physics teaching. *The Physics Teacher, 8,* 295–300.

III Conceptual Tools for Learning Science

Teachers need strategies to help students learn science meaningfully. In recent years, researchers have developed several powerful strategies for fostering meaningful science learning. Some of these capitalize on computers, whereas others capitalize on textbooks or simply willing minds. These strategies have a common goal of helping students' to construct their science knowledge and make sense of the natural world. The chapters in Part III highlight these research-based strategies.

9

The ThinkerTools Project: Computer Microworlds as Conceptual Tools for Facilitating Scientific Inquiry

Barbara Y. White
University of California at Berkeley

Learning physics is usually considered to be beyond the reach of most students. Various rationalizations have been put forward to justify this belief. The most frequent of these argues that solving physics problems requires abstract formal thinking, and therefore, it is not surprising that only high-ability students over the age of 15[1] correctly solve the type of problems presented to students on traditional physics tests (Shayer & Adey, 1981).

Research within the cognitive science and physics education communities paints an even grimmer picture. Of the small proportion of students who are motivated to take and pass traditional physics courses, an alarming proportion still maintain many of their misconceptions and do not acquire an understanding of the principles addressed in the course (e.g., Caramazza, McCloskey, & Green, 1981; Champagne, Klopfer, & Gunstone, 1982; Clement, 1982; diSessa, 1982; Larkin, McDermott, Simon, & Simon, 1980; McDermott, 1984; Trowbridge & McDermott, 1981; Viennot, 1979; White, 1983). The conclusion is that few students really learn physics through traditional physics courses.

Such findings have been used as the basis for recommending that physics be removed from elementary, middle, and even high school curricula—only college students who really need to learn physics, such as future scientists and engineers, should have to suffer through this most abstract and difficult of disciplines!

---

[1]That is, students who have reached the Piagetian developmental stage of *formal operational thinking* (Piaget & Garcia, 1964).

I argue that these conclusions are misguided. Physics is an ideal subject matter for introducing all students (regardless of whether or not they intend to become scientists or engineers) to the nature of scientific knowledge: its form, its evolution, and its application. Moreover, it is not inherently unlearnable. Students' difficulties in understanding physics arise, I argue, from deficiencies in the traditional definition of knowing physics and from deficiencies in traditional approaches to teaching it. In this chapter I illustrate that, by reconceptualizing what it means to understand physics as well as how it is taught, one can make the subject accessible and interesting to a wide range of students. Furthermore, one can use physics as a vehicle for introducing young students to the enterprise of science.

LEARNING PHYSICS

Traditional Approaches

Traditional approaches emphasize quantitative problem solving (Clement, 1981). A frequently applied instructional strategy is to introduce quantitative physical laws as constraint equations. Students then learn how these equations can be applied to solve problems. The technique typically involves matching the variables presented in the problem to the appropriate equation(s) and then performing algebraic transformations on the equations to solve for the unknowns. The difficulty is that such constraint-based formulations and the corresponding algebraic approaches to problem solving obscure underlying causal principles (Frederiksen & White, 1992; White & Frederiksen, 1990). They also do not correspond to how physicists reason when solving problems. The work of Chi, Feltovich, and Glaser (1981), deKleer and J. Brown (1985), and Larkin et al. (1980) reveals that expert problem solving within physical domains typically begins with a qualitative analysis of the problem. If the problem requires a quantitative solution, it is developed only after the problem has been analyzed and understood in qualitative terms.

This overemphasis on algebraic, constraint-based reasoning probably accounts for the finding that students can succeed in high school and even college physics courses while still maintaining many of their misconceptions and without acquiring an understanding of the physical principles addressed in the course. For example, many physics students make incorrect predictions about the trajectory of a ball when it is kicked off a cliff (McCloskey, 1983b). Such questions do not call for computation or the algebraic manipulation of formulas; rather, they require understanding the implications of the fundamental tenets of Newtonian mechanics. Students' failure to correctly answer such questions reveals a deficiency in their knowledge of the causal principles that underlie the formulas they have been taught. They have learned how to manipulate formal abstractions in order to solve problems, but they have not learned the meaning of the abstractions.

An Alternative Approach

Our approach focuses on learning how to construct causal models rather than on learning how to solve well-defined quantitative problems (White & Horwitz, 1988). It thus embodies a new perspective on understanding science, as well as a new view of the goals of science education. The emphasis is on understanding concepts and causal relationships, and on linking abstract formalisms with conceptual knowledge and with real-world phenomena. Formal representations and computational techniques, such as vectors and vector addition, play a key role in the evolution of this understanding. Their use, however, is in enabling students to carry out causal analyses of dynamic phenomena, rather than algebraic constraint analyses. As part of the learning process, students design representations and derive laws that operate on those representations, in order to make inferences about a system's behavior. Through this process, they acquire powerful conceptual models of domain phenomena that enable prediction and explanation. They also acquire metaknowledge about the form of scientific models and the process of constructing them. The thesis is that acquisition of such knowledge overcomes misconceptions and fosters an understanding of physics and scientific inquiry that older students taught with traditional methods appear to lack.

THE INSTRUCTIONAL APPROACH

We developed a constructivist approach to teaching science that incorporates a set of computer-based modeling tools along with a sequence of inquiry activities.

Increasingly Complex Microworlds. The primary conceptual tools are a series of interactive computer models: the ThinkerTools microworlds. Each successive microworld embodies an increasingly sophisticated model of how forces affect the motions of objects (e.g., Burton, J. Brown, & Fischer, 1984; Papert, 1980; White, 1981). It incorporates the concepts, causal relationships, and formal representations that students need to understand. The initial microworlds represent simple, idealized situations (i.e., motion in one dimension with no friction and with quantized impulses as the causal agents). By experimenting within such microworlds, students can gradually build on their prior knowledge (e.g., "impulses cause changes in velocity") toward a more sophisticated conception of force and motion (e.g., "forces cause accelerations"). The microworlds thus introduce key concepts and causal relationships in increasingly sophisticated forms. They also link abstract representations and computational mechanisms (such as vectors and vector addition) to concrete, dynamic phenomena. Through such linkages, the abstractions become concrete, manipulable, and meaningful.

Activities for Collaborative Inquiry.   In developing an instructional approach that incorporates this sequence of microworlds, we started from the premise that simply allowing children to play with the microworlds would not be sufficient for the development of powerful conceptual models. We argued that they need to be provided with experiences, which are initially very structured, that will enable them to assimilate and construct models. Thus, in addition to this sequence of microworlds, we also created a sequence of inquiry activities that focus on getting students to construct for themselves a set of conceptual models and an understanding of scientific modeling. These inquiry tasks are set in the context of a four-phase instructional cycle that involves (a) prediction, (b) experimentation, (c) formalization, and (d) generalization. This cycle repeats with each new microworld, and as the microworlds increase in complexity, so do the inquiry tasks.

Within this ThinkerTools curriculum, learning is always an active process in which the children are building on what they already know. The experiments and problems-solving tasks are often set in the context of computer games that are embedded in the microworlds. As the students play these games, they collaboratively formulate models and investigate the predictive power of alternative models. We thereby try to get students actively involved in scientific inquiry and play.

In order to provide a context for describing this inquiry-oriented instructional approach in more detail, I first describe Microworld 1. This microworld is a simple one-dimensional world in which there is no friction or gravity. The students' task is to control the motion of an object, *the dot*, by applying impulses to it (i.e., impulses are forces that act on an object for a specified — usually short — period of time, like a kick). In this microworld, students can apply impulses only to the right or to the left, and the impulses are always the same size. Thus, this first microworld is an idealized, one-dimensional world of quantized impulses.

Within the microworld, there are various representations of motion (see Fig. 9.1). First, there is the motion of the dot itself. There are also what we call *wakes* that provide a history of the dot's speed by leaving little dots on the screen at fixed time intervals. There is also a bar-graph speedometer, called a *datacross*, which enables students to see, whenever they apply an impulse, how it affects the speed of the dot.

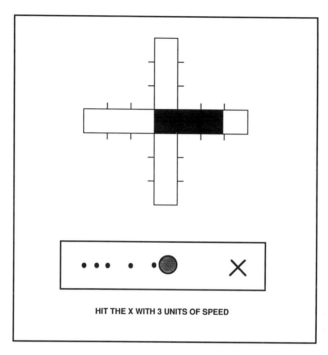

FIG. 9.1   The goal of this game is to make the dot hit the target with a specified velocity. In this case, the dot needs to be moving to the right with three units of speed when it hits the target.

The inquiry-oriented instructional approach that we developed incorporates four phases. This four-phase inquiry cycle is repeated with each new microworld in the sequence.

The Motivation Phase

In the first phase, the *motivation phase*, the teacher asks students to make predictions about the behavior of real-world objects. Questions were chosen, based on extensive interviews with sixth graders, to elicit disagreement. For example, students might be asked to imagine that there is an object resting on a table, and that the table is very smooth, so there is no friction. A blast of air is applied to the object. Then, as it is moving along, a blast of air, the same size as the first, is applied in the opposite direction. The question is, "What will the second blast of air do to the motion of the object?" The teacher simply records the students' reasoning and answers without commenting on their correctness or incorrectness. For instance, in response to the preceding question, some students say that the second blast of air will cause the object to turn around and go in the opposite direction.

Other students say that the second blast of air cancels the first and the object will stop. Still others say that it simply slows the object down, but the object keeps moving in the original direction. We hypothesized that such disagreement would motivate students because they know that they cannot all be correct, and thus they would want to find out who has the correct and incorrect beliefs about how forces affect motion. Further, because the questions are about the behavior of real-world objects, they create the potential for linking what happens in the computer microworld with what happens in real-world situations.

The Evolution Phase

In the second phase of the instructional cycle, the *evolution phase*, students go to the microworld and work together, usually in groups of two, on a series of game-like problem-solving activities. These activities are designed to help students derive the laws of the microworld for themselves. For example, in the first game (see Fig. 9.1), they have to make the dot hit a target while it is traveling at a given speed (e.g., set $V_x = 3$). If the dot is traveling at the given speed, the target "catches" the dot. If not, the dot crashes into the end walls and explodes. In the next game in the sequence, the end walls are removed and the students have to navigate the dot off the screen in order to be able to achieve the given velocity. When the dot is off the screen, the only way that the students can see the effects of the impulses they are applying is to look at the datacross (i.e., the bar-graph representation of the dot's speed). By focusing on this representation, they should notice that whenever they apply an impulse, it adds or subtracts a unit of speed from the dot's velocity. Through sequences of activities such as these, which make use of the alternative representations of motion displayed in the microworld, students potentially can determine the laws of the microworld for themselves. However, we do not rely, at least initially, on sixth graders being able to derive well-articulated laws. Thus, we go next to what is called the *formalization phase* of the instructional cycle.

The Formalization Phase

In this phase, the students work together at their computers, usually in small groups of three to five students. They are given a set of laws as possible descriptions of the behavior of the microworld. Their task is to sort the laws into two piles: those they think are correct and those they think are incorrect. For the laws they believe to be incorrect, they must be prepared to show the rest of the class a case where that law does not hold. In other words, they have to produce counterevidence to that particular law. For those they think are correct, they are asked to imagine that they can use only one of these laws to make predictions about the behavior of the dot in the microworld. The question they are asked is, "Which one of these laws would you pick and why?" After the class finishes debating in small groups, the whole class gets together and attempts to agree on the best law.

The sets of laws were carefully designed to elicit discussion about the properties of a useful scientific law. Some of the laws are inelegant (too long and difficult to remember); others are not precise. For example, "Whenever you apply an impulse to the dot, you change its speed" is correct, but it does not predict how the speed will change. Others are true but apply only in limited circumstances: For instance, "If the dot is moving to the right and you apply an impulse to the right, you will increase its speed" is correct, but it only applies when the dot is moving to the right. The law that we wanted students to select as the best always had the properties of being correct, simply stated, and generally applicable.

The Transfer Phase

The final phase of the instructional cycle focuses on applying the laws of the microworld to real-world situations. This *transfer phase* has two subphases. First, students are asked to recall the predictive questions that they were asked during the motivation phase, usually about a week before. Their task is to determine how the law, which the class later decided was the best law, would answer those questions. The teacher then points out that not everyone had given the same predictions as those generated by the law and asks them why that might be. Usually, at this point, one of the students will say something like, "Well, you asked us to imagine no friction, but that is hard to think about because it doesn't happen very often." The teacher then asks the students to go to the microworld and to experiment by putting in different values for friction to see if they can get the microworld to behave according to some of their intuitions. In this way, students begin to see the relationship between the microworld and the behavior of objects in the real world.

The second subphase of the transfer phase is concerned with getting students to relate laws learned in the microworld context to a variety of real-world situations. For example, the students are given experiments to engage in, such as controlling the motion of a bowling ball by hitting it with a rubber mallet, or experimenting with ping-pong balls and blow guns. In these activities, they are asked to think about the question, "Do the laws of the microworld help you to predict and control what happens in these real-world contexts?"

These four phases of the instructional cycle are repeated with each new microworld in the curriculum. Notice that this cycle relates to the classic conception of the scientific method: asking questions, doing experiments, formulating laws, and investigating how the laws generalize to different contexts. (This relationship is discussed later in the section concerned with facilitating scientific inquiry.)

THE MODEL PROGRESSION

This section describes the progression of microworlds and the corresponding desired evolution in the students' understanding of how forces affect the motion of objects.

Microworld 1: Understanding One-Dimensional Motion

In the first one-dimensional microworld, described previously, students are given tasks such as having to hit a target at a specified speed (see Fig. 9.1). Through such tasks, they can use the datacross representation (i.e., the bar-graph speedometer) and their knowledge of scalar arithmetic (e.g., $1 + 1 = 2$) to see that the effects of forces are additive. The law that they infer from interacting with this microworld is, "Whenever you apply an impulse to an object, it changes its speed. If applied in the same direction as the object is moving, it adds a unit to its speed, and if applied in the opposite direction, it subtracts a unit from its speed."

Microworld 2: Understanding Two-Dimensional Motion

The second microworld is a two-dimensional world in which students can apply impulses up or down, as well as to the left or right. In this microworld, students are introduced to yet another representation for the motion of objects: two arrows, one vertical and one horizontal, that remain constantly pointed at the dot. These arrows represent the horizontal velocity of the dot and the vertical velocity of the dot, that is, its orthogonal velocity components. Thus, in this microworld, students are exposed to four alternative representations for motion: the dot, its wakes, its arrows, and its datacross (see Fig. 9.2). These representations correspond to ways that physicists think about motion: (a) the speed and direction of an object's velocity, and (b) its orthogonal velocity components (i.e., its speed in the x dimension and in the y dimension). The speed and direction of the dot's velocity are represented in a dynamic form by the motion of the dot itself, and in a more abstract form by the dot's wake (i.e., the little dots that it leaves on the screen at fixed time intervals). The dot's orthogonal velocity components are represented in a dynamic form by the horizontal and

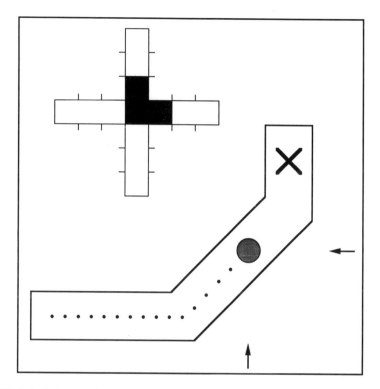

FIG. 9.2   This screen image illustrates the linked, alternative representations of motion employed within the microworlds (i.e., the moving dot and its wake, arrows, and datacross). In the task shown, the goal is to make the dot navigate the track and stop on the target.

vertical arrows that remain constantly pointed at the dot, and in a more abstract form by the datacross (where the horizontal bar shows the dot's speed in the horizontal dimension and the vertical bar shows the dot's speed in the vertical dimension).

Initially, students are encouraged to think in terms of orthogonal velocity components. They are given tasks where one student has to control the motion of the horizontal arrow and another student the motion of the vertical arrow. By performing such tasks, students should derive two principles. The first is that the law derived in the first microworld, concerning the additivity of impulses, applies to this new vertical dimension of motion. The second is that impulses applied in the vertical dimension have no effect on the dot's horizontal velocity, and vice versa. In other words, the dot's horizontal and vertical velocity components are independent of one another.

Later in the progression of tasks for Microworld 2, students go on to thinking in terms of the representation of motion as speed and direction, and to understanding how orthogonal velocity components combine to determine the speed and direction of the dot's motion. For example, in the task shown in Fig. 9.3, students have to set the datacross by giving it an amount of velocity in the vertical dimension and an amount of velocity in the horizontal dimension, such that when the dot is released, the resulting direction of motion will cause the dot to pass through the target. Through such game-like problem-solving activities, students learn to think in terms of both orthogonal velocity components and speed and direction of motion, as well as to translate between these two alternative ways of thinking about motion.

Microworld 3: Understanding Continuous Forces

The third microworld incorporates a model for reasoning about the effects of continuous forces. It is a one-dimensional microworld in which students can apply impulses only upward or downward. The purpose is to enable students to model a continuous force, such as gravity, in terms of a series of small impulses closely spaced in time. In this way, they can use their law about the additive effects of impulses to predict the effects of a constant force. They can thereby develop a conceptual model of a continuous process as a sequence of cause–effect events. This model is introduced via a limit process: Students are given the ability to change the rate at which impulses can be applied in the microworld. To elaborate, in the first two microworlds, if students hold down the fire button on the joystick (which is used to apply impulses), they get a series of impulses at the rate of one every three-quarters of a second. In Microworld 3, students can press specified keys to change the frequency with which impulses are applied. They can repeatedly double the rate at which impulses are applied, but every time

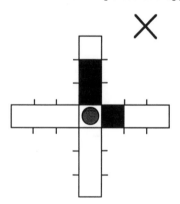

FIG. 9.3   The goal of this game is to set the dot's horizontal and vertical velocity, via the datacross, so that the dot will hit the target when it is released.

they do this, the size of the impulse is halved, so they end up having the same ultimate effect on motion. This new feature of Microworld 3 allows students to increase the rate at which impulses are applied and thereby enables students to approximate a continuous force by applying a series of small impulses closely spaced in time. Because they previously learned that the effect of each impulse is additive, they can use this law to develop a conceptual model of the additive effects of continuous forces.

To foster the evolution of this model, students are given experiments to perform and analyze such as, "Describe and explain what happens when you throw a ball up in the air. What happens to the motion of the ball and why?" They reason, for example, that "The ball will start by going up and will gradually slow down because gravity keeps pulling and adding another impulse down, and there will be an instant when the ball is stopped in the air, and then it will start coming down and will gradually speed up because gravity keeps adding another impulse down."

Microworld 4: Analyzing Trajectories

In the fourth and final microworld, students are required to utilize all of their knowledge acquired in the first three microworlds to analyze trajectory problems. In this two-dimensional microworld, gravity is acting in the vertical dimension. The students are asked to analyze problems such as, "If you have two balls sitting on the edge of a table, and you give one ball a large horizontal kick off the edge, and the other ball a small horizontal kick off the edge, and both kicks are applied at the same time, which ball lands first?" The somewhat counterintuitive answer is that both balls land at the same time (see Fig. 9.4). By consolidating what they learned in the prior microworlds, students have the knowledge needed to analyze such situations correctly.

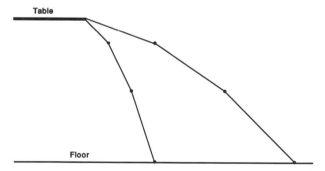

FIG. 9.4 A model-based prediction of the trajectories of two balls launched from a table at the same time with different horizontal velocities.

The Target Conceptual Model

The conceptual model students could evolve by interacting with this progression of microworlds and problem-solving activities would enable them to predict and explain how forces affect motion. For instance, they would understand the additivity of impulses. They would know about the independence of x and y motion. They could translate between alternative representations of motion, such as the component way of thinking about motion and the speed-and-direction way of thinking about motion. Finally, they could model continuous forces in terms of a series of small impulses closely spaced in time. The consolidation of this knowledge would produce quite a sophisticated conceptual model (see White, 1993b, for more detail). It would employ the kind of reasoning that physicists themselves use when, for example, analyzing projectile motion. Thus, I argue that through this progression of microworlds and problem-solving activities, combined with the inquiry activities embedded in the instructional cycle, students could acquire a powerful conceptual model for reasoning about force and motion.

INSTRUCTIONAL TRIALS

The ThinkerTools curriculum was implemented by a teacher who was responsible for five sixth-grade science classes in a middle school located in a middle-class Boston suburb. One of the five classes was used for a pilot trial of the first two modules of the ThinkerTools curriculum. Of the remaining four classes, two were used as a peer control group (containing 37 students), and the other two (containing 42 students) were given the ThinkerTools curriculum. In this school district, the students have a science class every school day for 45 minutes. The ThinkerTools curriculum took 2 months to complete and occupied the entire class period. Students in the control classes received the standard curriculum, which, at this point in the year, was devoted to a unit on inventions.

In addition to the peer control group of sixth-grade students, two further control groups were employed, consisting of high school physics students in the same school system. These students had chosen to enroll in physics course in the 11th or 12th grade. The first group consisted of two classes (containing 41 students) who had just completed 2½ months studying Newtonian mechanics using the textbook *Concepts in Physics* (Miller, Dillon, & Smith, 1980). The second group consisted of two classes (containing 45 students) who were at the very beginning of their physics course, before they had studied Newtonian mechanics.

The results are summarized with respect to a transfer test designed to measure students' understanding of Newtonian mechanics in real-world problem-solving contexts (additional results can be found in White, 1993b). This test was administered to the experimental group and the three control groups. It was composed of questions used by researchers in studying misconceptions among physics students (Clement, 1982; diSessa, 1982; McCloskey, 1983a, 1983b; McDermott, 1984; Minstrell, 1982, 1989; White, 1981, 1983). All of the problems were noncomputational and required application of the basic principles of Newtonian mechanics. An example is the spiral problem, shown in Fig. 9.5, in which students were asked to predict the trajectory of a ball when it emerges from passing through a spiral tube. The questions were thus simple predictive questions to which high school and college physics students frequently give wrong answers.

Figure 9.6 presents a summary of the results. The ThinkerTools students did significantly better on this transfer test than the high school physics students ($t[156] = 2.33$, $p = .02$), who were, on the average, 6 years older and had been taught about force and motion using traditional methods. Further, although both the high school physics course and the ThinkerTools curriculum produced significant improvements in performance on this test over their respective controls, the ThinkerTools curriculum produced significantly greater improvement than the high school physics course ($t[156] = 2.76$, $p = .007$). This result is somewhat surprising, because the high school students were older (which should make it easier for them to learn this material), and they were a self-selected group (i.e., they chose to take physics). Both these factors should favor the high school students learning more from their physics course. However, because there are at least three systematic differences between the ThinkerTools students and the high school physics students (age, selection, and treatment), one cannot

Imagine that you are looking down at a spiral tube lying flat on a table. A ball enters the tube. Which path does the ball take when it comes out of the tube?

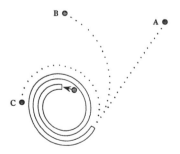

FIG. 9.5   The spiral problem.

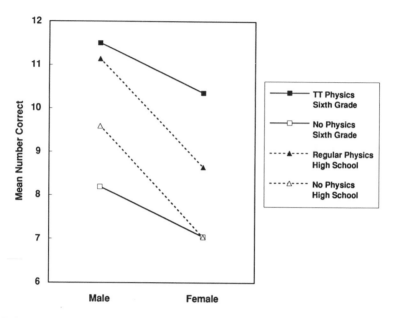

FIG. 9.6   Performance of the four groups on the transfer test, shown for each gender.

conclude from this result alone that the ThinkerTools curriculum is more effective in developing an understanding of force and motion. The result could be an age effect (older students learn less), or a selection effect (students who choose to take physics courses are poor learners), although these explanations are both counterintuitive. Fortunately, there is additional evidence supporting the conjecture that the difference in improvement is due to the curriculum itself, not to age difference or selection effects: In an earlier study, I tried similar microworld-based activities with high school physics students, and found the same dramatic improvements in performance on a similar test of force and motion problems (White, 1981, 1984).

A comparison of the four groups of students' performances on individual items on the transfer test revealed some interesting findings. Some of the most intriguing results of this item analysis (described further in White, 1993b) relate to problems where the ThinkerTools students did dramatically better than the high school physics students. Such differences occurred primarily on very simple problems, such as the one shown in Fig. 9.7, where students were asked to predict the trajectory of a ball that is kicked off the edge of a cliff, or to describe the speed of a ball as it falls to the ground. These are very simple problems, and it is not surprising that the Thinker-Tools students gave correct answers to such questions. What is surprising is that many of the high school physics students did not. It is as though the

Imagine that you kick a ball sideways off a cliff.
Which path does the ball take as it falls to the ground?

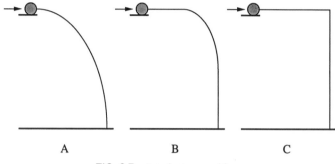

A   B   C

FIG. 9.7   A trajectory problem.

high school students could apply what they learned in physics class to formal problems, but not to simple, everyday situations. This result, although surprising, converges with other research in the cognitive science and physics education literatures (see McDermott, 1984).

The item analysis also indicated that many of the ThinkerTools students could apply the laws they learned to new contexts. For example, one of the new contexts for the ThinkerTools students was the problem shown in Fig. 9.8. In this problem, two boats are crossing two rivers; the only difference between the two rivers is that one has a current flowing and the other does not. This is a problem that requires understanding the independence of x and y motion for its correct solution. This principle is addressed in the ThinkerTools curriculum, but the ThinkerTools students had never before been asked to think about this principle in the context of boats crossing rivers. On this problem, the ThinkerTools students did as well as the high school physics students ($\chi^2[1, N = 82] = .05\ p = .83$), and the high school physics students did much better than the high school students who had not yet taken their physics course ($\chi^2 [1, N = 86] = 9.29, p = .002$). Performance on such questions indicates that many students in the Thinker-Tools group (ranging from 50% to 80%, depending on the question) were able to transfer what they learned from contexts presented in the curriculum to new contexts. I think three aspects of the instructional treatment are responsible for this result:

1. The approach introduces abstract, widely applicable representations such as the datacross. The students learn, in the transfer phase of the instructional cycle, that this representation can be used to describe the motion of many objects. The fact that this represen-

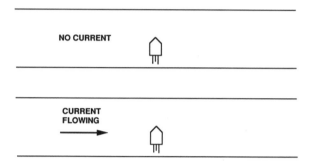

Suppose that we have two identical rivers with two identical boats trying to cross those rivers. The only difference is that one river has a current flowing and the other does not. Both boats have the same motors and leave at the same time. Which boat gets to the other side first?

NO CURRENT

CURRENT FLOWING

(a) The one crossing the river without a current flowing.

(b) The one crossing the river with a current flowing.

(c) Both boats get to the other side at the same time.

FIG. 9.8   The river crossing problem.

tation maps across different contexts may help students to realize that the laws and representations they have learned are generally applicable. In addition, the objects and events of the microworlds are discussed in generic terms. In other words, the object is called a dot, not a spaceship or a billiard ball. Similarly, forces are referred to as impulses, not as engine blasts or kicks. Referring to the objects and events of the microworlds in generic terms may help foster students' abilities to map the microworld model to different contexts.

2. Students formalize what they learn into laws that are simple to remember and generally applicable. In the formalization phase of the instructional cycle, students summarize what they have learned from interacting with the microworld into a law, for instance, "Impulses, depending on their direction, add or subtract a unit of speed to the appropriate velocity component." The laws give them a precise, concise means of computing the effects of impulses using the datacross representation. Acquisition of these representations and laws gives students a relatively simple knowledge structure that can apply across different contexts.

3. Students get practice with transfer. In the transfer phase of the instructional cycle, students apply the representations and laws to predict and control the motion of real-world objects. They thereby learn that their laws apply in a range of contexts, and they gain experience in transferring what they learn in one context (i.e, the computer microworld) to another context (i.e., a particular real-world situation).

I therefore conjecture that the representations used in the microworlds, combined with the formalization and transfer phases of the curriculum cycle, are responsible for the ThinkerTools students' ability to apply their knowledge to new contexts.

FACILITATING SCIENTIFIC INQUIRY

In addition to enabling students to understand and apply the principles underlying Newtonian mechanics, we had the symbiotic goal of helping them to learn about the form and evolution of scientific knowledge. In our pilot work on this project, we found that in certain key respects children are not born scientists. For instance, when we asked sixth graders, "What is meant by a scientific law?" we typically got responses like, "It is something you must obey or you will get in trouble." In other words, they think of laws as prescriptive, rather than descriptive. Thus, we concluded that scientific inquiry skills would have to be developed gradually — just as the knowledge of Newtonian mechanics had to be developed gradually. In this way, students would learn about scientific inquiry, and inquiry skills could play a role in helping students to develop an understanding of Newtonian mechanics.

Instructional Method

The instructional approach that we created aims to enable students to construct an understanding of physics for themselves via structured inquiry. The pedagogical techniques support the development of two key aspects of scientific expertise: (a) learning about the form of scientific knowledge, and (b) learning about the processes of scientific inquiry. In attempting to introduce these aspects of scientific expertise,[2] we took the approach of

---

[2]See Carey, Evans, Honda, Jay, and Unger (1989), Karmiloff-Smith (1988), D. Kuhn (1988), T. Kuhn (1970), Langley, Simon, Bradshaw, and Zytkow (1987), Rosebury, Warren, and

starting with a lot of structure and gradually removing it (as in the coaching and fading approach of Palincsar & A. Brown, 1984). As mentioned earlier, our four-phase instructional cycle—asking questions, doing experiments, formulating laws, and investigating generalizations—is related to the classic conception of the scientific method; that is, there is a correspondence between what the ThinkerTools students did to learn physics and what scientists do to discover new principles. However, in the initial stages of the curriculum, students were given questions to ask, experiments to do, laws to evaluate, and contexts in which to investigate generalizations. They were thus not initially making these decisions for themselves and were therefore not fully practicing scientific inquiry.

As the curriculum progressed, more and more of the inquiry process was turned over to the students. For instance, part way through the curriculum they were given experiments to do in the microworld context, but rather than being given possible laws to evaluate, they had to formulate their own. Later in the curriculum, they were asked to design an experiment using real-world objects, such as ping-pong balls and blowguns, that would help someone else to discover a principle that they had already discovered themselves. In this way, the students gained experience in formulating laws (with all of the other inquiry steps structured for them) and in designing experiments.

Results and Discussion

In presenting an overview of the results, I first focus on students' understanding about the form of scientific knowledge and then on their scientific inquiry skills. These results are presented in more detail in White (1993b).

Understanding the Form of Scientific Knowledge. Knowing the characteristics of a useful scientific law is an important aspect of scientific expertise. The instructional technique we developed was to present students with alternative laws for each microworld and ask them to select the best law. We observed that when students were evaluating these sets of laws, they spontaneously engaged in discussions concerning the simplicity of a law, the precision of its predictions, and its range of applicability. Each set of laws was carefully constructed to elicit such discussions, and this approach appears to have been highly successful.

The results indicate that the students were able to generate comments and discussion about the utility of laws proposed to describe the behavior of the microworlds (see White, 1993b). For instance, when asked to evaluate the

---

Conant (1992), and Siegler (1978) for further discussions concerning the nature, development, and teaching of scientific inquiry skills.

rule, "If you're stopped and you give an impulse to the right, and then you give an impulse to the left, you stop again," the sixth graders came up with an impressive range of responses. The most frequent was to provide a "proof" as to why the rule is correct: "That's a good rule because an impulse to the right and an impulse to the left cancel out." Another frequent type of response was to comment about the rule's properties such as its utility: "It is useful because it's true and that would be helpful, but it's bad because you need more rules. It doesn't say enough." These comments indicate the development of expertise about the nature of scientific knowledge and explanation.

Developing Scientific Inquiry Skills. Being able to develop and reason from counterevidence is a key scientific inquiry skill. It is important for students to learn that falsification is part of the process by which scientific knowledge evolves. For a rule to be a scientific law, it must have the potential to be proven wrong by counterevidence. The students were introduced to the concept of falsification by being asked to determine which of a set of possible laws for a given microworld were incorrect. For a law they judge to be incorrect, they have to be prepared to describe, using their conceptual model, or to demonstrate, using the microworld, a case where the law does not hold. In the initial stages of the curriculum, the incorrect laws were relatively easy to prove wrong. An example of such a law is, "Whenever you give the dot an impulse, it speeds up." We observed that when the students were evaluating the sets of laws, they were adept at coming up with cases that would falsify a particular law (see White, 1993b).

Students should also understand that the laws they are evolving are of increasingly general applicability, and that they should be able to apply them in new contexts. Based on our classroom observations and the results of the transfer test, we found that many students were indeed able to generalize the use of principles derived in the microworld contexts to a variety of simple real-world contexts. In the formalization phase of the instruction, they had successfully abstracted what they learned from the computer microworld into a set of laws and, in the transfer phase, learned how to map the laws onto different real-world problem-solving situations. Students also saw how these laws had to be refined as they were generalized to increasingly complex circumstances (in this case, the increasingly complex progression of microworlds).

However, when we looked at what the students did when they formulated laws and designed experiments for themselves, we found that there were limits to their scientific inquiry skills. In the context of the first microworld, for example, students were asked, at the end of the unit, to experiment by putting different amounts of friction into the microworld and to determine what would happen. We expected groups of students to come up with simple, qualitative laws such as, "The more friction you put in, the faster the dot slows down," or "The faster the dot goes, the more friction slows it down." They did indeed derive such laws. One group of students surprised us, however, by discovering a law that we had not discovered ourselves (see Horwitz, 1989). We call it the "linear friction law": In the microworld, the effect of friction is linearly proportional to the speed with which the object is moving. The consequence is that when students apply a sequence of impulses to the dot, it does not matter whether they apply them in quick succession or widely spaced in time; in either case, the dot will come to rest at the same point. The students discovered this fact, but they did not fully explore its implications (such as whether it means that the dot can stop only at certain locations on the screen), nor did they go on to investigate whether it is an accurate model of real-world friction (such as that which affects rolling balls or sliding hockey pucks).

As a further example of limited inquiry skills, in the fourth unit on analyzing trajectories, the students were asked to design an experiment. They had already determined the principles that affect trajectories and were asked to develop a game-like activity (using objects such as ping-pong balls, blowguns, and buckets) that would help someone to learn about trajectories. The activities they created were, for the most part, entertaining games, not good instructional experiments. Also, when evaluating each other's activities at the end of the period, their criteria for a good activity had more to do with its being enjoyable than instructive. Several groups of students did, however, design activities that involved systematic experimentation. In these activities, the player had to vary the angle at which he or she fired the blowgun and observe where the bucket had to be placed so that the ball would land in it. These loosely correspond to experiments the students did in the microworld, where they had to vary systematically the dot's horizontal velocity and then its vertical velocity.[3]

If one looks at the instructional approach, these limitations in the students' inquiry skills are understandable. The students were never given examples of good and bad experiments, as they were with laws. In fact, their primary perception of what they were doing in the microworlds was "playing fun games," not doing experiments. This was revealed in their answers to the opinion survey taken at the end of the course. For example, in response to the question, "What did you like about the course?" many

---

[3]The correspondence between blowguns and the microworlds students have been working with is not perfect. The blowgun delivers a fixed-sized impulse in whatever direction it is aimed. In the microworld, impulses can only be given in vertical and horizontal directions. Thus, in order to make the dot go at 45 degrees, it has to be given an impulse in the vertical and horizontal directions, which makes it go faster than a dot that has just been given a vertical impulse. In fairness to the students, this lack of correspondence between the blowgun and the microworld probably made it harder for them to design experiments.

students said, "I learned physics while playing fun games." In response to the question, "How could the course be improved?" many said, "More games and less talk." Further, students were never explicitly told that the four phases of the instructional cycle correspond to steps in the scientific method, and that they represent a particular kind of systematic inquiry. For instance, the students who discovered the linear friction law did not investigate the implications or generality of their law. Although they had had practice (in the transfer phase of the instructional cycle) in generalizing, it was not made explicit to them that they were testing the explanatory power of a law and that the generalization process plays a crucial role in scientific discovery. Therefore, it is perhaps not surprising that the students did not spontaneously explore the generality of laws they discovered.

Revising the curriculum to improve the development of students' scientific inquiry skills is the focus of our present work. These improvements include: (a) providing examples of good and bad experiments, as we had with laws; (b) making the goals of inquiry, such as generalization, explicit; (c) modeling the processes involved, such as experimental design and theory formulation; and (d) creating a gradual well-worked-out progression of scientific inquiry skills, as we had with models of force and motion.

GENERAL DISCUSSION

The most striking findings of this instructional study were the high level of interest and competence in "doing science" that the sixth graders exhibited. When we observed the classes, the majority of children were actively engaged in each of the phases of the instructional cycle: (a) making predictions, (b) working with their partners at the computer games and experiments, (c) collaborating with their groups to evaluate laws and representations, and (d) conducting experiments with real-world objects to investigate the utility of the laws and representations for modeling the behavior of the real world. Our conclusion is that this approach to science education has the potential both to motivate and to enable children to engage in the process of "doing science." It can develop inquiry skills, along with knowledge about the nature of scientific models and their creation, as well as nontrivial subject-matter expertise (in this case, a knowledge of the relevant physics).

An Alternative Approach to Teaching Science

The approach embodies a new perspective on understanding science, as well as a new view of the goals and methods of science education. It focuses on learning how to construct causal models, rather than on learning how to solve well-defined, quantitative problems. This focus is in keeping with the increasing emphasis on modeling and visualization that is occurring in the scientific disciplines due to the availability of powerful new technologies (Sabelli, 1992). It is also in keeping with recent views on how cognitive science research can contribute to educational reform (Carey, 1986; Champagne & Klopfer, 1984; Glaser, 1984; Resnick, 1983; Schoenfeld, 1990).

Acquiring Scientific Expertise.   Developing scientific expertise, as I have argued, involves more than memorizing definitions and formulas, and more than learning how to solve problems via constraint-based, algebraic reasoning. Our approach introduces students to models in which the representations are iconic and the reasoning used to make predictions and generate explanations is causal. This contrasts with "top-down" traditional approaches that start with more abstract algebraic representations and acausal constraint-based reasoning. It also contrasts with hands-on "bottom-up" approaches that start with manipulating the physical objects themselves instead of icons on a computer screen.

The use of iconic models has been investigated with regard to mathematics education (e.g., Feurzeig & White, 1983; Lampert, 1986; Ohlsson, 1987; Resnick & Omanson, 1987; Schwartz, 1989). For instance, Ginnsburg and Yamamoto (1986, p. 367) use the term *intermediary schemata* to refer to "artificially devised materials designed to promote the various areas of mathematical knowledge and the connections among them." The use of such models has also received attention recently from researchers interested in investigating the role that computer-based tools can play in science education (e.g., Kozma, 1992; Linn, Songer, Lewis, & Stern, 1993; Mandinach, 1989; Smith, Snir, Unger, & Grosslight, 1990; Wiser, 1988).

Our models are designed to facilitate a "middle-out" approach to science education. We create models that, if assimilated, enable children to build on the knowledge and reasoning forms they already possess, and to conceptualize domain phenomena at an intermediate level of abstraction (White, 1989, 1993a). The goal is to create a coherent link between real-world phenomena (e.g., kicking a ball) and computational formalisms (e.g., vector addition). In our approach, students are presented with iconic causal models and with tasks that involve mapping between the behavior of an icon (e.g., the dot) and the behavior of a more abstract representation (e.g., the datacross),[4] as well as with tasks that involve mapping between the behavior of the icon and the behavior of a real-world object (e.g., a ball).

---

[4]The datacross can also be regarded as iconic, and the reasoning used in working with the datacross to make predictions is a causal form of $F = ma$. One could eventually progress to the efficient but acausal form of reasoning that utilizes algebraic expressions, such as $F = ma$, and constraint-based reasoning.

We start at an intermediate level of abstraction with regard to both the form of representation and the form of reasoning used. We then use the instructional technique of giving students experience at mapping between these different representations to develop a connection between phenomena and formalism.

Acquiring Expertise at Teaching Scientific Inquiry.   The instructional cycle, inquiry activities, and microworlds provide models of the inquiry and subject-matter expertise. These are needed as a source of expertise, because most sixth grade teachers have never taken a physics course, and most do not possess the scientific inquiry skills that the curriculum tries to foster. We thus cannot depend on having the teacher demonstrate inquiry or subject-matter expertise, as can be done in the teaching of reading, writing, and arithmetic (Collins, J. Brown, & Newman, 1989). The teacher's primary role is to create a climate in which the participants listen to each other's ideas and collaborate effectively to help each other's understanding to evolve. Of course, ideally, the teacher would also be an expert in the inquiry process (Roth & Lindquist, 1992), and the ThinkerTools curriculum can be used to develop such expertise.

Both teachers involved in this project felt that they taught the Thinker-Tools curriculum successfully. The following presents some quotations from an interview with the teacher whose classes were the focus of the study presented in this chapter:

Question: How has the ThinkerTools Project been different from your normal teaching of science?

Answer: I think that this project is different in terms of watching how kids think. It's almost like being able to see a slice of the way they think . . . and I haven't had that experience before.

Question: What do you feel the computer provides?

Answer: For this particular project, I think it is essential. It would be absurd to try to teach this without the computer simulations. I liked it, because it didn't monopolize the program. It was part of it. It was a tool. It's made me far more enthusiastic about using computers with kids. I don't want to see these computers go! . . . I don't feel that the computer took my place. I think the computer was my assistant.

Question: Do you feel kids are developing understandings?

Answer: Yes, and some of their insights amaze me. They catch on to some of the things that, when I got involved in this project, I never thought about, and I gave some of the wrong answers. . . . I look at the kids right now responding to some of the same questions, and they are showing better insights than I did.

And, it is not embarrassing to me. It is neat to watch. It's funny; five years ago I could never have envisioned doing something like this. And, I can see five years down the road, that this is the way that things are going to be as far as I'm concerned.

Since the conclusion of this study, one of the participating school systems made the ThinkerTools curricular modules a part of its sixth-grade science curriculum. Because this school system has two sixth-grade science teachers, the second teacher had to pick up the ThinkerTools curriculum almost entirely on his own, relying on only minimal assistance from the other teacher, who participated in the original project. Despite having virtually no background in physics, he reports experiencing no unusual difficulty in teaching the lessons. Both teachers who taught the ThinkerTools curriculum after the project ended feel that the children enjoy the experience and learn a lot from it.

The ThinkerTools lesson plans were designed to introduce students to physics and to scientific inquiry. The instructional approach introduces the physics by starting with simplified microworlds and gradually progressing to more sophisticated ones. It introduces scientific inquiry by a sequence of increasingly challenging inquiry tasks in which students collaborate to create and revise conceptual models that embody their theories of force and motion. This approach appears to be beneficial not only for students but also for teachers. Thus, the primary focus of our future work is to create improved versions of the ThinkerTools curricular materials and teacher's guides that will help both students and teachers learn about physics, scientific inquiry, and constructivist approaches to education.

ACKNOWLEDGMENTS

The author is particularly indebted to her collaborator on this project, physicist Paul Horwitz. The study described in this chapter was sponsored by the National Science Foundation, under award number DPE-8400280 with the Directorate for Science and Engineering Education. Recent work on this project has been supported by a grant from the James S. McDonnell Foundation, under award number 9135. This chapter incorporates material from White (1993a, 1993b). The author is grateful to Barbara Boudreau, Carolee Matsumoto, and Marianne Haley from the Concord Public Schools, and Mildred Feloney, William Kroen, and Marilyn McGinn from the Cambridge Public Schools for their support and participation in this project. She is also grateful to Jack Lochhead and David Brown, who served as consultants; Craig Cohen and Geoffrey Pike, who helped in software development; and Jane Imai, who scored and tabulated the test results. Finally, the author would like to thank John Frederiksen and Michelle von Koch for their constructive comments on a draft of this chapter. To obtain additional information about this work, readers can write to the author at the School of Education, 4533 Tolman Hall, University of Calfornia, Berkeley, CA 94720.

REFERENCES

Burton, R., Brown, J., & Fischer, G. (1984). Skiing as a model of instruction. In B. Rogoff & J. Lave (Eds.), *Everyday cognition* (pp. 139–150). Cambridge, MA: Harvard University Press.

Caramazza, A., McCloskey, M., & Green B. (1981). Naive beliefs in "sophisticated" subjects: Misconceptions about trajectories of objects. *Cognition, 9*, 117–123.

Carey, S. (1986). Cognitive science and science education. *American Psychologist, 41* (10), 1123–1130.

Carey, S., Evans, R., Honda, M., Jay, E., & Unger, C. (1989). "An experiment is when you try it and see if it works": A study of grade 7 students' understanding of the construction of scientific knowledge. *International Journal of Science Education, 11*, 514–529.

Champagne, A., & Klopfer, L. (1984). Research in science education: The cognitive psychology perspective. In D. Holdzkom & P. Ludz (Eds.), *Research within reach: Science education*. Washington, DC: National Science Teachers Association.

Champagne, A., Klopfer, L., & Gunstone, R. (1982). Cognitive research and the design of science instruction. *Educational Psychologist, 17*, 31–53.

Chi, M., Feltovich, P., & Glaser, R. (1981). Categorization and representation of physics problems by experts and novices. *Cognitive Science, 5*, 121–152.

Clement, J. (1981). Solving problems with formulas: Some limitations. *Engineering Education, 72*(2), 158–162.

Clement, J. (1982). Students' preconceptions in elementary mechanics. *American Journal of Physics, 50*, 66–71.

Collins, A., Brown, J., & Newman, S. (1989). Cognitive apprenticeship: Teaching the craft of reading, writing, and mathematics. In L. Resnick (Ed.), *Knowing, learning, and instruction: Essays in honor of Robert Glaser* (pp. 453–494). Hillsdale, NJ: Lawrence Erlbaum Associates.

deKleer, J., & Brown, J. S. (1985). A qualitative physics based upon confluences. In D. G. Bobrow (Ed.), *Qualitative reasoning about physical systems*. Cambridge, MA: MIT Press.

diSessa, A. (1982). Unlearning Aristotelian physics: A study of knowledge-based learning, *Cognitive Science, 61*, 37–75.

Feurzeig, W., & White, B. (1983). *Development of an articulate instructional system for teaching arithmetic procedures* (BBN Report No. 5485). Cambridge, MA: Bolt, Beranek, & Newman.

Frederiksen, J., & White, B. (1992). Mental models and understanding: A problem for science education. In E. Scanlon & T. O'Shea (Eds.), *New directions in educational technology* (pp. 211–226). New York: Springer Verlag.

Glaser, R. (1984). Education and thinking: The role of knowledge. *American Psychologist, 39*(2), 93–104.

Ginnsburg, H., & Yamamoto, T. (1986). Understanding, motivation, and teaching: Comment on Lampert's "Knowing, doing, and teaching multiplication." *Cognition and Instruction, 3*(4), 357–370.

Horwitz, P. (1989). ThinkerTools: Implications for science teaching. In *The 1988 AETS yearbook. Information technology and science education* (pp. 59-70). Auburn, AL: Association for the Education of Science Teachers.

Karmiloff-Smith, A. (1988). The child as a theoretician, not an inductivist. *Mind and Language, 3*(3), 183-195.

Kozma, R. (1992, April). *Mapping external representations onto internal meaning: Toward a science of symbolic design.* Paper presented at the meeting of the American Educational Research Association, San Francisco.

Kuhn, D. (1988). *The development of scientific thinking skills.* San Diego: Academic Press.

Kuhn, T. (1970). *The structure of scientific revolutions* (2nd ed.). Chicago: University of Chicago Press.

Lampert, M. (1986). Knowing, doing, and teaching multiplication. *Cognition and Instruction, 3*(4), 305-342.

Langley, P., Simon, H., Bradshaw, G., & Zytkow, J. (1987). *Scientific discovery: Computational explorations of the creative process.* Cambridge, MA: MIT Press.

Larkin, J. H., McDermott, J., Simon, D. P., & Simon, H. A. (1980). Expert and novice performance in solving physics problems. *Science, 208,* 1335-1342.

Linn, M., Songer, N., Lewis, E., & Stern, J. (1993). Using technology to teach thermodynamics: Achieving integrated understanding. In D. Ferguson (Ed.), *Advanced technologies in the teaching of mathematics and science* (Vol. 107, pp. 5-60). Berlin: Springer- Verlag.

Mandinach, E. (1989). Model-building and the use of computer simulation of dynamic systems. *Educational Computing Research, 5*(2), 221-243.

McCloskey, M. (1983a). Intuitive physics. *Scientific American, 248*(4), 122-131.

McCloskey, M. (1983b). Naive theories of motion. In D. Gentner & A. Stevens (Eds.), *Mental models* (pp. 299-324). Hillsdale, NJ: Lawrence Erlbaum Associates.

McDermott, L. C. (1984). Research on conceptual understanding in mechanics. *Physics Today, 37,* 24-32.

Miller, F., Dillon, T., & Smith, M. (1980). *Concepts in physics* (3rd ed.). New York: Harcourt Brace Jovanovich.

Minstrell, J. (1982). Conceptual development research in the natural setting of the classroom. In M. Budd Rowe (Ed.), *Education in the 80's — Science.* Washington, DC: National Education Association.

Minstrell, J. (1989). Teaching science for understanding. In L. Resnick & L. Kloper (Eds.), *Toward the thinking curriculum: Current cognitive research* (pp. 129-149). Yearbook of the Association for Supervision and Curriculum Development. Alexandria, VA.

Ohlsson, S. (1987). Sense and reference in the design of interactive illustrations for rational numbers. In R. Lawler & M. Yazdani (Eds.), *AI and education* (Vol. 1). Norwood, NJ: Ablex.

Palincsar, A., & Brown, A. (1984). Reciprocal teaching of comprehension fostering and monitoring activities. *Cognition and Instruction, 1*(2), 117-175.

Papert, S. (1980). *Mindstorms: Computers, children, and powerful ideas.* New York: Basic Books.

Piaget, J., & Garcia, R. (1964). *Understanding causality.* New York: Norton.

Resnick, L. (1983). Mathematics and science learning: A new conception. *Science, 220,* 477-478.

Resnick, L., & Omanson, S. (1987). Learning to understand arithmetic. In R. Glaser (Ed.), *Advances in instructional psychology* (Vol. 3, pp. 41-95). Hillsdale, NJ: Lawrence Erlbaum Associates.

Rosebury, A., Warren, B., & Conant, F. (1992). Appropriating scientific discourse: Findings from language minority classrooms. *Journal of the Learning Sciences, 2*(1), 61-94.

Roth, K., & Lindquist, B. (1992, April). *Teaching for understanding in science: "But how can regular teachers do this?"* Paper presented at the meeting of the American Educational

Research Association, San Francisco.

Sabelli, N. (1992, April). *Sharing multiple complementary representations in teaching.* Paper presented at the meeting of the American Educational Research Association, San Francisco.

Schoenfeld, A. (1990). On mathematics as sense-making: An informal attack on the unfortunate divorce of formal and informal mathematics. In D. Perkins, J. Segal, & J. Voss (Eds.), *Informal reasoning and education* (pp. 311–343). Hillsdale, NJ: Lawrence Erlbaum Associates.

Schwartz, J. (1989). Intellectual mirrors: A step in the direction of making schools knowledge-making places. *Harvard Educational Review, 59*(1), 51–61.

Shayer, M., & Adey, P. (1981). *Towards a science of science teaching.* London: Heinemann.

Siegler, R. (1978). The origins of scientific thinking. In R. Siegler (Ed.), *Children's thinking: What develops?* (pp. 109–149). Hillsdale, NJ: Lawrence Erlbaum Associates.

Smith, C., Snir, J., Unger, C., & Grosslight, L. (1990, April). *Facilitating conceptual differentiation using conceptual models.* Paper presented at the meeting of the American Educational Research Association, Boston.

Trowbridge, D. E., & McDermott, L. C. (1981). Investigation of student understanding of the concept of acceleration in one dimension. *American Journal of Physics, 49*, 242–253.

Viennot, L. (1979). Spontaneous reasoning in elementary dynamics. *European Journal of Science Education, 1*, 205–221.

White, B. (1981). *Designing computer games to facilitate learning* (Tech. Rep. AI-TR-619). Cambridge, MA: Artificial Intelligence Laboratory, Massachusetts Institute of Technology.

White, B. (1983). Sources of difficulty in understanding Newtonian dynamics. *Cognitive Science, 7*(1), 41–65.

White, B. (1984). Designing computer activities to help physics students understand Newton's laws of motion. *Cognition and Instruction, 1*, 69–108.

White, B. (1989). The role of intermediate abstractions in understanding science and mathematics. *Proceedings of the Eleventh Annual Meeting of the Cognitive Science Society* (pp. 972–979). Hillsdale, NJ: Lawrence Erlbaum Associates.

White, B. (1993a). Intermediate causal models: A missing link for successful science education? In R. Glaser (Ed.), *Advances in instructional psychology* (Vol. 4, pp. 177–252). Hillsdale, NJ: Lawrence Erlbaum Associates.

White, B. (1993b). ThinkerTools: Causal models, conceptual change, and science education. *Cognition and Instruction, 10*(1), 1–100.

White, B., & Frederiksen, J. (1990). Causal model progressions as a foundation for intelligent learning environments. *Artificial Intelligence, 24*, 99–157.

White, B., & Horwitz, P. (1988). Computer microworlds and conceptual change: A new approach to science education. In P. Ramsden (Ed.), *Improving learning: New perspectives* (pp.). London: Kogan Page.

Wiser, M. (1988, April). *The differentiation of heat and temperature: An evaluation of the effect of microcomputer models on students' misconceptions.* Paper presented at the meeting of the American Educational Research Association, New Orleans, LA.

10 Concept Mapping: A Strategy for Organizing Knowledge

Joseph D. Novak
Cornell University

Concept maps are tools for organizing and representing knowledge. They include concepts, usually enclosed in circles or boxes of some type, and relationships between concepts or propositions, indicated by a connecting line between two concepts. Words on the line specify the relationship between the two concepts. We define *concept* as a perceived regularity in events or objects, or records of events or objects, designated by a label. The label for most concepts is a word, although sometimes we use symbols such as $+$ or Σ. *Propositions* are statements about some object or event in the universe, either naturally occurring or constructed. Propositions contain two or more concepts connected with other words to form a meaningful statement. Sometimes these are called semantic units.

Another characteristic of concept maps is that the concepts are represented in a hierarchical fashion with the most inclusive, most general concepts at the top of the map and the more specific, less general concepts arranged hierarchically below. The hierarchical structure for a particular domain of knowledge also depends on the context in which that knowledge is being applied or considered. Therefore, it is best to construct concept maps with reference to some particular situation or event that we are trying to understand through the organization of knowledge in the form of a concept map.

Another important characteristic of concept maps is the inclusion of *cross-links*. These are relationships between concepts in different domains of the concept map. Cross-links help us to see how some domains of knowledge represented on the map are related to each other. In the creation of new knowledge, cross-links often represent creative leaps on the part of the knowledge producer. There are two features of concept maps that are important in the facilitation of creative thinking: the hierarchical structure that is represented in a good map, and the ability to search for and characterize cross-links.

Final features that may be added to concept maps are specific examples of events or objects that help to clarify the meaning of a given concept. Figure 10.1 shows an example of a concept map that describes the structure of concept maps and illustrates the above characteristics.

Since 1964, our research program on science teaching and learning has been based on the learning psychology of David Ausubel (1963, 1968; Ausubel, Novak, & Hanesian, 1978). The fundamental idea in Ausubel's cognitive psychology is that learning takes place by the assimilation of new concepts and propositions into existing concept propositional frameworks held by the learner. The question sometimes arises as to the origin of the first concepts; these are acquired by children during the ages of birth to 3 years, when they recognize regularities in the world around them and begin to identify language labels or symbols for these regularities (Macnamara, 1982). This is a phenomenal ability that is part of the evolutionary heritage of all normal human beings. After age 3, new concept and propositional learning is mediated heavily by language, and takes place primarily by a *reception learning* process where new meanings are obtained by asking questions and getting clarification of relationships between old concepts and propositions and new concepts and propositions. This acquisition is mediated in a very important way when concrete experiences or props are available—hence the importance of "hands-on" activity for science learning with young children, but this is also true with learners of any age (Tan & Novak, in review). In addition to the distinction between the discovery learning process, where the attributes of concepts are identified autonomously by the learner, and the reception learning process, where attributes of concepts are described using language and transmitted to the learner, Ausubel made the very important distinction between rote learning and meaningful learning. Meaningful learning requires three conditions:

1. The material to be learned must be conceptually clear and presented with language and examples relatable to the learner's prior knowledge. Concept maps can be helpful to meet this condition, both by identifying large general concepts prior to instruction in more specific concepts, and by assisting in the sequencing of learning tasks though progressively more explicit knowledge that can be anchored into developing conceptual frameworks.
2. The learner must possess relevant prior knowledge. This condition is easily met after age 3 for virtually any domain of subject matter, but it is necessary to be careful and explicit in building concept

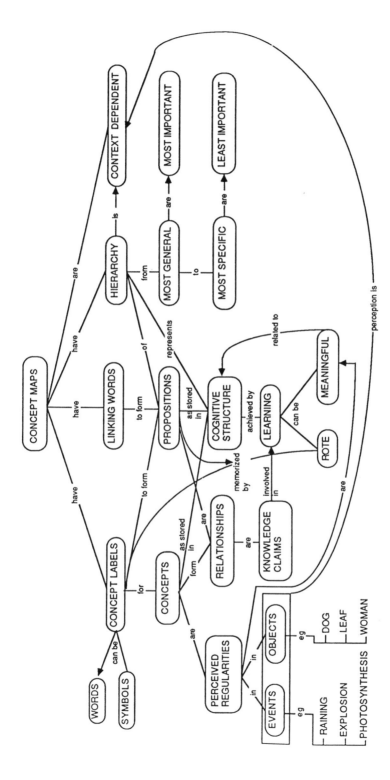

FIG. 10.1. Concept map showing the key features and ideas that are incorporated into concept maps.

frameworks if one hopes to present detailed specific knowledge in any field in subsequent lessons. We see, therefore, that conditions 1 and 2 are interrelated and both are important.

3. The learner must choose to learn meaningfully. The one condition over which the teacher has only indirect control is the motivation of students to choose to learn by attempting to incorporate new meanings into their prior knowledge, rather than simply memorizing concept definitions or propositional statements or computational procedures. The control over this choice is primarily in the evaluation strategies used, and typical objective tests seldom require more than rote learning (Holden, 1992). In fact, the worst forms of objective tests, or short-answers tests, require verbatim recall of statements, which is impeded by meaningful learning where new knowledge is assimilated into existing frameworks, making it difficult to recall specific, verbatim definitions or descriptions. This kind of problem was recognized years ago in Hoffman's *The Tyranny of Testing* (1962).

One of the powerful uses of concept maps is not only as a learning tool but also as an evaluation tool, thus encouraging students to use meaningful-mode learning patterns (Novak, 1990; Novak & Gowin, 1984). Concept maps are also effective in identifying both valid and invalid ideas held by students. They can be as effective as more time-consuming clinical interviews (Edwards & Fraser, 1983).

The important distinction between instructional approach and learning approach is illustrated in Fig. 10.2. Ideally, students would be engaged in high levels of meaningful autonomous discovery learning. In reality, this is both impractical and inefficient. Most school learning is necessarily of a reception nature, or a guided discovery nature. The use of concept mapping in instruction can facilitate both reception learning and discovery learning.

Another important advance in our understanding of learning is that the human memory is not a single "vessel" to be filled, but rather a complex set of interrelated memory systems. Figure 10.3 illustrates the three memory systems of the human mind. Although all memory systems are interdependent (and have information going in both directions), the most critical memory system for incorporating knowledge into long-term memory is the short-term or "working memory." All incoming information is organized and processed in the working memory by interaction with knowledge in long-term memory. The limiting feature here is that working memory can process only a relatively small number of psychological units at any one moment. This means that relationships among two or three concepts are about the limit of working memory processing capacity. Therefore, to

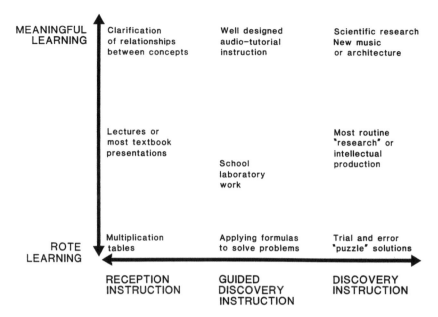

FIG. 10.2. The rote-meaningful learning continuum is distinct from the reception-discovery continuum for instruction. Both reception and discovery instruction can lead to rote learning or meaningful learning. Modified from Novak, 1977, p 101. Reproduced with permission.

structure large bodies of knowledge requires an orderly sequence of iterations between working memory and long-term memory as new knowledge is being received (Anderson, 1992). We believe one of the reasons concept mapping is so powerful for the facilitation of meaningful learning is that it serves as a kind of template to help to organize knowledge and to structure it, even though the structure must be built up piece by piece with small units of interacting concept and propositional frameworks. Many learners and teachers are surprised to see how this simple tool facilitates meaningful learning and the creation of powerful knowledge frameworks that not only permit utilization of the knowledge in new contexts, but also retention of the knowledge for long periods of time (Novak, 1990; Novak & Wandersee, 1991). Although there is still relatively little known about memory processes and how knowledge finally gets incorporated into our brain, it seems evident from diverse sources of research that our brain works to organize knowledge in hierarchical frameworks and that learning approaches that facilitate this process significantly enhance the learning capability of all learners.

Although it is true that some students have more difficulty building concept maps and using these, at least early in their experience, this appears to result primarily from years of rote-mode learning practice in school

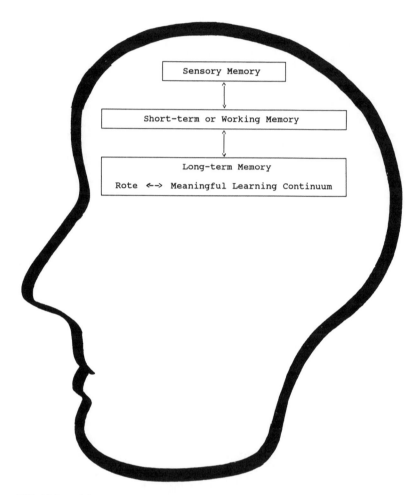

FIG. 10.3.   Schematic showing the three different memory systems that operate in human learning. In working memory, meaning construction occurs. From Novak, 1980 p. 281. Reproduced with permission.

settings rather than as a result of brain structure differences per se. So-called "learning style" differences are, to a large extent, differences in the patterns of learning that students have employed, varying from high commitment to continuous rote-mode learning to almost exclusive commitment to meaningful mode learning. It is not easy to help students in the former condition move to patterns of learning of the latter type. Although concept maps can help, students also need to be taught something about brain mechanisms and knowledge organization, and this instruction should accompany the use of concept maps.

EPISTEMOLOGICAL FOUNDATIONS

As indicated earlier, we defined concepts as perceived regularities in events or objects, or records of events or objects, designated by labels. What is coming to be generally recognized now is that the meaningful learning processes described earlier are the same processes used by scientists and mathematicians to construct new knowledge. In fact, I have argued that knowledge construction is nothing other than a relatively high level of meaningful learning (Novak, 1977, 1993). Nevertheless, the process of knowledge construction requires an interplay of a dozen or so elements that work interactively with one another during the process. D. Bob Gowin, now retired from Cornell University, invented a heuristic device to help students understand the nature of knowledge construction. Figure 10.4 shows the various elements involved in knowledge construction as represented in Gowin's Vee. We see that knowledge construction stands on "the point of the Vee" where events and objects are observed. The Vee heuristic illustrates that knowledge construction involves a framework of ideas illustrated on the left side of the Vee, as well as attitudes and values, which are used to guide the activities on the right side of the Vee. They are also used to select the events or objects to be observed, and to construct the focus questions we will ask. Our knowledge also helps determine the kind of records we will make, and frequently we draw on other domains of knowledge to construct instrumentation or to interpret results from instrumentation for making records. Much creative work in science involves clever ways to construct events or to record specific relevant data from those events. In fact, most of technology springs from the requirements that scientists have for generating events or making records of events. In the case of our research work, the tool of concept mapping sprang from the need in our cognitive learning studies to represent changes in conceptual understanding of science over a span of years (Novak & Musonda, 1991). The Vee heuristic was created as a tool in our efforts to understand why students gained so little competence in interpreting laboratory work and also tended to dislike laboratory work. When the Vee heuristic is employed with students in laboratory studies, they not only become much more successful and confident of their work, but also report more enjoyment of science labs (Robertson-Taylor, 1985).

The left side of the Vee could also be represented as a complex concept map. Figure 10.5 shows an illustration of a Vee diagram for a classroom study on the limits of short-term memory.

Other chapters in this book deal more extensively with the process of knowledge construction, but it is important to recognize that students who are taught to use concept mapping must also be taught to understand

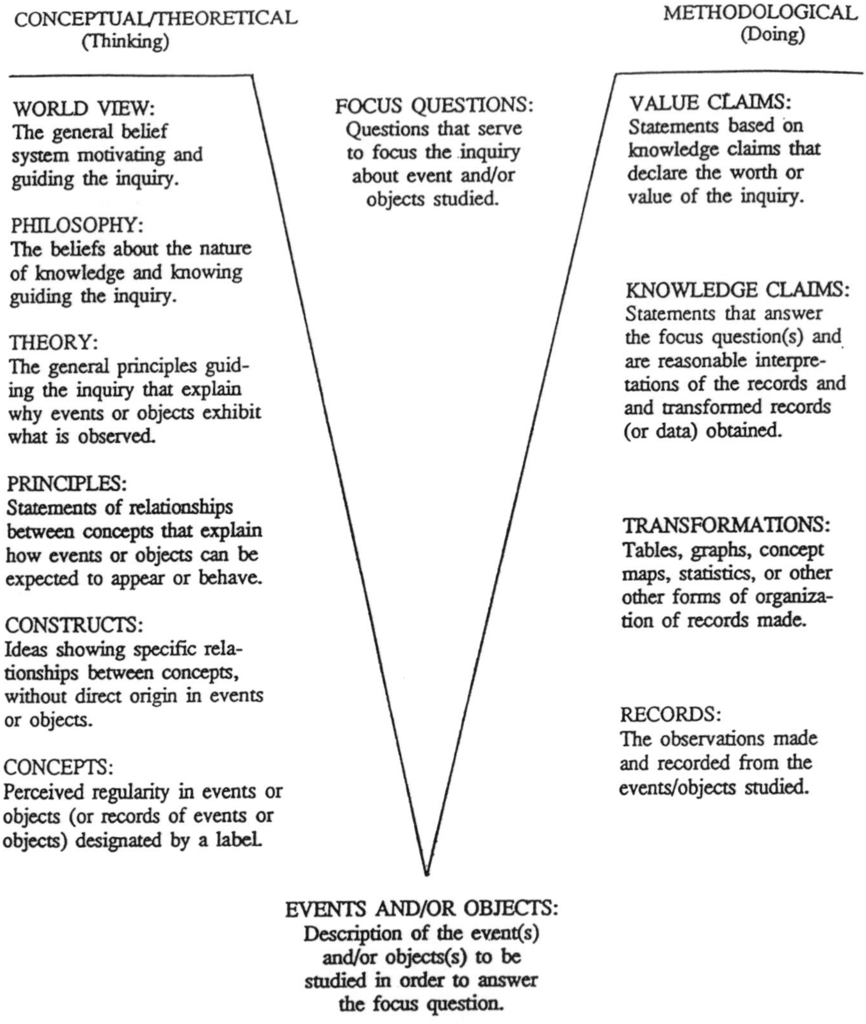

CONCEPTUAL/THEORETICAL
(Thinking)

METHODOLOGICAL
(Doing)

WORLD VIEW:
The general belief
system motivating and
guiding the inquiry.

PHILOSOPHY:
The beliefs about the nature
of knowledge and knowing
guiding the inquiry.

THEORY:
The general principles guiding the inquiry that explain
why events or objects exhibit
what is observed.

PRINCIPLES:
Statements of relationships
between concepts that explain
how events or objects can be
expected to appear or behave.

CONSTRUCTS:
Ideas showing specific relationships between concepts,
without direct origin in events
or objects.

CONCEPTS:
Perceived regularity in events or
objects (or records of events or
objects) designated by a label.

FOCUS QUESTIONS:
Questions that serve
to focus the inquiry
about event and/or
objects studied.

VALUE CLAIMS:
Statements based on
knowledge claims that
declare the worth or
value of the inquiry.

KNOWLEDGE CLAIMS:
Statements that answer
the focus question(s) and
are reasonable interpre-
tations of the records and
and transformed records
(or data) obtained.

TRANSFORMATIONS:
Tables, graphs, concept
maps, statistics, or other
other forms of organiza-
tion of records made.

RECORDS:
The observations made
and recorded from the
events/objects studied.

EVENTS AND/OR OBJECTS:
Description of the event(s)
and/or objects(s) to be
studied in order to answer
the focus question.

FIG. 10.4. Gowin's Vee heuristic, showing the epistemological elements involved in the construction of new knowledge. All elements interact with one another in the process of constructing new knowledge or value claims or in seeking understanding of these for any set of events and questions.

constructivist epistemology. Regarding this objective, "one hand washes the other," because the use of concept mapping helps students understand the constructed concept and propositional nature of knowledge, and, in turn, that understanding facilitates their skill and commitment to concept mapping.

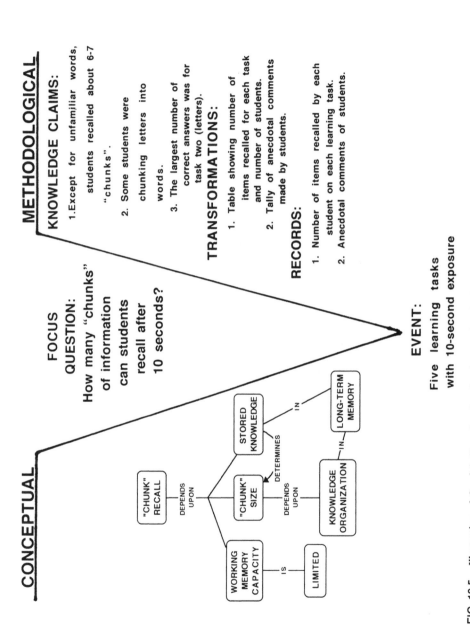

FIG. 10.5. Illustration of Gowin's Vee, showing the elements involved in understanding the limitation of short-term memory.

237

CONSTRUCTING GOOD CONCEPT MAPS

In learning to construct a concept map, it is important to begin with a domain of knowledge that is very familiar to the person constructing the map. Because concept map structures are dependent on the context in which they will be used, it is best to identify a segment of a text, a laboratory activity, or a particular problem set that one is trying to understand. This creates a context that will help to determine the hierarchical structure of the concept map. It is also helpful to select a limited domain of knowledge for the first concept maps.

Once a domain has been selected, the next step is to identify the key principles or propositions that apply to this domain. These principles could be listed, and then from this list key concepts can be extracted. Because each principle contains two or more concepts, one can simply go through the list of principles to identify the concepts. Once the key concepts are identified, a rank order should be established from the most general, most inclusive concept, for this particular problem or situation, to the most specific, least general concept. Although this rank order may be only approximate, it helps to begin the process of map construction.

The next step is to construct a preliminary concept map. This can be done by writing all of the concepts on self-adhesive notes, or preferably by using a computer software program.[1] Self-adhesive notes allow one to move concepts around easily, and this is necessary as one begins to struggle with the process of building a good hierarchical organization. Computer software programs are even better in that they allow moving of concepts together with linking statements. They also permit a computer printout that can be done in laser format, producing a nice product.

The next step is to make a preliminary concept map of the concepts identified and to label linking lines. The link words serve to form propositions from individual concepts and thus are essential to convey the meanings expressed in a concept map.

It is important to recognize that a concept map is never finished. After a preliminary map is constructed, it is always necessary to revise this map. Good maps usually undergo three to many revisions. This is one reason why computer software is helpful.

After a preliminary map is constructed, cross-links should be sought. These are links between different domains of knowledge on the map that help

---

[1]We will provide a copy of C-Map to any interested persons if they will send a 3½-inch floppy disk formatted for a Macintosh computer. Because formatting varies from computer to computer, we ask that your floppy be formatted, and we will return it with C-Map and some simple documentation for the use of this program. Please enclose $2.00 (U.S. funds) for mailing and processing.

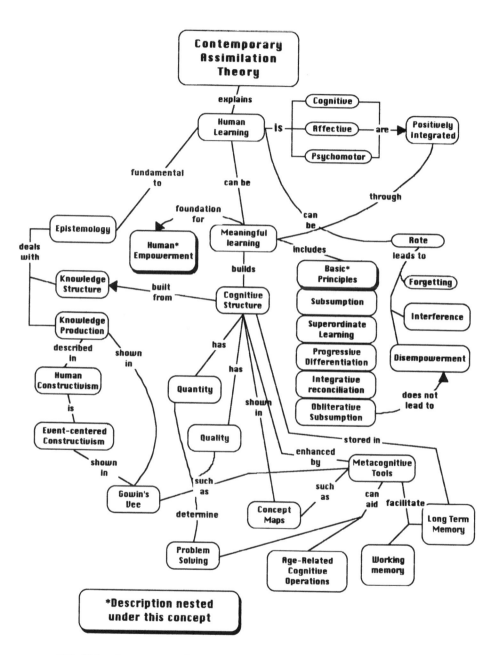

FIG. 10.6. Concept map of Ausubel's assimilation theory, showing the highly integrated set of concepts and propositions involved in his theory of cognitive learning.

to illustrate how these domains are related to one another. Finally, the map should be revised, concepts positioned in ways that lend to clarity, and a "final" map prepared. If computer software is used, one can go back and change the size and font style to "dress up" the concept map. Figure 10.6 presents a concept map using MacFlow that has the features suggested above.

It is important to help students recognize that all concepts are in some way related to one another. Therefore, it is necessary to be selective in identifying cross-links and as precise as possible in identifying linking words that connect concepts. In addition, one should avoid "sentences in the boxes" because this usually indicates that a whole subsection of the map could be constructed. "String maps" illustrate either poor understanding of the material or an inadequate restructuring of the map. Figure 10.7 shows an example of a string map.

Students often comment that it is hard to add linking words onto their concept map. This is because they only poorly understand the relationship between the concepts, and it is the linking words that specify this relationship. Once students begin to focus in on good linking words, and also identification of good cross-links, they can see that every concept could be related to every other concept. This also produces some frustration, and they must choose to identify the most prominent and most useful cross-

FIG. 10.7.   "String map" produced by a child from concept words supplied following a field trip to a paper mill. This child was an excellent oral reader, but her reading comprehension was poor. From Novak and Gowin, 1984, p. 108. Reproduced with permission.

links. This process involves what Bloom (1956) identified as high levels of cognitive performance, namely, evaluation and synthesis of knowledge. Concept mapping is an easy way to achieve very high levels of cognitive performance, when the process is done well. This is one reason concept mapping can be a very powerful evaluation tool.

MACRO AND MICRO CONCEPT MAPS

In curriculum planning, concept maps can be enormously useful. They present in a highly concise manner the key concepts and principles to be taught. The hierarchical organization of concept maps suggests more optimal sequencing of instructional material. Because the fundamental characteristic of meaningful learning is integration of new knowledge with the learners' previous concept and propositional frameworks, proceeding from the more general, more inclusive concepts to the more specific information usually serves to encourage and enhance meaningful learning. Thus, in curriculum planning, we need to construct a global "macro map" showing the major ideas we plan to present in the whole course, or in a whole curriculum, and also more specific "micro maps" to show the knowledge structure for a very specific segment of the instructional program. Figure 10.8 shows a macro map constructed by the faculty of Cornell's College of Veterinary Medicine to show the knowledge structure for the entire four-year curriculum. Figure 10.9 shows a micro map constructed to show the key ideas needed to recognize, understand, and treat a specific disease, Lyme borreliosis. The concepts of Fig. 10.9 link into the "lower level" concepts of treatment, prevention, and clinical exam on Fig. 10.8. Other links and cross-links could be identified.

Using concept maps in planning a curriculum or instruction on a specific topic helps to make the instruction "conceptually transparent" to students. Many students have difficulty identifying and constructing powerful concept and propositional frameworks, leading them to see science learning as a blur of myriad facts or equations to be memorized. If concept maps are used in planning instruction and students are required to construct concept maps as they are learning, previously unsuccessful students can become successful in making sense out of science and acquiring a feeling of control over the subject matter (Bascones & Novak, 1985; Novak, 1991).

FACILITATING COOPERATIVE LEARNING

There is a growing body of research that shows that when students work in small groups and cooperate in striving to learn subject matter, positive cognitive and affective outcomes result (Johnson, Maruyama, Johnson, Nelson, & Skon, 1981). In our work with both teachers and students, small groups working cooperatively to construct concept maps have proven to be

242

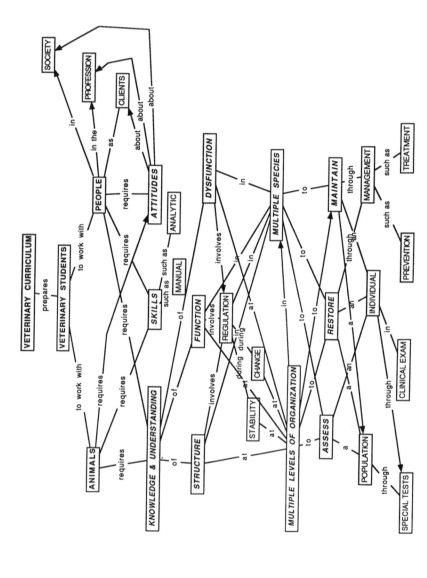

FIG. 10.8. Concept map prepared by faculty to show the major ideas in a curriculum for the Cornell College of Veterinary Medicine.

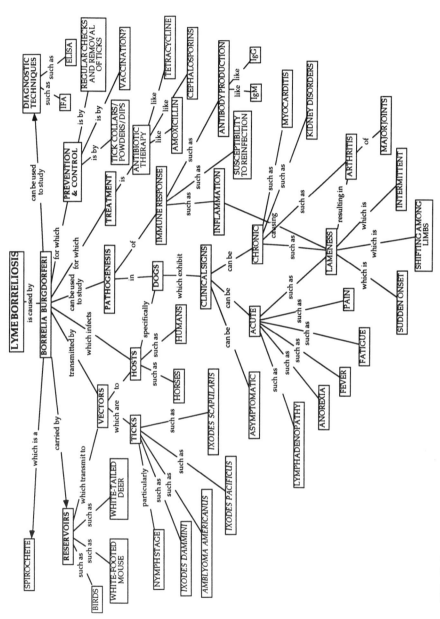

FIG. 10.9. Concept map for a very specific instructional segment in veterinary medicine dealing with Lyme borreliosis.

243

useful in many contexts. For example, the concept maps shown in Fig. 10.8 and 10.9 were constructed by faculty working together to plan instruction in veterinary medicine. In my own classes, and in classes taught by my students, small groups of students working collectively to construct concept maps can produce some remarkably good maps. In a variety of educational settings, concept mapping in small groups has served us well in tasks as diverse as understanding ideas in assimilation theory and clarifying job conflicts for conflict resolution in profit and nonprofit corporations.

CONCEPT MAPS FOR EVALUATION

We are now beginning to see in many science textbooks the inclusion of concept mapping as one way to summarize understandings acquired by students after they study a unit or chapter. Change in school practices is always slow, but it is likely that the use of concept maps in school instruction will increase substantially in the next decade or two. When concept maps are used in instruction, they can also be used for evaluation. There is nothing written in stone that says multiple choice tests must be used from grade school through university, and perhaps in time even national achievement exams will utilize concept mapping as a powerful evaluation tool. This is a chicken-and-egg problem because concept maps cannot be required on national achievement tests if most students have not been given opportunities to learn to use this knowledge representation tool. On the other hand, if state, regional, and national exams would begin to include concept maps as a segment of the exam, there would be a great incentive for teachers to teach students how to use this tool. Hopefully, before the return of Halley's comet in 2061, this will come to pass.

REFERENCES

Anderson, O. R. (1992). Some interrelationships between constructivist models of learning and current neurobiological theory, with implications for science education. *Journal of Research in Science Teaching*, 29(10), 1037–1058.

Ausubel, D. P. (1963). *The psychology of meaningful verbal learning*. New York: Grune & Stratton.

Ausubel, D. P. (1968). *Educational psychology: A cognitive view*. New York: Holt, Rinehart & Winston.

Ausubel, D. P., Novak, J. D., & Hanesian, H. (1978). *Educational psychology: A cognitive view* (2nd ed.). New York: Holt, Rinehart & Winston. Reprinted, New York: Werbel & Peck, 1986.

Bascones, J., & Novak, J. D. (1985). Alternative instructional systems and the development of problem-solving skills in physics. *European Journal of Science Education*, 7(3), 253–261.

Bloom, B. S. (1956). *Taxonomy of educational objectives — The classification of educational goals*. New York: David McKay.

Edwards, J., and Fraser, K. (1983). Concept maps as reflectors of conceptual understanding. *Research in Science Education*, *13*, 19–26.

Hoffman, B. (1962). *The tyranny of testing*. New York: Corwell-Collier.

Holden, C. (1992). Study flunks science and math tests. *Science, 26*, 541.

Johnson, D., Maruyama, G., Johnson, R. Nelson, D., & Skon, L. (1981). The effects of cooperative, competitive and individualistic goal structure on achievement: A meta-analysis. *Psychological Bulletin, 89*, 47–62.

Macnamara, J. (1982). *Names for things: A study of human learning*. Cambridge, MA: MIT Press.

Novak, J. D. (1977). *A theory of education*. Ithaca, NY: Cornell University Press.

Novak, J. D. (1980). Learning theory applied to the biology classroom. *American Biology Teacher, 45*(5), 280–285.

Novak, J. D. (1990). Concept maps and Vee diagrams: Two metacognitive tools for science and mathematics education. *Instructional Science, 19*, 29–52.

Novak, J. D. (1991). Clarify with concept maps. *Science Teacher, 58*(7), 45–49.

Novak, J. D. (1993). Human constructivism: A unification of psychological and epistemological phenomena in meaning making. *International Journal of Personal Construct Psychology, 6* 167–193.

Novak, J. D., & Gowin, D. B. (1984). *Learning how to learn*. New York Cambridge University Press.

Novak, J. D., & Musonda, D. (1991). A twelve-year longitudinal study of science concept learning. *American Educational Research Journal, 28*(1), 117–153.

Novak, J. D., & Wandersee, J. (Eds.). (1991). Special issue on concept mapping. *Journal of Research in Science Teaching, 28*, 10.

Robertson-Taylor, M. (1985). *Changing the meaning of experience: Empowering learners through the use of concept maps, Vee diagrams and principles of educating in a biology lab course*. Unpublished doctoral thesis, Cornell University.

Tan, S. K., & Novak, J. D. (in review). Students' meanings of understanding in the physics classroom. *Journal of Research in Science Teaching*.

11 Teaching Science with Analogies: A Strategy for Constructing Knowledge

Shawn M. Glynn
University of Georgia

Reinders Duit
IPN, University of Kiel, Germany

Rodney B. Thiele
Curtin University of Technology, Australia

Many of Galileo Galilei's (1564–1642) colleagues at the University of Padua in the Republic of Venice believed that the earth is standing still, not rotating on its own axis. Galileo could not accept this view. In an effort to convince Galileo, his colleagues argued that if the earth were rotating on its axis, a rock dropped from a tower would not land directly at the foot of the tower. They reasoned that if the earth were rotating, the tower would continue to move while the rock was falling through the air, with the result that the rock would hit the ground far away from the tower's foot. Because this obviously doesn't happen—the dropped rock actually lands directly at the tower's foot—the colleagues concluded that the tower and the earth could not be moving. The colleagues saw no reason to change their belief that the earth and the tower connected to it are standing still.

Galileo countered that the earth, the tower, and a rock held at the top of the tower are all moving forward with uniform velocity. When the rock is dropped, it gains downward velocity, but it doesn't give up its forward velocity. The downward and forward velocities are independent. Because the earth, tower, and rock have the same forward velocity, Galileo argued, the rock will not be left behind by the earth and tower but will land at the foot of the tower. Furthermore, he explained, because the colleagues share the forward motion of the earth, tower, and rock, they are not in a position to observe the effects of the earth's movement.

To further explain his view to his colleagues, Galileo drew on an analogy. He compared the scenario with the earth, tower, and rock to a another scenario, one involving a sailing ship. Galileo asked his colleagues to imagine a rock being dropped from the top of the ship's mast. Galileo said that, regardless of whether the ship is standing still or moving forward with constant speed in still water, the rock always lands at the foot of the mast.

The tower in the first scenario corresponds, of course, to the ship's mast. The analogy is powerful because it introduces a new feature: a ship that can be either standing still or moving. The mast, unlike the tower, is connected to the ship, a body that the colleagues can view either in motion or standing still. In either event, the dropped rock lands at the foot of the mast. By means of this powerful analogy, Galileo successfully countered the argument of his colleagues and advanced his views concerning the rotation of the earth and moving frames of reference.[1]

ANALOGIES: TOOLS FOR SCIENTIFIC THINKING

Just as they did in Galileo's time, scientists still make frequent use of analogies. In fact, throughout the history of science, analogies have played an important role in explanation, insight, and discovery (Hesse, 1966; Hoffman, 1980). It is not surprising, therefore, that science teachers and textbook authors routinely use analogies to explain complex concepts to students. Often, teachers and authors are unaware that they are using analogies — they do it automatically. Throughout their lessons, especially when responding to students' questions, teachers regularly preface their explanations with colloquial expressions such as: "It's just like," "It's the same as," "It's no different than," and "Think of it as." In textbooks, authors use more formal expressions like "Similarly," "Likewise," "Along related lines," "In comparison to," and "In contrast with." These expressions are all ways of saying, "Let me give you an analogy."

Unfortunately, teachers' and authors' analogies may do more harm than good (Duit, 1991; Gilbert, 1989; Thagard, 1992; Treagust, Duit, Joslin, & Lindauer, 1992). That is because teachers and authors, lacking guidelines for using analogies, sometimes use them unsystematically, often causing confusion and misconceptions in their students. The distinctions among a target concept, features of the concept, examples of the concept, and an analogy become blurred in students' minds. One solution, of course, would be to advise teachers and authors not to use analogy. That would be unrealistic because teachers and authors, like all human beings, are predisposed to think analogically, and they will use analogies, consciously or unconsciously, during explanation. The better solution is to introduce teachers and authors to a strategy for using analogies systematically to

---

[1]This story was based on the dialogue (p. 126) in Galileo Galilei (1632/1967, p. 126) and an interpretation of this dialogue (Unit 1, pp. 105–106) by Rutherford, Holton, & Watson (1975, Unit 1, pp. 105–106).

explain fundamental concepts in ways that are meaningful to students because the strategy allows students to construct new knowledge by comparing it to their prior knowledge.

This chapter describes the role of analogies in instruction and presents new research on the Teaching-with-Analogies model (Glynn, 1991, 1994; Glynn, Law, & Gibson, 1994). Task analyses of textbooks and exemplary teachers have been conducted to develop this model. The purpose of this model is to provide teachers and textbook authors with guidelines for constructing analogies and strategically using them during science instruction to build on what students already know. The task analyses examine how exemplary teachers and authors construct effective analogies that help students activate, transfer, and apply relevant existing knowledge when learning from textbooks.

Learning Science Meaningfully: Constructing Relations

Meaningful learning is the process of integrating new knowledge with existing knowledge (Glynn & Muth, 1994). This process is complex and is the result of an interaction of key cognitive processes, such as forming images, organizing, and drawing analogies (Anderson & Thompson, 1989). The interaction of these processes leads to the construction of conceptual relations.

Science students should not be viewed as human video cameras, passively and automatically recording the information transmitted by teachers and textbooks. On the contrary, science students are active consumers of information, "informavores" if you will, who—when learning meaningfully—will challenge the information they are presented, struggle with it, and try to make sense of it by integrating it with what they already know.

One of the questions most often asked by both new and seasoned science teachers is, "How can I help my students learn concepts meaningfully?" The answer is to help students learn concepts *relationally*, not by rote (Glynn, Yeany, & Britton, 1991). That is, students should learn concepts as organized networks of related information, not as lists of facts. Science teachers often realize this, but are not sure how to facilitate relational learning in their students, particularly when the number of students in a class is large, syllabi are rigid, time is short, and concepts are complex. Complex concepts are the rule rather than the exception in biology (e.g., photosynthesis and mitosis—meiosis), chemistry (e.g., chemical equilibrium and atomic structure), physics (e.g., gravitational potential energy and electromagnetic induction), earth science (e.g., plate tectonics and precipitation), and astronomy (e.g., the sun and planetary motion). In one form or another, many of these concepts are introduced to children in the elementary school years; by high school, all students are expected to be scientifically literate, that is, to understand complex concepts such as these. So teachers at all levels play a critical role in ensuring that students have a meaningful (relational) understanding of fundamental science concepts. To be successful in this role, teachers need powerful instructional strategies.

Strategies for Learning Conceptual Relations

Studies of experts and novices in fields such as physics (Chi, Feltovich, & Glaser, 1981) and biology (Feltovich, 1981) have shown that experts are experts, not just because they know more facts than novices, but because their knowledge exists in the form of interrelated networks. The relations in and among conceptual networks are of many kinds, including hierarchical, exemplifying, attributive, causal, correlational, temporal, additive, and adversative. In an expert, these relations contribute to a high-performance human "information-processing system." This system includes a working-memory component, analogous to a small cognitive workbench on which only a few cognitive operations can be performed at a time, and a long-term memory component, analogous to a set of file cabinets or a computer hard disk. Long-term memory provides raw material (knowledge) for working-memory operations and stores the products of those operations. The construction of conceptual relations enhances an expert's working-memory and long-term memory performance. Because the expert's knowledge is relational, it is easily stored, quickly retrieved, and successfully applied. Unfortunately, a student's knowledge is all too often rote learned, the consequence of which is a system of knowledge that is easily forgotten and is not readily transferable to new, related situations that the student may encounter.

Teachers and textbook authors need powerful instructional strategies to help develop a student's information processing system into that of an expert. *Concept mapping* (Novak, 1990) and *teaching with analogies* (Glynn, 1991) are two such strategies. Concept mapping facilitates the learning of relations within a conceptual network. But what about relationships among different, but in some ways similar, conceptual networks? How can teachers and authors develop such relationships and use them to bridge conceptual networks? Teaching with analogies can provide answers to these questions.

TEACHING WITH ANALOGIES: NEED FOR A MODEL

The role of analogical thinking in teaching and learning science has received increasing attention in recent years (Brown, 1993; Clement, 1989, 1993;

Gentner, 1989; Lawson, 1993). Research findings suggest that teachers and text authors often use analogies, but use them ineffectively (Duit, 1991; Duit & Glynn, 1992; Glynn, Britton, Semrud-Clikeman, & Muth, 1989; Halpern, 1987; Halpern, Hansen, & Riefer, 1990; Thagard, 1992; Thiele & Treagust, 1991; Treagust et al., 1992; Vosniadou & Schommer, 1988). Sometimes the analogies that teachers and textbook authors use to explain new concepts are clear and well developed, but at other times they are vague and confusing. Teachers and textbook authors need a model to guide their construction of instructional analogies systematically. Analogies could then be custom tailored to suit students' own background knowledge. In response to this need, research on a Teaching-with-Analogies model was initiated (Glynn, 1989a, 1989b, 1991; Glynn et al., 1989; Harrison & Treagust, 1993; Thiele & Treagust, 1991).

Definition of Analogy

In the Teaching-with-Analogies model, an analogy is drawn by identifying similarities between two concepts. In this way, ideas can be transferred from a familiar concept to an unfamiliar one. The familiar concept is called the *analog* and the unfamiliar one the *target*. Both the analog and the target have *features* (also called *attributes*). If the analog and the target share common or similar features, an analogy can be drawn between them. A systematic comparison, verbally or visually, between the features of the analog and target is called a *mapping*.

An abstract representation of an analogy, with its constituent parts, appears in Fig 11.1. As can be seen in Fig. 11.1, the analog and target often are examples of a *superordinate* (higher order or cross-domain) concept.

An example of an analogy can be found in the high school textbook, *Physical Science* (Alexander et al., 1988), in which the familiar concept *bookcase* is the analog and the concept *Bohr's model of the atom* is the target. In the context of Rutherford's earlier model and Schrödinger's later one, Bohr's model is explained in the following way:

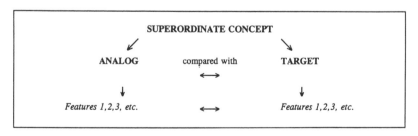

FIG. 11.1.   Abstract representation of an analogy, with its constituent parts. Analog features are mapped onto target features. The analog and target are subordinate to a superordinate concept.

According to the Bohr model, the electrons in an atom are not whirling around the nucleus in a random way. Instead, electrons move in paths. Each path is a certain distance from the nucleus. Compare Bohr's model to a bookcase. . . . Just as each shelf is a certain distance from the floor, each path is a certain distance from the nucleus. Also, the distance between one path and the next is not the same for each path, just as the shelves in some bookcases are not the same distance from each other. The paths in which electrons circle the nucleus are called energy levels. Electrons are found in energy levels, not between them, just as books are found on bookcase shelves, not floating between shelves. (p. 85)

An analogy can be drawn between the bookcase and the atom because they share the similar features mapped in Fig. 11.2. Although a word mapping of features is sometimes sufficient for an analogy to be drawn, additional graphic or pictorial mappings are desirable because they activate the cognitive process of forming mental images. Students also can form better representations of the analogy. Figure 11.3 depicts the analogy in pictorial form.

The analog (bookcase) and the target (Bohr's atom) are examples of a superordinate concept we call a *tiered holding system*. Often, it is hard to identify and label the superordinate concept in an analogy that spans different conceptual domains. In such cases, teachers and textbook authors should try to create a verbal label, even when it sounds a bit peculiar.

It is worth the trouble to identify and name the cross-domain superordi-

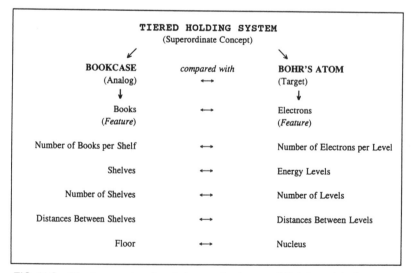

FIG. 11.2.   Word-mapped analogy between a bookcase and Bohr's model of an atom. The superordinate concept is "tiered holding system."

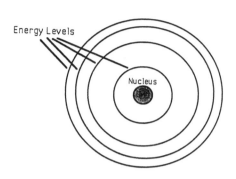

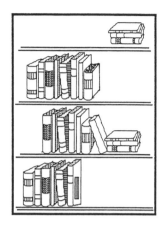

FIG. 11.3.   Pictorial analogy between a bookcase and Bohr's model of an atom.

nate concept because that concept can suggest subordinate concepts that also can be used as analogs. For example, concepts subordinate to "tiered holding system" include "ladder" and "staircase." Depending on the purposes of the teacher or author, these could be better analogs than a bookcase.

No analog maps onto the target perfectly; if the target and analog were identical, they would be the same concept. Every analog breaks down at some point, and no two analogs are alike. For these reasons, teachers and authors should try to suggest several analogs to students. Each analog has its corresponding and noncorresponding features; some analogs will be better for some purposes than others. For example, if the purpose is to demonstrate, by analogy, how an electron in a generic atom undergoes de-excitation, a staircase analog can be more useful than a bookcase. The staircase represents an atom and the steps represent the possible energy levels that an electron can occupy (see Fig. 11.4). A ball falling from step to step represents an electron undergoing the process of de-excitation. A similar but more detailed version of this analogy is described by Jordan, Watson, and Scott (1992). When teaching university general-studies astronomy and physics classes, they used a specially constructed set of stair steps as an analog for a generic atom. The instructor — taking the role of an electron — jumps from a lower step to a higher one or vice versa. Jordan et al. explained:

Each step represents a possible energy level that an electron can have in our atom. The lowest energy level is on the floor and represents the ground state. The highest energy level is located at the top step. The region between the steps represents the differences in the energies of the two levels. This region is painted with a color that represents the wavelength of the energy—the photon—emitted by the atom as an electron changes orbits or steps. On the front is the color of the transition to the next step (state). On the side are colors that represent wave-lengths of photons emitted by the atom as electrons change their orbits (step) to the ground state, as well as to other energy levels. (p. 42)

Our stair-steps model, like an atom, has discrete energy values. . . . The person playing the role of the electron must be on one step (energy level) or another, not between steps. Our generic atom, in other words, is quantized. This simple analogy gives students a better understanding of what is going on inside an atom.

An instructor plays the role of an electron in an atom that is undergoing the process of de-excitation. When he jumps from the top step to the middle step, he will emit a photon (throw a ping-pong ball) with the energy and wave-length (color) equivalent to the difference between the two steps. (p. 44)

Jordan et al. cautioned that their stair-step analog is simple and far from a true representation of an atom. At the same time, they believed the analog serves its purpose well in providing a visual demonstration of how energy is released during de-excitation in an atom.

In summary, when students are provided several analogs—such as the bookcase and staircase analogs of the Bohr atom—they can focus on the target concept from several perspectives and thereby come to a more complete understanding of the target. Furthermore, when students are thinking in terms of several analogs, they are less likely to equate any one analog with the target. The additional analogs need not be developed in the

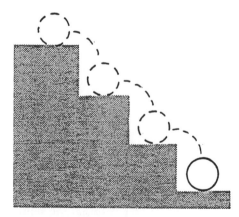

FIG. 11.4. A ball falling down a staircase is similar to an electron in an atom that is undergoing the process of de-excitation.

same detail as the primary analog. A sentence or two emphasizing their unique features often will be sufficient.

The identification and labeling of a superordinate concept can prompt students to generalize and transfer what they have learned to other related concepts, not just features. That allows us to expand the earlier definition of an analogy: An analogy is a process of identifying similarities among two or more concepts. In other words, an analogy may involve an entire family of concepts, with concepts varying in the degree of family resemblance they share among themselves.

Analogical Transfer: Bridging Concepts

An effective analogy puts new ideas into terms already familiar to students. An analogy drawn by a teacher or author between a concept covered earlier in a course and one covered later is particularly effective because there is some assurance that the earlier concept is familiar to every student. For example, in *Conceptual Physics*, Hewitt (1987) explained the concept *gravitational potential energy* in Chapter 8 and used it again in Chapter 33 to introduce students to the concept *electrical potential energy*:

> Recall from Chapter 8 the relation between work and potential energy. Work is done when a force moves something in the direction of the force. An object has potential energy by virtue of its location, say in a force field. For example, if you lift an object, you apply a force equal to its weight. When you raise it through some distance, you are doing work on the object. You are also increasing its gravitational potential energy. The greater the distance it is raised, the greater is the increase in its gravitational potential energy. Doing work increases its gravitational potential energy.

> In a similar way, a charged object can have potential energy by virtue of its location in an electric field. Just as work is required to lift an object against the gravitational field of the earth, work is required to push a charged particle against the electric field of a charged body. (It may be more difficult to visualize, but the physics of both the gravitational case and the electrical case is the same.) The electric potential energy of a charged particle is increased when work is done to push it against the electric field of something else that is changed. (pp. 501–502)

Ideally, an analogy effectively drawn between two concepts will help students transfer their existing knowledge to the understanding, organizing, and visualizing of new knowledge. The result is often a high order, relational understanding; that is, the students see how the features of a concept fit together and how the concept in question connects to other concepts. Students will be more likely to generalize their understanding to a superordinate concept, such as that of potential energy. They also will be more likely to transfer their understanding to other instances of the superordinate concept, such as elastic potential energy and chemical potential energy, and see the similarities among different examples of potential energy, such as a lifted stone, a charged battery, a drawn arrow, and an unstruck match.

Effectiveness of an Analogy: Shared Features

The effectiveness of an analogy generally increases as the number of similar features shared by the analog and target increases. For example, teachers and textbook authors have traditionally used a camera as an analog to describe the structure and function of the human eye, because the two concepts share so many similar features. Consider the following excerpts from Hewitt's (1987) *Conceptual Physics*:

> In many respects the human eye is similar to the camera. The amount of light that enters is regulated by the *iris*, the colored part of the eye which surrounds the opening called the *pupil*. Light enters through the transparent covering called the *cornea*, passes through the pupil and lens, and is focused on a layer of tissue at the back of the eye — the *retina* — that is more sensitive to light than any artificial detector made. . . . In both the camera and the eye, the image is upside down, and this is compensated for in both cases. You simply turn the camera film around to look at it. Your brain has learned to turn around images it receives from your retina!

> A principal difference between a camera and the human eye has to do with focusing. In a camera, focusing is accomplished by altering the distance between the lens and the film. In the human eye, most of the focusing is done by the cornea, the transparent membrane at the outside of the eye. Adjustments in focusing of the image on the retina are made by changing the thickness and shape of the lens to regulate its focal length. This is called *accommodation* and is brought about by the action of the *ciliary muscle*, which surrounds the lens. (pp. 450–451)

The analogy between the camera and the eye is a powerful one because the analog and the target share many features shared by the two concepts. The camera is an effective analog, however, only when students are familiar with its many features, especially those related to its internal structure. Hewitt ensured his students' familiarity with the features of the camera by explaining its components in a section titled "Some Common Optical Instruments" that preceded the section on "The Eye."

Another powerful analogy, one with many corresponding features, is that between a mechanical pump and the human heart. Many authors and teachers assume that students are familiar with the features of a pump. This assumption is often unjustified. Students might well be familiar with the pump-to-heart analogy, but that doesn't mean they have a clear understanding of how a pump works. Regardless of an analog's many shared features and frequent connection with a target concept, authors and teachers should always take the time to ensure that students are familiar with the features of the analog before they attempt to draw an analogy. This may be done using pictorial analogies where possible, providing a clear description of the relevant analog features, and, in the classroom setting, questioning the students concerning aspects of the analog prior to mapping the shared features.

It is possible to draw a good analogy on the basis of a few similar features, or even one feature, if it is directly relevant to the goal of instruction. For example, consider the following analogy from Smallwood and Green's (1968) chapter on "The Molecules of Life" in their high school textbook, *Biology*:

> Most carbohydrate molecules can be compared to a freight train that is made up of boxcars linked together. Carbohydrate molecules are usually long chains of simple sugars bonded together. We call these large carbohydrate molecules **polysaccharides**. (p. 54)

The preceding analogy is simple; the train and boxcars correspond to the carbohydrate molecule and the sugars, respectively. Despite its simplicity, the analogy is effective because it maps a familiar mental picture (a freight train) onto the target concept (a carbohydrate molecule). The analogy helps the students to quickly visualize the general structure of the molecule.

The instructional value of an analogy decreases if it is difficult to identify and map the important features shared by the analog and the target. For example, consider this explanation of gravity and "black holes" in a physical science textbook:

> To understand black holes, astronomers study what happens when gravity is very strong. An object with a huge mass has such strong gravity that it bends space around it. The curved space bends any light that passes by. (Pasachoff, Pasachoff, & Cooney, 1983, p. 466)

The teacher's edition to this textbook provides teachers with the following question and analogy, presumably to aid them in their explanation of the effects of gravity:

> Is space curved or does gravity "pull on" the light? Analogy: two men walk side by side, ten feet apart, each perpendicular to the equator. To their

surprise, they collide upon reaching the north pole. Question: Did gravity pull them together, or is the earth curved? (p. 467)

The answer to the preceding question is clear: The earth is curved. But what is not clear is how the features of the analog—two men walking apparently parallel to each other and perpendicular to the equator until they collide at the north pole—correspond to the target concept, the effect of gravity on space and light. In this analogy, there is a strong likelihood that misconceptions will be formed.

Misconceptions Caused by Analogy: The Dark Side

The advantage of teaching with analogy is that it capitalizes on students' relevant existing knowledge. Learning becomes relational rather than rote, and therefore it is more meaningful. Like playing with an Erector set, the process of joining new knowledge to existing knowledge is intrinsically motivating. Analogical thinking is also efficient, helping us to understand new phenomena and solve new problems by drawing on our past experiences. This is the bright side of analogical thinking. There is a dark side as well. When students overgeneralize and map noncorresponding features of concepts, misconceptions can result (Thagard, 1992). This dark side of analogical thinking is an unfortunate fact of life.

On the first day of a science course, some high school teachers and college professors routinely advise their students: "Forget what you think you know about how the world works. You'll learn how it really works in this course." These professors and teachers have a poor understanding of how students learn meaningfully. Meaningful learning requires that students' existing knowledge be taken into account, not ignored. Conceptual bridges must be built between existing knowledge and new knowledge; analogy plays an important role in the construction of these bridges. Trying to avoid analogy is, to use another analogy, like throwing the baby out with the bath water. Human beings seem to have a natural bent for analogical thinking; we are, in effect, "hard wired" to think analogically. Even very young children reason analogically, as illustrated by Jean Piaget's (1962) observation of his daughter Jacqueline when she was 2 years and 10 months old:

J. had a temperature and wanted oranges. It was too early in the season for oranges to be in the shops and we tried to explain to her that they were not yet ripe. "They are still green. We can't eat them. They haven't yet got their lovely yellow color." J. seemed to accept this, but a moment later, as she was drinking her camomile tea, she said, Camomile isn't green, it's yellow already. . . . Give me some oranges. (p. 231)

Effective teachers and textbook authors capitalize on analogical thinking rather than ignore it. They make systematic use of analogy and emphasize to students that analogical thinking is powerful, but limited, and that wrong ideas can arise when an analogy is carried too far. For example, Miller, Dillon, and Smith (1980), in their textbook *Concepts in Physics*, explained to students:

> Models and analogies can be of great value in physics if they are used with care and discrimination. It is important, for example, to guard against the danger of believing that a model or analogy is an exact representation of some physical system. One should always regard a model critically and remember that an analogy means no more than: under certain special conditions, the physical system being studied behaves as if . . . (p. 253)

Analogies are double-edged swords. An analog can be used to explain and even predict some aspects of the target concept; however, at some point, every analogy breaks down and, if the analogy is carried beyond that point, misconceptions may begin to form. Because two concepts are never completely identical, differences always exist among their defining features. For example, consider an analogy used to explain drug overdose from a chapter on "Drugs and Behavior" in the high school textbook, *Biology: An Everyday Experience* by Kaskel, Hummer, and Daniel (1988). One of the accompanying figures is of a partially stoppered sink, with water flowing into the sink and out of it at the same rate. The other figure is of an overflowing sink, with more water flowing into it than can drain out. The explanation in the text reads:

> The body balances the amount of drug entering and leaving it. Think of the water going into the sink as a drug entering the body. The leaking stopper stands for the organ removing the drug. If the water entering the sink is equal to the water leaving it, the water will not overflow. Nor will the sink become empty. The same type of thing happens with a correct drug dose. With the proper drug dose, the amount of drug entering the body equals the amount leaving it.

> What happens if a person does not take the correct drug dose? A drug overdose could result. An *overdose* is the result of too much of a drug in the body. Let's look at the sink example again. [The figure] shows what might lead to a drug overdose. Too much of a drug is added to the body. The body cannot get rid of the drug fast enough, and a drug overdose results. (p. 332)

The preceding analogy, drawn between water in a sink and a drug in the body, could easily lead to a misconception. Although the authors note, "Drugs taken into the body soon leave it or change into a different form," the analog nevertheless promotes the misconception that a prescription or nonprescription drug flows through the body without interacting physically and chemically with its constituents. Unless cautioned otherwise by the authors or teachers, students could assume that a drug such as alcohol poses few risks if it flows through them and soon exits in urine.

A careful examination of all features of an analogy is a prerequisite to using it effectively in instruction. When teachers and authors use an analogy, they should anticipate analogy-caused misconceptions and elimi-nate them by pointing out to students where the analogy breaks down. Teachers should engage their students in a discussion in which the limita-tions of the analogy are identified.

TEACHING-WITH-ANALOGIES MODEL: RESEARCH AND DEVELOPMENT

Research on a Teaching-with-Analogies model began with a task analysis of elementary school, middle school, high school, and college science text-books; the analysis identified how 43 textbook authors used analogies to explain new concepts to students (Glynn, 1991; Glynn et al., 1989). The task analysis of textbooks has now been supplemented by an analysis of the lessons of exemplary science teachers (Glynn, 1994; Glynn et al., 1994).

Task Analysis: A Research Method

A knowledge acquisition technique, *task analysis*, was used in the present research "with the intent of modelling an individual expert's thinking" (Wiggs & Perez, 1988, p. 267). A task analysis (Gagne, 1985; Gardner, 1985), also called a procedural analysis, is a technique that "identifies and structures the basic processes that underlie task performance . . . trying to document the basic processes that are involved in performing a cognitive task" (Goetz, Alexander, & Ash, 1992, p. 360). A task analysis of how experts perform a cognitive task leads to a representation of the experts' knowledge and, eventually, to a model of the task that includes the operations carried out in the performance of the task. For example, a task analysis of expert writers led Flower and Hayes (1981) to a model of competent expository writing; the model has subsequently played an important role in the instruction of novice writers (Hayes & Flower, 1986). Likewise, in our research, task analyses of science textbooks and exemplary teachers have led to a model for teaching with analogies—a model that provides less experienced authors and teachers with guidelines on how to use analogies effectively.

Research Findings: Analogies in Textbooks

A task analysis was conducted on the analogies in 43 elementary school, high school, and college textbooks (see Glynn, 1991; Glynn et al., 1989). The sentences comprising the analogies in each textbook were examined. For each sentence, or group of topically related sentences called statements, the question was asked: "What is the author's intention here?" This question, alternatively stated, is: "What operation in support of the analogy is the author performing?" The statements were sorted into categories on the basis of perceived similarity, and the categories were labeled in terms of the operations they represented. A summary of these data for all textbooks indicated that the statements fell into six main categories. These categories and the operations they represent are shown in Table 11.1. Together, these six operation form the basis of the Teaching-with-Analogies model. The order of the six operations listed in Table 11.1 is only approximate. The authors actually varied with respect to the order in which they carried out operations, the number of operations they carried out, and the number of times they carried out any given operation.

Although all of the textbook authors were considered to be experts, the analysis identified the analogies drawn by Hewitt (1987), author of *Conceptual Physics*, as being among the best. He consistently used the six operations listed in Table 11.1, and drew analogies not only between concepts, but between principles and formulas as well. For example, in *Conceptual Physics*, he drew a detailed analogy between Newton's law of gravitation and Coulomb's law of electrical force. A graphic map of this analogy appears in Fig. 11.5.

In his text, Hewitt introduced the target concept, Coulomb's law, by reminding students of the analog concept, Newton's law, which he had explained in an earlier chapter:

> Recall from Newton's law of gravitation that the gravitational force between two objects of mass m_1 and mass m_2 is proportional to the product of the masses and inversely proportional to the square of the distance d between them: $F = G (m_1 m_2/d^2)$, where G is the universal gravitational constant. (pp. 482–483)

TABLE 11.1
Operations in the Teaching-with-Analogies Model

1. Introduce target concept.
2. Cue retrieval of analog concept.
3. Identify relevant features of target and analog.
4. Map similarities.
5. Indicate where analogy breaks down.
6. Draw conclusions.

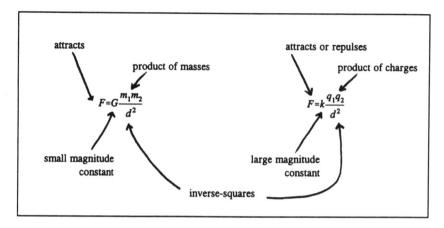

FIG. 11.5. Comparison of two inverse-square laws: Newton's law of gravitation and Coulomb's law of electrical force.

Hewitt did not just remind students of the analog, Newton's law; he briefly retaught it, identifying the key features in the analog. Hewitt knew that some students will have forgotten Newton's law, entirely or in part, and they will not take the time to flip back to the earlier chapter, so he refreshed their memory for them. Next, Hewitt identified the features of the target concept, Coulomb's law:

> The electrical force between any two objects obeys a similar inverse-square relationship with distance. . . . **Coulomb's law** states that for charged particles or objects that are small compared to the distance between them, the force between the charges varies directly as the product of the charges and inversely as the square of the distance between them. The role that charge plays in electrical phenomena is much like the role that mass plays in gravitational phenomena. Coulomb's law can be expressed as: $F = k (q_1q_2/d^2)$ where d is the distance between the charged particles; q_1 represents the quantity of charge of one particle and q_2 the quantity of charge of the other particle; and k is the proportionality constant. (p. 483)

Then Hewitt mapped the similar features of the concepts. He was careful to point out where the analogy breaks down. By doing so, he reduced the likelihood that students will overgeneralize from the analog to the target concept and form some misconceptions:

> The proportionality constant k in Coulomb's law is similar to G in Newton's law of gravitation. Instead of being a very small number like G, the electrical proportionality constant k is a very large number. . . . So Newton's law of gravitation for masses is similar to Coulomb's law for electric charges. Whereas the gravitational force of attraction between a pair of one-kilogram

masses is extremely small, the electrical force between a pair of one-coulomb charges is extremely large. The greatest difference between gravitation and electrical forces is that while gravity only attracts, electrical forces may either attract or repel. (pp. 483–484)

Finally, Hewitt drew main conclusions for students about both the target concept (electrical force) and the analog (gravitational force):

Because most objects have equal numbers of electrons and protons, electrical forces usually balance out. Any electrical forces between the earth and the moon, for example, are balanced. In this way the much weaker gravitational force, which attracts only, is the predominant force between astronomical bodies.

Although electrical forces balance out for astronomical and everyday objects, at the atomic level this is not always true. The negative electrons of one atom may at times be closer to the positive protons of a neighboring atom than to the electrons of the neighbor. Then the attractive force between these charges is greater than the repulsive force. When the net attraction is sufficiently strong, atoms combine to form molecules. The chemical bonding forces that hold atoms together to form molecules are electrical forces acting in small regions where the balances of attractive and repelling forces are not perfect. (pp. 484–485)

To illustrate the implications of his conclusions, Hewitt provided students with a computational example in which he compared the electrical and gravitational forces between the proton and the electron in a hydrogen atom. By means of this example, he showed students that the electrical force in the hydrogen atom is much greater than the gravitational force — so much so, that the gravitational force is negligible. Hewitt also pointed out to students that the similarity between the law of gravitational force and the law of electrical force may point the way to new discoveries in science:

The similarities between these two forces have made some physicists think they may be different aspects of the same thing. Albert Einstein was one of these people; he spent the later part of his life searching with little success for a "unified field theory." In recent years, the electrical force has been unified with the "weak force," which plays a role in radioactive decay. Physicists are still looking for a way to unify electrical and gravitational forces. (p. 484)

Hewitt's use of analogies is exemplary, but many authors use analogies ineffectively. The task analysis of 43 science textbooks revealed many instances in which authors suggested a sketchy analogy to students, and then abandoned the analogy, leaving students to make sense (or nonsense) out of it for themselves. Under these conditions, students could identify irrelevant features of the target and analog concepts, map these features, fail to realize where the analogy breaks down, and draw wrong conclusions about the target and analog. In other words, the misguided use of analogies by some authors could actually promote misconceptions in students.

Research Findings: Teachers' Analogies

The task analysis of textbook analogies was supplemented by a task analysis of the lessons of 10 exemplary science teachers (see Glynn, 1994; Glynn et al., 1994). The exemplary science teachers were from public middle and elementary schools. The teachers were identified as exemplary by means of awards and the judgments of principals, other teachers, and university teacher educators. All classes were multicultural, with 18–25 students in each class. The lessons were observed and videotaped; a task analysis of the lessons was conducted. The teachers later reenacted their lessons in a video studio and were asked to explain the decisions they made during the course of their lessons (using methods and instructions described in Afflerbach & Johnston, 1984; Glynn, Muth, & Britton, 1990; Muth, Glynn, Britton, & Graves, 1988).

Each teacher was asked to "select a lesson and make the best possible use of analogy-based activities to elaborate on a key concept that the students had read about in their textbooks." For example, one of the teachers, Martha Gilree, taught an earth science lesson on the structure of the earth. She baked layered cupcakes for her students and explained that the cupcakes were analogs of the earth, with the four layers corresponding to the crust, mantle, outer core, and inner core of the earth. Using straws, the students took "core samples" from the cupcakes, examined the samples, and compared them to representations of the earth in their textbooks.

Another teacher, Joe Conti, taught a biology lesson on natural selection and the concept of survival of the fittest. He took his children outside to an area of green grass where earlier he had scattered an equal number of green, brown, and red uncooked noodles. He explained that the noodles were analogs for different colored grasshoppers and that the students were hungry birds who preyed on the grasshoppers. The students "caught as many grasshoppers" as they could in the next 5 minutes and returned to the classroom, where a tally revealed that fewer green grasshoppers were caught than brown, and fewer brown than red. Joe then explained to his students how a trait such as coloration can increase or decrease the probability a species will survive in a given environment.

Still another teacher, Becky Wheeler, taught a physical science lesson on optics. She and her students built a simple, working camera and she used this camera to explain optic principles. She then explained that the camera is an analog for the human eye and, using a physical model of the eye, she compared its features to those of the camera. She then went on to teach the optics principles common to the camera and eye.

A task analysis was conducted on the videotaped statements and actions that made up the lessons of the 10 exemplary teachers. In each lesson, a statement was one to a few sentences on either a target concept (e.g., the eye), an analog concept (e.g., the camera), or a conceptual feature (e.g., the lens). For each statement, the question was asked: "What operation is the teacher performing?" The statements were sorted into categories, tallied, and summarized for all teachers.

The teachers were found to use the six operations that the authors did, in addition to several others. For example, some identified concepts that are superordinate to the target and analog concepts: The science of optics is superordinate to the concepts of eye and camera. These operations were relevant to the analogies, but not essential, so they were not added to those already in the Teaching-with-Analogies model (see Table 11.1).

Thirty-five sample statements and the six corresponding operations for the lesson on optics taught by Becky Wheeler are presented in Table 11.2. (The operation numbers in Table 11.2 correspond to those in Table 11.1). Becky Wheeler, like the other teachers, carried out the operations in an order that roughly corresponds to the order in Table 11.1. The teachers' statements, which were spontaneous and oral, were more difficult to categorize than the written statements of the authors. The content and grammar of the teachers' statements were less structured and precise than those of the authors. In addition, the teachers' statements frequently included questions that the students were asked to answer; after the students answered, the teacher then provided feedback. For example, Becky Wheeler mapped similarities (Operation 4) between an eye and a camera and asked students to draw conclusions (Operation 6): "Think about the parts we just talked about . . . an eyelid. . . . What could we compare the eyelid to on this camera? [The students responded "Shutter!"] Yes, the shutter." As a result of this interactive questioning, two-operation statements were more common among teachers than authors.

As can be seen in Table 11.2, the primary analogy is drawn between a camera and the human eye; however, it is important to note that there are secondary analogies as well. These include comparing the eyeball to a ping-pong ball, the optic nerve fibers to a cable, and the eye itself to a plastic model and to a traffic light. The other lessons were similar in this respect: Each included a primary analogy, but also made use of several related, secondary analogies.

Research Implications

The task analyses of textbooks and exemplary teachers indicated that, in actual practice, the order in which the six operations are carried out can

TABLE 11.2
Becky Wheeler's Lesson on Optics: Statements and Corresponding Operations

One of the things we're going to learn today is what the eye looks like. [Operation 1]

If I were to take out my eye or anyone else's eye and put it on a plate, they'd look pretty much the same; they'd be about the same size. [Teacher shows ping-pong ball; Operations 2 and 3]

What do you call the eye, generally? How would you refer to the eye if you took it out like this? Yes, an eyeball. [Operation 2]

We call it a ball because it's round and actually this ping-pong ball is about the same size as the eye. [Operations 3 and 4]

How many of you think you know what this is? [Teacher shows a glass lens; Operation 2]

Actually, if you wanted to know what the eye looks like, the lens of it looks like this. [Operation 3]

Now, it's not exactly the same material because the eye is made of soft tissue and this is made of glass. It looks a lot like this but it's not this big; this is much bigger. [Operation 5]

Okay, let's look at a model of our eye. [Teacher shows plastic model of eye; Operation 2]

We can see this white part, which is sort of a tough tissue and it's called the sclera. [Operation 3]

You can see this bulging part. Put your finger on your eye and move it right and to the left. Can you feel the bulge? Who knows what that bulge is called? Yes, the cornea. [Operation 3]

The part that goes around the pupil and changes the size of the hole is the iris—that controls the amount of light and changes the size of the pupil. [Operation 3]

Actually, it can get as tiny as the end of a pencil and as large as about the size of the eraser on the other end. [Teacher shows and compares pencil features; Operations 2 and 4]

The clear transparent part on the front is called the aqueous humor. [Operation 3]

Inside your eye is a gel-like solution called the vitreous humor and it helps to give the eye its shape. [Operation 3]

The light has to come in; it goes through the pupil . . . and finally it gets to the back of the eye. What is that called? Okay, the retina. [Operation 3]

A lot of times we compare the eye to a camera. [Operation 2]

Think about the parts we just talked about . . . an eyelid . . . what could we compare the eyelid to on this camera? Yes, the shutter. [Teacher shows and compares camera; Operations 4 and 6]

On the camera, what do you have that controls the light that goes into it, comparable to the iris that controls the amount of light going into the eye? Yes, the aperture. [Operations 4 and 6]

The lens, we said, is an important part of the eye; and of course, the camera has a lens [Operation 4]

You told me that you have a retina on the back of your eye that's light sensitive? What do you have that controls the light that goes into it, comparable to the iris that controls the amount of light going into the eye? Okay, light sensitive paper—the film. [Operations 4 and 6]

On our retinas we have special nerve cells that can pick up black and white color. These are called rods, and we have some cells called cones that pick up colors. So on a camera, what do you think we could use to compare to the rods? [Operations 4 and 6]

Now the optic nerve in our eye takes the message to the brain; you know the camera doesn't have that. [Operation 5]

(Continued)

TABLE 11.2 (Continued)

Okay, the vitreous humor—that's part of the eye, but it's not a part of the camera. [Operation 5]

Does anyone know what I have here? A pinhole camera. [Teacher shows homemade, tube-like pinhole camera; Operation 2]

What do you think this part, the shutter, would be compared to? Yes, the eyelid. [Operations 4 and 6]

Then we've got the little pinhole, the aperture; what could we compare that to? The pupil, the iris working together. [Operations 4 and 6]

On the very back, we have the light-sensitive paper; what part of the eye would you compare that to? Yes, the retina. [Operations 4 and 6]

Okay, there's a wonderful part of your eye that controls the lens—so that the lens in your eye is different from the lens in a camera. In the lens in a camera you have to have a way of adjusting it to make it focus, but the lens in our eye has special muscles called ciliary muscles. They can make the lens flat and they can make the lens thin. [Operation 5]

Okay, the retina on the back of the eye is different from the film of the camera because it's very small. . . . [Operation 5]

It's actually about the size of a postage stamp. [Operations 2 and 4]

All of the nerve fibers come together and form something like a cable; that is where the optic nerve attaches. [Operations 2 and 4]

[Teacher shows poster of traffic signal and eye; string represents light rays.] All of the light rays are coming from this red light . . . when it comes it's straight and when it gets to this area, it is going to bend so that it ends up here on the back of the eye. [Operation 2]

Now, what has happened to the image? Yes, it's turned upside-down. [Operation 6]

[Teacher shows a glass lens.] This is just like the lens in your eye: Light travels in a straight line, comes through the lens. [Operation 2]

Look at me through this lens; how do I appear to you? [Students look and see upside-down image of teacher; Operation 6]

Note. See Table 11.1 for descriptions of Operations 1–6.

vary. It is usually important, however, for the teacher or textbook author to perform all of the operations. If the teacher or textbook author were to perform only some of the operations, leaving some to the student, it is possible that the student might fail to perform an operation or might perform it poorly. The result could be that the student will misunderstand the concept being taught. Misunderstanding is less likely to occur, of course, when teachers and authors have explained the operations in the Teaching-with-Analogies model to their students and cautioned them about the limitations of analogies.

It is reasonable to assume that teachers and textbook authors will use the process of analogy more effectively if they keep the Teaching-with-Analogies model in mind. They can mentally check off the six operations in the model when constructing an analogy to explain a new concept. When an author doesn't perform some of the operations in the model and the analogy suffers as a result, the teacher can perform them for the students. Or, when the author's analogy is effective and the teacher wants to extend it, the teacher can use the model for this purpose, thus increasing the instructional value of the analogy.

The teacher also can modify the model in response to student characteristics and instructional goals. Harrison and Treagust (1993) carried out an extensive case study in which an experienced science teacher was trained with the Teaching-with-Analogies (TWA) model and used it to teach a lesson on optics and the refraction of light. Harrison and Treagust modified the model by reversing the order of the final two operations (see Table 11.1). As noted previously, the order of the operations varies in practice. Regarding the effectiveness of the model, they concluded:

> Based on the data collected over four lessons . . . it is asserted that in this instance, with this teacher, a systematic approach like the modified TWA model is a practical and achievable means for improving the use of analogies in science classrooms. . . . At the conclusion of three episodes during which Mrs. Kay used the modified TWA model, she appeared to be competent and fluent in its use and the students responded positively to the resultant analogical instruction. As shown by this data, there was a consistently high level of understanding encountered during the interviews. In the described lesson, Mrs. Kay felt that the students had understood refraction better than on any previous occasion that she had taught this concept. Based on our studies with this teacher and five other teachers, it is predicted that the majority of practicing teachers would require extended practice combined with critical feedback in order to integrate the modified TWA model into their pedagogical repertoire. (p. 1293)

Teachers also are encouraged to use the model to construct additional analogies to complement an author's analogy. Several analogies constructed for the same concept can help the students view the target concept from different perspectives. The analogies function like conceptual lenses, with each one bringing different features of the concept into sharper focus. For example, several analogies can be used to discuss views of how galaxies are arranged in the universe:

> Astrophysicists closing in on the grand structure of matter and emptiness in the universe are ruling out the meatball theory, challenging the soap bubble theory and putting forward what may be the strongest theory of all: that the cosmos is organized like a sponge.

> This new concept holds that a surprisingly complex arrangement of clustered galaxies stretches in connected tubes and filaments from one end of the universe to the other and that galaxy-free voids form an equally complex, equally well-connected structure.

> Far more rapidly than was possible a few years ago, scientists are assembling data from the most distant galaxies to produce a picture of the universe's

structure. The sponge idea is meant to resolve a clash between views of the universe as clumps of matter on an empty background (the meatball concept), or as empty voids carved out of a full background (the bubbles concept). ("Sponge concept," 1986, p. 7)

All three analogies—meatball, soap bubble, and sponge—are useful in explaining views of how galaxies are arranged. These views are similar but have some important differences. Each analogy, with its particular constellation of features, has its own explanatory power.

FUTURE DIRECTIONS FOR RESEARCH: STUDENT-GENERATED ANALOGIES

The research described in this report has focused on how teachers and textbook authors can construct effective analogies to help students comprehend textbook concepts. Future research also will focus on determining how students can construct effective analogies for themselves, independently of teachers and textbook authors. Research and development will be carried out on a modified form of the Teaching-with-Analogies model called the *Learning-with-Analogies model*. It is anticipated that students who are taught how to use a Learning-with-Analogies model will be able to interpret, criticize, and extend analogies provided by authors and teachers.

A lively class discussion in which an analogy is dissected by students who understand the Learning-with-Analogies model could help students to better understand the target concept and, at the same time, help the teacher to diagnose misconceptions the students might have. For example, middle-school teachers sometimes compare baking a cake to the process of photosynthesis (Glynn, 1989b). This analogy helps teachers to identify those students who mistakenly believe that plants get their food directly from the soil (i.e., eating "plant food") rather than making their own food from raw materials in the air and soil (i.e., water and carbon dioxide). Most students have seen their mother baking a cake and therefore are familiar with the analog. By asking students to explain how baking a cake is like photosynthesis, teachers identify students who have misconceptions about photosynthesis. Teachers then use the analog to correct the misconception. This analogy, like all analogies, breaks down at various points, and teachers can use these points to further assess students' true understanding of the target, photosynthesis.

Students could use a Learning-with-Analogies model as a guide when constructing their own analogies. For example, students seeking an alternative to the baking-a-cake analog for photosynthesis might use a building-a-house analog to construct their own analogy: raw materials (lumber +

nails + shingles) + energy from a carpenter = final product (house) + waste products (sawdust + scrapwood). The final and waste products correspond to sugar and oxygen, respectively (see Kaskel et al., 1988, pp. 360–362, for a detailed version of this analogy).

Even when authors and teachers have provided analogies for a particular concept, it is advantageous for students to construct their own analogies because then students must use their own relevant knowledge. This ensures that the analogies will be meaningful. In addition, students who can construct their own analogies become more independent in their learning. They can tackle new concepts on their own, using analogical reasoning as a way of understanding those concepts.

CHAPTER SUMMARY

Just as in Galileo's time, the science teachers and textbook authors of today routinely use analogies to explain complex concepts to students. Unfortunately, teachers' and authors' analogies may do more harm than good. Lacking guidelines for using analogies, teachers and authors sometimes use them unsystematically, causing confusion and misconceptions in their students.

This chapter provided an overview of the Teaching-with-Analogies model, a strategy that uses analogies systematically to explain fundamental concepts in ways that are meaningful to students. This model, developed from task analyses of textbooks and exemplary teachers, provides guidelines for strategically using analogies during science instruction. The model shows how exemplary teachers and authors help students to activate, transfer, and apply relevant existing knowledge when learning new knowledge.

Task analyses of textbooks and exemplary teachers' lessons revealed six operations that ideally should be carried out when teaching with analogies:

1. Introduce target concept.
2. Cue retrieval of analog concept.
3. Identify relevant features of target and analog.
4. Map similarities.
5. Indicate where analogy breaks down.
6. Draw conclusions.

Textbook authors and teachers will use analogies more effectively if they keep the six operations of the Teaching-with-Analogies model in mind.

Any given analogy has its own strengths and limitations. Several analogies constructed for the same concept can help the students to view the target concept from different perspectives. The analogies function like conceptual lenses, with each one bringing different features of the concept into sharper focus.

Future research will focus on determining how students can construct effective analogies for themselves, independently of teachers and textbook authors. Research and development has begun on a variation of the Teaching-with-Analogies model called the Learning-with-Analogies model. It is anticipated that students who are taught how to use the Learning-with-Analogies model can better interpret, criticize, and extend analogies provided by authors and teachers. Students can also use the Learning-with-Analogies model as a guide when constructing their own analogies.

ACKNOWLEDGMENTS

The work reported herein was prepared with partial support to the first author from the National Reading Research Center (NRRC) of the Universities of Georgia and Maryland. It was supported under the Educational Research and Development Centers Program (PR/Award no. 117A20007) as administered by the Office of Educational Research and Improvement, U.S. Department of Education. The findings and opinions expressed here do not necessarily reflect the position or policies of the National Reading Research Center, the Office of Educational Research and Improvement, or the U.S. Department of Education. An earlier version of this work was published by the first author as an NRRC Reading Research Report, No. 15, Spring 1994, Athens, GA: Universities of Georgia and Maryland.

REFERENCES

Afflerbach, P., & Johnston, P. (1984). Research methodology: On the use of verbal reports in reading research. *Journal of Reading Behavior, 16*, 307–322.

Alexander, P., Fiegel, M., Foehr, S. K., Harris, A. F., Krajkovich, J. G., May, K. W., Tzimopoulos, N., & Voltmer, R. K. (1988). *Physical science.* Lexington, MA: Silver, Burdett & Ginn.

Anderson, J. R., & Thompson, R. (1989). Use of analogy in a production system architecture. In S. Vosniadou & A. Ortony (Eds.), *Similarity and analogical reasoning* (pp. 267–297). Cambridge: Cambridge University Press.

Brown, D. E. (1993). Refocusing core intuitions: A concretizing role for analogy in conceptual change. *Journal of Research in Science Teaching, 30*, 1273–1290.

Chi, M. T. H., Feltovich, P. J., & Glaser, R. (1981). Categorization and representation of physics problems by experts and novices. *Cognitive Science, 5*, 121–152.

Clement, J. (1989). Learning via model construction and criticism. In J. A. Glover, R. R. Ronning, & C. R. Reynolds (Eds.), *A handbook of creativity: Assessment, theory, and research* (pp. 341–381). New York: Plenum.

Clement, J. (1993). Using bridging analogies and anchoring intuitions to deal with students' preconceptions in physics. *Journal of Research in Science Teaching, 30,* 1241-1257.

Duit, R. (1991). On the role of analogies and metaphors in learning science. *Science Education, 75,* 649-672.

Duit, R., & Glynn, S. M. (1992). Analogien und Metaphern, Brücken zum Verständnis im schülergerechten Physikunterricht [Analogies and metaphors, bridges to understanding in student-oriented physics instruction]. In P. Häußler (Ed.), *Physikunterricht und Menschenbildung* (pp. 223-250). Kiel, Germany: Institut für Pädagogik der Naturwissenschaften.

Feltovich, P. J. (1981). *Knowledge based components of expertise in medical diagnosis* (Tech. Rep. No. PDS-2). Pittsburgh: University of Pittsburgh Learning Research and Development Center.

Flower, L. S., & Hayes, J. R. (1981). A cognitive process theory of writing. *College Composition and Communication, 32,* 365-387.

Gagne, R. M. (1985) *The conditions of learning and theory of instruction.* New York: Holt.

Galilei, G. (1967). *Dialogue concerning the two chief world systems — Ptolemaic & Copernican* (S. Drake, Trans.). Berkeley, CA: University of California Press. (Original work 1632)

Gardner, M. K. (1985). Cognitive psychological approaches to instructional task analysis. In E. W. Gordon (Ed.), *Review of research in education* (pp. 157-196). Washington, DC: American Educational Research Association.

Gentner, D. (1989). The mechanisms of analogical learning. In S. Vosniadou & A. Ortony (Eds.), *Similarity and analogical reasoning* (pp. 199-241). Cambridge: Cambridge University Press.

Gilbert, S. W. (1989). An evaluation of the use of analogy, simile, and metaphor in science texts. *Journal of Research in Science Teaching, 26,* 315-327.

Glynn, S. M. (1989a, January). *Conceptual explanations in high school physics textbooks: A Teaching-with-Analogies model.* Paper presented at the meeting of the American Association of Physics Teachers, San Francisco.

Glynn, S. M. (1989b). The Teaching-with-Analogies (TWA) model: Explaining concepts in expository text. In K. D. Muth (Ed.), *Children's comprehension of text: Research into practice* (pp. 185-204). Newark, DE: International Reading Association.

Glynn, S. M. (1991). Explaining science concepts: A Teaching-with-Analogies model. In S. M. Glynn, R. H. Yeany, & B. K. Britton (Eds.), *The psychology of learning science* (pp. 219-240). Hillsdale, NJ: Lawrence Erlbaum Associates.

Glynn, S. M. (1994, April). *Analogy: Conceptual tool for teaching science.* Paper presented at the meeting of the American Educational Research Association, Anaheim, CA.

Glynn, S. M., Britton, B. K., Semrud-Clikeman, M., & Muth, K. D. (1989). Analogical reasoning and problem solving in science textbooks. In J. A. Glover, R. R. Ronning, & C. R. Reynolds (Eds.), *A handbook of creativity: Assessment, theory, and research* (pp. 383-398). New York: Plenum.

Glynn, S. M., Law, M., & Gibson, N. (1994, March). *Teaching-with-Analogies: Task analyses of exemplary science teachers.* Paper presented at the meeting of the National Association for Research in Science Teaching, Anaheim, CA.

Glynn, S. M., & Muth, K. D. (1994). Reading and writing to learn science: Achieving scientific literacy. *Journal of Research in Science Teaching, 31,* 1057-1073.

Glynn, S. M., Muth, K. D. & Britton, B. K. (1990). Thinking out loud about concepts in science text: How instructional objectives work. In H. Mandl, E. De Corte, S. N. Bennett, & H. F. Friedrich (Eds.), *Learning and instruction: European research in an international context* (Vol. 2, pp. 215-223). Oxford, England: Pergamon Press.

Glynn, S. M., Yeany, R. H., & Britton, B. K. (1991). A constructive view of learning science. In S. M. Glynn, R. H. Yeany, & B. K. Britton (Eds.), *The psychology of learning science* (pp. 3-19). Hillsdale, NJ: Lawrence Erlbaum Associates.

Goetz, E. T., Alexander, P. A., & Ash, M. J. (1992). *Educational psychology.* New York:

Merrill.

Halpern, D. (1987). Analogies as a critical thinking skill. In D. Berger, K. Pezdek, & W. Banks (Eds.), *Applications of cognitive psychology* (pp. 75–86). Hillsdale, NJ: Lawrence Erlbaum Associates.

Halpern, D. F., Hansen, C., & Riefer, D. (1990). Analogies as an aid to understanding and memory. *Journal of Educational Psychology, 82,* 298–305.

Harrison, A. G., & Treagust, D. F. (1993). Teaching with analogies: A case study in grade-10 optics. *Journal of Research in Science Teaching, 30,* 1291–1307.

Hayes, J. R., & Flower, L. S. (1986). Writing research and the writer. *American Psychologist, 41,* 1106–1113.

Hesse, M. B. (1966). *Models and analogies in science.* Notre Dame, IN: University of Notre Dame Press.

Hewitt, P. G. (1987). *Conceptual physics.* Menlo Park, CA: Addison-Wesley.

Hoffman, R. R. (1980). Metaphor in science. In R. P. Honeck & R. R. Hoffman (Eds.), *Cognition and figurative language* (pp. 393–423). Hillsdale, NJ: Lawrence Erlbaum Associates.

Jordan, T. M., Watson, J., & Scott, R. (1992). The stair-step atom. *Science Teacher, 59*(1), 42–46.

Kaskel, A., Hummer, P. J., & Daniel, L. (1988). *Biology: An everyday experience.* Columbus, OH: Merrill.

Lawson, A. E. (1993). The importance of analogy: A prelude to the special issue. *Journal of Research in Science Teaching, 30,* 1213–1214.

Miller, F., Dillon, T. J., & Smith, M. K. (1980). *Concepts in physics.* New York: Harcourt Brace Jovanovich.

Muth, K. D., Glynn, S. M., Britton, B. K., & Graves, M. (1988). "Thinking out loud" during text study: Attending to important ideas. *Journal of Educational Psychology, 80,* 315–318.

Novak, J. D. (1990). Concept mapping: A useful tool for science education. *Journal of Research in Science Teaching, 27,* 937–949.

Pasachoff, J. M., Pasachoff, N., & Cooney, T. M. (1983). *Physical science.* Glenview, IL: Scott, Foresman.

Piaget, J. (1962). *Play, dreams, and imitation in childhood.* New York: Norton.

Rutherford, F. J., Holton, G., & Watson, F. G. (1975), *Project physics.* New York: Holt, Rinehart & Winston.

Smallwood, W. L., & Green, E. R. (1968). *Biology.* New York: Silver Burdett.

Sponge concept of universe replaces meatball, soap bubble theories. (1986, November 9). *The Atlanta Journal and Constitution,* p. 7a. (reprinted from *The New York Times*)

Thagard, P. (1992). Analogy, explanation, and education. *Journal of Research in Science Teaching, 29,* 537–544.

Thiele, R. B., & Treagust, D. F. (1991). Using analogies in secondary chemistry teaching. *Australian Science Teachers Journal, 37*(2), 10–14.

Treagust, D. F., Duit, R., Joslin, P., & Lindauer, I. (1992). Science teachers' use of analogies: Observations from classroom practice. *International Journal of Science Education, 14,* 413–422.

Vosniadou, S., & Schommer, M. (1988). Explanatory analogies can help children acquire information from expository text. *Journal of Educational Psychology, 80,* 524–536.

Wiggs, C. L., & Perez, R. S. (1988). The use of knowledge acquisition in instructional design. *Computers in Human Behavior, 4,* 257–274.

12 Science Textbooks: Their Present Role and Future Form

Arthur Stinner
The University of Manitoba, Canada

> The research on textbook quality indicated that there is little
> good to say about an instructional tool that is relied on so
> heavily. . . . There was little text devoted to science, technol-
> ogy, and society issues; scientific literacy; inquiry; . . . and
> concepts were not placed in historical context. Elementary
> texts required reasoning beyond the capabilities of the stu-
> dents.
>
> . . . It strikes me that looking for ways to improve a method
> of instruction that has been consistently proven to be less
> successful than other methods is a strange activity for science
> educators. . . . Responsible science educators should not ca-
> pitulate to poor practice because it is the reality. They should
> continue to argue for good practice and conduct research that
> makes the implementation of that practice easier for teachers.
> (Baker, 1991, p. 367)

Baker (1991) made the foregoing observations following a summary of
research on textbooks in the journal *Science Education*. Baker's observations are consistent with a widely held view that in science teaching the
textbook plays a dominant role and dictates both what is taught in science
and how it is taught (Shymansky & Kyle, 1992; Wheatley, 1991; Yager,
1983, 1992; Yore, 1991). Ten years ago, Yager (1983) summarized research
on science textbooks. His conclusions seem to be, to a large extent, as valid
today as they were then. He stated that the most significant decision science
teachers make is the choice of a textbook. Yager argued that textbooks

275

imprison science teachers in a belief that the instructional sequence of assign, recite, and test is guaranteed to produce knowledge. He went on to emphasize that direct experience is almost never offered, and laboratory work, if it occurs at all, is of the deductive-verification type. He claimed that high reliance on textbooks does not seem to produce scientifically and technologically literate graduates. Yager concluded cryptically that "The status of science education can be summarized in a single word: textbooks" (Yager, 1983, p. 578).

One of the serious shortcomings of most textbooks seems to be that they implicitly or explicitly promote the empiricist-inductivist picture of science, namely, the belief that laws and discoveries are a guaranteed consequence of systematic observation that is based on a specifiable scientific method (Shelley, 1989; Stinner, 1989; Yager, 1983). Another shortcoming of many textbooks is the implication that a clearly presented lesson that is based on the instructional mode of lecture, question, and answer is guaranteed to produce knowledge. Moreover, textbooks in general are content driven. Chiapetta, Sethna, and Fillman (1991) examined chemistry textbooks and found that "all of the chemistry textbooks deemphasize science as a way of thinking" (p. 949). They argued that if content coverage drives chemistry courses, students will not become scientifically literate in the broad sense recommended by the National Science Teachers Association.

Historians and philosophers of science, however, tell us that scientific concepts and theories do not follow from observation in a simple inductivist manner and that scientists in fact study a world of which they are a part, and not a world from which they are apart. This picture of science requires that students learn to look at scientific data with their ideas that are based on their personal experience and understanding. At the same time, cognitive scientists tell us that knowledge is actively constructed by the child and not passively received from the environment (Driver, 1989; Hewson & Thorley, 1989). Learning is now generally seen as an adaptive process in which the learner's conceptual schemes are progressively reconstructed in keeping with a wider range of experiences (Driver, 1989).

A discernible shift is now taking place in how science educators and science teachers view the relevance of recent findings in the history and philosophy of science (Arons, 1989; Jordan, 1989; Rohrlich, 1988; Stinner, 1992). An equally important shift is occurring in how science educators view the nature of the learning process (Kyle, 1991; O'Loughlin, 1992). There is even evidence that these important findings and views are becoming known to classroom science teachers and textbook authors.

Why have such important findings and arguments about the nature of science and the nature of the learner not made a greater impact on science textbook authors and on science teachers? In trying to answer this question, Shymansky and Kyle (1992) reminded us, "most science education research produces knowledge in the context of a system clinging to tradition" (p. 756). One important aspect of this tradition is connected to the prevalent use of textbooks.

A textbook-centered science teaching culture rests on two presuppositions: that there is a specifiable scientific method that guarantees success, and that the expert is able to break down the content into teachable units that can be sequenced for the consumption of the learners. The learners therefore are indoctrinated into an unskeptical acceptance of an inductivist-empiricist picture of science. Moreover, learning is seen as a slow accumulation of knowledge through practice, where the learner is assumed to be, in the John Locke tradition, a *tabula rasa* (Wheatley, 1991). Science teachers learn their science from textbooks and obtain their early teaching practices in textbook-oriented classrooms. They then teach from textbooks that largely emphasize memorization of scientific facts in an ongoing rhetoric of information.

This chapter examines two parallel views, those of Thomas Kuhn and William Whewell, of the role of science textbooks. Kuhn's insightful and influential comments about the role of the textbook in science education are compared with William Whewell's ideas about good pedagogy in physics education. Thomas Kuhn is a leading contemporary historian and philosopher of science, whereas William Whewell was the premier British philosopher of science of the nineteenth century who wrote the first important physics textbooks. Both were deeply concerned about how students learn concepts in science education and both had a great deal to say about the relationship between what may be called the *logical plane of activity* and the *evidential plane of activity* of science. It is argued that good science teaching not only has to pay more attention to how these planes are related but also must recognize and respect the third plane of activity, namely, the *psychological plane of activity*. Later, a conceptual model (Stinner, 1992) that relates these three planes of activity is presented. Many researchers have found that a sound understanding of science concepts generally cannot be developed from textbook use alone (Baker, 1991; Loewenberg-Ball & Feiman-Nemser, 1988; Renner, Grybowski, & Marek, 1990). In the following sections I expand on the foregoing and conclude with some plausible recommendations for improving the future form of science textbooks.

WILLIAM WHEWELL AND THE FIRST PHYSICS TEXTBOOKS

The first widely used textbooks in elementary physics in the English-speaking world were written by William Whewell. In the preface of his *An*

Elementary Treatise of Dynamics (first published in 1823), he especially complimented the continental mathematicians for their analytical skills "in compressing the whole science into a few short formulae" (Whewell, 1850, p. 41). In spite of this tribute, Whewell was deeply concerned about the seductive powers of the finished product of mathematics in the teaching of physics. He argued that students should learn concepts outside the grip of a mathematical formulation. He thought that if they did not struggle through appropriate arguments based on intuition, space, and geometry first, they would only "learn to reason by means of symbols . . .; and by means of the general rules of combining and operating upon such symbols; without thinking of anything but these rules" (Whewell, 1850, p. 41).

Whewell put his pedagogical principle into practice of placing intuition, geometric reasoning, and prealgorithm discussion before the finished product of mathematical formulation. Although it is arguable that textbooks in physics that followed were modeled after his, many of Whewell's pedagogic devices to explicate concepts prior to the presentation of the finished product were dropped. In these later textbooks (see, e.g., *Natural Philosophy* by John Sangster, 1864), authors first stated the principles, definitions, and laws and then, sequencing the problems, asked students to work them out as an exercise.

In contrast to Whewell's treatment, extensive discussion of the origin of and the evidential basis for mathematical formulations was discontinued. In these texts, example problems are worked out to illustrate the application of formulas. It seems that "post-Whewellian" texts are the prototypes for today's physics texts, and they may have set the tone for the format of science texts in general.

SCIENCE TEACHING AND SCIENCE TEXTBOOKS

The teaching of science in general and of physics in particular has been a textbook-centered affair in the English-speaking world since Whewell's textbooks appeared in the 1820s. To be sure, we have made some progress since then. Most modern textbooks attempt to provide the student with a link between what is considered an established scientific fact of a topic and the concrete level of evidential and experiential support given to it. However, science textbook writers as well as science teachers seem to emphasize the finished product of scientific fact and mathematical formulation in the teaching of physical science. Students, in turn, are trapped by the efficiency of memorizing the scientific fact and the efficacy of applying the formulas in solving exercise problems. The correct solution of the exercise problems then provides evidence for the teacher of the teaching effectiveness, and it gives the student a sense of confirmation of mastery and understanding of the material (Hewitt, 1990; Stinner, 1992; von Baeyer, 1990).

This overemphasis of the mathematical formulation of a topic at the expense of the appropriate evidence to support it is apparent in the study of the physical sciences, especially in elementary physics. Former science (physics) students will no doubt remember in particular solving countless problems by using formulas based on laws, principles, and definitions, and performing experiments to verify these laws. Newton's second law, for example, has been proved by generations of students, whether this proof involved the use of Atwood's machine, Fletcher's trolley, or the use of the electronic air table. Newton's first law, the textbook may have told us, is just a special case of the second law. But does that follow deductively? Can we perform experiments to "prove" the first law? Did Newton use inductive reasoning in arriving at these laws? If so, how is it that his laws are used as one would use a deductive system in geometry, as Whewell, among others, insisted could be done?

The historically oriented Harvard Project Physics series does consider such questions, but most textbooks seldom do. If they occasionally do occur, then the answers to them are given in footnotes, or in brief historical references, but they are seldom seriously discussed. Science teachers in general, of course, are the product of textbook-centered teaching. It is therefore not surprising that they, too, tend to bypass such questions.

Moreover, there is evidence to indicate that many students studying science see little connection between their experiences and ideas about the world and what they learn in science textbooks (von Aufshnaiter & Schwedes, 1989). One suspects at the outset that what lies at the heart of this problem is a sense of disconnectedness between the logic of the textbook and what counts for the student as good reasons for believing the science that is presented.

TEXTBOOK-CENTERED TEACHING AND NORMAL SCIENCE

Thomas Kuhn argued in his influential work *The Structure of Scientific Revolutions* that textbook-centered teaching provides the basis for initiation into the normal science activity of the working scientist. Indeed, according to Kuhn, textbooks are pedagogic vehicles for the perpetuation of normal science. He stressed that scientists seem to "agree about what it is that every student of the field must know" (Kuhn, 1962, p. 44). Though it is generally true that different science textbooks in a given science display different subject matter, they do not differ in substance and conceptual structure.

Moreover, Kuhn believed that scientists learn their science through a study of the application of a theory to some concrete range of natural phenomena, and "never learn concepts, laws, and theories in the abstract and by themselves" (1962, p. 46). Similarly, he maintained that students of physics learn physics by studying specific applications and concrete examples—what he calls *exemplars*—or "the concrete problem-solutions that students encounter from the start of their scientific education, whether in laboratories, on examinations, or at the end of chapters in science texts" (1962, p. 46). Kuhn noted that rarely do we find in textbooks a description of the sort of problems that the professional may be asked to solve.

Both Kuhn and Whewell promote frequent contact between the logical-mathematical and the evidential-experiential levels of activity when engaged in sequencing problems. Whewell argued for premathematical experience as evidence for an underlying rule. Kuhn, on the other hand, seemed to emphasize postmathematical formulation, by way of exemplars, to demonstrate the wide applicability of an underlying rule.

For Kuhn, the contact between the two planes of activity meant being engaged in solving problems based on the commonly recognized exemplars of a science. It should be stressed, however, that Kuhn did not see this activity as the kind of algorithmic problem solving that seems to be at the heart of conventional science (physics) teaching. Rather, he argued that "by doing problems the student learns consequential things about nature" (p. 188). In elementary physics, for example, these are the problems that are related to such exemplars as the inclined plane, billiard ball collisions, the conical pendulum, and Atwood's machine. These problems, Kuhn insisted, should be developed and sequenced so that the laws (e.g., Newton's second law, $F = ma$) are not seen as a finished product of mathematical formulation to be committed to memory and then applied to problems algorithmically. Rather, Kuhn argued that students should learn to think of such laws as symbolic generalizations that gain new meanings in different contexts.

This suggests that Newton's second law, for example, could be introduced first in middle school as a verbal statement given by students. These statements should be based on students' own experiences, observations, and intuitive understanding related to motion that can be easily studied, such as the motion of cars and the motion of dynamic carts. The law then could be reintroduced in senior high school, beginning with a proportionality statement, followed by Newton's own version, namely, as force (unbalanced) in terms of rate of change of momentum, and later as the familiar $F = ma$. The context now is shifted to well-designed experiments, such as the motion of a dynamic cart being pulled by a constant tension that is attached to a ticker timer. Finally, in college, students are introduced to yet another level of symbolic generalization of this law, namely, a differential equation, in connection with the solution of the period of a pendulum.

Unfortunately, Kuhn's argument that "doing problems is learning consequential things about nature" may be true only in a restricted sense. Only secure science teachers implement such a recommendation by providing mostly consequential problems. The unfortunate consequence for many students is that doing problems means memorizing scientific facts and practicing algorithms.

A PEDAGOGICAL DILEMMA

Whewell argued for frequent contact with the evidential plane of activity in the teaching of physics. To accomplish this he advocated the explication of concepts by appealing to the student's experience and intuition prior to the final mathematical formulation (Whewell, 1850). He seemed to have assumed that this would be a straightforward pedagogical task.

Kuhn argued that because textbooks have been so successful in producing competent puzzle-solvers in normal science, namely, the working scientist, textbook-centered teaching must also be successful in teaching science in general, namely, to the science student. However, some studies suggest that most scientists working today decided to become scientists early in life, before encountering textbook-centered science teaching (Rigden Tobias, 1991). Later, as students, they may see a connection between textbook science and their own self-initiated involvement with scientific ideas (von Aufshnaiter & Schwedes, 1989).

Kuhn was very explicit on this, that by learning the exemplars of a science, students should be able to make contact with an evidential base in a way that makes sense to them. It seems, however, that most students fail to make this contact, and the normal pattern of science learning is memorization and algorithm recitation. In other words, students seem to make a clear distinction between school science and everyday science.

One of the reasons for the failure of science teaching to help students make contact with appropriate evidence is that some science teachers have inadequate background knowledge themselves and consequently find it difficult to make connections with the student's evidential-experiential level of activity. Although this may not be the case for science specialists in high school, it is arguably so in the lower grades, especially in early years science. Another important reason may well be the insufficient attention given to the question of how students learn science concepts.

Clearly, both Whewell and Kuhn are deeply concerned about how students learn concepts in science education. However, neither Whewell's pedagogical emphasis on intuition, geometric reasoning, and prealgorithm discussions nor Kuhn's account of the role of textbooks and exemplars in science education explicitly discussed the third plane of activity, namely, the psychological plane. This plane involves activities related to the way students learn concepts in science. Textbooks usually leave the pedagogy, or the question of just how students learn science, to the science teacher.

In planning successful science teaching, then, science teachers need to pay attention to all three planes of activity, namely, the logical, the evidential, and the psychological (see Fig. 12.1). In preparation for a discussion of how this model (called the *LEP conceptual model*) is used with preservice teachers, a brief description of the three planes of activity and how they are related is now given.

THE LOGICAL PLANE

On this plane of activity one finds the finished conceptual products of a science, such as laws, principles, models, theories, and facts. The concepts of chemical valence, specific heat, Newton's second law, $F = ma$, the principle of conservation of energy, the Bohr model of the atom, Mendel's

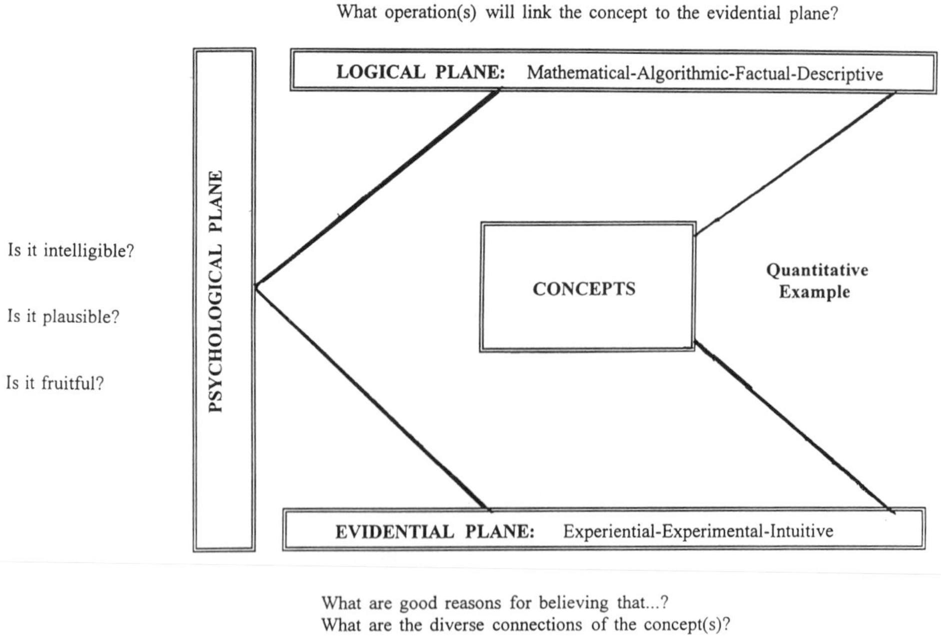

FIG. 12.1   A model for concept development in science.

laws of inheritance, the Hardy-Weinberg law in genetics, the kinetic-molecular theory of gases, and the scientific fact that the electron is the basic electric charge are all found on the logical plane.

The basic question on this plane is: "What operation(s) will link the concept to the evidential plane?" The answer to this question is important, because it determines to what extent the activity on the logical plane relates to the evidential plane. I show later, in preparation for working out an example, that valid operations can range from instrumental to "paper-and-pencil" operations. So far the examples given have been physics examples. In order to describe the three planes of activity and how they are related, however, general science examples are necessary (see Fig. 12.1; also see Stinner, 1992). The following examples, one taken from each of physics, chemistry, and biology, respectively, are good illustrations of the textbook's major preoccupation with the logical plane. These are: in physics, the mathematical formulations of Newton's second law of motion; in chemistry, the rules for chemical combination based on the notion of valence of the elements; and in biology, the circulation of the blood.

Newton's second law of motion is usually given fully developed, with little preamble to the presentation of the mathematical formulation, sometimes as early as Grade 9. The operations that link the law with the evidential plane are mostly given implicitly in terms of working out textbook problems. Moreover, the kinds of questions we asked earlier in connection with this law are seldom posed. Experimental activity, if any, is of the "to verify Newton's second law" type. Students then solve a host of problems from the textbook dealing with motion and forces.

In the chemistry example a definition of *valence* is given and the algorithm for combining such elements as oxygen and hydrogen are laid out. The operations that are supposed to connect valence with the evidential plane are usually (inappropriately) given in terms of the Bohr model of the atom, and students are taught to relate the number of outer shell electrons with valence. The Bohr model then is supposed to be the evidential connection for the rules of combining elements, but an abstract model like the Bohr model of the atom cannot be considered as evidence. This topic is usually discussed in Grade 11 chemistry, but unfortunately it is often taken up in detail as early as in Grade 8.

The circulation of the blood is generally discussed in Grade 8. Students memorize "scientific facts" from diagrams and descriptions in the text. The operations that link the conception to the evidential plane, if given at all, will refer to pumps and closed systems. Sometimes teachers may show large scale models of the circulatory system. Students memorize a great number of facts and study schematics depicting the circulation of the blood. Students must accept, on faith, that the blood circulates throughout the body.

THE EVIDENTIAL PLANE

On the evidential plane of activity one finds the experimental, intuitive, experiential connections that support the laws, principles, and facts accumulated on the logical plane (see Fig. 12.1). The first question to be asked on this plane is, "What are good reasons for believing that . . .?" Here science teachers should be looking for evidence that "makes sense" to the student. The second question to be asked is, "What are the diverse connections of this conception?" On this plane, provision needs to be made to show that the concept is valid when used in seemingly disparate areas in scientific inquiry. Moreover, the more diverse connections there are, the firmer will be the conception in the student's mind.

Thus, when presenting the topic of motion and forces, essentially Newton's second law, students should be given the opportunity to consider everyday examples of motion. This should be done in response to such questions as "Do you require a force to produce motion?" and "What are good reasons for believing that only an unbalanced force produces an acceleration?" In response to such questions, simple experiments should be designed, sometimes initiated by the teacher but more often by the student. The typical textbook experiments of the kind "To verify Newton's second law" should be avoided. We should also delay the presentation of the finished product of the mathematical formulation of Newton's laws, such as $F = ma$.

Before presenting these formulas, however, the teacher should consider the question, "What are the diverse connections that led Newton to his second law?" Historically, there were three empirical connections: the motion of the pendulum, the results of collisions between hardwood balls attached to two pendula, and the motion of the conical pendulum.

These seemingly disparate phenomena were finally united conceptually by essentially one equation. In other words, the results of these experiments plus the scientific imagination of a Newton produced the equation of motion $F = ma$. Of course, it is not suggested that students should be asked to recapitulate historical high-grade scientific thinking when they are working on the evidential plane. However, discussing the evidential basis for the finished mathematical product, such as $F = ma$, is a splendid science story and can be very motivating as well as illuminating (Stinner, 1993). However Newton's laws of motion are introduced, care must be taken that the teacher does not simply provide the student with the formula without adequate evidential argument, and explicitly say or imply that such laws are inductively arrived at from experimental data alone.

The concept of *valence* is generally taught by introducing ad hoc rules for writing simple compounds, such as HCl and H_2O, sometimes as early as

Grade 8 or 9. This is done without any evidential basis other than the appeal to the simplified Bohr model of the atom. Science teachers find that students respond to this kind of "evidence" with questions that can be translated to mean "why should I believe this?" or "provide me with good reasons for believing. . ." Unfortunately, some science teachers' stock response here would be, "Hydrogen has one electron in the outer shell and therefore has a valence of $+1$ and chlorine has seven electrons in the outer shell therefore has a valence of -1. . ." Junior high school students simply do not see the abstract model of the Bohr atom as properly placed on the evidential plane (Vogelezang, 1987). Many students respond with confusion and, ultimately, with boredom.

Again, as in the case of our example of Newton's second law from physics, a historical approach could be appropriate here. The concept of valence was well established and diversely connected, long before Bohr's model of the atom was established in 1913. Originally the "combining power" of elements was connected to the two cornerstones of chemistry, namely, the principle of conversation of mass, and the law of definite and multiple proportions. To illustrate these, teachers can use ordinary materials found in the kitchen, such as table salt, vinegar, baking soda, Alka Selzer, and sugar. Simple preliminary experiments could be devised to show the difference between a mixture and a solution, and the difference between a chemical and physical reaction. Later, an experiment showing the chemical combining weights of two elements, for example, that of sulfur and iron, and a demonstration of the electrolysis of water can be added. Moreover, the experiments of Gay-Lussac with combining volumes of gases and the theoretical arguments of Avogadro should be discussed. On the basis of such experiments and discussions, and only after a clear (pre-Bohr atom) understanding of the concepts of element and compound has been achieved, should the students proceed to write the formulas of simple compounds.

The circulation of the blood is studied almost exclusively by memorizing "facts" and schemata from textbooks. The questions one asks on this plane are generally not answered to the satisfaction of the student. For example, most textbooks make little or no attempt to recapitulate Harvey's original arguments of why the blood must circulate. Thus the opportunity to involve the student in one of the first "thought experiments" in biology is missed. Teachers and students could also read and discuss the arguments of Harvey based on a historical setting as depicted in an excellent article by F. Kilgour in *Scientific American* (1956).

A common misunderstanding is that thought experiments are highly theoretical and abstract. However, students find the classic thought experiments in physics often more compelling than concrete demonstrations.

Harvey's thought experiment to prove that the blood must circulate is no exception because the arguments appeal to physical principles of conservation of mass (Matthews, 1989; Stinner, 1990).

THE PSYCHOLOGICAL PLANE

In this plane science teachers pay attention to the students' prescientific knowledge, and to their previous school science. Here we study the responses they have to some key questions we shall pose in testing their readiness to accommodate a concept. Textbooks generally are not directly concerned with the questions asked on this plane. This lack of concern for students' prior knowledge suggests that most science teachers engaged in textbook-centered teaching pay little or no attention to how students' preconceptions interact with what is being taught (see Fig. 12.1).

The three key questions on this plane, intended for making connections between the evidential plane and the logical plane, are based on the work of Posner, Strike, Hewson, and Gertzug (1982) and partly based on suggestions made with regard to the phrasing of subsidiary questions by Hewson and Thorley (1989). The first key question sets the necessary precondition for a conception to be considered at all: The student must find a conception *intelligible* before any meaningful teaching can take place. For example, going back to our first example, a student may not find the mathematical formulation of Newton' second law, $F = ma$, intelligible; that is, he or she cannot solve problems involving $F = ma$ consistently without using a mnemonic or without slavishly following an algorithm. Therefore, if the first question cannot be answered with certainty, we cannot proceed to the second question, which sets the stage for establishing plausibility. The student then cannot go beyond meaningless algorithm recitation on the logical plane, because a connection with the evidential plane is not possible.

In the chemistry example involving the concept of *valence*, teachers encounter similar hurdles. Students in a Grade 8 class often find the Bohr model unintelligible; that is, they simply may not be able to make sense of the connection between an electron state of the outer orbit with the "combining power" of the element when writing chemical formulas. Students also may find the Bohr model not *plausible*. After all, they have no evidential basis for believing in such a model.

The circulation of the blood as a concept is found to be intelligible and plausible by most students, especially after a discussion of Harvey's arguments. It is always astounding to see the delight on the faces of fledgling science teachers when they are first exposed to Harvey's simple but compelling thought experiment.

Ideally, of course, one wishes to see every concept carried through to satisfying the requirements of the third question, that of *fruitfulness*. In the physics example, that would mean being able to apply Newton's second law in a wide variety of situations, including linear motion, circular motion, and simple circular satellite motion. In the chemistry example, that might involve the student consciously trying to understand such phenomena as electrolysis, electroplating, and how experimental evidence suggests the concepts of electrovalence and covalence. Finally, in the biology example, the student might want to know how diseases spread throughout the body, and what might be the underlying causes of heart attacks and strokes. Only when students can see new connections, perceive a variety of possibilities, and come up with new ideas is a concept firmly established in the mind of the student.

PREPARING TO USE THE LEP MODEL

Preservice teachers in science education at the University of Manitoba have used the three planes of activity for the last 3 years (what we now simply call the LEP model) for mapping out action plans for teaching concepts in science. The following comments are based on experiences and responses of students about the strengths and weaknesses of the model.

First, preservice science education students are presented with arguments that concepts are central and are fundamental agents of thought. Second, arguments are given and research evidence presented for claiming that sound understanding of science concepts cannot be attained from a textbook alone, unless students find a way to link prior knowledge to the new concept presented in the text (Pines & West, 1986; Renner et al., 1990; Vachon & Haney, 1991; Wandersee, 1988). Finally, the LEP conceptual model is presented as one instructional strategy to help students as well as teachers to facilitate conceptual development by linking prior knowledge to a new concept in an appropriate way.

To begin, concepts should be thought of as existing in networks. For example, the higher order concept of Newton's second law of motion subsumes the concepts of force, mass, and acceleration by way of a mathematical relationship.

Concepts, such as mass, velocity, force, comet, atom, density, light year, plate tectonics, and kinetic energy, are best thought of as abstractions that have attributes of regularity or structure that can be represented symbolically (Novak & Gowan, 1984). Rudolf Carnap (1966), an influential contemporary philosopher of science, conveniently divided science concepts into three main groups: *classificatory* (taxonomy in botany), *comparative* (warmer, heavier, longer), and *quantitative* (assigning a number to the weight of an object). The first is qualitative, the second intermediate between qualitative and quantitative, and the third must have clear procedures for assigning a numerical value. Carnap argued that qualitative, comparative concepts are useful, can be operationalized, and are often precursors to quantitative concepts. Thus, the comparative concept "warmer" eventually developed into the quantitative concept "temperature." Similarly, before the concept of weight became a quantitative concept, the comparative concepts of heavier, lighter, and equal in weight had to be established. Carnap's ideas of establishing empirical procedures for transforming qualitative concepts to quantitative ones are important for science teachers. These procedures help them guide students from intuitive qualitative concepts to quantitative concepts used in science. Implicit in Carnap's presentation is the use of verbal arguments rooted in personal experience that lead to self-confident application of the symbolic representations of science such as Newton's second law.

At this point preservice students are reminded that concepts are generally built up from more elemental notions. For example, the concept of density is based on the special relationship between mass and volume that determines the physical property of density. Clearly, mass and volume themselves are concepts, but more elemental than the concept of density. Indeed, the conditions of the LEP model require that if these elemental concepts are not intelligible to students, then they cannot understand the concept of density (see example worked out in Stinner, 1992).

What, then, are the special requirements for a concept to be acceptable as a scientific concept?

To answer this important question, it is recommended that the reader refer to Percy Bridgman (1952) and Gerald Holton (1980) for clarification, because of the seminal and important work they did on the nature of science concepts. Bridgman believed "we do not know the meaning of a concept unless we can specify the operations which were used by us or our neighbor in applying the concept in any concrete situation" (Bridgman, 1952, p. 3). In other words, for a concept to be bona fide scientific, a necessary but not sufficient condition is that a concept have an operational aspect. Holton (1980) went further and argued that for a concept in science to be bona fide the concept must be operationalizable (in one form or another), quantitatively determinable, and diversely connected. Holton stressed that operationally definable concepts do not by themselves guarantee us a science. Concepts must also have a quantitative character. Finally, concepts may be quantitative and meaningful, but still not be qualified to be included into science. Concepts must also be connected in a fruitful and consistent way to all aspects of science.

Preservice students generally find that operationalizing a concept like density is the most difficult part of the activity in fulfilling the requirement of the LEP model. Further referral to Bridgman's ideas then clarifies the task of finding an operational statement that links the theoretical (the logical plane) with observational evidence (the evidential plane).

Bridgman, in elucidating the nature of operationalizing science concepts, argued that there are two kinds of valid operations, namely, instrumental and noninstrumental. *Instrumental* operations assign a numerical value to the concept, for example, finding the density of a metal to be 7,000 kg/m3. *Noninstrumental*, or what he called *mental operations*, on the other hand, are represented by "paper-and-pencil" activities, which may include verbal and mental operations. Moreover, in the noninstrumental category of mental operations one should include the use of models and analogical reasoning.

This approach to operationalizing a concept ensures a wide latitude for establishing a relationship between the logical and evidential planes of activity. Thus, the degree of eventual success of operationalizing such common concepts as the three examples used (Newton's second law, chemical valence, and the circulation of the blood) depends on one's background knowledge and on one's ability to construct arguments that may involve models and analogies (see worked-out example in Stinner, 1992).

SCIENCE TEXTBOOKS, PRESENT PROBLEMS, AND THEIR FUTURE FORM

Many research studies suggest that concepts in science cannot be successfully taught from the textbook alone. Renner et al. (1990) investigated whether sound understanding of science concepts develops from textbook use. They selected four concepts from middle school, namely, expansion, the Doppler effect, flotation, and kinetic energy. Renner et al. judged the expansion concept concrete and the other three formal, with the Doppler effect the most formal. Specifically, they investigated how textbooks can be used to develop theories, skills, and classroom strategies that would promote effective science reading and reading comprehension.

These concepts are suitable for the LEP model and are among those analyzed by my preservice students. Some have already used this model in junior high school in teaching these very concepts.

It was not surprising, therefore, that Renner et al. found that very few junior high school students showed even a partial understanding of the Doppler effect and only a few demonstrated a good understanding of the expansion concept. In all, they found that when students study the four concepts as given in a textbook, 61% of the students showed no understanding or showed misunderstanding. The combined percentage of partial understandings and sound understandings responses was 28%. They concluded, "Those data do not constitute a positive recommendation for using a science textbook as the focus of science teaching nor, in all probability, the manner in which it was used" (p. 51).

Because prior knowledge based on direct experience of the concept to be understood determines the student's comprehension, Renner et al. recommended laboratory, demonstrations, and other activities prior to reading the text. They concluded, "teachers can no longer adopt a textbook and follow it straight through" (p. 51).

Science educators generally recognize that science teachers encounter two kinds of knowledge when they are teaching scientific concepts. There is children's *intuitive knowledge*, based on sense-making activities involving the environment as well as interactions with parents, peers, and media, and then there is *formal knowledge*, a product of planned instruction, or what we generally call *school science* (Pines & West, 1986).

Flick (1991) also reminded science teachers that they must pay attention to these two ways of knowing. Students are expected to formulate new ideas in terms introduced by the textbook. However, forcing students to think in textbook terms separates the use of direct experience into two categories, namely, the experiences that are used to support personal beliefs and those used as referents for scientific meanings.

Wandersee (1988) found that even at the college level only 6% of students in his study made a conscious effort to link prior knowledge to the new concepts when they were reading a textbook. Because most science teaching is textbook-centered on the college level, Wandersee recommends, for one thing among others, that instructors "teach students to consciously attempt to link new concepts in a textbook to prior knowledge" (p. 81).

Finally, Chiappetta et al. (1991) analyzed a wide range of science textbooks from grades seven through to twelve. In evaluating these textbooks they used four categories of scientific literacy: (a) *the knowledge of science, (b) the investigative nature of science, (c) science as a way of thinking, and (d) interaction of science, technology, and society* (STS). The first category involves "facts, concepts, principles, laws, theories, etc. . . . the transmission of scientific knowledge where the student received information" (p. 943). The second category refers to "the intent of the text to stimulate thinking and doing by asking the student to 'find out' " (p. 943). The third category is connected with the intent of the text to illustrate "how science in general or a certain scientist in particular went about 'finding out' " (p. 943). The last category is checked if "the intent of the text is to illustrate the effects or impacts of science on society" (p. 944).

It is relevant to discuss briefly the detailed results of investigating high school chemistry textbooks in this study. It was found (not surprisingly) that the first category, the knowledge of science involving facts, principles, and laws, typifies the content of most of these textbooks (about 70% to 90%), namely, the transmission of information to be learned by the student. Only about 15% of texts were devoted to the second category, namely, the investigative nature of science. The third category, science as a way of thinking, was very poorly represented, ranging from 0% to 6%. Finally, the fourth, category, the STS connection, ranged between 4% and 12%. It is probably safe to conjecture that physics and biology textbooks would not fare much better.

Clearly, the first category of science literacy as outlined by Chiappetta et al. is related to the logical plane in the LEP model. The second category can be roughly compared to the evidential plane in the LEP model. To a great extent the evidential plane also accommodates the third category, because a complete evidential argument in response to the question "What are good reasons to believe that . . .?" almost always connects to historical account of the idea discussed. The second question on the evidential plane, "What are the diverse connections of the concept or conception?" pays attention to the STS connection.

The findings of the research reviewed point to a general failure of textbook-centered science teaching. What then must be done to raise teachers' awareness of this issue and bring about significant change in curriculum design?

My preservice students have attempted to use the LEP model in the teaching of main concepts in science in middle school. We have gathered evidence, based on individual and group discussions prior to and after the use of the model, that preservice teachers first develop a good awareness of the already mentioned dimensions of scientific literacy. Later, and more significantly, they seem to develop better ideas of how to engage students' preconceptions, set realistic goals for the acquisition of concepts, and ensure student involvement. In order to formalize the use of the model and obtain a database for classroom application, a summer institute for inservice teachers was planned, to be followed by field testing in the schools.

We are now hypothesizing that science instruction in a real classroom setting can be significantly enhanced and enriched by the systematic use of the LEP model. Essentially, the model will engage the teacher in four activities:

1. Referring to the preconceptions of students and testing for their readiness for conceptual change (psychological plane).
2. Examining the statements made in the textbook (logical plane) and providing evidence for these statements (evidential plane).
3. Finding diverse connections in science and technology (evidential plane).
4. Working with the model, which will also engage the teacher in narrating the historical development of an idea.

The LEP model points to the need to change the present form of the science textbook, beginning with the recognition by science teachers of the general failure of textbooks to significantly address and coherently incorporate three kinds of knowledge:

1. The findings of modern learning theories about the nature of the learning process, especially the importance of paying attention to students' preconceptions, to identify them, respect them, and then to build on them,
2. The contemporary picture of the nature of science, especially the understanding that scientific conceptions, principles, theories, and laws are not enshrined but are evolving, that they do not follow simply from observation in an inductivist manner,
3. The diverse connections between scientific conceptions and discoveries, and technology and society.

Textbook authors should take this knowledge into account in shaping the textbook of the future. Briefly going beyond the framework of this discussion, one hopes that they will also reconsider the rhetorical language of textbook writing. Strube (1989) investigated the language of physics textbooks. He recommended that textbook authors pay attention to style, assume less formality and project more warmth, place more emphasis on verbal argumentation, and reduce the number of new terms introduced. He found that authors are generally remote and anonymous, tend to overemphasize logical arguments, use a style that is rigid and inappropriate to the students' world, and provide the student with definitions that are short and easy to remember whereas explanations given are long and complex.

Textbook authors also should temper their tendency to give logical and rational reconstruction of scientific discoveries and theory building with the humanizing effect of using actual case studies. Sutton (1989), as well as Stinner and Williams (1993), focused on the interplay of experiments and theory in science textbooks. They recommended case histories to dispel the message that, if appropriate experiments are carried out, discoveries are sure to follow. Finally, textbook authors should incorporate existing and emerging technologies with pedagogically sound suggestions as to how they can be used.

There are already hopeful signs that such recommendations are being considered in designing science textbooks. Recently, Duit, Häussler, Mikelskis, and Westphal (1994) published a newly designed textbook for elementary physics that specifically paid attention to the LEP conceptual model discussed in this chapter, as well as to the recommendations made by Strube and Sutton. The Duit et al. (1993) textbook also implemented a constructivist, conceptual-change model that took into account students' prior conceptions (Duit, Haussler, Lauterbach, Mikelskis, & Westphal, 1992).

IMPLICATIONS FOR SCIENCE EDUCATION

The consistent use of a conceptual model in the the teaching of science, such as the LEP conceptual model, in conjunction with present teaching aids and materials, seems to make teachers aware of the proper role of textbooks. Teachers begin systematically to refer to what learning theories say about concept formation and become aware of the importance of what the historians and philosophers have said about the nature of science.

The expectation when applying the LEP conceptual model is that teachers will reflect on the concept they are about to teach (i.e., its place, origin, and relationship to theory) and operationally link the concept to the evidential plane. This reflection will encourage teachers to collect appropriate evidence that "makes sense" to the student, in answer to the questions, "What are good reasons for believing that . . .?" and "What are the diverse connections of the concept?" Finally, it is hoped that teachers will map out the many connections between the activities on the evidential and the logical planes, filtered through the requirements of the psychological plane (see detailed example worked out in Stinner, 1992).

Teachers should venture beyond a limited understanding of science as an empirical-inductive enterprise. Teacher educators should encourage teachers to consider the three planes of activity outlined here. In addition, the use of the LEP model will also encourage teachers to consult diverse texts and other sources that deal with historical contexts and philosophical issues of science. Finally, science teachers should collaborate with their colleagues on an ongoing basis in finding new and fresh evidential material. The use of the LEP model helps clarify relationships between experiment, hypothesis, and theory in scientific inquiry. The LEP model acts as a heuristic device that allows an eclectic discussion of philosophical issues independent of a school of thought. The LEP model also fosters repeated excursions into historical background, which generates interest for the teacher and the student alike.

Indeed, one of the strengths of making contact with the evidential plane is that it inevitably draws us into a historical consideration of the origin of a concept. This was the case with each of the examples we discussed: Newton's second law of motion in physics, the concept of valence in chemistry, and the concept of circulation of the blood in biology. In each case, the teacher would be encouraged to research the historical contexts to provide appropriate evidence for what the students are given on the logical plane. This kind of activity and reflection would influence the teacher and change his or her view and understanding of science. In fact, one could claim that by using this approach, "science teachers are being challenged to present science as it 'really' is, rather than promote a mythic, textbook science" (Martin & Brouwer, 1990, p. 554).

The textbook of the future will need to consciously incorporate the findings of the history and philosophy of science as well as those of contemporary learning theories, along the lines suggested by this chapter. To achieve that, textbook authors must use a model for conceptual change, such as the LEP model, that guides them toward developing an appropriate format and a new role for the science textbook. Such a model should make connections with the history and philosophy of science as well as with contemporary learning theories. However, these connections should be "natural," an intrinsic part of the "story-line" of the text, and not in separate blocks as an aside, placed there only for interested students to consider.

Perhaps what we need is a new version of the widely used PSSC physics text of the 1960s that physics teachers enjoyed but students generally found difficult to read. The new version must make the material interesting and motivating to students. One way this can be done is by emphasizing science–technology–society (STS) connections in the text (Stinner & Williams, 1993).

The science textbook will probably be with us for some time to come. It may even be necessary for the education of the scientist, as some authorities seem to believe (Brackenridge, 1989). Textbook-centered teaching, however, must be revised to produce greater numbers of creative scientists and scientifically literate citizens. To achieve this, science teachers and textbook authors must recognize and understand the two-way passage from the logical plane to the evidential plane, filtered through the requirements of the psychological plane. Recognition and understanding of this passage by teachers and authors may change the format and the role of textbooks in the future.

REFERENCES

Arons, A. B. (1989). Historical and philosophical perspectives attainable in introductory physics courses. *Educational Philosophy and Theory, 20,* 13–23.

Baker, D. (1991). Special issue on research summary. *Science Education, 75,* 359–367.

Brackenridge, B. J. (1989). Education in science, history of science, and the textbook. *Interchange, 20,* 71–80.

Bridgman, P. (1952). *The nature of our physical concepts.* New York: Philosophical Library.

Carnap, R. (1966). *An introduction to the philosophy of science* (pp. 51–53). New York: Basic.

Chiappetta, E. L., Sethna, G. H., & Fillman, D. A. (1991). A qualitative analysis of high school chemistry textbooks for scientific literacy themes and expository learning aides. *Journal of Research in Science Teaching, 28,* 939–951.

Duit, R., Haussler, P., Lauterbach, R., Mikelskis, H., & Westphal, W. (1992, July). *Bringing issues of "girl suited" science teaching, STS, and constructivism together in a new physics textbook for "normal classes."* Paper presented at the annual meeting of the Australian Science Education Research Association (ASERA) in Hamilton, New Zealand.

Duit, R., Haussler, P., Mikelskis, H., Westphal, W. (1994). *Physik — Um die Welt zu begreifen.* Frankfurt, Germany: Diesterweg.

Driver, R. (1989). Students' conceptions and the learning of science. *International Journal of*

Science Education, 11, 481–490.

Flick, L. (1991). Where concepts meet percepts: Stimulating analogical thought in children. *Science Education, 75*, 215–230.

Hewitt, P. G. (1990, May). Conceptually speaking. *Science Teacher, 57*(5), 35–57.

Hewson, P. W., & Thorley, R. H. (1989). The conditions of conceptual change in the classroom. *International Journal of Science Education, 11*, 541–553.

Holton, G. (1980). *Thematic origins of scientific thought*. Cambridge, MA: Harvard University Press.

Jordan, T. (1989). Themes and schemes: A philosophical approach to interdisciplinary science teaching. *Synthese*, 80, 63–79.

Kuhn, T. (1962). *The structure of scientific revolutions*. Chicago: University Press.

Kilgour, F. (1956). William Harvey. *Scientific American, 194*(6), 57–62.

Kyle, W. (1991). The reform agenda and science education: Hegemonic control vs. counter-hegemony. *Science Education, 75*, 403–411.

Loewenberg-Ball, D., & Feiman-Nemser, S. (1988). Using textbooks and teaching guides: A dilemma for beginning teachers and teacher educators. *Curriculum Inquiry, 18*, 401–423.

Martin, B., & Brouwer, W. (1990). Authentic science: A diversity of meanings. *Science Education, 74*, 541–554.

Novak, J., & Gowin, D. (1984). *Learning how to learn*. Cambridge: Cambridge University Press.

Matthews, M. R. (1989). History & philosophy in science teaching. *Interchange, 20*, 3–15.

Novak, J., & Gowin, D. (1984). *Learning how to learn*. Cambridge: Cambridge University Press.

O'Loughlin, M. (1992). Rethinking science education: Beyond piagetian constructivism toward a sociocultural model of teaching and learning. *Journal of Research in Science Teaching, 29*, 791–820.

Pines, L., & West, L. (1986). Conceptual understanding and science learning. *Science Education, 70*, 583–604.

Posner, G. J., Strike, K. A., Hewson, P. H., & Gertzog, W. A. (1982). Accommodation of a scientific conception: Toward a theory of conceptual change. *Science Education, 66*, 211–227.

Renner, W. Abraham, M. R., Grybowski, E. B., & Marek, E. A. (1990). Understandings and misunderstandings of eighth graders of four physics concepts found in textbooks. *Journal of Research in Science Teaching, 27*, 35–54.

Rigden, J. S., & Tobias, S. (1991). Tune in, turn off, drop out. *Sciences, January*, 16–20.

Rohrlich, F. (1988). Four philosophical issues essential for good science teaching. *Educational Philosophy and Theory, 20*, 1–6.

Sangster, J. (1864). *Natural philosophy*. Cambridge, England: Cambridge University Press.

Selley, N. J. (1989). The philosophy of school science. *Interchange, 20*, 24–32.

Shymansky, J., & Kyle, W. 1992. Establishing a research agenda: Critical issues of science curriculum reform. *Journal of Research of in Science Teaching, 29*, 749–778.

Stinner, A. (1989). The teaching of physics and the contexts of inquiry: From Aristotle to Einstein. *Science Education, 73*, 591–605.

Stinner, A. (1990). Philosophy, thought experiments and large context problems in the secondary school physics course. *International Journal of Science Education, 12*, 244–257.

Stinner, A. (1992). Science textbooks and Science teaching: From logic to evidence. *Science Education, 76*, 1–16.

Stinner, A. (1993). A brief history of force. *Physics in Canada, 49*, 135–145.

Stinner A., & Williams, H. (1993). Concept formation, historical context, and science stories. *Interchange, 24*, 87–104.

Strube, P. (1989). The notion of style in physics textbooks. *Journal of Research in Science Teaching, 26*, 291–299.

Sutton, C. (1989). Writing and reading science: The hidden message. In R. Millar (Ed.), *Doing science: Images of science in science education* (pp. 137–159). London: Falmer Press.

Vachon, M., & Haney, R. (1991). A procedure for determining the level of abstraction of science reading material. *Journal of Research in Science Teaching*, 28, 343–352.

Vogelezang, M. J. (1987). Development of the concept 'chemical substance'—Some thoughts and arguments. *International Journal of Science Education*, 9, 519–528.

Wandersee, J. (1988). Ways students read texts. *Journal of Research in Science Teaching*, 25, 69–94.

von Aufshnaiter, S., & Schwedes H. (1989). Play orientation in physics education. *Science Education*, 73, 467–479.

von Baeyer, H. C. (1990). Two-way street. *Sciences, November*, 13–15.

Wheatley, G. (1991). Constructivist perspectives of science and mathematics learning. *Science Education*, 75, 9–21.

Whewell, W. (1823). *An elementary treaties of dynamics*. Cambridge, England: Cambridge University Press.

Whewell, W. (1850). *Of a liberal education*. London: Parker.

Yager, R. (1983). The importance of terminology in teaching K-12 Science. *Journal of Research in Science Teaching*, 20, 577–588.

Yager, R. (1992). Viewpoint: What we did not learn from the 60's about science curriculum reform. *Journal of Research in Science Teaching*, 29, 905–910.

Yore, L. (1991). Secondary science teachers' attitudes toward and beliefs about science reading and science textbooks. *Journal of Research in Science Teaching*, 28, 55–72.

IV Assessing Learners' Science Knowledge

Assessment should be an integral part of science instruction that helps students and teachers to achieve their goals by providing systematic feedback throughout the course of instruction. The view that students must actively construct their knowledge for it to be meaningful is encouraging teachers to use more authentic assessments such as portfolios, interviews, and objective questions that tap higher order thinking skills rather than rote learning. Authentic assessments are "built into" instruction and provide opportunities for students to learn through the process of assessment itself. The chapters in Part IV highlight innovative, research-based techniques for authentically assessing students' understanding of science.

13 Moving Toward a Portfolio Culture in Science Education

Drew H. Gitomer
Educational Testing Service

Richard A. Duschl
University of Pittsburgh

Portfolios have received an increasing amount of attention not only as a way of documenting student learning but also as a tool for changing instructional practice in fundamental ways. Benefits cited have included students taking more responsibility for their own learning by assessing their own work, learning and its assessment being viewed as a developmental process that occurs over extended time periods, and the encouragement of learning activities that are consistent with current notions of how people learn and what is worth learning (Camp, 1993; Gitomer, 1989; Paulson, Paulson, & Meyer, 1991; Tierney, Carter, & Desai, 1991; Wolf, Bixby, Glenn, & Gardner, 1991). The most frequent use of portfolios has been in the area of language arts (e.g., Belanoff & Dickson, 1991; Camp, 1993; Tierney et al., 1991), although portfolio approaches are being applied across all academic disciplines. For example, a number of statewide assessment systems now include mathematics portfolios (e.g., Koretz, Stecher, & Deibert, 1993).

In this chapter, we discuss the evolution of portfolio practice in middle school science classrooms. We are exploring and developing our ideas in the context of Project SEPIA (Science Education through Portfolio Instruction and Assessment), a project funded by the National Science Foundation and conducted in the Pittsburgh Public Schools, a large urban setting.

The most important point we can make is that a successful science portfolio is not merely an interesting assessment technique that simply can be placed within a traditional science classroom. Instead, good portfolio practice requires fundamental changes in conceptions of science and science teaching, in ideas about learners and learning, and of course in the practice and function of assessment. Taken together, these changes manifest themselves in a rethinking of the purpose and nature of curriculum, leading to what we have called a *portfolio culture* (Duschl & Gitomer, 1991; Gitomer, Grosh, & Price, 1992). A portfolio culture is a learning environment in which students are engaging in learning activities consistent with current psychological philosophical, historical, and sociological conceptions of the growth of scientific knowledge (Duschl, 1990; Duschl & Hamilton, 1992; Laudan, 1977, 1984; Shapere, 1987), teaching is organized to encourage conceptual change, learners are active constructors of meaning (Posner, Strike, Hewson, & Gertzog, 1982; Strike & Posner, 1992), and assessment is an invaluable tool that teachers as well as students use to help make instructional decisions. The label "culture" is meant to convey an image of a science classroom that reflects a comprehensive and continual interplay between teacher, student, and curriculum. Two basic and distinguishing characteristics of the portfolio culture classroom are the assessment-based interactions teachers have with students to monitor meaningful learning, and the project orientation of instructional activities and tasks. Together, these characteristics mediate instructional activities and teacher decision making in ways that facilitate the development of students' depth of knowledge in principled ways.

The purpose of this chapter is to describe the nature of changes occurring in middle school science classrooms — changes that affect teaching practices, curriculum, and learners themselves. In the next section, we briefly overview the theoretical framework that guides the development of a portfolio culture, focusing on changes in conceptions of science, learning, and assessment. We then describe and illustrate central features of a portfolio culture by examining how these ideas are manifest in a prototype curriculum unit. In the final section, we reflect on our progress to date, on future directions for SEPIA, and on recommendations and cautions to others contemplating involvement in portfolio culture science education.

THEORETICAL UNDERPINNINGS OF A PORTFOLIO CULTURE

A portfolio culture is predicated on adopting beliefs and practices of science education that differ markedly from traditional classrooms. We can assign those changes to three broad categories: (a) changing conceptions of science, science thinking, and goals for science education, (b) changing conceptions of student learning and appropriate instruction, and (c) changing the role and practice of assessment. All three areas of change act together in the formation of a classroom that moves toward the establishment of a portfolio culture.

Changing Conceptions of Science, Science Thinking, and Goals for Science Education

In the 1950s a very important paper was being researched and written by Joseph Schwab. It asked a very simple but at the same time complex question, "What do scientists do?" The foundation of the paper was an examination of some 2,000 scientific research papers, contemporary as well as historical. The preceding question became the title of an article (Schwab, 1960) representing the seed of Schwab's thinking about two very significant ideas about science education. One of the contributions is his explanation of the role of inquiry in science and in science education. The second is the distinction he made between two aspects of scientific knowledge — syntactic and semantic structures of knowledge. *Syntactic knowledge* is concerned with the rules of how one comes to comprehend and justify knowledge claims and methods in science (e.g., a set of experiments that provide evidence supporting a particular theory). *Semantic knowledge* refers to the content and meaning of scientific knowledge claims (e.g., the planets revolve around the sun; atomic particles are made up of quarks).

Work by Schwab (1962) and T. Kuhn (1962/1970) made clear that the development of both these forms of knowledge is quite dynamic. They noted that there are periods in which members of the scientific community are in agreement about the background knowledge and critical problems within their respective domains of inquiry, which, in turn, establishes the important questions and activities within the domain. During normal or stable times, scientific activities turn to the refinement of established knowledge claims.

But the review of historical documents and actual practice of scientists revealed that there are also times when members of a scientific community are in disagreement about what are the appropriate background knowledge and critical problems that should guide the design of investigations and the evaluation of evidence and knowledge claims. During these periods of flux, the activities among scientists are considered to be revolutionary and fluid.

The view of science as inquiry is one we have adopted in SEPIA, accepting the general proposition that science curricula should reflect the nature of science. Implications of this position for classroom practice are:

1. Learners should acquire knowledge and science experiences through investigation procedures similar to those scientists employ.
2. Learners should understand that the knowledge being acquired from an investigation is subject to change and reformulation.
3. Practice should be guided by accepted rules of practice (i.e., syntactic knowledge).

4. Knowledge and investigations should be shaped by prevailing meanings and background knowledge of the scientific discipline (i.e., semantic knowledge).

Although many curriculum projects in the past endorsed the first of these tenets, most also subscribed to a version of scientific knowledge that supported only a stable or normal view of scientific inquiry (Duschl, 1985, 1990; Nadeau & Desautels, 1984; Russell, 1981). Students were not in an environment in which the dynamic nature of scientific knowledge was given high status. Exploration and the development of processes of science focusing on data gathering were taking place, but meaning-making through data analysis and reasoning via scientific argumentation have been lagging behind. D. Kuhn (1993) maintained that learners are not being provided the opportunities to develop the requisite reasoning skills to move from scientific data to scientific conclusions. Kuhn and others (e.g., Toulmin, 1958) called the move from data to conclusions *scientific argumentation* and claimed that such argumentation is a crucial, but absent, element of K–12 science classrooms.

Science instruction has been and continues to be dominated by the teaching of facts, hypotheses, and theories, for the contribution each makes to establishing modern knowledge. Schwab (1964) called it the "rhetoric of conclusions," whereas Duschl (1990) called it "final form science." How scientific knowledge came to exist (i.e., what arguments give rise to our scientific knowledge claims) is treated as a nonissue. Consequently, an incomplete picture of science is presented to students. Learners are provided with instructional tasks designed to teach what is known by science. A large part of this instruction involves teaching students processes that justify what we know: teaching the "what" without teaching about the "how." Kilbourn (1982) coined the term *epistemological flatness* to describe science curriculum materials or instruction strategies that do not give a complete picture of the concepts being taught. Too often, he argued, science instruction is taken out of context and presented without the critical background material necessary to meaningfully understand the meanings or transitions of science. Educators are left with the problem of making fluid inquiry a part of science instruction.

The ideas of T. Kuhn and Schwab, as novel as they were, did very little to shed light on the precise ways in which fluid inquiry takes place or revolutions in science come about. As philosophers of science examined the history of scientific thinking, they recognized that scientific change did not always progress in the manner suggested by T. Kuhn. Rather than theory changes always driving changes in methods and research aims, it was discovered that often, changes in methodologies or questions (aims) led to changes in theory.

Laudan (1984) conceived of scientific progression as more piecemeal in nature. Sometimes changes in methods lead to new theories, or even new goals. For example, we can examine the role British physicists played in the revival of the idea of continental drift and the development of plate tectonic theory. The aim of these scientists was, initially, to obtain evidence about their dynamo theory to explain the earth's magnetic field. To do this, an instrument called the astatic magnetometer was constructed. These scientists did not find the evidence for their magnetic theory, but did discover that the instrument designed to test theories about the magnetic core of the earth could also be used to determine the remnant magnetism of rocks.

The astatic magnetometer was an invaluable instrument in expanding the geophysical knowledge about the earth. Subsequent studies of continental rocks in England, India, and North America produced a set of anomalous data that required a restructuring of prevailing theory about geologic dynamics. This is an example of how a change in method (using the astatic magnetometer to measure rocks) led to a change in aims (physicists turning their attention from a classical problem of magnetism to the problem of continental drift) that, in turn, led to a total restructuring of our knowledge of the earth (see Takeuchi, Uyeda, & Kanamori, 1967, for a full account of this episode of scientific discovery).

Of course, sometimes changes in goals or aims of research lead to new theories and methods. One only has to look at the impact that acquired immune deficiency syndrome (AIDS) has had in moving scientists to ask new questions. These questions have led to the design and application of new research tools, as well as significant theoretical contributions to immunology and other related fields.

In order to be consistent with views of scientific thinking, a portfolio culture needs to adopt a view of science that has the following characteristics (characteristics that are too frequently missing from most science classrooms):

1. The aims that a theory is intended to support need to be clear to students. Whether doing experiments or reading text, students should know the larger questions that justify the scientific work.
2. The significant pieces of evidence, methodological developments, or changes in aims that led to a presented theoretical position must be clear to students and used in scientific arguments.
3. Attempts should be made to confront the particular theoretical conceptions that students bring to the learning situation.
4. Theories should be presented not as final-form truth, but as present-day best thinking about a problem that surely will undergo revision.

5. Processes should not be presented as theory independent. General processes of observation and drawing conclusions, for example, are skills that are heavily influenced by theoretical perspectives (Hodson, 1992). What one chooses to observe and how that observation is conducted, for example, are determined by the theoretical orientation and conceptual understanding one has. Theoretical understanding determines what is important to observe. Therefore, processes must be considered in the context of different conceptual contexts (e.g., observing in biological field studies is very different than observation in a mechanics study).

CHANGING CONCEPTIONS OF STUDENT LEARNING AND APPROPRIATE INSTRUCTION

If science as a discipline has been redefined as being more dynamic and interactive, so too has the learning of science been reconceptualized. Interestingly, growth of scientific knowledge within individuals shows similar patterns to the growth of science as a body of knowledge (Carey, Evans, Honda, Jay, & Unger, 1989; Duschl, Hamilton, & Grandy, 1990; Rissland, 1985; Vosniadou & Brewer, 1987). Where traditional science essentially has tried to teach students the content of science, ignoring what the student brings to the learning situation, current constructivist views emphasize the understanding that students bring to a task.

Individuals hold certain theoretical positions and use their theoretical understanding to incorporate and assimilate new information. Much of learning is thought of as a process of transfer, implying that one can only learn by making sense of new information through the use of already learned concepts (e.g., Vosniadou & Ortony, 1989). New concepts can build on old concepts, or there can be such inconsistency between old and new concepts that cognitive restructuring is required.

As an example, many students believe that the earth is a very stable, static body. Although this theoretical position may undergo some refinement (e.g., there are rare perturbations called earthquakes), the primary belief that the earth is unchanging remains. And why not? Virtually everything in the child's experience confirms the stability of the earth. Is there anything more certain than that the mountains you see today will be there tomorrow? Minor changes in an individual's theoretical position, such as the acknowledgment of earthquakes, are known as weak restructuring. The new concepts essentially build on already established concepts. Strong restructuring occurs when the individual's theoretical position is no longer viewed as useful or tenable. A new theoretical position then replaces the previous theory. An example of strong restructuring would be when an individual rejects the theoretical position that the earth is a stable body.[1]

Viewing science learning as conceptual change rather than conceptual innoculation from teacher and textbook to student has a number of significant implications for how science instruction ought to proceed. Teaching for conceptual change in a classroom setting is a very complex task. Posner, Strike, Hewson, and Gertzog (1982) asserted that learners will change their commitment to particular ideas when four conditions are met:

1. Existing ideas must be found to be unsatisfactory.
2. The new idea must be intelligible, coherent, and internally consistent.
3. The new idea must be plausible.
4. The new idea must be preferable to the old viewpoint on the grounds of perceived elegance, parsimony, and/or usefulness.

The Posner et al. model of conceptual change has its roots in the early view of scientific thinking discussed. In this model, considerations of theoretical adequacy are the driving force for the development of scientific thinking. Embracing more current views (e.g., Laudan, 1984) recognizes the importance of aims and methods in supporting conceptual development as well. Maintaining the triadic relationship between theories, aims, and methods is a critical focus of the portfolio culture (Duschl & Gitomer, 1991). Student conceptual development demands an understanding of the justification for methods and their relationship to a set of aims. Theories without aims lead to decontextualized learning. Applications of methods without aims and theoretical positions result in impoverished skill execution.

In a portfolio culture, we adopt the view that the goal of science education is to help students develop concepts, theories, strategies, practices, and beliefs that are consistent with scientific ways of knowing, arguing, and exploring. To do this, we recognize two principles.

The first principle is that students come into a learning situation with strong theoretical (albeit nonscientific) positions or conceptual structures. These structures guide the way new information is processed. Thus, instruction must allow students to voice, and teachers to recognize and act on, these theoretical positions in order to effect change in student conceptions.

---

[1]Interestingly, as this chapter is being revised, Jupiter is being bombarded with large fragments of a comet. For the first time, the technology is available to document the effects of this kind of event. How will this well-publicized occurrence affect nonscientists' conceptions of the stability of the universe?

The second principle is that students construct understanding through a progressive change in conceptual structures. A large part of the instructional task involves eliciting student conceptions and then providing instructional events that will move students to positions that are more conceptually developed and scientifically consistent.

CHANGING THE ROLE AND PRACTICE OF ASSESSMENT

Traditional assessment strategies (e.g., end-of-unit tests, standardized tests, chapter tests, etc.) have been used to serve the purposes of individuals who function outside of the classroom — principals, superintendents, and local, district, and state supervisors. When careful thought is given to how assessment can serve the needs of students and teachers, very different, complex, and concomitant considerations for the roles of teachers, of learners, and of subject matter must take place as well.

Students are exceptionally adaptive creatures. Through the curriculum, instruction, and assessment, students obtain a very clear view of what matters and adapt their strategies accordingly. What matters is always implicit in student activities, but sometimes it is explicit as well. When we talk about "what matters," we are talking about the criteria that are used to consider student performance.

Unfortunately, what matters most in many science classrooms is not reflective of the preceding discussion of scientific thinking and learning at all. Instead, what we observe are criteria that value the rote memorization of facts and the rote application of procedures. In response, then, we often see students unwilling to stay with a curriculum topic for more than a few days. Even in classrooms that promote "hands-on" activities, students learn quickly that they will do well if they engage in and complete the activity. If students observe (not necessarily understand) the intended result, and describe the phenomena employing science terms, then the activity is deemed successful. Criteria associated with more legitimate forms of scientific thinking (e.g., using evidence to support a knowledge claim, considering alternative explanations) are ignored in the typical science classroom. From rote forms of instructional and assessment practice arises the inevitable complaint that "students don't really care about understanding, they just want to get the grade." Well, the students shouldn't be blamed if they've learned to play a game where rewards accrue from rote memorization and rote execution of prespecified procedures. The students will change only when the game rules are revised.

In a science portfolio culture, we adopt the view that assessment must meet three conditions. First, assessment should attend to knowledge and skills that are deemed important within the discipline. Therefore, learning to use evidence to support an argument would be a target of assessment; memorizing the periodic table would not.

Second, assessment should contribute to instruction and learning. Satisfying this condition requires a rethinking of assessment. If assessment is to contribute to instruction, it cannot occur only at the end of a unit or semester. Assessment after the instruction is over does not allow for the assessment to contribute to any instructional decisions. All that can be said is the degree to which a student mastered some amount of content. Assessment must be a continuous process that facilitates "on-line" instructional decision making in the classroom.

Assessment that contributes to instruction and learning must also provide information that forms the basis for instructional decisions. Unfortunately, most traditional forms of assessment do not furnish such information. In the common assessment approach, student responses are marked as correct or incorrect and the student's grade is essentially the sum of correct answers. Typically missing is any information about how the student sees the problem, what the student knows about the content being tested, and where difficulties for the student may lie. Therefore, assessment in a portfolio culture must provide the type of information that will support a conceptual change learning environment. Implicit in this view of instruction is that students are not simply receivers of assessment information, but are themselves active participants in the assessment process.

The third condition of assessment in a portfolio culture is that assessment should contribute to an accountability process within an educational system. Assessment ought to inform an educational institution, whether it be a school, district, or state, about how a science program is functioning. Rather than simply asking whether students are scoring higher than students in another institution or than students from another year, it is important that assessment provide information about what opportunities students have had in science, where they are succeeding, and where they are having difficulty. Further, an accountability process ought to provide information that helps an institution make decisions about how it will improve itself (Darling-Hammond, 1993; Gitomer, 1991).

In the following section, we describe some of the features and provide examples of an assessment system we have been developing in SEPIA. The work here reflects a partnership with a group of middle school teachers in the Pittsburgh Public Schools. The ideas about a portfolio culture have been evolving and continue to evolve. Therefore, the following represents our current thinking about portfolio culture in middle school science classrooms.

FEATURES OF A PORTFOLIO CULTURE

Deciding What Is Important — Moving Toward Classroom Criteria

As noted earlier, what is deemed important in science classrooms is often beside the point when viewed from the perspective of science. SEPIA is being conducted in a district that has embraced a hands-on view of science, stressing student experience with carrying out investigations and reporting results of those investigations. What is valued and rewarded is the doing of the investigation, the completion of any lab sheets and summary questions (although not necessarily accurately), and the successful mastery of short-answer tests that assess knowledge of concepts associated with the investigations.

The SEPIA project has asserted that such a view of science is incomplete. Not only do we want students doing investigations, but we want students to reason about their investigations and argue for a particular point of view. Furthermore, investigations that are done only because they are the next unit in the curriculum are not adequately motivated. We argue that the investigations students engage in should grow out of their scientific reasoning. That is, students ought to be engaging in the practice of making explanations that are supported, tested, and confronted by their investigations.

Changing the nature of what counts as quality work is inherent in a science portfolio culture. SEPIA has focused on defining what counts through the establishment of a set of public criteria. The criteria extend far beyond the forms of criteria operating in most science classrooms and are consistent with quality scientific thinking. The role of the teacher is to make these criteria the currency of the classroom, the public expression of what matters and what is valued. As students learn these criteria, they not only learn the rules of the game in the classroom, they also learn what is valued in the scientific discipline.

A sample set of criteria that we are developing in SEPIA is presented in Table 13.1. Together with the criteria are sets of questions that students and teachers can ask as explanations are considered. Notable characteristics of these criteria are:

Criteria Are Scientifically Consistent.   These criteria can be legitimately applied to any scientific argument, explanation, or experiment, whether developed by a student or a practicing scientist. The criteria are consistent with models of scientific thinking discussed previously, reflecting the values present in the scientific community, rather than only being valued in the classroom. Any scientist will consider a theoretical explanation in terms of clarity, coherence, explanatory power and accuracy, and so forth. The

TABLE 13.1
SEPIA Criteria for Explanations

Relationships
    How do these terms go together?
    Why do they belong together
    Is there a name we can give to the relationship?
    Is there anything that does not belong?
    How are things alike?
Clarity
    Is it clear?
    What does it tell someone?
    What makes it clear to someone else?
Consistency with evidence
    How is the statement supported by observations?
    How is the statement supported by the observations of others?
    How is the statement supported by lab data?
    How does evidence from nature support the statement?
    How well does your statement reflect the data?
Use of examples
    Can you give an example?
    Why is it a good example for this purpose?
    Is there a better example for this purpose?
    Can you think of an original example?
Making sense
    Is this what you expected?
    Are there any surprises here?
    Is there anything that does not fit?
    Does your hypothesis make sense given what you know?
    Can you predict what will be the outcome?
Acknowledging alternative explanations
    How else can this be explained?
    Is your explanation or hypothesis plausible – can it happen?
    What does this explanation say that the other doesn't?
Elaboration of a theme
    How is this term related to something we did before?
    Is it familiar? If so, how?
    How is it related to anything you did in another class?
Accuracy
    Is the statement consistent with other information on the same topic?
    How does your model compare with other models?
    How does it compare with other representations?

criteria do not reflect a model of science that is static and only values the recall of information and reenactment of previous experiments. Rather, the criteria promote modification of existing explanations and consideration of alternative explanations.

Criteria Are Dynamic.   Although the collective essence of these criteria has remained consistent, their organization has undergone modification and will likely continue to undergo change. No claim is made that the list of criteria in Table 13.1 is complete or optimal for every classroom situation. At this point, though, this list is useful for communicating the desired attributes of student performance.

Criteria Are Public.   Earlier, we discussed how students often derive the criteria operating in a classroom implicitly from the activities in which they are asked to engage. Fundamental to the portfolio culture is the principle that the criteria must be public and explicit and used in reflection on student work. The teaching task involves helping students come to understand what these criteria denote and getting students to internalize these criteria as they engage in and evaluate their own work.

Criteria Evolve from Student Work.   Criteria such as these can only be applied if students are engaged in activities that have some scientific integrity to them. If students are only asked to recall isolated facts, then it is impossible to apply the criteria such as coherence to student responses. If students are only asked to see the "right" answer, then we are unable to examine student ability to entertain and evaluate alternative hypotheses. Thus, SEPIA-like criteria cannot be dropped into a traditional science classroom without wholesale changes occurring in the type of work that students are asked to produce.

Criteria Generalize Beyond Specific Tasks or Content Areas.   These criteria are not specific to any single field or topic of science. Whether one is considering genetics or mechanics, these criteria are applicable. What may shift across given topics is how criteria are satisfied. For example, the idea of precision in field biology is qualitatively different from the idea of precision for physicists in a fusion laboratory. The specifics that would satisfy any of these criteria, of course, are ultimately dependent on the scientific content of the area itself. Importantly, though, ideas such as consistency with evidence, explanatory power, and coherence provide a basis for discussing any scientific performance, regardless of topic.

Generating Student Work

SEPIA teachers have made great strides in getting students to produce work that is consistent with the criteria we are attempting to establish in the classroom. Essentially, students are becoming more facile in "showing what they know." Teachers, having made a commitment to encourage students to express their understanding, are now considering ways to act effectively on this information. Several examples are presented to illustrate some successful classroom techniques.

SEPIA teachers, like many of their colleagues, have been leery of asking students to do much writing in the science classroom. Students typically don't write very much, nor do they write very well. Scoring such responses has been seen as time-consuming and not very enlightening.

One of the things learned from the writing reform movement, though, is that developing writers must have a clear purpose and audience for an effective communication (e.g., Bereiter & Scardemalia, 1982). In typical science writing, the audience is the teacher (who is assumed to know the material already), and the purpose is to convince the teacher that the student has sufficient familiarity with the material. Contrast this with a communication in which a student is genuinely trying to explain something to someone unfamiliar with the material. Capitalizing on this notion, SEPIA teachers have invented various writing tasks in which audience and purpose are clearer, resulting in more effective communication. In the example in Fig. 13.1, the teacher asked a student to write a letter to a sibling or friend explaining a concept he has studied, in this case sound. Several features are notable in this writing. First, the student actually writes quite a bit. Second, his willingness to write and explain an idea provides a much clearer window into his understanding. Although he has some notion that sound is differentially transmitted through different states of matter, this knowledge is very fragile, as evidenced by his conception that sound will travel better through a brick wall surrounded by air than it will through air. Having this student's work accessible can support a teacher who asks a student to reconcile an explanation with evidence acquired from real-world experience (applying the criteria of consistency with evidence). Without the evidence contained in the explanation, such a question is likely never to be raised. Contrast the amount of insight that can be gained from this type of response with that which can be obtained through a more traditional item such as:

Sound travels fastest in _____ .

a. gas   b. liquid   c. solid

Scientists, and student scientists, are not always best able to represent their ideas in written, verbal form. Pictures, graphs, physical models, simulations, and oral communications are frequently employed to express ideas. Often, combinations of modalities are used (e.g., graphical and verbal). SEPIA teachers have encouraged students to represent their understanding using multiple forms of representation. In Figs. 13.2 and 13.3, we can see student drawings/explanations to describe the Earth's movement around the sun as an explanation for seasons. In Fig. 13.2, we see one student who has a before and after unit depiction of the concepts needed to explain the cause of seasons and the cause of night and day

(d)

FIG. 13.1.   Illustration to accompany this example of student writing from a SEPIA explanation task: "Dear Ralph, Sound has many different parts. Sound travels by sound waves. The sound waves can only travel by mediums (solids, liquids or gases). [See figure parts a, b, and c, respectively.] Sound travels fastest through solids. Sound travels slowest through gases. Sound travels slower through liquids than solids, but faster through liquids than gases. Intensity is the loudness of sounds. Loudness is measured in decibels. Sound is how high or low the pitch of something is. A tuning fork is an instrument based on pitch. [See figure part d.] The smaller the tuning fork the higher the pitch. The bigger the tuning fork the lower the pitch. The vibrations on a tuning fork can also tell something about the pitch. The more vibrations the higher the pitch. The less vibrations the lower the pitch."

and another student who has a final drawing accompanied by a written statement on the same set of concepts. Comparing the before and after work, it is clear how much the student has learned. Yet, at the same time, the comparison points out some continuing sources of confusion. For example, the prime meridian that runs from the north pole to the south pole is oriented parallel to the direction of the sun rays, rather than perpendicular. Additionally, it is not clear from the drawing that this student comprehends the notion of direct and indirect sunlight. The second student (Fig. 13.3), while elaborating on the meaning of indirect and direct sunlight in the written statement, evidences at least some difficulty in understanding the orientation of the earth's axis. Thus, this type of student work permits a teacher and students to have a much greater understanding of how a student is thinking and making meaning from science content. It enables and enriches assessment opportunities that can inform subsequent instructional activities and tasks. Such opportunities might include:

1. Grouping students with dissimilar responses and then asking them to arrive at a consensus representation or drawing.
2. Conducting a class discussion around two or three different models/depictions of indirect and direct sunlight or the proper orientation the earth has with the sun.
3. Asking students follow-up questions or pointing out uses of facts or information that draw on established criteria of science learning (e.g., in the written statement our writer attempts to be precise about the angle of the tilt of the axis and the length of the year).

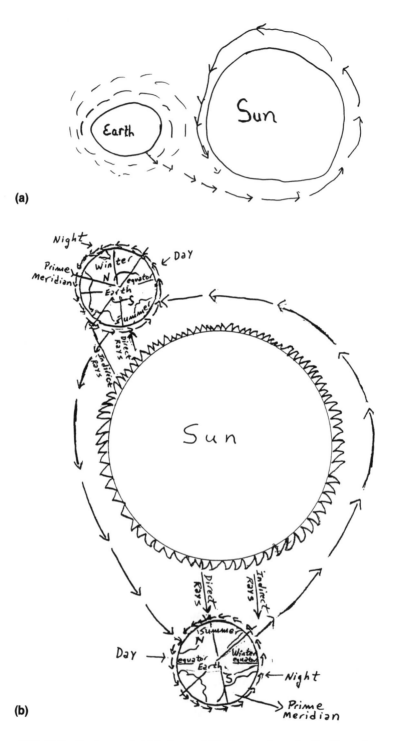

FIG. 13.2.   Student work (a) before and (b) after a unit on the Earth's motion.

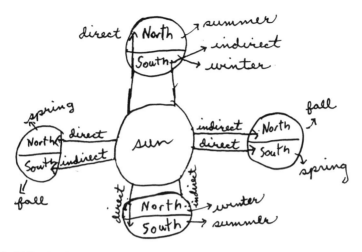

FIG. 13.3.   Student illustration for this explanation of the earth's seasons: "What is revolution and what does it cause? Revolution is when something goes around something like a racecar going around a racetrack or the earth going around the sun. Revolution causes the seasons. The earth is tilted on its axis (23½°). The rays from the sun are either direct or indirect and they depend if the Southern Hemisphere is facing more towards the sun or if the Northern Hemisphere facing more towards the sun. When it's spring in the Northern Hemisphere it's fall in the Southern Hemisphere. The Northern Hemisphere and southern Hemisphere always have the opposite seasons. It takes the earth 365 days (1 year) to go around the sun."

Taken together, instructional steps are a direct outcome of teacher assessment decisions that begin to alter the dynamics of the classroom learning environment. The public expression of what matters and what is valued begins to change. As students learn the criteria, they not only learn the rules of the game in the classroom, they also learn what is valued in the scientific discipline.

Gaining access to such student information through letter writing and drawings and then using this information is a complex cognitive task for SEPIA teachers. Even the initial step of reviewing student work employing the criteria in Table 13.1 requires fundamental changes in the learning environment, changes we are only beginning to see effectively implemented (Duschl & Gitomer, in press). This central challenge faces the SEPIA project, and all other projects that are considering portfolios and performance assessments as instructional vehicles.

Portfolio Beginnings: Integrating Curriculum and Assessment

Moving from facts and procedures to models, explanations, and experimentation necessitates the reformulation of curriculum. In SEPIA, we have developed a prototype sixth-grade curriculum unit around the topic of buoyancy that moves us closer to what a portfolio culture curriculum might look like. The "Vessels" unit has the following logical structure:

Anchoring the Task.   Bransford and colleagues (Cognition and Technology Group, 1990, 1992) discuss the importance of anchoring instruction in a meaningful context. Students should have a sense of why instructional concepts and skills might be useful. The "Vessels" unit is anchored through the problem-solving task of having students work out the design of a vessel that will have maximum carrying capacity for a city planning agency. The letter introducing the task is presented in Fig. 13.4. From looking at the design packet information in the letter, note that it is not enough just to design a vessel with maximum capacity, but the students must also demonstrate their understanding of scientific principles related to vessel design.

Generating a Diversity of Ideas.   The students each design an aluminum foil vessel and test the carrying capacity of the vessel by placing weights in the vessel until it sinks in a container of water. They then calculate the weight needed to sink the vessel and also determine the dimensions of the vessel (bottom surface area and height of sides). Along with the actual vessel, students have also written initial thoughts on the features important to a successful vessel. At that point, a class graph is created in which students physically place their boat on a graph plotting the weight to sink the boat. The result is a wall chart of aluminum foil vessels that typically looks something like Fig. 13.5. Vessels differ not only in width, length, and shape, but also in terms of height and thickness of sides and symmetry of the design.

Assessment: Acting on Student Work.   The graph provides the basis for a critical event in the portfolio culture classroom *the assessment conversation* (Duschl & Gitomer, in press). This conversation serves multiple purposes. One is to find out what students know. A second is to create opportunities for students to engage in and learn processes of scientific explanation, argument, and presentation. The teacher models the use of the classroom criteria to evaluate and respond to student comments. Students are expected to use the criteria as a basis for responding to other students' comments as well. A third purpose of the assessment conversation is to use scientific reasoning frameworks to move from the initial diversity of ideas existing in a classroom to a view that represents a consensus by virtue of its scientific plausibility. Here is an annotated illustration of how such an assessment conversation might work in a SEPIA classroom based on the vessel graph:[2]

---

[2]The excerpt here is not a direct record of a classroom conversation. Rather, it represents and idealized version based on observations of classroom and goals of the project.

T: Based on the graph, who has any ideas about what features of a boat contribute to its carrying capacity? [An open question that encourages a diversity of ideas.]

S1: The bigger the boat, the more it carries.

T: What do you mean by bigger? Can you be more precise? [Appeal to criteria of clarity.]

S1: The area of the bottom is bigger.

T: Does the data on the graph support the idea that if the boat has a bigger bottom it will have a larger carrying capacity? [Appeal to the criteria of consistency with evidence.]

S2: Kind of, except that some of the boats with the biggest bottoms don't hold as much as some of the others.

T: Can you point to two boats that support your idea that big bottom boats don't hold as much as others? Are there any boats in the same part of the graph that have very different designs but held the same weight? [Appeal to criteria use of examples and consistency with evidence.]

S2: Yeah, the 301 to 400 part, that has boats with different designs.

T: Why might that be? Are there other ideas about what might affect a vessel's carrying capacity? [Appeal to criteria of consistency with evidence, acknowledging alternative explanations and making sense or coherence.]

S3: It seems like the boats in the 301 to 400 place with the big bottoms that don't hold as much have real low sides.

T: Good. Can we say that the height of the sides is related to carrying capacity? [Appeal to acknowledging alternative explanations, consistency with evidence.]

S3: Well, kind of, but it's not like the boats with the highest sides always carry more weight. See if you look at the 401 to 500 column, there are two boats that have about the same sides but the bigger bottom boat held more.

T: Okay, so far we've said that both size of the bottom and height of the sides are kind of related to carrying capacity, but not for all cases. Does anyone have a new explanation that might account for all of our findings? [Appeal to criteria of interconnectedness, consistency with evidence, making sense or coherence.]

S4: Well, it seems like you want to have a boat with a big bottom, but you can't have the sides too low, so that the best boats have big bottoms, but also sides that are pretty high. Since you have to have high sides, you can't have the biggest bottoms.

City of Pittsburgh
Sofia Maslow, Mayor

Department of City Projects
Land Use Planning Program
1600 W. Rosedale St.
Pittsburgh, PA 15219

<u>RE: Request for Design Plans</u>

Dear Applicant:

The purpose of this letter is to provide you with information for submitting a bid to the City. I am pleased to learn that you and your staff will be submitting hull design plans to be used for building a fleet of river-going vessels. In order to assist you with the development of your design plans, let me tell you how we intend to use the vessels.

The City intends to build office complexes, apartments, shopping centers, marinas, and playgrounds on Herrs Island. Herrs Island is an island on the Allegheny River up the river from the 16th Street Bridge. In fact, the 31st Street Bridge directly crosses Herrs Island. We think the total project will take 10 years to complete. The best way to deliver construction materials - sand, cement, lumber, bricks, cinder blocks, pipe, etc. - is using the river. The bridges that go to the island will not hold up after 10 years of traffic from heavy truckloads of materials. Therefore, we feel it is in the City's best interest to build its own fleet of vessels.

The contract for supplying the construction materials has been awarded to Best Construction Materials Supply Co. which is located on the Monongahela River. The main function of the vessels will be to take materials between the Mon River and the Allegheny River. Attached is a print of a map of the Point which shows the locations of Best Construction and Herrs Island.

As you can tell, the ability to carry materials is important. The successful plan will be one that explains how a vessel hull should be designed so it stays afloat while carrying the most load. In order to make the competition fair, we are asking all bidders to design hull models using aluminum foil that is the same size.

After completing your investigation, the packet of information you submit to the City should contain the information and materials in the items listed below.

(Continued)

Only complete packets will be considered. We want to hire the firm that can design the best hull. But the City must have confidence that the designers understand and can explain why a vessel will float and carry a load. Without this explanation, the City can't be certain the design model you submit will work.

Design Packet Items

1. A sketch of the vessel hull.
The sketch should be neat and have the height, length and width of the vessel labeled.

2. A scale model of the vessel.
The scale model should be made of aluminum foil. It will represent the hull of the vessel. It should be made as best as you can to look like the sketch you submit.

3. Sketches of the vessel hull in water with and without a load
These two sketches should be side by side on the same piece of paper. Using arrows, science terms and the names of forces, label the sketches to explain the forces that keep the vessel afloat. Please mark the water line.
These sketches are a very important part of the design packet. We want to hire the firm that understands and can best explain why vessels float.

4. A report of tests and results.
Please list the tests, experiments, and investigations you performed. Then provide the a report of results. For example, what is the mass in grams (g) that it took to sink your vessel. Include in your packet any tables, graphs, or test design sketches you think will demonstrate you have thought through the problem carefully.

Good luck!

Sincerely,

Peter Remraf, Project Manager
Herr's Island Development Proposal

FIG. 13.4. Introductory letter from the "Vessels" unit.

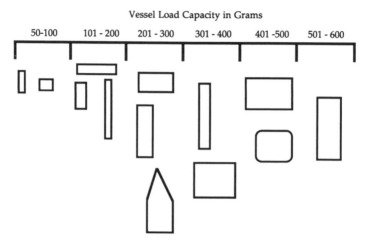

FIG. 13.5. This graph represents a physical display of aluminum vessels in the classroom on a bulletin board or blackboard. It is used during an assessment conversation to compare and contrast design features of vessels.

The approach shown here; in which the teacher is directing the assessment conversation, is only one of several classroom arrangements that we are exploring. We are finding evidence that classroom conversations are increasingly taking on the characteristics of assessment conversations (Gitomer, Zohar, Chang, & Duschl, 1994). Other models include having students work in pairs or small groups to come to a consensus view through criteria-based assessment conversations and then replicating that process within the larger classroom. Whatever the setting, the critical features include the generation of a diversity of ideas, the examination of those ideas using classroom criteria, and the development of a synthesis of ideas that moves toward group consensus that is supported by the application of classroom criteria.

Reasoning to Investigations. A problem that we have noted in most science classrooms is that student investigations are typically motivated by the curriculum and sequence of lesson plans. Very rarely are investigations the outgrowth of student reasoning processes. In a portfolio culture, we encourage the bidirectionality of reasoning and investigations.

As illustrated already, alternative hypotheses are typically generated in this type of venture. The assessment conversation is intended to come to terms with some of this diversity, but should certainly not be seen as an endpoint. Instead, the result of the assessment conversation is, in reality, a new working hypothesis. Therefore, as scientists, it is necessary to take new conceptualizations and test them. Therefore, in the vessels project, students work in groups to build new vessels, testing their newly developed ideas about what contributes to a vessel's carrying capacity. The results of these investigations are then made public and explored to a given level of satisfaction, given curricular goals and developmental expectations.

Another direction we have taken has been to use the diversity of ideas as a way of structuring cooperative groups in the classroom. If one student believes that X is caused by Y and another believes that X is not caused by Y, then it makes sense to have these students work together, with the teacher's help, to develop an investigation that will address the discrepant views. Typically, the diversity of views can be anticipated, allowing for a sense of what shape these investigations are likely to take. So, for example, in the "Vessels" unit we developed a set of mini-units that are independent explorations of the effect of bottom surface area, height of sides, shape of vessel, thickness of sides, and so forth. When these ideas naturally emerge from the graphing discussion, teachers are prepared to put students together in groups to explore particular hypotheses. The students then bring the results of each individual experiment to the larger classroom.

Public Presentation of Ideas.   In the portfolio culture, as in the culture of science, ideas are ultimately considered in public forums. We are beginning to explore possible ways for students to publicly describe the results of their work, both in written and oral forms. In the "Vessels" project, students create a design packet that serves as a proposal to the city agency "sponsoring" this effort. In addition, oral presentations and descriptions of the work are also being explored. The purpose of these public presentations is to not only promote science presentation skills in written and oral form, but also to serve as a celebratory event for all the hard work that students have done. For the student, as well as a scientist, it is very rewarding to be able to present to others the results of one's good thinking and to get positive feedback from peers and others. Too often in the science classroom there is no opportunity for these types of celebrations. To the extent that celebrations are meaningful, it is because students have been held to high expectations and made significant progress in their thinking.

CAVEATS AND CONCLUSIONS

The view of science education espoused here is extremely difficult to realize in traditional classrooms in traditional schools. We have been fortunate to work with a group of exceptional teachers, yet we have had to encounter and overcome a number of significant hurdles in our research and development effort. Although we have accomplished much, we still have a good way to go before we have realized a true transformation of significant numbers of classrooms into a portfolio culture that is dedicated toward a conceptual change model of teaching. For those considering moving toward a portfolio culture model, we would recommend the following based on our experiences:

Starting Small and Familiar.   Trying to restructure the dynamics of classrooms, curricula content, and assessment procedures is a mammoth task that can rapidly become overwhelming, resulting in frustration and rejection. We have had more success starting with curriculum units that are already comfortable for teachers, and then slowly building in elements of a portfolio culture. For example, it is illuminating just to begin to ask questions of students that really probe what students understand with respect to some curricular unit. Getting students to show what they know is revealing, surprising, an interesting challenge for students, and often makes inadequacies in the current curriculum immediately apparent.

Because a portfolio culture implies a radical change for most teachers, it means that new routines must be learned and new logistics must be mastered. Therefore, starting with one class and one unit makes more sense than trying to implement a wholesale shift for all students across the entire curriculum. Again, such valiant attempts are doomed to failure. It is much more feasible to establish workable routines in a limited way and then expand the portfolio culture as it becomes more efficiently executed. By the end of the second year of SEPIA, teachers had become sufficiently immersed in the project to design and implement a comprehensive curriculum unit on acids and bases without the assistance of the research team.

Teacher Collaborations.   Critical to this effort has been the opportunity for teachers to get together regularly, share their experiences, and discuss student work. Discussions of student work have led to the development of criteria and the building of expectations for students. Additionally, successful initiatives of one teacher are rapidly borrowed by others when these lines of communication are available. It is essential that discussions around portfolio culture be grounded in student work, continually considering the science program in terms of what students are being asked to do and what they are doing. To ignore student work is to keep the discussion only at a philosophical level where each individual tends to have an individual interpretation of criteria, objectives, and the like. Grounding the discussion in student work helps to develop shared meaning, for ideas can be illustrated by and referenced to concrete examples of student performance. Providing these opportunities has time and economic consequences that have to be addressed by a school system.

Science Support.   Unfortunately, it is well documented that many teachers of science, especially those in elementary and middle schools, are inadequately prepared in their knowledge of the content matter of science (National Science Foundation, 1980). It is essential that the portfolio culture help teachers to continually develop their knowledge of science. We see this happening in several ways. First, discussions of student work that includes teachers, administrators, and perhaps outsiders (university people, community scientists) are an excellent and nonthreatening way to understand both science content and the teaching of that content. Looking at work may reveal misconceptions that are not unique to a student, but are also shared by individuals looking at that work. Collectively, a group expertise can gradually be established.

Second, explicit efforts are needed to provide teachers with curricular support, in terms of concepts, materials, and a clear sense of the conceptual difficulties students are likely to encounter. This support can be provided in written materials, but is likely to be more effective if discussed in face-to-face interactions.

Third, a portfolio culture necessarily implies a deeper understanding of a smaller number of concepts as coverage is reduced. One benefit for teachers is that such a move means that a smaller number of content areas need to be understood. In the curriculum we have been working with, there are 24 discrete units, a breadth that is virtually impossible for anyone to master competently. If we reduce the number of units significantly, then there is an increased possibility of grasping the core issues and concepts of each unit.

Rethinking Classroom Routines. For many teachers there is a discernible gap between the management of classroom behavior and the management of ideas. In many classrooms, teachers spend a great deal of time working on classroom behavior management that includes handling of materials, lab procedure protocols, and general student conduct expectations. Only after these are established do many teachers begin to explore science concepts. For a portfolio culture learning environment, we believe it is necessary that management of both forms be addressed simultaneously from the first day of school. Students need to know that ideas as well as behavior are the basis or currency of the classroom. Balancing these two complementary goals is often difficult for teachers.

In summary, we believe a portfolio culture can support the scientific conceptual growth of students by embracing a model of science and of learning that is more consistent with current notions of each, respectively. However, moving toward a portfolio culture presents significant challenges for teachers, administrators, and researchers, for it represents radical restructuring of science education and of classrooms. Much more is involved than introducing a new curriculum or new assessment technique into an existing classroom structure. Portfolio culture represents fundamental change in operative belief systems, and these are never easily transformed.

ACKNOWLEDGMENTS

Funding for this work is supported by the National Science Foundation (MDRI-9055574) to the University of Pittsburgh and Educational Testing Service. The views expressed here are those of the authors and do not imply any endorsement by NSF. We thank Ken Adams, Agnes Curry, Terry Golden, Jim Gray, Ron Karas, Michele Mackey, Nikki Rosato, Wanda Simmons-Barnes, and Gene Tabone, teachers in the Pittsburgh Public Schools, for all their contributions to the project. We also appreciate the assistance of Doris Litman, Ruth Martin, and Rich Matthews from the Pittsburgh Science Center, as well as Suhail Baloch, Bob Faux, Jay Freundlich, Leslie Petasis, Linda Reams, Mike Smith, and Sibel Erduran from the University of Pittsburgh. Finally, we are grateful to Samuel Palmer for assistance with the chapter's figures.

REFERENCES

Belanoff, P., & Dickson, M. (1991). *Portfolios: Process and product.* Portsmouth, NH: Boynton/Cook.

Bereiter, C., & Scardemalia, M. (1982). From conversation to composition: The role of instruction in a developmental process. In R. Glaser (Ed.), *Advances in instructional psychology* (Vol. 2, pp. 1–64). Hillsdale, NJ: Lawrence Erlbaum Associates.

Camp, R. (1993). The place of portfolios in our changing views of writing assessment. In R. E. Bennett & W. C. Ward (Eds.), *Construction versus choice in cognitive measurement* (pp. 183–212). Hillsdale, NJ: Lawrence Erlbaum Associates.

Carey, S., Evans, R., Honda, M., Jay, E., & Unger, C. (1989). "An experiment is when you try it and see if it works": A study of grade 7 students' understanding of the construction of scientific knowledge. *International Journal of Science Education, 11,* 514–529.

Cognition and Technology Group at Vanderbilt University. (1990). Anchored instruction and its relationship to situated cognition. *Educational Researcher, 19,* 2–10.

Cognition and Technology Group at Vanderbilt University. (1992). Anchored instruction in science and mathematics: Theoretical basis, developmental projects, and initial research findings. In. R. A. Duschl & R. J. Hamilton (Eds.), *Philosophy of science, cognitive psychology, and educational theory and practice* (pp. 244–273). Albany, NY: SUNY Press.

Darling-Hammond, L. (1993). Reframing the school reform agenda: Developing capacity for school transformation. *Phi Delta Kappan, 74,* 752–761.

Duschl, R. (1985). The changing concept of scientific observation. In R. Bybee (Ed.), *Science technology society: 1985 yearbook of the National Science Teachers Association* (pp. 60–69). Washington, DC: National Science Teachers Association.

Duschl, R. (1990). *Restructuring science education: The role of theories and their importance.* New York: Teachers College Press—Columbia University.

Duschl, R., & Gitomer, D. (1991). Epistemological perspectives on conceptual change: Implications for educational practice. *Journal of Research in Science Teaching, 28,* 839–858.

Duschl, R. A., & Gitomer, D. H. (in press). Strategies and challenges to changing the focus of assessment and instruction in science classrooms. *Educational Assessment.*

Duschl, R., & Hamilton, R.(Eds.). (1992). *Philosophy of science, cognitive psychology, and educational theory and practice.* Albany, NY: SUNY Press.

Duschl, R. Hamilton, R., & Grandy, R. (1990). Psychology and epistemology: Match or mismatch when applied to science education? *International Journal of Science Education, 12*, 220–243.

Gitomer, D. H. (1989). *Developing a portfolio culture that enables learners.* Paper presented at the National Summit Conference on the Arts and Education, Washington, DC.

Gitomer, D. H. (1991). The art of accountability. *Teaching Thinking and Problem Solving, 13*, 1–9.

Gitomer, D. H., Grosh, S., & Price, K. (1992). Portfolio culture in arts education. *Art Education*, 7–15.

Gitomer, D. H., Zohar, A., Chang, M., & Duschl, R. A. (1994). *The impact of portfolio culture practices on classroom discourse.* Paper presented at the annual meeting of the American Educational Research Association, New Orleans.

Hodson, D. (1992) Assessment of practical work: Some considerations in philosophy of science. *Science & Education, 1*, 115–144.

Kilbourn, B. (1982). Curriculum materials: Teaching, and potential outcomes of students: A qualitative analysis. *Journal of Research in Science Teaching, 19*, 675–688.

Koretz, D., Stecher, B., & Deibert, E. (1993). *The reliability of scores from the 1992 Vermont portfolio assessment program* (Tech. Rep. No. 355). Los Angeles: University of California, Center for Research on Evaluation, Standards, and Student Testing: Center for the Study of Evaluation.

Kuhn, D. (1993). Science as argument: Implications for teaching and learning scientific thinking. *Science Education, 77*, 319–338.

Kuhn, T. (1962/1970). *The structure of scientific revolutions (2nd ed.).* Chicago: University of Chicago Press.

Laudan, L. (1977). *Progress and its problems.* Berkeley: University of California Press.

Laudan, L. (1984). *Science and values: The aims of science and their role in scientific debate.* Berkeley: University of California Press.

Nadeau, R., & Desautels, J. (1984) *Epistemology and the teaching of science.* Ottawa: Science Council of Canada.

National Science Foundation. (1980). *What are the needs in precollege science, mathematics, and social science education? Views from the field.* Washington, DC: U.S. Government Printing Office.

Paulson, F. L., Paulson, P. P., & Meyer, C. A. (1991). What makes a portfolio a portfolio? *Educational Leadership, 48*, 60–63.

Posner, G., Strike, K., Hewson, P., & Gertzog, W. (1982). Accommodation of a scientific conception: Toward a theory of conceptual change. *Science Education, 66*, 211–227.

Rissland, E. (1985). The structure of knowledge in complex domains. In S. Chipman, J. Segal, & R. Glaser (Eds.), *Thinking and learning skills* (Vol. 2, pp. 107–125). Hillsdale, NJ: Lawrence Erlbaum Associates.

Russell, T. (1981). What history of science, how much, and why? *Science Education, 65*, 51–64.

Schwab, J. (1960). What do scientists do? *Behavorial Science, 5*, 1–27.

Schwab, J. (1962). The teaching of science as inquiry. In J. Schwab & P. Brandwein (Eds.), *The teaching of science* (pp. 3–103). Cambridge, MA: Harvard University Press.

Schwab, J. (1964). The structure of the natural sciences. In G. W. Ford & L. Pugno (Eds.), *The structure of knowledge and the curriculum* (pp. 31–49). Chicago: Rand McNally.

Shapere, D. (1987). Method in the philosophy of science and epistemology: How to inquire about inquiry and knowledge. In N. Nersessian (Ed.), *The process of science* (pp. 1–38). Dordrecht: Martinus Nijhoff.

Strike, K., & Posner, G. (1992). A revisionist theory of conceptual change. In R. Duschl & R. Hamilton (Eds.), *Philosophy of science, cognitive psychology, and educational theory and practice* (pp. 147–176). Albany, NY: SUNY Press.

Takeuchi, H., Uyeda, S. & Kanamori, H. (1967). *Debate about the earth: Approach to geophysics through analysis of continental drift.* San Francisco: Freeman, Cooper.

Tierney, R. J., Carter, M. A., & Desai, L. E. (1991). *Portfolios in the reading-writing classroom.* Norwood, MA: Christopher Gordon.

Toulmin, S. (1958). *The uses of argument.* Cambridge: Cambridge University Press.

Vosniadou, S., & Brewer, W. F. (1987). Theories of knowledge restructuring in development. *Review of Educational Research, 57,* 51–67.

Vosniadou, S., & Ortony, A. (1989). *Similarity and analogical reasoning.* New York: Cambridge University Press.

Wolf, D. P., Bixby, J., Glenn, J., & Gardner, H. (1991). To use their minds well: Investigating new form of student assessment. In G. Grant (Ed.), *Review of research in education* (Vol. 17, pp. 31–74). Washington, DC: American Educational Research Association.

14 Diagnostic Assessment of Students' Science Knowledge

David F. Treagust
Curtin University of Technology, Perth, Australia

Science education reforms taking place in the United States (American Association for the Advancement of Science, 1993; Shymansky & Kyle, 1992), Australia (Australian Education Council, 1992), England (Department of Education and Science, 1991), and other countries indicate an increasing awareness that the science curriculum offered in schools is not meeting the needs of society today and is likely to be inadequate for the future. A related component of this reform concerns making judgments about students' performance as they learn about the curriculum. In most of these reports about curriculum reform, the concerns about examinations and testing are usually presented as refinements of existing technical testing procedures. However, research suggests that current assessment procedures distort and narrow instruction, misrepresent the nature of the subject, and underscore inequities in access to education. Furthermore, current assessment procedures are claimed to not provide valid measures of what students know, and to provide no opportunity for students and teachers to be involved in discussions about the work being assessed (Lorsbach, Tobin, Briscoe, & LaMaster, 1992; Wolf, Bixby, Glenn, & Gardner, 1991).

Wolf et al. (1991) recommended that alternative forms of assessment are needed that might permit the assessment of thinking rather than of the possession of information. These alternative assessment procedures are presented in a context of learning and include performance tasks and portfolio-like components. Assessment by performance tasks requires students to write, read, and solve problems in genuine rather than artificial ways. Portfolio-based assessment involves a structured sampling of a student's earlier and later work on, for example, selected science problems

327

taken from different topics. Wolf et al. (1991, p. 33) claimed that a shift in this direction of assessment "might enable teachers to develop sophisticated clinical judgements about students' understanding of significant ideas and processes and encourage educators to discuss, rather than simply measure, educational progress."

These alternative forms of assessment are different from those generally used by science teachers in that standard tests are largely paper-and-pencil collections of individual items with single correct answers presented without a surrounding context. A change in this direction of assessment is highly recommended by many authors, but a considerable amount of in-service education about their use will be needed before such alternative forms of assessment become the norm, or at least begin to be used by teachers with any confidence. The supporters of these different approaches to assessment have neglected to consider that alternative forms of current assessment procedures also can assess thinking in a context.

Many of the concerns about testing just described can be addressed by teachers using a substantially different type of multiple choice assessment items that are thoroughly grounded in recent research findings in science education. The basis for this type of assessment argues that teachers must learn about the intuitive knowledge base that students have already constructed if they want to understand students' thinking of science concepts. The research that informs this position is a constructivist approach to learning, which has been elaborated by many authors such as Driver (1986) and Tobin (1993).

During the past two decades, research in science education has provided data to conclusively claim that students bring with them to science lessons certain ideas and notions that are well established but that are frequently inconsistent with the ideas of teachers and scientists. The large body of literature in this field has been summarized by Confrey (1990), Driver and Erickson (1983), and Pfundt and Duit (1994). Students' conceptions that are different from those generally accepted by the scientific community have been given different terms, often depending on the author's view of the nature of knowledge and its construction. Terms such as *misconceptions, preconceptions, alternative frameworks, children's science,* or *students' science* are all commonly used. The term *misconception* receives much less attention than it did 10 years ago and is now generally reserved for alternative conceptions that arise as a result of instruction. In this chapter, students' ideas that are different from scientists' ideas are called *alternative conceptions* or *students' conceptions* to acknowledge that students have constructed their own understanding of the concepts under consideration.

The usual means for obtaining information about students' conceptions, either prior to or following formal instruction, has been through individual student interviews, an approach for probing children's thinking developed by Piaget. A variety of interview formats or procedures for conducting these interviews has been developed, with interviews-about-instances and interviews-about-events being perhaps the most common (see Bell, Osborne, & Tasker, 1985). As valuable as interviews are, it is often difficult for practicing secondary science teachers to conduct them, particularly when time is limited and class enrollments are high.

In advocating different assessment procedures to probe students' understanding of scientific concepts, Simpson and Arnold (1982, p. 181) recommended that information "relating to peculiar and erroneous information held to be true by pupils" should be included in tests that depart from the usual norm-referenced paradigm. This line of research in assessment has included the development of multiple choice tests items that have distractors based on students' conceptions. Researchers currently involved in this line of diagnostic assessment include Hestenes (Halloun & Hestenes, 1985; Hestenes, Wells, & Swackhamer, 1992), Tamir (Amir, Frankl, & Tamir, 1987; Amir & Tamir, 1990), and Treagust (Haslam & Treagust, 1987; Peterson, Treagust & Garnett, 1989; Treagust, 1989).

The development of multiple choice instruments to identify students' conceptions has the potential to make a valuable contribution to the field of alternative assessment. A further important point is that such instruments can help science teachers use the findings of this research to inform their teaching. Results from science education research do take considerable time to be used by teachers, and the development of instruments incorporating research findings, which can be readily utilized in the classroom, would appear to be one way of greatly improving the rate of this application.

As is shown in this chapter, alternative conceptions held by students can be identified by administering specifically designed pencil-and-paper multiple choice instruments that assess understanding in limited and clearly defined content areas. Such instruments can be used for diagnostic purposes rather than for summative assessment, and help the teacher to begin to address existing students' conceptions that are not compatible with scientific conceptions. These existing conceptions may be influenced by earlier teaching and learning prior to commencing the topic, or may have occurred following teaching of the topic. It is, however, well documented that the task of changing students' conceptions is not easy, because these conceptions have been constructed and successfully used by students to explain their daily experiences. Further, students' alternative conceptions often have been incorporated securely into cognitive structure, and teacher's learning about students' conceptions does not lead directly to improved instruction (Hashweh, 1986). Nevertheless, a teacher needs a starting place for addressing known students' conceptions and/or misconceptions, and a multiple choice diagnostic instrument, informed by research in students' learning problems in a particular content area, would appear to provide a relatively straightforward approach to such assessment. Another viable aspect of developing the instruments is that they can be used by other researchers in studies using large populations where it is less practical to use interviews.

Of direct concern in this chapter is the application of a constructivist perspective to the complex problems of assessment of two science content areas. The topics selected for discussion are photosynthesis and respiration in plants, and covalent bonding and structure in chemistry. The two topics are central to an understanding of biology and chemistry, respectively. The chapter first describes a procedure used in developing the diagnostic instruments that examine and identify students' conceptions. This procedure can be utilized by science teachers to develop their own test instruments, but it does require a lot of time. Next, I discuss how the two instruments can be used by teachers to diagnose students' thinking about the content of these topics.

DEVELOPMENT OF THE DIAGNOSTIC INSTRUMENTS

The development of the diagnostic instruments for identifying students' conceptions in specific science content areas comprises 10 steps involving three broad areas: defining the content, obtaining information about students' conceptions, and developing a diagnostic instrument.

Defining the Content

The first four steps are concerned with defining the conceptual boundaries of the topic pertinent to a particular grade level or levels. These steps involve the identification of propositional content knowledge statements and the development of a concept map.

Step 1: Identifying Propositional Knowledge Statements. The importance of identifying propositional knowledge statements in curriculum development and teaching has been described by Finley and Stewart (1982). Using this technique, 46 propositional knowledge statements were identified for photosynthesis and respiration in plants (see Table 14.1), and 33 propositional knowledge statements were identified for the covalent bonding and structure topic.

Step 2: Developing a Concept Map. A map of concepts that relate to the topic under investigation at a particular level of instruction is developed (Novak, 1991; Novak & Gowin, 1984). For example, the concept map of the covalent bonding and structure topic, which includes most of the proposi-

TABLE 14.1
Propositional Statements Representing Knowledge Required to Comprehend
the Mechanisms of Photosynthesis and Respiration in Plants

P 1	Chlorophyll gives green color to the leaves and to the stems.
P 2	Chloroplasts are found in plant cells containing chlorophyll.
P 3	Photosynthesis takes place only in the presence of light energy.
P 4	Photosynthesis takes place mainly in the leaves (but green stems make food too).
P 5	Carbon dioxide is taken in by the green leaf (or green stem) during the process of photosynthesis.
P 6	Water is absorbed through the roots of the plant.
P 7	The four essential factors for photosynthesis in plant cells are light energy, chlorophyll, carbon dioxide, and water.
P 8	Glucose and oxygen are produced during photosynthesis.
P 9	Oxygen gas is given off by the green leaves (or green stems) during the process of photosynthesis.
P10	Plants use glucose molecules to derive energy for growth, transport, reproduction, etc.
P11	Glucose molecules that are not used immediately by the plant form starch.
P12	Glucose is converted to starch for storage in the cells.
P13	Starch is converted back to glucose to supply energy for the plant's growth etc.
P14	Photosynthesis may be represented by the equations:

$$\text{Carbon dioxide} + \text{water} \xrightarrow[\text{chlorophyll}]{\text{light energy}} \text{glucose} + \text{oxygen gas}$$

or

$$CO_2 + H_2O \xrightarrow[\text{chlorophyll}]{\text{light energy}} C_6H_{12}O_6 + O_2$$

or

$$6CO_2 + 6H_2O \xrightarrow[\text{chlorophyll}]{\text{light energy}} C_6H_{12}O_6 + 6O_2$$

P15	Photosynthesis is the process by which green plants containing chlorophyll are able to trap light energy, and use it to combine carbon dioxide and water to make simple sugars (plant food) such as glucose and to produce oxygen gas.
P16	In some simple plants (some seaweeds) brown and red chloroplasts (other types of chlorophyll) are present, which absorb the light for photosynthesis. This is to make better use of the light, mainly blue, available in deep water.
P17	Green plants use some of the oxygen produced during photosynthesis. The extra oxygen goes into the air.
P18	The rate of photosynthesis increases when light intensity increases.
R 1	Every living cell respires.
R 2	All organisms, plants and animals, respire continually.
R 3	Respiration is a chemical process in which chemical energy, stored in food, is released, using oxygen, so that cells can use it in other ways.
R 4	Plants and animals need energy to live and grow.
R 5	During respiration plants derive energy from glucose.
R 6	Glucose is used up during respiration.

(Continued)

TABLE 14.1 (*continued*)

R 7	The end products of respiration are energy, carbon dioxide, and water. This process may be represented by the equation:

$$\text{Glucose} + \text{oxygen} \longrightarrow \text{energy} + \text{carbon dioxide} + \text{water}$$

R 8	Carbon dioxide is present in the atmosphere.
R 9	Oxygen is present in the atmosphere.
R10	Oxygen is taken in during respiration.
R11	Roots of plants obtain oxygen from the soil air.
R12	The oxygen dissolved in soil water diffuses into the root cells whereas carbon dioxide produced from the root cells diffuses out.
R13	Oxygen molecules enter the leaf through the stomata (pores).
R14	Carbon dioxide produced during respiration diffuses out through the stomata.
R15	Stomata (pores) are present on the leaf surface. Gases diffuse in and out of the stomata.
R16	The symbol of oxygen gas is O_2. The symbol for carbon dioxide is CO_2.
R17	Both plants and animals release carbon dioxide during respiration.
R18	Carbon dioxide is the only gas that will react with clear lime water to turn it "milky white."
R19	Carbon dioxide will react with bromothymol blue (BTB) solution to change its color from blue to green when there is a small amount of CO_2, and from blue to yellow when there is much CO_2.
R20	All living things derive their energy from glucose molecules by a process of respiration in which oxygen is used.
R21	If an organism cannot obtain energy it will die.
R22	Breathing is a method of taking air into the body to provide the important oxygen that the body needs to carry out the process of respiration in cells. Breathing is a physical process whereas respiration is a chemical process.
PR 1	In bright daylight photosynthesis in plants occurs at a much greater rate than respiration.
PR 2	At night, if there is no light energy at all, photosynthesis ceases while respiration continues.
PR 3	During the day when photosynthesis is occurring more oxygen is produced than is used by respiration.
PR 4	Photosynthesis is a constructive process that may lead to increase in mass.
PR 5	Respiration is a destructive process that may lead to decrease in mass.
PR 6	Respiration and photosynthesis in terms of products and reactants are reverse reactions of each other; the products of one are used as reactants of the other.

Note. P indicates propositions required to comprehend the mechanism of photosynthesis, R propositions required to comprehend the mechanism of respiration, and PR proposition required to comprehend the relationship between photosynthesis and respiration.

tional knowledge statements, is shown in Fig. 14.1. As with the development of propositional knowledge statements, this activity enables the researcher to carefully consider the extent of the content that has been selected for instruction.

Step 3: Relating Propositional Knowledge to the Concept Map. The propositional knowledge statements are related directly to the concept map

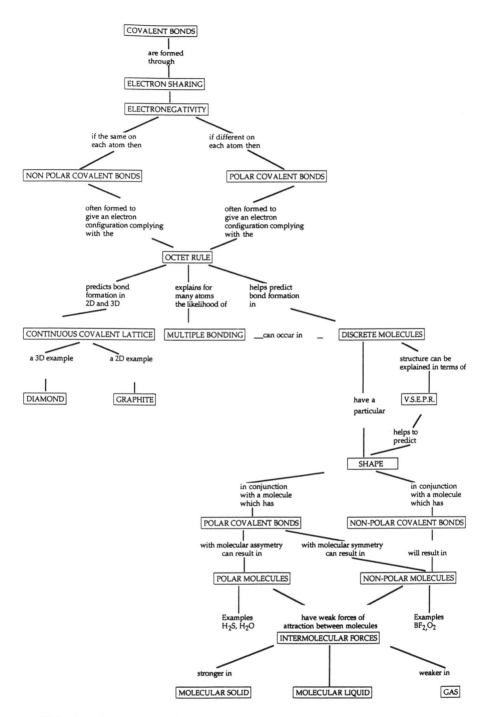

FIG. 14.1 Concept map with propositional knowledge statements related on to the diagnostic instrument" "Covalent Bonding and Structure."

to ensure that the content being examined is internally consistent. This is a reliability check that the underlying concepts and propositional statements are covering the same topic area. To ensure that the concept area is properly documented, it is essential that there is a representative covering of concepts and propositional statements for each topic under investigation.

Step 4: Validating the Content. The propositional statements and the concept map are content validated by subject matter experts who may be science educators, secondary science teachers, and university science specialists. Any discrepancies or irregularities are deleted, and the list of propositional statements and the concept maps are corrected and modified. In this way, the knowledge being examined is documented so that all questions developed for the multiple choice instrument relate clearly to the concepts being taught. An essential feature of this development is that the content and concepts to be investigated are scientifically accurate as far as the particular level of study being assessed. The final revised list of propositions and the concept map reflect the input from experts in these content areas.

Obtaining Information About Students' Conceptions

The second broad area in the process of developing a diagnostic instrument to evaluate students' conceptions involves three steps. Initially, a thorough examination of the relevant research literature is made. Then data from interviews and from free responses on open-ended pencil-and-paper questions are obtained to identify students' understanding of science content that they have studied or are about to study. In this way, a typical range of students' conceptions of the topic is determined.

Step 5: Examining Related Research Literature. Before commencing new efforts to identify problems and/or students' conceptions in the science topic being investigated, the related literature dealing with research on students' conceptions is examined. At the time of development of the instruments, a review of the literature did not identify any research on students' conceptions on covalent bonding and structure. On the other hand, considerable research was available concerning students' conceptions of photosynthesis and respiration in plants. These research findings and others concerning young people's ideas about plants have been reviewed recently by Wood-Robinson (1991). By examining the descriptions of students' conceptions and those areas with conceptual difficulty, it is possible to begin to build up a base of information for developing multiple choice items based on students' conceptions.

Step 6: Conducting Unstructured Student Interviews.   In order to gain a broad perspective of students' understanding of the science topics under investigation, unstructured tape-recorded interviews are conducted with students who have recently completed the topic. These interviews help to identify students' alternative conceptions, and areas of misunderstanding and/or misconceptions. Examples of open-ended questions are, "What is a covalent bond?", "Why do molecules have different shapes?", "How does a plant obtain food?", or "Explain what happens when plants respire." Students' responses are probed further, and any alternative conceptions or differences in thinking compared to the teacher are noted. This part of the instrument development could be conducted with interviews-about-events or interviews-about-instances cards, but in this instance I have described a more open-ended approach.

Step 7: Developing Multiple Choice Content Items with Free Response.
Items of a multiple choice nature are written based on the topic being taught. Each item is based on a limited number of propositional statements and is designed to address students' conceptions and misconceptions encountered in the literature and the interviews. Each multiple choice item is followed by a space for the student to complete the reason why the particular option of the multiple choice was selected. After a series of items has been developed that is representative of the topic, the instrument is given to a class of students who have studied the topic. Students' conceptions as well as acceptable scientific conceptions become evident in the free-response answers. This technique is common in students' conceptions research and has been described in much detail in the literature.

Developing a Diagnostic Instrument

The third broad area for the instrument construction involves the development of two-tier items, of which the first tier requires a content response and the second tier requires a reason for the response. The responses generated from Steps 5, 6, and 7 are used to produce the second tier of the items.

Step 8: Developing the Two-Tier Diagnostic Instruments.   A two-tier diagnostic instrument is developed from the multiple choice items with a design comparable to the format of the Test of Logical Thinking (Tobin & Capie, 1981). In this design, the first part of each item on the instrument is a multiple choice content question having usually two or three choices. The second part of each item contains a set of four possible reasons for the answer given to the first part. The reasons consist of the designated correct answer, together with identified students' conceptions and/or misconceptions. The reasons are from the students' responses given to each open-response question as well as information gathered from the interviews and the literature. When more than one alternative conception is given, these are included as separate alternative reason responses. Students' answers to each item are considered to be correct only if both the correct choice and correct reason are given.

Step 9: Designing a Specification Grid. A specification grid is designed to ensure that the diagnostic instrument fairly covers the propositional knowledge statements and the concepts on the concept map underlying the topic. The items in the instrument on photosynthesis and respiration in plants were content validated against the propositional statements, and the final arrangement is shown in Table 14.2.

Step 10: Continuing Refinements. Successive refinements of the two-tier multiple choice items with different classes ensure that the instrument as a whole can be used for diagnosing students' alternative conceptions in the topic being assessed. The development of these instruments to date has shown that each item can be successfully refined to improve its diagnostic nature. There is no shortcut to obtain initial information on student responses other than to thoroughly review the students' conceptions literature, interview students, and collect data by pencil-and-paper open-ended

TABLE 14.2

Specification Grid of Propositional Knowledge Statements for Each Item in "What Do You Know About Photosynthesis and Respiration in Plants?"

	Propositional Knowledge Statements		
Item	Photosynthesis	Respiration	Relationship Between Photosynthesis and Respiration in Plants
1	P3 P5 P15	(R2)	(PR3)
2	(P3) (P5)	R2 R10	
3	(P3)	R2 R10 R14	
4	(P3)(P5)	R17	(PR1)
5		R1 R2 R4	
6		R1 R4 R22	
7	(P3)	R4 R5 R7	
8	(P3)	R2 R4 R20	
9	(P14)	R5 R6 R7 R10	(PR6)
10	P8 P9 P14 P15	(R7)	(PR6)
11	P7 P14 P15 P18		
12	P5 P15		(PR1)(PR4)
13	P3	R2 R20 R21	PR2

Note. The propositional knowledge statements in parentheses are implicitly addressed by the item.

items. Each administration of the instrument to different groups of students provides improvements for diagnostic assessment of students' conceptions by each item.

ASSESSMENT OF STUDENTS' UNDERSTANDING
IN BIOLOGY

An instrument, "What Do You Know About Photosynthesis and Respiration in Plants?" (Haslam & Treagust, 1987), was developed to examine students' conceptual understanding of photosynthesis and respiration in plants. The propositional knowledge statements shown in Table 14.1 represent the level of understanding of the mechanism of photosynthesis, the mechanism of respiration, and the relationships between photosynthesis and respiration, as expected from study during the first 3 years of high school (ages 12–15 years). Consequently, there are some restrictions on the content presented at this level of science. For example, proposition P8 does not consider that carbohydrates other than glucose are produced during photosynthesis, and proposition P11 does not consider that plants store lipids as well as starch, because these aspects are not part of the curriculum in Grades 8–10.

The instrument was administered to students in Grades 8–10 in one school and to students in Grades 11 and 12 in three schools from comparative socioeconomic areas. The students in Grades 11 and 12 are more homogeneous than students in earlier years of secondary schooling because they have chosen to study biology and, as a result of their previous grades, have been accepted to do so. Difficulty indices of the items in the instrument ranged from 0.12 to 0.78 and discrimination indices ranged from 0.36 to 0.60. These data indicate that the items have a wide range of difficulty and that they all discriminated in an acceptable manner between students who understood the concepts investigated and those who did not understand. Following administration of the instrument to a total of 441 students in Grades 8–12 in Western Australian schools, 17 alternative conceptions were identified (see Table 14.3) across all five grade levels.

The second item of this instrument (see Table 14.4), which investigates students' understanding of the gas being taken in by plants when there is no light energy, illustrates how the data from these items are obtained and can be interpreted. Specifically, item 2 addresses the following four propositional knowledge statements:

R2: All organisms, plants and animals, respire continually.

R10: Oxygen is taken in during respiration.

P3: Photosynthesis takes place only in the presence of light energy.

P5: Carbon dioxide is taken in by the green leaf (or green stem) during the process of photosynthesis.

TABLE 14.3

Percentage of Secondary Students with Alternative Conceptions of
Photosynthesis and Respiration in Plants Identified by the
Two-Tier Diagnostic Instrument

	Grade				
Students' Alternative Conceptions	8 (n = 137)	9 (n = 88)	10 (n = n = 99)	11 (n = 68)	12 (n = 49)
Photosynthesis					
Photosynthesis occurs in green plants all the time.	21	14	11	9	0
Photosynthesis can occur when there is no light energy.	27	25	19	3	0
Green plants make their food from oxygen gas in the presence of light energy.	25	13	18	10	2
Nongreen plants like fungi that do not contain chlorophyll or similar pigments can also photosynthesize.	17	12	19	7	0
The most important benefit to green plants when they photosynthesize is the production of energy for plant growth.	22	28	30	34	31
The most important benefit to plants when they photosynthesize is the removal of carbon dioxide from the air through the leaf's stomates.	22	23	25	12	2
Respiration					
Respiration in green plants take place only during the day.	21	11	17	0	0
Respiration does not take place in the presence of light energy.	14	12	18	12	0
Carbon dioxide is used in respiration when there is no light energy to photosynthesize.	11	21	11	9	6
Oxygen gas is used in respiration, which only occurs in green plants when there is no light energy to photosynthesize.	12	11	23	34	15
Green plants stop photosynthesizing when there is no light energy at all so they continue to respire and give off oxygen gas.	21	34	20	16	4
Green plants respire only when there is no light energy.	18	21	25	20	10

(Continued)

338

TABLE 14.3 (*continued*)

Students' Alternative Conceptions	Grade				
	8 *(n = 137)*	*9* *(n = 88)*	*10* *(n = n = 99)*	*11* *(n = 68)*	*12* *(n = 49)*
Respiration in plants takes place in the cells of the leaves only, because only leaves have special pores to exchange gases.	29	47	41	34	8
Respiration in green plants provides energy to live and is a chemical process by which plants manufacture food from water and carbon dioxide.	11	9	12	9	2
Respiration in green plants is the taking in of carbon dioxide and giving off of oxygen gases through plant stomates.	18	9	24	16	0
Green plants respire only at night (when there is no light energy).	24	42	34	23	12
In the process of respiration carbon dioxide and water are used by the green plant to produce energy, during which time glucose and oxygen waste are produced.	15	20	25	19	6

As shown in Table 14.2, the first two propositional knowledge statements are addressed directly by item 2, whereas the second two statements are addressed implicitly. The results indicate that this sample of students does not have a clear understanding of the process of photosynthesis and supports the usual problem that students believe plants photosynthesize and animals respire. Further analysis of the data provides valuable information about students' thinking in this context.

When the first part of the item only is taken into consideration (end column of Table 14.4), the results show that there is generally an increasingly correct response choice from Grades 8–12 (39%, 44%, 41%, 65%, 88%) about oxygen gas being taken in by green plants when there is no light energy. However, when students' reasoning for their choice in the first part of the item is taken into consideration, the correct response is much lower (9%, 11%, 7%, 28%, 65%). While there is generally less selection of

TABLE 14.4
Percentage of Secondary Students Selecting Alternative Responses on Item
Number 2 from the Diagnostic Test on Photosynthesis and
Respiration in Plants

Which gas is taken by green plants in large amounts when there is no light energy at all?
(1) carbon dioxide gas
(2) oxygen gas
The reason for my answer is because:
(A) This gas is used in photosynthesis, which occurs in green plants all the time.
(B) This gas is used in photosynthesis, which occurs in green plants when there is no light energy at all.
(C) This gas is used in respiration, which occurs in green plants when there is no light energy to photosynthesize.
(D) This gas is used in respiration, which takes place continuously in green plants.

Grade Level	Number of Students	Content Choice	Reason Choice				No Reason	Total (%)
			A	B	C	D		
8	137	1	14	17	11	16	3	61
		2	7	10	12	9[a]	1	39
9	88	1	11	6	21	17	1	56
		2	3	19	11	11[a]	–	44
10	99	1	8	11	11	25	4	59
		2	3	8	23	7[a]	–	41
11	68	1	7	1	9	18	–	35
		2	2	1	34	28[a]	–	65
12	49	1	–	–	6	6	–	12
		2	–	–	15	65[a]	8	88

Note. "-" No responses in this category. [a]The correct choice and reason response.

alternative reasons at each successively higher year level, it is not until Grade 12 that responses indicate that this sample of students has an adequate understanding about respiration in plants.

The results of administering the diagnostic instrument provide data that show that in Grades 8–11, and in some cases in Grade 12 also, a high percentage of students held alternative conceptions. Based on the responses to item 2, the selection of choice A in the second tier, irrespective of which gas was considered to be present in large quantities, diagnoses that substantial numbers of students in Grades 8–10 (21%, 14%, 11%) believed that photosynthesis occurs in plants at all times. Examining responses to choice B in the second tier, again irrespective of which gas was considered to be present in large quantities, shows that a substantial number of these students (27%, 25%, 19%) believed that photosynthesis can occur when there is no light energy.

Choice 1C diagnoses that 11%, 21%, and 11% of students in Grades

8–10 believed that carbon dioxide is used in respiration when there is no light energy to photosynthesize. A similar percentage chose 2C (12%, 11%, 23%), indicating that they believed that oxygen gas is used in respiration that only occurs in green plants when there is no light energy to photosynthesize. In making choice 2C it is instructive to see that 34 % and 15% of Grades 11 and 12 students believed that respiration and photosynthesis are not occurring at the same time.

Examining the data from the instrument as a whole shows that the two most consistent student conceptions were related to understanding whether plants respire during the day and/or the night, and the relationship between respiration and photosynthesis. In addition, high proportions of students did not comprehend that respiration is an energy conversion process, viewed photosynthesis as an energy-providing process, and considered respiration and breathing to be synonymous. Students' attempts to understand the concepts of photosynthesis and respiration in plants result in many concepts that are not well articulated and others that are erroneous but still firmly held by some students in Grades 11 and 12.

These results are perhaps surprising when one realizes that respiration is frequently taught as an identified topic as early as Grade 8 and is addressed throughout biology classes in later years of the students' secondary schooling. Nevertheless, the findings illustrate students' alternative conceptions, misconceptions, and lack of understanding that respiration in plants is an ongoing continuous process during both light and dark conditions.

ASSESSMENT OF STUDENTS' UNDERSTANDING IN CHEMISTRY

The diagnostic instrument "Covalent Bonding and Structure" (Peterson, Treagust, & Garnett, 1987), consisting of 15 items, was developed to examine students' conceptual understanding of six areas of chemistry, namely, bond polarity (three items), molecular shape (five items), polarity of molecules (three items), lattices (two items), intermolecular forces (two items), and the octet rule (two items). Each item is based on a problem-centred situation and examines a limited number of previously content-validated propositional knowledge statements. The first tier of each item consists of a content question having two, three, or occasionally four choices; the second part of each item contains four possible reasons for the answers given in the first tier, which included the correct answer and three alternative reasons involving students' conceptions.

The instrument was used to collect data from students who previously had received instruction about covalent bonding and structure while enrolled in chemistry during the last two years of high school. The students, of whom 159 were in Grade 11 and 84 in Grade 12, attended 14 different classes in five different schools. Analysis of the data showed that the items ranged in difficulty from 0.13 to 0.60 and that the discrimination indices ranged from 0.32 to 0.65, all items being acceptable discriminators. The seventh item of this diagnostic instrument (see Table 14.5) assesses students' understanding of intermolecular forces and is based on three propositional knowledge statements:

Intermolecular forces, or weak forces of attraction, exist in varying degrees between molecules.

Whether a substance composed of molecules exists as a solid, liquid, or gas at room temperature will depend on the magnitude of the intermolecular forces between molecules.

Molecular substances with high melting and boiling points have strong intermolecular forces between molecules.

The majority of students in both grades (88%, 98%) responded correctly that intermolecular forces account for the difference in state of hydrogen

TABLE 14.5

Percentage of Students Selecting Alternative Responses on Item Number 7 from the Diagnostic Instrument on Covalent Bonding and Structure

Water (H_2O) and hydrogen sulfide (H_2S) have similar chemical formulas and have V-shaped structures. At room temperature, water is a liquid and hydrogen sulfide a gas. The difference in state between water and hydrogen sulfide is due to the presence of strong intermolecular forces between
(1) H_2O molecules
(2) H_2S molecules
Reason
(A) The difference in strength of the intermolecular forces is due to differences in the strength of the O-H and S-H covalent bonds.
(B) The bonds in H_2S are easily broken, whereas in H_2O they are not.
(C) The difference in strength of the intermolecular forces is due to the difference in polarity of the molecules.
(D) The difference in strength of the intermolecular forces is due to the fact that H_2O is a polar molecule, and H_2S is a nonpolar molecule.

Grade Level	Number of Students	Content Choice	Reason Choice				Total (%)
			A	B	C	D	
11	159	1	14	49	11[a]	14	88
		2	4	4	3	1	12
12	84	1	23	17	33[a]	25	98
		2	0	0	2	0	2

[a] *The correct choice and reason response*

sulfide and water at room temperature. Almost all these chemistry students were aware of the relationship that exists between the strength of the intermolecular forces and the melting point/boiling point of a substance. However, only 11% and 33%, respectively, correctly understood why this relationship exists. A large percentage of students in Grade 11 (63%, i.e., 14% + 49%) and Grade 12 (40%, i.e., 23% + 17%) selected choices 1A or 1B, which relate to the strength of intramolecular bonds. These students appeared to hold an alternative conception of why molecules are either in liquid or vapor phase at room temperature. This conception was identified easily by the teachers using this item. Indeed, the major alternative conception being addressed, which was identified by interview and in the free-response format in the development of this item, related to the common misunderstanding that "intermolecular forces are the forces within a molecule."

A second alternative conception addressed in choice B of item 7 was that "covalent bonds are broken when a substance changes state." This alternative conception, selected by 49% of Grade 11 students and 17% of Grade 12, indicated these students have not understood the nature of intermolecular forces compared with the forces within a molecule. The alternative conception is similar to that reported by Osborne and Cosgrove (1983), where students considered that the bonds in water molecules were broken when water changed state.

Analysis of incorrect combinations of the items following administration of the instrument of these Australian student groups has resulted in the identification of 14 alternative conceptions in the six conceptual areas (see Table 14.6) that make up the diagnostic instrument. For example, students' ability to establish the correct polarity of a bond was unexpectedly low. In this sample, 33% and 23% of students in Grades 11 and 12, respectively, appeared to have correctly related electron sharing to covalent bonds, but had not considered the influence of electronegativity and the resultant unequal sharing of the electron pair on bond polarity. One common student conception relating to the shape of molecules was that the "repulsion between bonds" determined molecular shape. This explanation was given by 38% and 25%, respectively, of Grade 11 and Grade 12 students to justify a linear structure of SCl_2. Similar results have been obtained from students in schools and universities in Australia, the United States, and Thailand.

USING THESE INSTRUMENTS FOR ASSESSMENT AND TEACHING SCIENCE

Recommended reforms in science education usually give more attention to the curricula than to new assessment procedures. The new approach described in this chapter would appear to address many of the concerns

TABLE 14.6

Percentage of Grade 11 and 12 Students with Alternative Conceptions Identified from the Diagnostic Instrument on Covalent Bonding and Structure

Students' Alternative Conceptions	Grade 11 (n = 159)	Grade 12 (n = 84)
Bond polarity		
Equal sharing of the electron pair occurs in all covalent bonds.	33	23
The polarity of a bond is dependent on the number of valence electrons in each atom involved in the bond.	22	16
Ionic charge determines the polarity of the bond.	26	0
Molecular shape		
The shape of a molecule is due to equal repulsion between the bonds.	46	25
Bond polarity determines the shape of a molecule.	23	27
The V-shape in a molecule of the type SCl_2 is due to repulsion between the nonbonding electron pairs.	19	22
Molecules of the shape SCl_2 are linear due to repulsion between two S-Cl bonds.	38	25
Intermolecular forces		
Intermolecular forces are the forces within a molecule.	14	23
Covalent bonds are broken when a substance changes state.	49	17
Polarity of molecules		
Nonpolar molecules form when the atoms in the molecule have similar electronegativities.	40	34
Molecules of the type OF_2 are polar, as the nonbonding electrons on the oxygen form a partial negative charge.	32	15
Octet rule		
Nitrogen atoms can share five electron pairs in bonding.	15	20
Lattices		
High viscosity of some molecular solids is due to strong bonds in the continuous covalent lattice structure.	27	16
Strong intermolecular forces exist in a continuous covalent solid.	48	33

about current assessment practices by overtly assessing the outcomes of thinking within a specified context rather than assessing knowledge of information.

By using these diagnostic instruments at the beginning or on completion of a specified topic, a science teacher can obtain clearer ideas about the nature of the students' understanding and the existence of any alternative conceptions or misconceptions in the topic being studied. Once students' alternative conceptions are identified, science instruction can be modified to remedy the problem by developing and/or utilizing alternative teaching approaches that specifically address students' alternative conceptions or misconceptions. For example, as described earlier, based on the results of the item on intermolecular forces, it is apparent that science teachers need to pay more attention to the essential meaning of intermolecular forces and intramolecular forces and to illustrate the different concepts clearly with good examples. Without this happening, it is evident that this alternative conception or misunderstanding will be retained. Similarly, the results obtained from administering the item on respiration in plants illustrate clearly that this sample of students has a lack of understanding that the respiration process is ongoing and continuous.

The students' conceptions identified by these diagnostic instruments are often well known to experienced teachers, but are appreciated by less experienced teachers only after instruction has been completed. In the latter instance, there is no possibility to consider students' conceptions of the phenomena and to incorporate these in the teaching process. Research evidence also suggests that experienced teachers frequently do not appreciate the problems encountered by students in learning complex science concepts. There are two reasons for this. First, regular approaches to instruction do not probe sufficiently for reasoning of answers, and second, the usual assessment procedures do not demand such detailed explanations of phenomena. I must, however, caution that the use of these diagnostic instruments and subsequent change in teaching emphasis do not guarantee that alternative conceptions or misconceptions will not be constructed and retained by students.

REFERENCES

American Association for the Advancement of Science. (1993). *Benchmarks for science literary: Project 2061*, New York: Oxford University Press.
Amir, R., Frankl, D. R., & Tamir, P. (1987). Justifications of answers to multiple choice items as a means for identifying misconceptions. In J. D. Novak (Ed.), *Proceedings of the Second International Seminar on Misconceptions and Educational Strategies in Science and Mathematics* (Vol. I, pp. 15-26). Ithaca, NY: Cornell University.
Amir, R., & Tamir, P. (1990, April). *Detailed analysis of misconceptions as a basis for developing remedial instruction: The case of photosynthesis*. Paper presented at the annual meeting of the American Educational Research Association, Boston. (ED 319 635)
Australian Education Council. (1992, July). *National statement on science for Australian schools*. Canberra: Author.
Bell, B., Osborne, R., & Tasker, R. (1985). Finding out what children think. In R. Osborne & P.Freyberg, *Learning in science* (pp. 151-165). Auckland, New Zealand: Heinemann.
Confrey, J. (1990). A review of the research on student conceptions in mathematics, science and programming. In C. B. Cazden (Ed.), *Review of research in education* (pp. 3-56). Washington, DC: American Educational Research Association.
Department of Education and Science. (1991). *Science for ages 5 to 16 (1991): Proposals of the Secretary of State for Education and the Secretary of State for Wales*. London: Author.
Driver, R. (1986). A constructivist approach to curriculum development in science. *Studies in Science Education, 13*, 105-122.

Driver, R., & Erickson, G. (1983). Theories-in-action: Some theoretical and empirical issues in the study of students' conceptual frameworks in science. *Studies in Science Education, 10,* 37–60.

Finley, F. N., & Stewart, J. (1982). Representing substantive structures. *Science Education, 66,* 593–611.

Halloun, I. A., & Hestenes, D. (1985). The initial knowledge state of college physics students. *American Journal of Physics, 53,* 1043–1055.

Hashweh, M. Z. (1986). Toward an explanation of conceptual change. *European Journal of Science Education, 8,* 229–249.

Haslam, F., & Treagust, D. F. (1987). Diagnosing secondary students' misconceptions of photosynthesis and respiration in plants using a two-tier multiple choice instrument. *Journal of Biological Education, 21,* 203–211.

Hestenes, D., Wells, M., & Schwackhamer, G. (1992). Force concept inventory. *Physics Teacher, 30,* 141–158.

Lorsbach, W., Tobin, K., Briscoe, C., & LaMaster, S. U. (1992). An interpretation of assessment methods in middle school science. *International Journal of Science Education, 14,* 305–317.

Novak, J. (1991). Clarify with concept maps: A tool for students and teachers alike. *Science Teacher, 58*(7), 45–49.

Novak, J. D., & Gowin, D. B. (1984). *Learning how to learn.* Cambridge: Cambridge University Press.

Osborne, R. J., & Cosgrove, M. M. (1983). Children's conceptions of the changes of state of water. *Journal of Research in Science Teaching, 20,* 825–838.

Peterson, R. F., Treagust, D. F., & Garnett, P. J. (1989). Development and application of a diagnostic instrument to evaluate grade 11 and 12 students' concepts of covalent bonding and structure following a course of instruction. *Journal of Research in Science Teaching, 26,* 301–314.

Pfundt, H., & Duit, R. (1994). *Bibliography: Students' alternative frameworks and science education* (4th ed.). (IPN Reports-in-Brief.) Kiel, Germany: Institute for Science Education, University of Kiel.

Shymansky, J. A., & Kyle, W. C., Jr. (1992). Establishing a research agenda: Critical issues of science curriculum reform. *Journal of Research in Science Teaching, 29,* 749–778.

Simpson, M., & Arnold, B. (1982). The inappropriate use of subsumers in biology learning. *European Journal of Science Education, 4,* 173–182.

Tobin, K. G. (1993). *The practice of constructivism in science education.* Washington, DC: American Association for the Advancement of Science.

Tobin, K. G., & Capie, W. (1981). The development and validation of a group test of logical thinking. *Educational and Psychological Measurement, 11,* 413–423.

Treagust, D. F. (1989). Development and use of diagnostic tests to evaluate students' misconceptions in science. *International Journal of Science Education, 19,* 159–169.

Wolf, D., Bixby, J., Glenn, J., III, & Gardner, H. (1991). To use their minds well: Investigating new forms of student assessment. In G. Grant (Ed.), *Review of research in education* (pp. 31–74). Washington, DC: American Educational Research Association.

Wood-Robinson, C. (1991). Young people's ideas about plants. *Studies in Science Education, 19,* 119–135.

15 Interviewing: A Technique for Assessing Science Knowledge

Beverley Bell
University of Waikato, Aotearoa New Zealand

Interviewing is a technique that researchers in science education use to find out what students are thinking. Interviewing can also be used by teachers as a part of their teaching and assessing to find out what students are thinking. By means of interviews, we can find out the ideas, beliefs, experiences, and feelings the students bring with them to a lesson. This assessment before teaching can be called *diagnostic assessment*. We may find out during a lesson the understandings the students are constructing from the teaching and learning activities. Assessment during learning can be called *formative assessment*. And we may find out at the end of a teaching episode what the students have learned. Assessment after learning can be called *summative assessment*. In summary, one way to access and assess the thinking of students is to attend to their talking in an interview situation.

We are also teaching when we are responding to the talking and thinking of the students. If we have elicited the thinking of the students, then we can use that information as feedback in the teaching and learning process. There is no point in collecting the information in the first place if we are not going to use it. Just listening to the students is only one aspect of teaching; we also need to react or respond to the outcome of our assessing students' thinking.

This chapter looks at interview situations and the ways in which we can attend to and respond to students' ideas in the classroom before, during, and after a teaching episode.

WHY DO WE NEED TO FIND OUT WHAT OUR STUDENTS ARE THINKING?

Students come to lessons with their own understandings and explanations of their biological, physical, and technological worlds. From an early age, they have been making sense of the phenomena around them. A young child develops understandings about hot and cold, about moving things, and about the pets in the home; however, these existing ideas are often not the same as the ideas currently accepted by scientists. For example, many students view a cat as an animal, but they do not view a butterfly as an animal (Bell, 1981). Others may think of gravity as being due to the atmosphere and think that there is no gravity on the moon (Stead & Osborne, 1981). Many students hold a view that there is air or oxygen or water vapor between the particles of air (Osborne & Schollum, 1983). These ideas can be called *children's science* or *alternative conceptions* (Gilbert & Watts, 1983). Background information on children's science and alternative conceptions can be found in Osborne and Freyberg (1985), Claxton (1991), Driver (1983), Duckworth, Easley, Hawkins, and Henriques (1990), Bell (1993a), White (1988), and Northfield and Symington (1991).

The ideas brought by students to the classroom are not just material for interesting stories to tell when we meet with teacher colleagues; these ideas are important because they influence what learning will occur or not. For example, many students view animals only as large, four-legged, furry creatures, such as cows, horses, dogs, lions, and cats; smaller creatures, such as worms, butterflies, and spiders, may be called insects, but not animals. If a teacher asks students to collect some animals for tomorrow's lesson and suggests to the students that they look in the long grass on the school grounds, the response by a student who views animals as large, four-legged, furry creatures will differ from that of another student who views, as does a biologist, worms, spiders, and beetles as animals (Bell & Barker, 1982).

The following is a quotation from a high school teacher at a teacher development meeting, run as part of a research project (Bell, 1993b). She had found that one of her students (aged 13 years) held an alternative view of the particulate nature of air and was sharing with the group of teachers what had been taking place in the classroom:

> I found that really difficult with the [air topic], and I kept on going. We went for days before we sort of got there. With the kid's idea, that air, there is no space between air, air is full. And I kept on giving him another experiment, and they [the other students] wouldn't come to the right conclusion, so I would have to try something else again. And I'd started earlier with the meths and water, you know 50 mls meths, 50 mls water. And sort of didn't get

anywhere. . . . I did the tube with the hydrochloric acid and the ammonia [at] one end. Obviously air can get out of the cotton wool there. . . . I went on to what I wanted to say for sublimation, which was putting the bung in the top of a boiling tube and having the iodine, sort of the same. Well, what happened, well we got this purple gas. How could it get there if it was full of air already? Well I shuffled around a bit, and I said well okay, if it's a gas and they are all joined together, cause that's their idea, I said what would you expect? And they said, it would come back together, back to one. . . . And finally, you know, three days later, we finally got the idea that we could actually have this purple gas going between the spaces in air, that there must be spaces there, cause it could get there. But it took a long time. It was really hard to keep thinking of things to try and get that idea across.

One of the teachers in the group asked if she had discussed the compressibility of gases with the students. The teacher replied:

Yes, we had done that earlier. But you know, it's like having a big balloon, and you push it and it occupies a smaller space, and heat it up, it occupies a bigger space, so that wasn't anything to do with spaces. . . . Well, they had, they had that oxygen and nitrogen in the air occupied space, that atom, that particle occupied a space and next door to it was another atom, you know touching it, and next door was another atom touching it, so that there were actually no spaces between them. . . . You can squeeze the air, and you can make all the particles smaller. I think their concept was more like you can get a sponge, and you can squish a sponge down . . . so that it occupies less space. But they had that concept even though we had done it with solids . . . like you can squeeze a balloon, you know push a balloon into a box, [and it] will occupy a smaller space. And they just weren't having that you actually had spaces and the things were coming closer together.

Her comments indicated that the students had alternative ideas and were unaccepting of the scientifically accepted ideas being taught. She went on to comment: "Well I think, [normally] I probably wouldn't have really gone to that extent to find out where they were at, and really considered and understood where they were at as well. I presumed that they had some concepts, but obviously they didn't."

During science lessons, students can construct unanticipated meanings. They are using their existing knowledge, which may be alternative ideas to those of scientists, to make sense of in-class experiments or practical work. For example, two students carrying out an electrolysis investigation thought that their equipment wasn't working because bubbles were occuring at only one of the two electrodes (Osborne & Freyberg, 1985). Their expectations were that bubbles of gas should appear on both electrodes. This was not the understanding that the teacher was hoping the students would construct during the practical. In fact, the students had a view of electric current known as the "clashing currents" model. In this model, the current flows from both terminals of a dry cell, along the wires, to clash in a light bulb, for example. In the electrolysis investigation, the students were expecting the current from each terminal to clash with the electrolyte to produce bubbles.

If we view students as coming to science lessons with their own meanings for words and explanations of why things behave as they do, then learning can be viewed as conceptual change. That is, learning is occuring when students are developing and changing their existing knowledge (Bell, 1993a; Driver & Bell, 1985; Osborne & Wittrock, 1985). Teaching can be viewed as helping students to develop their existing ideas and not only as the transmission of new ideas. Teaching that takes into account students' thinking can be summarized as teaching that helps students to clarify their own and others' ideas, be aware of cognitive dissonance, construct new conceptions, restructure existing conceptions, and accept new ideas and use them in familiar and new situations (see Bell, 1993b; Driver, 1988; Osborne, Bell, & Gilbert, 1983). A teacher who is helping students to develop their own ideas and understandings needs to know before, during, and after a teaching episode what the students are thinking and what learning is occurring.

Biddulph, Bell, and Carr (1989), Biddulph (1989), and Begg (1991) suggested that to assess students' learning in terms of conceptual change, information on students' thinking is needed in three situations: before, during, and after teaching. In each of these three situations, the needed information can be obtained by answering the following key questions.

Before Teaching (Diagnostic Assessment)

To find out what ideas, beliefs, opinions, and experiences their students bring to the lesson, teachers can ask such questions as:

- What does the literature say about the likely views students will have on the topic?
- What are the students' interests and memories associated with a topic?
- What are students' ideas prior to teaching—their existing conceptions on the topic?
- What are the genuine questions students are likely to have about this topic?
- What are the students' possible answers to some of their own questions?

With the information obtained through asking these questions, teachers can then plan their teaching to take into account the students' thinking rather than ignore it.

During Teaching (Formative Assessment)

To find out what the students are thinking during a teaching episode, teachers can ask the following questions:

- What questions are the students asking? Are they genuine and puzzling ones?
- What possible explanations or answers are the students proposing?
- Are the students seeking, listening to, and considering the ideas of other students?
- Are the students relating what they already know to the new ideas that they are learning?
- What clarification are the students seeking, and from whom?
- What are the students discussing and challenging when they talk with each other?
- Are the students able to devise their own investigations to test out ideas?
- Are the meanings that the students are constructing similar to the intended ones?
- Are the students changing their conceptions?
- Can the students give reasons for a change in ideas or for continuing to hold the same ideas?
- Are the students exploring and investigating beyond the topic and the school program?
- Can the students identify and comment on their ideas before and after an investigation?
- Are the students reflecting on how and what they are learning?

In monitoring students' thinking during the lesson, teachers can plan and modify their teaching to best promote conceptual change. Having ascertained what the students are thinking, they can respond while the teaching is still in progress.

After Teaching (Summative Assessment)

At the end of the teaching, teachers can ask the following questions to find out what the students learned and what conceptual changes occurred:

- What are the students' ideas when the teaching episode has finished (their "after-views")?
- How do the students' after-views compare with their before-views? That is, what conceptual change has occurred?

- How do the students' after-views compare with the intended learning outcomes in the curriculum schemes?
- Can the students use their newly learned ideas in unfamiliar situations and with confidence?
- What needs to be recorded or reported for student documentation?

Teachers may also be seeking information to evaluate the learning experiences and activities. They are constantly reviewing the teaching and learning activities to see if they worked with respect to students' conceptual development and if they will use the activities in that format next time. Some questions to ask to evaluate the activities are:

- Which activities are suitable for promoting conceptual development and change?
- Are the students able to learn in an area of interest to them, within the main topic?
- Do the students have the opportunity to express their own ideas and views about the phenomena being studied, and therefore for their ideas to be identified?
- Do the learning activities help the students find answers to their questions?
- Were the students' understandings challenged in a supportive way where appropriate?
- Were the students helped to refine their ideas in the light of evidence and discussion?

Interviews may be used to find out different aspects of students' understanding. White and Gunstone (1992, pp. 3–5) described seven types of knowledge that make up a person's conceptual understanding: propositions, strings, images, episodes, intellectual skills, motor skills, and cognitive strategies. In an interview situation, we may find out about students' understanding of concepts—the perceived instances and noninstances and the criteria used to decide if something is an instance or not. An example would be the student who categorized a snail as a noninstance of the concept "animal" because it was small. However, we may also obtain information about the propositions (facts, opinions, or beliefs) held by the students—such as, water contains hydrogen and oxygen—or strings, such as a scientific law or the mnemonic to remember the elements in the periodic table. Students' understanding elicited in an interview may also include images or mental representations, such as the feel of the furry tomentum on a daisy leaf or the mental picture of sandstone strata in a road cutting. Exploring students' understandings many mean finding out about episodes in the students' memory. Episodes are "memories of events that you think happened or that you witnessed" (White & Gunstone, 1992, p. 4), such as the memory of the field trip to the sand dunes or the lightning and thunder in a violent storm. An interview may also elicit students' intellectual skills (the capacity to carry out classes of mental tasks, such as categorizing creatures into animals or not animals) or motor skills (the capacity to carry out classes of physical tasks, such as cutting up a vegetable). In an interview, we may find out about students' cognitive strategies (broad skills used in thinking and learning, such as maintaining attention to the task at hand). In summary, an interview is one way of finding out about many aspects of a student's understanding, and this information is needed if students' thinking is to be taken into account in our teaching.

FINDING OUT WHAT THE STUDENTS ARE THINKING BEFORE AND AFTER TEACHING

In this section, we explore how teachers can use interviews to find out what their students are thinking before and after a teaching episode. An interview may be viewed as a conversation with a student or with a group of students in order to listen and to find out what they are thinking. A characteristic of the interview is that the students are doing most of the talking and the teacher most of the listening. There are several points to keep in mind when planning and conducting an interview, related to the purpose of the interview, the wording of the interview questions, putting the students at ease, recording the interviews, and keeping the conversation going. Each of these is discussed in turn.

The Purpose of the Interviews

During an interview, the goal is to find out what the student is thinking, not just whether they have the "right" answer. The interview is a teaching situation only in that we are listening to the student; it is not an opportunity to guide students by careful questioning to the "right answer."

The Wording of the Interview Questions

The wording of the questions in the interview is important to find out what a student is thinking. For example, in an interview to find out a student's ideas about gravity, the student might be shown a picture of the moon and asked, "I am interested in your meaning of the word *gravity*. Can you tell me about gravity on the moon?" This interview question is open ended and gives the student an opportunity to talk about gravity on the moon in her or his own words.

Questions to avoid are ones that seek to find out if the student has the "right answer," such as, "Do you know if there is gravity on the moon?" Other questions to avoid include "teaching" questions that are designed to lead the student to the "right" answer: "Do you think there is gravity on the moon? Have you seen the film of the men walking on the moon? Did they float around or could they stand upright?"

In an interview situation, the questions asked are "genuine" ones—genuine in that we do not know the answer to our question when we ask it. A typical teaching question might be, "What color does iodine turn with starch?" As teachers we already know the answer, and we are asking it to see if the students know the "right" answer too. Contrast that question with this one: "I am interested in your meaning of the word *energy*. Can you tell me about energy in this picture of a fire?" In this case, the teacher did not know the answer to her question in advance.

Care needs to be taken to ask only one question at a time. It is easy to string several questions together in an attempt to clarify the first question; however, students may find this confusing.

Putting the Students at Ease

When teachers start interviewing students, the students may be unsure of this new activity and comprehend the situation in terms of past experiences. They may seek affirmation from the teacher that they are giving the "right" answers or they may try to work out what the teacher wants in order to please the teacher. They may feel uncomfortable about being singled out for a special "talk" and wonder if they have done something wrong to merit this "remedial" attention. It is therefore helpful to explain to each student why she or he is being interviewed and why the teacher is using a new teaching activity:

> Tom, I'm wanting to try out a new teaching activity and wonder if you can help me. I am interested to find out your own ideas about the topic for our next science module on floating and sinking. I am interested in your own ideas about floating and sinking so that I have a better idea about what activities to use in the lessons. Will you help me?

It is unusual in classrooms for teachers to value and give so much attention to students' views. When teachers do this, some students may relish the increased attention, and some may not. When we change our teaching, we have to give the students time to change also.

Recording the Interview

At times, it is helpful to record the interview on audiotape so that the conversation can be listened to at a later stage. Often, interesting aspects of students' views are picked up when the tape is replayed. In audiotaping an interview, the student needs to: (a) be asked for permission first, (b) have a portion of the tape played back before he or she leaves, and (c) receive a copy of the transcript to make changes to before the data are used. It is helpful to discuss with the student your interpretation of the tape, so the student can validate your theoretical ideas. The main concern here is an ethical one of who owns the data. Because the students generated the data, they own them, and need to be given opportunities to exercise control over the data.

Interviews are best conducted in a quiet place, such as the library or an office or the back of a classroom.

Keeping the Conversation Going

When interviewing a student, it is often best to sit at a table, beside the student, and to have some activity or object to take the focus of the interview away from the interviewer and interviewee dichotomy. For example, in the interview-about-instances technique (Osborne & Gilbert, 1980), the student is given a set of cards with line drawings or simple pictures on them, depicting instances and noninstances of a single concept such as "floating and sinking," "animal," "gravity," "force," or "living." For each card, the student is first asked a question to see if the student categorizes the picture as an instance or noninstance of the concept. For example, with respect to the pictures relating to "burning" in Fig. 15.1, the question asked is: "I am interested in your meaning of burning. In your meaning of the word, would you say burning is taking place?" The student is then asked to give reasons for the answer given: "What tells you that?"

It is often difficult for teachers to just listen to students and not ask leading questions. It helps to rote learn some phrases (called *view-finders*) to say in the interview to keep students talking. Often the phrases are colloquial expressions. Examples of view-finders are:

That's an interesting idea. I wonder if other people think like that?
What would happen if . . .
Can you tell me more about that?
What tells you that?
Can you think of other examples when that might happen too?
I don't quite understand. Could you explain that to me again?

Repeating a student's answer back to her or him, with a questioning intonation, may keep the student talking. For example:

Student: I am not too sure but I think the sun is living. It reproduces.

Teacher: Reproduces?

"In your meaning for burning, would you say burning is taking place here?"

FIG. 15.1.   Interview-about-instances on burning. Adapted from Biddulph (1991), by permission.

Student: Yes, the sunspot could be little suns. And it gives off wastes—the gases. But it doesn't have cells. Too hot. I don't know if it is or it isn't.

In most interviews, probe questions are helpful to query a contradiction, to question the student on an aspect of the concept that he or she hasn't volunteered but that he or she may have ideas on, or to check out an aspect of children's science from another student. For example:

Student: No, the spider is not an animal.

Teacher: All spiders or just the small one in the picture?

Giving the students enough time to think and respond is important. The interview is to find out their ideas, and the message being conveyed is that their ideas are valuable. A rushed interview is likely to send mixed messages. The tone of your voice and the speed of talking is important also. Silences are valuable in that they can indicate the student is thinking and formulating a reply. It may help to use such comments as, "Remember, I am interested in your own ideas here, so take your time." However, some students may become more and more quiet, shy, reticent, or lose confidence. It is best to tactfully draw the interview to a close so as not to cause the student stress and discomfort.

At the end of an interview, a student may ask you for your views on floating and sinking, for example, or may wish to ask you a question about the purpose of the interview, having been through it. Conversations are reciprocal, and it is helpful to interpersonal relationships if the interviewer is prepared to self-disclose his or her ideas after the main part of the interview is over.

At times, it may be useful to interview students in pairs or groups of three or four. The advantages are that the students may act as catalysts to each other's thinking and the group situation may make the students feel more at ease. However, dominant group members can silence other members who would otherwise have something interesting to say.

Further reading on the interviewing techniques of teachers who have a constructivist view of learning and assessment can be found in Bell, Osborne, and Tasker (1985) and White and Gunstone (1992, pp. 65–97).

At times, conducting interviews may be too time-consuming, particularly if the views of the whole class are to be elicited. Another technique to elicit students' ideas and explanations is the survey, based on the research findings on students' alternative views. An example of a survey based on the findings of the interview-about-instances with many students is given in Table 15.1. Other techniques to find out students before- and after-views include concept mapping, brainstorming, creative writing, drawings, word association, and question production. These are explained in a New Zealand Ministry of Education guide (1990), and by White and Gunstone (1992) and Grant, Johnson, and Sanders (1990).

The information about students' thinking before and after a teaching episode can be used to assess the learning that has occured and to make decisions about learning activities. For example, before a unit of work on photosynthesis, a teacher may wish to find out students' views on how plants make their food. The information may be used to plan teaching

TABLE 15.1
Survey About Burning

1. When a candle is alight, does it need air?
   (a) No, not really.
   (b) Yes, to help the flame, but nothing happens to the air, except that it gets a bit hot.
   (c) Yes, and some of the air gets changed into something else.
2. What happens to the wax when a candle is alight?
   (a) It is burned up in the flame.
   (b) It is not burned up, but it holds up the burning wick.
   (c) It melts and stops the wick from burning too fast.
   (d) It just drips down the side of the candle.
3. Just above the flame of a gas cooker it is HOT.
   What is it that is hot?
   (a) The air.
   (b) The air, and also the gas that comes from the cylinder.
   (c) The gas that comes from the cylinder.
   (d) The air, and other gases.
4. A saucer held above a candle flame gets black.
   What is the blackness?
   (a) The heat burning the saucer.
   (b) The flame scorching the china.
   (c) Bits of stuff from the flame.
   (d) Dirt from the candle.
   (e) Dust from the air.
5. What do you think is needed to get a fire going?
   (a) Two things: paper and matches.
   (b) Three things: paper, matches, and wood.
   (c) Two things: a fuel, and something to light it with.
   (d) Three things: fuel, heat, and air.
   (e) Three things: fuel, matches, and something to burn it in.
   (f) Two things: a lighter, and some gas.
6. What happens to wood when it is burned in a fire?
   (a) It changes into gases, ash, and water.
   (b) It gets black and gives off smoke.
   (c) It disappears, except for the ash that is left.
   (d) It turns into heat and smoke mostly.
   (e) It shrinks into ashes and black bits.
7. What questions do you have about burning?

Note. Adapted from Biddulph (1991), by permission.

activities that take into account students' alternative ideas about plant nutrition. In addition, students' before- and after-views can be compared to assess the conceptual change in students' thinking. The after-views of the students may also be compared to the scientifically accepted ones. The students may not have acquired the scientifically acceptable view, but a comparison of before- and after-views may indicate a movement toward the accepted scientific view. Students often gain much from comparing their own before- and after-views in a self-assessment activity.

FINDING OUT AND RESPONDING TO STUDENTS' IDEAS DURING TEACHING

"Interviews" conducted during a teaching episode can give a teacher information about the new understandings the students are constructing. Interviewing students during a lesson is usually more informal and resembles a conversation with the students about what they are doing and thinking. For example, a teacher may ask a student about the results of an investigation or enter into a discussion of a student's ideas about plant feeding. In monitoring the students' thinking and understanding during a lesson, a teacher can make decisions about future teaching activities so as to facilitate learning. There is no need to gather this information if we are not going to do something in response to it. In taking into account students' thinking, we are facilitating learning and we are responding to the students' thinking, rather than rigidly following a predetermined teaching package.

In responding to students, we are creating a supportive atmosphere. Our listening during a lesson communicates that we are accepting of students' ideas as their contribution to the conversation. Our listening also helps students to value their own ideas. It communicates to the students that we consider their ideas, regardless of scientific "correctness," to be worthy of the teacher's and class' attention and consideration. Listening to students talk about their ideas also gives attention to students and helps them feel that they have something to contribute. The teacher is not the only one in the classroom who has something of interest and value to contribute.

If we are listening to students, then they are talking, and this has many benefits. It can help students develop and change their own ideas and it can help them develop their thinking skills. This may happen in a semistructured 15-minute interview using the interview-about-instances technique, and it can happen during mini-interviews in lessons. When we talk with students about their understandings, we may be doing any of the following: helping the students clarify and reflect on their ideas, challenging the students' ideas, giving the students further information to consider, helping the students to change their ideas, helping the students find answers for their questions, getting the students thinking for themselves, helping the students test out their own ideas, or helping the students to reflect on their own ideas about learning.

During lessons, teachers can be monitoring student talk for indicators that learning is occuring. In addition, aspects of the learning environment are attended to for information about whether learning is occurring (Bell & Pearson, 1992). For example, if the students are enjoying their work, are cooperating with other students, have ownership of their work, have confidence in themselves as learners, are interested in the topic being studied, and have increased involvement and engagement in the learning task, teachers often infer that learning is occurring. This information can be obtained by talking with students during the lessons, not about management matters (Are you nearly finished? Do you need some help with that equipment? Has everyone in your group had a turn with the burette?), but about students' thinking (That's an interesting idea. Tell me more about that. What happened when you added the water?). The students' enjoyment, involvement, confidence, and cooperation are often conveyed in their answers.

We also can find out what learning is actually occuring by talking with students during lessons. Some New Zealand elementary, middle, and high school teachers who take into account students' thinking were asked how they knew if their students were learning or not (Bell, 1993b). They commented that one way they ascertained learning outcomes during a lesson was by talking with and listening to students. In other words, their information about what the students had learned was obtained not just by watching students. For example, the following six quotes from the high school teachers show that by listening to students, the teachers were able to ascertain that the students were:

Learning New Ideas.

There is a girl in the class, who doesn't say anything, she is very reticent. . . . She is a lovely person and she really tries hard to do the work, but I was just blown away when she [finally said something]. One of the better kids had been explaining about pulse rate and how the muscular walls of the arteries pump, kept the blood and it was the pumping of the walls that you could feel. And I just said "Has anybody got any other information to add to that?" And away she went talking about how the heart fitted into it all. It was quite surprising because I hadn't spent a lot of time talking with her or a lot of time initially with her before when we were doing the research. But somewhere out of it all she had got it all together.

Asking Questions.

When people are asking questions I think better learning is going on. When you are talking about something or something is being opened up in the classroom, some phenomenon, some idea, if they start asking questions and the questions are their questions that tie things into their life and the things that are going on in their life, whether it is with their family or what they have been doing—I think that is when learning is occurring.

Thinking About the Learning Process.

The [16-year-old students] have got an exam in a couple of weeks time and, one of the things she [a student] was saying to me was "how do you actually learn for exams?" And we talked about some study techniques and she said "You know, it is really interesting, the work that we did on our own, that interactive material [from the research project]." She said, "I am having no trouble at all with that." She said, "It is there, I understand it, it makes sense to me, I can retain it," but she said, "When I look at some of the work that we did prior to that or some of the other things that we have done and" she said "it is really hard to learn that." So there is [sic] those sorts of comments.

Transferring Ideas and Linking New Ideas With Existing Ones.

When I first got them . . . [now] you might be talking about one topic and they stop and they say, "But that is part of this topic we did before and that also ties back in from somewhere in the first term's work," and their minds appear to be ticking over because they are dredging up first term work and fitting it in and things aren't box sections. They are able to flow over their ideas and put things together and that is with the kids' comments, what they say, and it is the first time I have noticed so much of that.

When students take something that you are talking about, come back and tell you about something in their own environment which ties into that, there has got to be learning going on. That is one way of telling, when they actually are approaching you on an informal basis and tying in what you are talking about in the classroom with what is in their life, then they have made a link between what you are talking about here and really you are separating out the intricacies of what you are talking about in the classroom, you get down to the nuts and bolts of things, normally. And so if they are getting some of the nuts and bolts and they are actually tying in in their environment things that are going on, that is good. "Sir, I get an electric shock when I touch the electric fence," and so we can talk about [what] electricity is and things like that and "Well why do you get a shock and why do you get a bigger shock when you have got wet feet or wet gumboots or if you are wearing dry gumboots why don't you get a shock," and they ask you those things. Learning is going on there.

Retaining New Ideas.

They will then look at the newspaper and tell me that . . . they actually associate what they have got in here, in this classroom, with what is outside more. . . . They recall things, not necessarily recall things, probably some of them could have recalled things that they learned anyway, but they keep things in their minds longer. . . . You could be finished [with] a unit and maybe three or four weeks later they find something that is relevant and so they mention it again. So that is a different kind of learning, it is not pigeon hole learning. One difference is that [of] today's electricity—"I have done electricity and I want the next thing," but more "We were looking at irons and what happens with machines and things and oh goodness Mum got a new iron and it did this and I wonder if that is because . . . and I will tell Mrs. C—and that is a while later. So that is not necessarily more learning, it is not necessarily they know more about electricity but it is more that the things stay in the front of their mind. It seems to be more useful. Does that make sense?

These teachers were able to make these comments because they listen to students talking in their classrooms. In order for this to happen, the students have to have opportunities and encouragement to talk about their own ideas, to listen to and consider the views of others, to reflect on their own ideas, to construct and test out new ideas, to accept new ideas and to use them with confidence. This tends to happen when the teacher is listening to the students rather than doing most of the talking, and when the teacher is responding to the students' thinking and talking rather than just transmitting expert information or following a predetermined teaching package. The learning activities that enable the students to think and talk about their thinking (and for the teacher to listen and interact with students' thinking) include brainstorming, the post-box technique, the interactive teaching approach, small group discussion work, open-ended problem solving, and student-initiated investigations. Details on these teaching and learning activities can be found in Bentley and Watts (1989), White and Gunstone (1992), Biddulph and Osborne (1984), Grant et al. (1990), Jones (1989), Biddulph (1991), Hume (1992), the Learning in Science Project (Energy) (1989), and Cosgrove, Osborne, and Forret (1989).

CONCLUSION

Teaching that is based on a constructivist view of learning is teaching that takes into account students' thinking. An interview is one way for teachers to find out what students are thinking. By using interviews, teachers are effectively operating as researchers. By researching the thinking of students before and after a teaching episode, teachers can find out how their students' understanding has changed. By researching students' under-standing during a lesson, teachers are able to respond to and interact with their students' thinking and make decisions about learning activities that may further facilitate conceptual development.

REFERENCES

Begg, A. J. C. (1991, April). *Assessment and constructivism.* Paper presented to the ICMI Study on Assessment in Mathematics Education and Its Effects, Calonge, Spain.
Bell, B. (1981). When is an animal not an animal? *Journal of Biological Education, 15* (3), 213–218.
Bell, B. (1993a). *Children's science, constructivism and learning in science.* Geelong, Victoria,

Australia: Deakin University Press.

Bell, B. (Ed.). (1993b). *I know about LISP but how do I put it into practice?* Final Report of the Learning in Science Project (Teacher Development), Centre for Science and Mathematics Education Research, University of Waikato, Hamilton, Aotearoa New Zealand.

Bell, B., & Barker, M. (1982). Towards a concept of animal. *Journal of Biological Education, 16* (3), 197–200.

Bell, B., Osborne, R., & Tasker, R. (1985). Finding out what children think. In R. Osborne & P. Freyberg (Eds.), *Learning in science* (pp. 151–165). Auckland: Heinemann.

Bell, B., & Pearson, J. (1992). "Better" learning. *International Journal of Science Education, 14* (3), 349–361.

Bentley, D., & Watts, M. (1989). *Learning and teaching in school science: Practical alternatives.* Milton Keynes, U.K.: Open University Press.

Biddulph, F. (1989). *Primary science education: criteria that would suggest worthwhile learning is occurring.* Unpublished paper, University of Waikato, Hamilton, New Zealand.

Biddulph, F. (1991). *Burning: A science unit for 10 to 13-year-olds.* Hamilton, New Zealand: Centre for Science and Mathematics Education Research, University of Waikato.

Biddulph, F., Bell, B., & Carr, M. (1989). *Constructivist assessment.* Unpublished paper, Centre for Science and Mathematics Education, University of Waikato, Hamilton, New Zealand.

Biddulph, F., & Osborne, R. (1984). *Making sense of our world: An interactive teaching approach.* Hamilton: Centre for Science and Mathematics Education Research, University of Waikato.

Claxton, G. (1991). *Educating the inquiring mind: The challenge for school science.* New York: Harvester Wheatsheaf.

Cosgrove, M., Osborne, R., & Forret, M. (1989). *Electric current: Developing learners' views.* Hamilton, New Zealand: Waikato Education Centre, University of Waikato.

Driver, R. (1983). *The pupil as scientist.* Milton Keynes, U.K.: Open University Press.

Driver, R. (1988). Theory into practice II: A constructivist approach to curriculum development. In P. Fensham (Ed.), *Development and dilemmas in science education,* (pp. 133–149). London: Falmer Press.

Driver, R., & Bell, B. (1985). Students' thinking and the learning of science. *School Science Review, 67* (240), 443–456.

Duckworth, E., Easley, J., Hawkins, D., & Henriques, A. (1990). *Science education: A minds-on approach for the elementary years.* London: Lawrence Erlbaum Associates.

Gilbert, J., & Watts, M. (1983). Conceptions, misconceptions and alternative conceptions: Changing perspectives in science education. *Studies in Science Education, 10,* 61–98.

Grant, P., Johnson, L., & Sanders, Y. (1990). *Better links: Teaching strategies in the science classroom.* Parkville, Victoria: STAV Publishing.

Hume, A. (1992). *Earthquakes: An interactive science resource for teachers.* Hamilton, New Zealand: Centre for Science and Mathematics Education Research, University of Waikato.

Jones, A. (1989). *Teaching physics from technological applications: A guide for teachers.* Hamilton, New Zealand: Centre for Science and Mathematics Education Research, University of Waikato.

Learning in Science Project (Energy). (1989). *Energy for a change: A guide for teachers.* Hamilton, New Zealand: Centre for Science and Mathematics Education Research, University of Waikato.

Northfield, J., & Symington, D. (1991). *Learning in science as viewed as personal construction: An Australasian perspective* (Monograph no. 3). Perth, Australia: Key Centre for School Science and Mathematics, Curtin University of Technology.

New Zealand Ministry of Education. (1990). *Learning in science: A professional development guide for teachers of science.* Wellington, New Zealand: Learning Media.

Osborne, R., Bell, B., & Gilbert, J. (1983). Science teaching and children's views of the world.

European Journal of Science Education, 5(1), 1–5.

Osborne, R., & Freyberg, P. (1985). *Learning in science: The implications of children's science.* Auckland: Heinemann.

Osborne, R., & Gilbert, J. (1980). A technique for exploring students' views of the world. *Physics Education, 50*(6), 376–379.

Osborne, R., & Schollum, B. (1983). Coping in chemistry. *Australian Science Teachers Journal, 29*(1), 13–24.

Osborne, R., & Wittrock, M. (1985). The generative learning model and its implications for science education. *Studies in Science Education, 12*, 59–87.

Stead, K., & Osborne, R. (1981). What is gravity: Some children's ideas. *New Zealand Science Teacher, 30*, 5–12.

White, R. (1988). *Learning science.* Cambridge, MA: Basil Blackwell.

White, R., & Gunstone, R. (1992). *Probing understanding.* London: Falmer Press.

Author Index

Y

Yaakobi, D., 140, *154*
Yager, R. E., 35, 40, *57*, *58*
Yager, R., 275–276, *296*
Yamamoto, T., 222, *227*
Yap, K. C., 18, *33*
Yeany, R. H., 3, 18, 24, *30*, *33*, 70, *84*, 249, *272*

Yore, L. D., 18, *33*
Yore, L., 275, *296*

Z

Zemansky, M., 180, *198*
Zohar, A., 127, *130*, 320, *325*
Zylbersztajn, A., 160, *177*
Zytkow, J., 217, *226*

Subject Index